C++
FAQs

SECOND EDITION

C++ FAQs

SECOND EDITION

Marshall Cline

Greg Lomow

Mike Girou

ADDISON–WESLEY

An imprint of Addison Wesley Longman, Inc.

Reading, Massachusetts • Harlow, England • Menlo Park, California
Berkeley, California • Don Mills, Ontario • Sydney
Bonn • Amsterdam • Tokyo • Mexico City

Many of the designations used by manufacturers and sellers to distinguish their products are claimed as trademarks. Where those designations appear in this book, and Addison Wesley Longman Inc. was aware of a trademark claim, the designations have been printed with initial caps or in all caps.

The authors and publisher have taken care in the preparation of this book, but make no expressed or implied warranty of any kind and assume no responsibility for errors or omissions. No liability is assumed for incidental or consequential damages in connection with or arising out of the use of the information or programs contained herein.

The publisher offers discounts on this book when ordered in quantity for special sales. For more information, please contact:

AWL Direct Sales
Addison Wesley Longman, Inc.
One Jacob Way
Reading, Massachusetts 01867
(781) 944-3700

Visit AW on the Web: www.awl.com/cseng/

Library of Congress Cataloging-in-Publication Data

Cline, Marshall P.
    C++ FAQs / Marshall Cline, Greg Lomow, Mike Girou.—2nd ed.
        p.   cm.
    Includes index.
    ISBN 0-201-30983-1
    1. C++ (Computer program language)   I. Lomow, Greg A.   II. Girou, Mike.   III. Title.
    QA76.73.C153C55   1999
    005.13'3—dc21   98–38674
                                                                 CIP

Text printed on recycled and acid-free paper.
ISBN 0201309831
3 4 5 6 7 8   CRS 02 01 00 99
3rd Printing November 1999

For MaryElaine, David, Elizabeth, Gabrielle,
Peter, Katherine, and Brandon.

—Marshall

For Barb, Lonnie, and Mac; and to the caregivers and
animals at <u>PIGS, A Sanctuary</u> and <u>Farm Sanctuary</u>.

—Greg

For Beverly, Christian, James, Kelly, and Tamie.

—Mike

Contents

Chapter 3   Understanding the Management Perspective   43

Chapter 4 The Architectural Perspective   **51**

Part II   **Object-Oriented Design**   **61**

Chapter 5 Object-Oriented Fundamentals   **63**

Chapter 6   Specification of Observable Behavior   83

Chapter 7   Proper Inheritance   95

Chapter 10   Testing Strategies   143

Part III   Language Facilities   153

Chapter 11   References   155

Chapter 12 New and Delete   165

Chapter 13 Inline Functions   183

Chapter 14 Const Correctness   193

Chapter 15   Namespaces   207

Chapter 16 Using Static 217

Chapter 20   Constructors and Destructors   269

Chapter 21   Virtual Functions   287

Chapter 22   Initialization Lists   301

Chapter 23   Operator Overloading   315

Chapter 24   Assignment Operators   327

Chapter 25   Templates   343

Chapter 28 Containers   387

Part IV   Topics   **401**

Chapter 29   Mixing Overloading with Inheritance   403

Chapter 30   The Big Three   415

Chapter 31   Using Objects to Prevent Memory Leaks   433

Chapter 34   COM and Active X   481

Chapter 35 Transitioning to CORBA   527

Chapter 36   C Language Considerations   535

Chapter 37   Private and Protected Inheritance   545

Chapter 38   Pointers to Member Functions   553

Chapter 39   The Transition to OO and C++   559

Acknowledgments

This second edition reflects the help and advice of many people. We are particularly indebted to Bjarne Stroustrup and Andrew Koenig for their inspiration and advice over the years. Paul Abrahams, Michael Ball, Ian Long, John Kwan, Jason Pritchard, Christopher Van Wyk, and Steve Vinoski were particularly helpful in the development of this edition. We appreciate the support and insights of our colleagues and associates, including Mathew Denman, Mike Ferretti, Peter Jakab, Charles Martin, Robert Martin, Chris Rooney, Dave Stott, Ioannis Tollis, John Vlissides, Jim Watson, Claudia Woody, Demetrios Yannakopoulos, and Howard Young. Debbie Lafferty was a tremendous supporter during both editions of this book, and we will always be grateful for her help and patience.

Special thanks from Marshall to David W. Bray for showing me the realities of self-directed thinking, to Doug Lea for daily email at 5:30 A.M. (you get an A++), to Jamshid Afshur, Jr. for a million and one suggestions via email, and to my colleagues at Clarkson University. Thanks to all of my students and the many wonderful supporters of the electronic FAQ. Most of all, thank you to MaryElaine and to David, Elizabeth, Gabrielle, Peter, Katherine, and Brandon; you make it worth the trouble.

Special thanks from Greg to Brian Unger and Graham Birtwistle for introducing me to Simula 67 and object-oriented programming in 1981, long before it became fashionable. Thank you Brian Unger and Marshall Cline for giving me the opportunity to pursue interesting projects in stimulating work environments. Also, thanks to my colleagues from the University of Calgary, Jade Simulations, Paradigm Shift, Inc., and MT Systems Company for their assistance and support over the years. Thank you, Barb, for all of your support and for putting up with my unusual work arrangements and bizarre schedules.

Special thanks from Mike to Dix Pettey for showing me what research is all about, to John Schmidt for teaching me to be practical, and to Len Gollobin for showing me how to look at problems the right way. The University of Missouri Mathematics

Department will always occupy a special place in my heart for both personal and professional reasons. Thanks to my children, Beverly and James, for putting up with a father whose efforts have not always matched his intentions, and to my special friends Christian, Kelly, and Tamie for being part of my life.

Marshall
Greg
Mike

Part I

Preliminaries

Chapters 1 through 4 present an introduction to C++ that provides the basis for understanding the rest of the material in this book. This part also provides professional programmers with insight into how their managers and technical leaders view life. This material is intended to help developers understand how their organization works so they can participate more fully in the decision-making process.

Chapter 1

Introduction

What is the purpose of this chapter?

To explain what the book is all about, how it is related to the electronic FAQ and the first edition, and what conventions are used.

This chapter discusses the purpose of the book and the conventions it follows. This chapter also discusses our approach to FAQs and why you should buy this book if you have the first edition or have access to the electronic FAQ.

What are C++ FAQs?

Frequently Asked Questions that should be asked about object-oriented programming and C++.

Each FAQ provides specific guidance in the form of in-depth answers. Many FAQs also provide a complete, working program that illustrates the principles espoused by the FAQ. The word FAQs is pronounced like "facts."

These FAQs aren't necessarily questions people have asked; rather, they are the questions people should ask. Although we never say it publicly, most of these FAQs are based on dumb things we see people do on a fairly regular basis. We got tired of explaining the same fundamental notions over and over again and decided to write them down in this book.

On the other hand, you have taken a step toward OO and C++ competence by purchasing this guidebook; now take the next step by reading and understanding its message.

FAQ 1.03

Who is the target audience for this book?

Professional software developers.

This book is aimed at developers including programmers, architects, and designers. It is a fine way for the experienced programmer to learn object-oriented C++. This book is not for beginners who are just learning to program since it assumes previous programming background. Familiarity with C wouldn't hurt but is not absolutely necessary.

FAQ 1.04

Is this a book about C++ per se?

This is a C++ book with a twist.

This book focuses on the object-oriented aspects of C++. Thus, whenever you see the word "C++," you should assume that the words "object-oriented" are present (and we'll occasionally inject the words "object-oriented" as a reminder to the reader).

This book focuses on practical ways to use C++; it does not explore all of the dark corners of the language beloved by "language lawyers." In this way, this book is not the traditional C++ book written from the perspective of the language and stressing the syntax and features of C++ in all their gory detail. Instead, this book concentrates on the key aspects of C++ (such as its OO features) and how to apply them effectively. Another reason for this approach is that the language is so large that it is hard for developers to understand what is relevant and how to apply it.

In this vein, one of the main contributions of this book is to focus on the moral use of C++ rather than simply describing the legal use of C++. In this context, using C++ morally means adhering to a programming discipline (i.e., a subset of all possible combinations of all the constructs of C++) that is relatively risk-free (whereas using C++ legally simply refers to any use of the language that the compiler accepts). We have found that many of the problems that developers run into stem from trying to combine

C++ features in incompatible and seemingly random ways; therefore using C++ morally is vital to using C++ effectively.

This book also tries to bridge the gap between software architecture and OO design and C++ programming (see Chapter 4).

FAQ 1.05

Why do developers need a guidebook for C++ and OO technology?

Learning to use C++ and OO properly is a long journey with many pitfalls.

Because of the sophistication and complexity of C++, developers need a road map that shows how to use the language properly. For example, *inheritance* is a powerful facility that can improve the clarity and extensibility of software, but it can also be abused in ways that result in expensive design errors.

The field of object-oriented technology is large, evolving, and heterogeneous. Under these circumstances, a guidebook is essential. These FAQs cover the latest innovations so that you don't have to stumble around for years learning the same lessons others have already learned. The FAQs also expose incorrect and questionable practices.

To be effective, programmers need to understand the language features and how the features of the language can be combined. For example, pointer arithmetic and the *is-a* conversion (see FAQ 2.24) are both useful, but combining them has some subtle edge effects that can cause big problems; see FAQ 8.16. Similar comments apply when combining overloading and overriding (FAQ 29.02), overriding and default parameters, abstract base classes and assignment (FAQ 24.05), and so on. So it is not enough to understand each feature of C++.

FAQ 1.06

What kind of guidance is given in the answers to these FAQs?

Explanations of language features, directions for using these features properly, and guidelines indicating programming practices to avoid.

The FAQs can be divided into roughly three categories:

1. FAQs that explain what a particular language feature is and how to use it in compliance with C++ semantics.

2. FAQs that explain how to use C++ properly. Some of these answers deal with only a single language feature, while others explain how to use several different language features in concert. Combining language features allows sophisticated designs that can simultaneously satisfy multiple technical requirements and business goals.

3. FAQs that expose poor programming practices. These show design and programming practices that are legal in C++ but should be avoided because they can lead to programs that are bug-ridden, hard to comprehend, expensive to maintain, difficult to extend, and lacking reuse value.

FAQ 1.07

What is the electronic FAQ and why buy this book when the electronic FAQ is free?

The electronic FAQ is a set of C++ questions and answers, originally prepared and distributed on the Internet by Marshall Cline. The Internet version is currently updated and distributed by Marshall and is available through the news group comp.lang.c++. This book has substantially more material than the electronic FAQ.

This book and the electronic FAQ were inspired by a seemingly unquenchable thirst among C++ developers for more and better information about C++ through comp.lang.c++. Addison-Wesley decided to provide an expanded form of that information in book format.

This book covers a broader range of topics and goes into greater depth than the electronic FAQ. It provides deeper coverage of the key points with extensive new examples.

Most of the programming examples are working, stand-alone programs, complete with their own `main()`, all necessary `#include` files, and so on. All examples have been compiled directly from the source text of the book; those that are complete programs have also been run.

FAQ 1.08

Why should you buy this edition if you already have a copy of the first edition?

Because the world has changed and you want to keep up with technology.   *new*

The OO world and the C++ language have changed significantly in the last few years. There are new language constructs such as Run Time Type Identification (RTTI) and namespaces. The Standard Template Library (STL) is a massive addition to the C++ body of essential knowledge. Design notation has apparently standardized on the Unified Modeling Language (UML). Java, CORBA, and ActiveX are now topics that every C++ developer needs to understand. The goal of this second edition is to bring you up to speed on all of these new developments while still keeping the pithy style and FAQ format that was so well received in the first edition.

Finally, the second edition is much more self-contained than the first, with lots of syntax and semantics. We've appreciated all your comments and suggestions and have tried to accommodate them wherever possible.

FAQ 1.09

What conventions are used in this book?

The undecorated word *inheritance* means "public inheritance." Private or protected inheritance is referred to explicitly.

Similarly the undecorated term *derived class* means "public derived class." Derived classes produced via private or protected inheritance are explicitly designated "private derived class" or "protected derived class," respectively.

The class names `Base` and `Derived` are used as hypothetical class names to illustrate the general relationship between a base class and one of its (publicly) derived classes.

The term *out-lined function* indicates a function that is called via a normal `CALL` instruction. In contrast, when an *inlined function* is invoked, the compiler inserts the object code for that function at the point-of-call.

The term *remote ownership* is used when an object contains a pointer to another object that the first object is responsible for deleting. The default destruction and copy semantics for objects that contain remote ownership are incorrect, so explicit controls are needed.

To allow compilation while simplifying the presentation to the reader, examples that use the standard library have a line that says `using namespace std;`. This dumping of the entire standard namespace is acceptable as a short-term conversion technique or as a pedagogical aid, but its use in production systems is controversial. Most authorities recommend introducing class names as needed or using the `std::` qualifier.

The term *OO* is used as an abbreviation for "object-oriented."

The term *method* is used as a synonym for "member function."

`NULL` is used rather than 0 to make the code more readable. Organizational standards and guidelines should be consulted before the reader continues this practice.

The term *C programming language* refers to the ISO version of C.

The compiler is assumed (per the C++ Standard) to insert an implicit `return 0;` at the end of `main()`.

The intrinsic data type `bool` is used, which has literal values `true` and `false`. For compilers that don't have a built-in `bool` type, insert the following at the beginning of each example:

```
typedef char bool; const bool false = 0; const bool true = 1;
```

The expression `new MyClass`, where `MyClass` is some type, is assumed to throw an exception if it runs out of memory—it never returns `NULL`. Most compilers implement this correctly, but some do not.

Most examples use `protected:` data rather than `private:` data. In the real world, this is appropriate for most developers and most applications, but framework developers probably should not use `protected:` data, since this would create a data coupling between the derived classes and the `protected:` data of the base class. In general, framework developers should use `private:` data with `protected:` access functions.

Type names (names of classes, structs, unions, enums, and typedefs) start with a capital letter; preprocessor symbols are all capitals; all other identifiers start with a lowercase letter. Data member names and class-scoped enumerations end with a single underscore.

It is assumed that the file extensions `.cpp` and `.hpp` are appropriate. Some compilers use a different convention.

Universal Modeling Language (UML) notation is used to express design relationships.

The following priorities were used in designing the examples: (1) unity of purpose, (2) compactness, and (3) self-contained functionality. In other words, each example demonstrates one basic point or technique, is as short as possible, and, if possible, is a complete, working program. The examples are not intended for plug-in reuse in industrial-strength settings because balancing the resultant (subtle) tradeoffs would conflict with these priorities.

To avoid complicating the discussions with finding the optimal balance between the use of `virtual` and `inline` for member functions, `virtual` is used more often than strictly necessary (see FAQ 21.15). To achieve compactness, some member functions are defined in the class body even if they wouldn't normally be `inline` or even if moving them down to the bottom of a header file would improve specification (see FAQ 6.05). Uncalled functions are often left undefined. Some functions that are called are also undefined, since compactness is a higher priority than self-contained functionality. Also for compactness, examples are not wrapped in preprocessor symbols that prevent multiple expansions (see FAQ 2.16).

The examples put the `public:` part at the beginning of the class rather than at the end of the class. This makes it easier for those who simply want to use the class as opposed to those who want to go in and change the internal implementation of the class. This is normally the right tradeoff since a class is normally used a lot more often than it is changed.

It is assumed that the C++ compiler and standard library are both compliant with the Standard and work correctly. In the real world, this is probably not a safe assumption, and you should be cautious.

Chapter 2

Basic C++ Syntax
and Semantics

What is the purpose of this chapter?

To present the fundamentals of C++ syntax and semantics.

This chapter provides a brief overview of C++ syntax and semantics. It covers topics such as `main()`, creating and using local, dynamically allocated, and static objects, passing C++ objects by reference, by value, and by pointer, default parameters, C++ stream I/O, using classes with operator overloading, using templates, using `auto_ptr` to prevent memory leaks, throwing and catching exceptions, and creating classes including member functions, const member functions, constructors, initialization lists, destructors, inheritance, the is-a conversion, and dynamic binding.

Experienced C++ programmers can skip this chapter.

What are the basics of `main()`?

It's the application's main routine.

Object-oriented C++ programs consist mostly of classes, but there's always at least one C-like function: `main()`. `main()` is called more or less at the beginning of the program's execution, and when `main()` ends, the runtime system shuts down the program. `main()` always returns an `int`, as shown below:

```
int main()
{
  // ...
}
```

`main()` has a special feature: There's an implicit `return 0;` at the end. Thus if the flow of control simply falls off the end of `main()`, the value 0 is implicitly returned to the operating system. Most operating systems interpret a return value of 0 to mean "program completed successfully."

`main()` is the only function that has an implicit `return 0;` at the end. All other routines that return an `int` must have an explicit `return` statement that returns the appropriate `int` value.

Note that this example shows `main()` without any parameters. However, `main()` can optionally declare parameters so that it can access the command line arguments, just as in C.

FAQ 2.03

What are the basics of functions?

new

Functions are one of the important ways to decompose software into smaller, manageable chunks. Functions can have return values (for example, a function that computed a value might return that value), or they can return nothing. If they return nothing, the return type is stated as `void` and the function is sometimes called a procedure.

In the following example, function `f()` takes no parameters and returns nothing (that is, its return type is `void`), and function `g()` takes two parameters of type `int` and returns a value of type `float`.

```
void f()
{
  // ...
}

float g(int x, int y)
{
  float sum = x + y;
  float avg = sum / 2.0;
```

```
    return avg;
}

int main()
{
  f();
  float z = g(2, 3);
}
```

FAQ 2.04

What are the basics of default parameters?

C++ allows functions to have default parameters. This is useful when a parameter *new*
should have a specified value when the caller does not supply a value. For example, suppose that the value 42 should be passed to the function f() when the caller does not
supply a value. In that case, it would make the calling code somewhat simpler if this
parameter value were supplied as a default value:

```
void f(int x=42);  ◄──── Declare the default parameter(s) in the function declaration

void f(int x)  ◄──────── Don't repeat the default parameter(s) in the function definition
{
  // ...
}

int main()
{
  f(29);  ◄─────────────── Passes 29 to f()
  f();  ◄───────────────── Passes 42 to f()
}
```

FAQ 2.05

What are the basics of local (auto) objects?

C++ extends the variable declaration syntax from built-in types (e.g., int i;) to *new*
objects of user-defined types. The syntax is the same: TypeName VariableName.
For example, if the header file "Car.hpp" defines a user-defined type called Car, objects
(variables) of class (type) Car can be created:

```
#include "Car.hpp"  ◄──────── Define class Car

void f()
```

```
{
    Car a;                          1: Create an object
    a.startEngine();                2: Call a member function
    a.tuneRadioTo("AM", 770);       3: Call another member function
}                                   4: Destroy the object

int main()
{
    f();
}
```

When control flows over the line labeled *1: Create an object,* the runtime system creates a local (auto) object of class Car. The object is called a and can be accessed from the point where it is created to the } labeled *4: Destroy the object.*

When control flows over the line labeled *2: Call a member function,* the startEngine() member function (a.k.a. method) is called for object a. The compiler knows that a is of class Car so there is no need to indicate that the proper startEngine() member function is the one from the Car class. For example, there could be other classes that also have a startEngine() member function (Airplane, LawnMower, and so on), but the compiler will never get confused and call a member function from the wrong class.

When control flows over the line labeled *3: Call another member function,* the tuneRadioTo() member function is called for object a. This line shows how parameters can be passed to member functions.

When control flows over the line labeled *4: Destroy the object,* object a is automatically destroyed. If the Car class has some special cleanup activities that need to take place when an object goes away, the writer of the class would include a *destructor* in the class and the runtime system would automagically call the destructor (dtor) when the object goes away; see FAQ 20.03. Local objects such as a are sometimes called automatic objects or stack objects, and they are said to go out of scope at the } line.

UML uses the following notation to show a class Car that contains member functions startEngine() and tuneRadioTo():

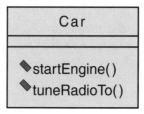

What are the basics of constructing objects using explicit parameters?

Constructors are special member functions that are called to initialize an object. If parameters are needed, the parameters can be supplied in the parentheses, (). If no parameters are needed on a local object, parentheses must not be provided. Here is an example:

```cpp
#include "Car.hpp"

void f()
{
   Car a;                    1: Create a "default" Car object
   Car b(100, 73);          2: Pass explicit parameters to Car's constructor

   // ...
}

int main()
{

   f();
}
```

When control flows over line 1, a local `Car` object is created and initialized by the class's *default constructor*. The default constructor is the constructor that can be called with no parameters (see FAQ 20.08).

When control flows over line 2, another local `Car` object is created and initialized, this time by passing two `int` parameters to a constructor of class `Car`. The parameters (`100, 73`) are presumably used to set up the object (e.g., initial values for various state variables). Line 1 and line 2 probably call different constructors (but see FAQ 2.04 on default parameters).

Note that in the following example b is not a `Car` object. Instead b is a function that returns a `Car` by value.

```cpp
void g()
{
   Car a;          a is a Car object
   Car b();        b is not a Car object!
}
```

FAQ 2.07

What are the basics of dynamically allocated (new) objects?

 C++ allows objects to be allocated dynamically using the new operator. Dynamic allocation is also known as allocating from the heap. As shown, a Car object can be allocated from the heap using the syntax new Car(). The result is stored in a CarPtr pointer. CarPtr is an alias for an auto_ptr, which is a "safe pointer type." The typedef syntax establishes this alias relationship.

```
#include <memory>  ◄──────────── This gets the definition for auto_ptr
#include <string>
using namespace std;

#include "Car.hpp"
typedef auto_ptr<Car> CarPtr;

void f()
{
   CarPtr p(new Car());  ◄──────────── 1: Create an object
   p->startEngine();  ◄──────────── 2: Call a member function
   p->tuneRadioTo("AM", 770);  ◄──── 3: Call another member function
}  ◄──────────────────────────── 4: Destroy the Car object

int main()
{
   f();
}
```

When control flows over the line labeled *1: Create an object,* an object is created dynamically (from the heap). The object is pointed to by the pointer p. The object can be accessed from the point it is created until the CarPtr is destroyed at the } (line 4). Note however that the CarPtr can be returned to a caller. This line is analogous to (*but not interchangeable with*) the C code p = malloc(sizeof(Car)). Note that parameters can be passed to the constructor; e.g., p = new Car(100, 73);.

When control flows over the line labeled *2: Call a member function,* the startEngine() member function is called for the object pointed to by p. The line labeled *3: Call another member function* is similar, showing how to pass parameters to member functions of dynamically allocated objects.

When control flows over the line labeled *4: Destroy the Car object,* the Car object pointed to by p is destroyed. If the Car class has a destructor, the runtime system automagically calls the destructor (dtor) when control flows over this line.

Note that dynamically allocated objects don't have to be destroyed in the same scope that created them. For example, if the function said return p;, the ownership of the Car object is passed back to the function's caller, meaning that the Car object won't be destroyed until the } of the caller (or the caller's caller if the caller does like-wise, and so on):

```
CarPtr g()
{
  CarPtr p(new Car());
  // ...
  return p;          The caller is now responsible for deleting the Car object
}

void h()
{
  CarPtr p = g();    Ownership is transferred from g() to h() here
  // ...
}                    The Car object dies here
```

Note to C programmers: It is generally considered bad form to use raw `Car*` pointers to hold the result of the `new Car()` operation. This is a big change from the way pointers are handled in the C language. There are many reasons for this change: the C++ approach makes "memory leaks" less likely (there is no explicit use of `free(p)` or `delete p`, so programmers don't have to worry about accidentally forgetting the deallocation code or jumping around the deallocation code), the C++ approach makes "dangling references" less likely (if C-like `Car*` pointers are used, there is a chance that someone will inadvertently access the memory of the `Car` object after it is deleted), and the C++ approach makes the code "exception safe" (if a C-like `Car*` were used, any routine that could throw an exception would have to be wrapped in a `try ... catch` block; see FAQ 2.23).

FAQ 2.08

What are the basics of local objects within inner scopes?

C++ local objects die at the } in which they were created. This means they could die before the } that ends the function:

new

```
#include "Car.hpp"

void f()
{
  Car a;

  for (int i = 0; i < 10; ++i) {
    Car b;       1: Create a Car object on each iteration
```

```
    // ...
}  ◄──────── 2: Each iteration's b dies here

    // ...
}  ◄──────── 3: Object a dies here

int main()
{
    f();
}
```

The line labeled 1: *Create a Car object on each iteration* is within the loop body, so a distinct Car object that is local to the loop body is created on each iteration.

Note that C++ allows loop variables (`int i` in the example) to be created inside the `for` parameters. Loop variables that are declared this way are local to the loop: they cannot be accessed after the } that terminates the `for` loop. This means that a subsequent `for` loop could use the same loop variable. Note that this is a new language feature, and compilers may not uniformly support this rule in all cases.

Also notice that, unlike C, variables do not have to be declared right after a {. It is not only allowable but also desirable to declare C++ variables just before they are first used. Doing so allows their initialization to be bypassed if the section of code they are in is bypassed, and it allows the introduction of other runtime variables in their initialization if the code is not bypassed. So there is never anything to lose, indeed there is sometimes something to gain, by declaring at first use.

FAQ 2.09

What are the basics of passing objects by reference?

Passing objects by reference is the most common way to pass objects to functions. C programmers often have a hard time adjusting to pass-by-reference, but it's generally worth the pain to make the transition.

```
#include "Car.hpp"

void f(Car& a)
{
    a.startEngine();  ◄──────── Changes main()'s x object
    // ...
}

void g(const Car& b)  ◄──────── Note the const
{
```

```
      b.startEngine();  ◄──────  Error: Can't change an object via a const reference
      // ...
   }
   main()
   {
     Car x;
     f(x);
     g(x);
   }
```

Function f() illustrates pass-by-reference (the & between the type name and the parameter name indicates pass-by-reference). In this case, a is main()'s x object—not a copy of x nor a pointer to x, but another name for x itself. Therefore anything done to a is really done to x; for example a.startEngine() actually invokes x.startEngine().

Function g() illustrates pass-by-reference-to-const. Parameter b is the caller's object, just as before, but b has an additional restriction: it can only inspect the object, not mutate the object. This means g() has a look-but-no-touch agreement with its callers— g() guarantees to its callers that the object they pass will not be modified. For example, if a programmer erroneously called b.startEngine(), the compiler would detect the error and would issue a diagnostic at compile time (assuming startEngine() is not a const member function; see FAQ 2.17). Reference-to-const is similar in spirit to pass-by-value (see FAQ 2.10), but is implemented much more efficiently.

FAQ 2.10

What are the basics of passing objects by value?

Beware: passing objects by value can be dangerous in some situations. Often it is better to pass objects by reference-to-const (FAQ 2.09) than to pass them by value. For example, pass-by-value won't work if the destination type is an abstract base class (see FAQ 2.24) and can result in erroneous behavior at runtime if the parameter's class has derived classes (see FAQ 24.12, 28.04). However if the class of the parameter is guaranteed not to have derived classes, and if the function being called needs a local copy to work with, pass-by-value can be useful.

new

```
   #include "Car.hpp"

   void f(Car a)
   {
     a.startEngine();  ◄──────  Changes a local copy of the original object
   }
```

```
int main()
{
  Car x;
  f(x);
}
```

Since f()'s a is a copy of main()'s x, any changes to a are not reflected in x.

FAQ 2.11

What are the basics of passing objects by pointer?

new Passing objects by pointer is not commonly used. The most common approaches are pass-by-reference and pass-by-auto_ptr. Pass-by-reference is used when the caller wants to retain ownership of the object (that is, when the caller wants to access the object after the call returns to the caller). Pass-by-auto_ptr is used when the caller wants to transfer ownership of the object to the called routine (that is, when the caller wants the object to get deleted before the called routine returns to the caller):

```
#include <memory>
using namespace std;

#include "Car.hpp"
typedef auto_ptr<Car> CarPtr;

void f(Car& c)
{
  c.startEngine();
  // ...
}  ◄———————— The Car object is not deleted at this line

void g(CarPtr p)
{
  p->startEngine();
  // ...
}  ◄———————— The Car object is deleted at this line

int main()
{
  CarPtr p(new Car());
  f(*p);  ◄——— Pass-by-reference; *p can be used after this line
  g(p);   ◄——— Pass-by-auto_ptr; *p cannot be used after this line
}
```

If the intent is for the caller to retain ownership of the object, pass-by-reference should generally be used. If the intent is for the ownership to be passed to the called routine, pass-by-auto_ptr should be used. About the only time pass-by-pointer should be used is when (1) the caller should retain ownership and (2) the called routine needs to handle "nothing was passed" (i.e., the NULL pointer) as a valid input. In the following example, note the explicit test to see if the pointer is NULL.

```cpp
#include <memory>
using namespace std;

#include "Car.hpp"
typedef auto_ptr<Car> CarPtr;

void h(Car* p)
{
  if (p == NULL) {
    // ...
  } else {
    p->startEngine();
    // ...
  }
}                          As in pass-by-reference, the Car object is not deleted at this line

void i()
{
  h(NULL);                 NULL is a valid parameter to function h()

  CarPtr p (new Car());
  h(p.get());              Pass-by-pointer; *p can be used after this line
  // ...
}                          The Car object is deleted at this line
```

FAQ 2.12

What are the basics of stream output?

C++ supports C-style output, such as the printf() family of functions. However it is often better to use the native C++ output services. With the native C++ output services, output is directed to an output stream object. For example, cout is an output stream object that is attached to the process's standard output device, often to the terminal from which the program is run. Syntactically these C++ output services look as if they're shifting things into the output stream object. The <iostream> header is needed when using these services:

```
#include <iostream>
using namespace std;

int main()
{
  cout << "Hello world\n";                    ———— Line 1
  cout << "Hello world" << '\n';              ———— Line 2
  cout << "Hello world" << '\n' << flush;     ←—— Line 3
  cout << "Hello world" << endl;              ———— Line 4
}
```

Line 1 prints the string "Hello world" followed by a newline character, '\n'. This is analogous to the C statement, fprintf(stdout, "Hello world\n"); thus cout is analogous to C's stdout, and cerr (not shown) is analogous to stderr.

Line 2 is logically equivalent to line 1: it prints the string "Hello world," then it prints a newline character, '\n'. This shows how the << operator can be cascaded—allowing multiple things to be printed with the same statement. This is analogous to the C construct fprintf(stdout, "%s%c", "Hello world", '\n').

Line 3 also prints "Hello world" followed by a newline, but then it flushes the output buffer, forcing the characters to be sent to the operating system. This is normally not necessary with cout, but when output is being sent to a file it can be important to flush the output buffers at certain times, such as just before abort() is intentionally called. In C, flushing an output buffer is accomplished by calling fflush(stdout). Note that flushing the I/O buffers too much can slow down the application.

Line 4 is a shorthand version of line 3. The symbol endl prints a newline character, '\n', followed by a flush symbol. Because endl flushes the buffer, it shouldn't be used very often since it can slow down the application.

FAQ 2.13

What are the basics of stream input?

C++ supports C-style input, such as the scanf() family of functions. However it is often better to use the native C++ input services. With the native C++ input services, information is read from an input stream object. For example, cin is an input stream object that is attached to the process's standard input device, often to the keyboard from which the program is run. Syntactically these C++ input services look as if they're shifting things from the input stream object. The <iostream> header is needed when using these services (the example uses stream output to prompt for the stream input):

```
#include <iostream>
#include <string>
using namespace std;

int main()
{
  cout << "What's your first name? ";  ◄——— Line 1
  string name;  ◄————————————————————————— Line 2
  cin >> name;  ◄————————————————————————— Line 3

  cout << "Hi " << name << ", how old are you? ";
  int age;
  cin >> age;  ◄—————————————————————————— Line 4
}
```

Line 1 prints the prompt. There is no need to `flush` the stream since `cout` takes care of that automatically when reading from `cin` (see the `tie` member function in the `iostream` documentation for how to do this with any arbitrary pair of streams).

Line 2 creates a `string` object called `name`. Class `string` is a standard class that replaces arrays of characters. `string` objects are safe, flexible, and high performance. This line also illustrates how C++ variables can be defined in the middle of the routine, which is a minor improvement over the C requirement that variables be defined at the beginning of the block.

Line 3 reads the user's first name from the standard input and stores the result in the `string` object called `name`. This line skips leading whitespace (spaces, tabs, newlines, and so on), then extracts and stores the whitespace-terminated word that follows into variable `name`. The analogous syntax in C would be `fscanf(stdin, "%s", name)`, except the C++ version is safer (the C++ `string` object automatically expands its storage to accommodate as many characters as the user types in—there is no arbitrary limit and there is no danger of a memory overrun). Note that an entire line of input can be read using the syntax `getline(cin, name);`.

Line 4 reads an integer from the standard input and stores the result in the `int` object called `age`. The analogous syntax in C would be `fscanf(stdin, "%d", &age)`, except the C++ version is simpler (there is no redundant `"%d"` format specifier since the C++ compiler knows that age is of type `int`, and there is no redundant address-of operator (`&age`) since the compiler passes the parameter age by reference).

FAQ 2.14

What are the basics of using classes that contain overloaded operators?

 They're easy to use. But when you create your own, make sure the operators are intuitive and natural.

Here is an example that uses the standard `string` class:

```
#include <iostream>
#include <string> ◄───────────────────────── Defines class string
using namespace std;

void f(const string& firstName, const string& lastName)
{
  string fullName = firstName + " " + lastName; ◄─────── Line 1
  cout << "Your full name is " << fullName << "\n"; ◄───── Line 2
}

int main()
{
  f("Charlie", "Brown");
  f("Fred", "Flintstone");
}
```

The `f()` function takes two `string` objects that will remain unchanged (`const string&`; see FAQ 2.09).

Line 1 concatenates the first name, a space, and then the last name. This uses the overloaded + operator associated with class `string`.

Line 2 prints the resulting full name. This uses the overloaded << operator associated with class `string`.

FAQ 2.15

What are the basics of using container classes?

 Templates are one of the most powerful code reuse mechanisms in C++. The most common use for templates is for containers. Container classes are used to create objects that hold other objects. There are many different container templates, including linked lists, vectors (arrays), sets, and maps. Container templates allow programmers to get the benefits of sophisticated data structures, such as binary trees that always stay balanced, hash tables, skip lists, and splay trees, without having to know anything at all about the details of those data structures.

Templates look a little funny at first, but they're not that much different from normal classes once you get used to them. The only strange part is the angle brackets: a vector of Car is declared using the syntax vector<Car>. The typedef syntax is used for convenience: it creates easy-to-read synonyms such as CarList.

```
#include <vector>  ◄─────────────── Get the standard vector template
#include <string>  ◄─────────────── Get the standard string class
#include <algorithm>
using namespace std;

#include "Car.hpp"  ◄─────────────── Get the user-defined Car class
typedef vector<Car>     CarList;  ◄───── Synonym for convenience
typedef vector<string> StringList;  ◄───── Synonym for convenience

int main()
{
  CarList x;  ◄─────────────── Create a vector of Car objects
  Car a, b, c;
  x.push_back(a);  ◄─────────────── Append object a to the CarList x
  x.push_back(b);
  x.push_back(c);
  // ...

  StringList y;  ◄─────────────── Create a vector of string objects
  y.push_back("Foo");  ◄─────────────── Append string "Foo" to the StringList y
  y.push_back("Bar");
  y.push_back("Baz");
  sort(y.begin(), y.end());  ◄─────── Sort the StringList y
  // ...
}
```

This sample code creates two vector objects: x is a vector of Car objects and y is a vector of string objects. This is analogous to creating two C-like arrays (Car x[3]; and string y[3];), but vector objects are more flexible, they can grow to an arbitrary size, they are safer, and they have a lot more services associated with them. See FAQ 28.13.

UML uses the following notation to show a template vector along with instantiations of that template vector<Car> and vector<string>.

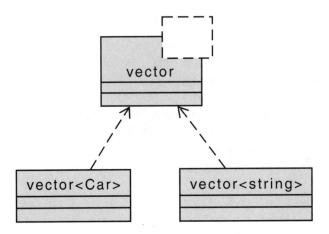

FAQ 2.16

What are the basics of creating class header files?

 The first step is to remember `#ifndef`.

When creating a class header file, the first thing to remember is to wrap the header in `#ifndef`, `#define`, and `#endif` lines, just as with C header files. The following shows the skeleton of the header file that defines C++ class `Car`.

```
#ifndef CAR_HPP
#define CAR_HPP

class Car {
public:
          ←——————  The member functions for Car objects are declared here
protected:
          ←——————  The data members for Car objects are declared here
};
#endif
```

This code might be stored in the header file `"Car.hpp"`.

The `public:` and `protected:` parts of the class are different: normal user code (e.g., `main()`) can access only `public:` features. If normal user code tries to access anything in the `protected:` part, the user code would get a compile-time error (not a warning: a true error, something that would have to be fixed before getting the code to compile). This is called *encapsulation,* and is described further in FAQ 5.16.

Although `public:` and `protected:` are quite different with respect to encapsulation, they are very similar otherwise. The `public:` part can also contain data, and the `protected:` part can also contain member functions. In fact, they are completely symmetrical: data and member functions can be declared in either section. It's generally considered unwise (and unnecessary) to create `public:` data, but `protected:` member functions are fairly common and quite useful. For example, `protected:` member functions can be helper functions that are used mainly by the `public:` member functions (analogous to `static` functions within a module in C).

FAQ 2.17

What are the basics of defining a class?

By convention, the `public:` part goes first. The following example shows the header file that defines C++ class `Car`.

new

```
#ifndef CAR_HPP
#define CAR_HPP

#include <string>

class Car {
public:
  virtual void startEngine();                              ← Line 1
  virtual bool isRunning() const;                          ← Line 2
  virtual void tuneRadioTo(const string& band, int freq);  ← Line 3
protected:
  bool isRunning_;                                         ← Line 4
  bool radioOnAM_;
  int  radioFreq_;
};
#endif
```

Line 1 declares a member function of class `Car`. This member function doesn't take any parameters. Note that C programmers use `(void)` to declare a function that takes no parameters, but this is not necessary in C++. Be warned that some C++ developers consider the `(void)` syntax in C++ code to be an indicator that the author of the code is still a warmed-over C programmer—that the author hasn't yet made the paradigm shift. This is an unfair judgment, but it might be wise to use `()` rather than `(void)` in C++ code.

Line 2 declares another member function, this time returning a `bool` (the `bool` data type has two values: `true` and `false`). The member function's name is designed to make sense in an `if` statement, e.g., `if (myCar.isRunning()) ...` The `const` on the right side means that the member function is an inspector—it promises not to change the object. This lets users know that the `Car` object won't suddenly change inside a statement such as `if (myCar.isRunning())`. It is a good idea to mark every member function that is logically an inspector with a `const`; otherwise the compiler will give error messages when someone calls one of these member functions via a reference-to-const or a pointer-to-const (see FAQ 2.09, 2.11).

Line 3 declares another member function, this time taking two parameters. Member functions that don't have a `const` on the right side are known as mutator member functions, since they can change the object. For example the statement `myCar.tuneRadioTo("AM",770)` probably makes changes to the `Car` object called `myCar`.

Line 4 declares a data member. By convention, data member names end with an underscore. This particular data member is presumably used by the `isRunning()` member function.

UML uses the following notation to show a class `Car` that contains member functions `startEngine()`, `isRunning()`, and `tuneRadioTo()`, and that contains data members called `isRunning_`, `radioOnAM_`, and `radioFreq_`:

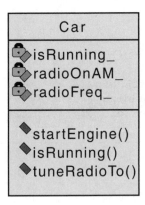

FAQ 2.18

What are the basics of defining member functions?

Member functions are normally defined in the source file associated with the class (but see FAQ 13.01. For example, if the header file is called `"Car.hpp"`, the source file might be called `"Car.cpp"`. Here is an example of the header file `Car.hpp`:

```
#ifndef CAR_HPP
#define CAR_HPP

class Car {
public:
  virtual void startEngine();          Declare a member function
  // ...
protected:
  bool isRunning_;
  bool radioOnAM_;
  int  radioFreq_;
};

#endif
```

Here is an example of the source file Car.cpp:

```
#include "Car.hpp"                    Get the Car class

void Car::startEngine()               Define a member function
{
  isRunning_ = true;
  // ...
}
```

The line void Car::startEngine() tells the compiler that this is the definition of the startEngine() member function from the Car class. If this just said void startEngine() { ... } the compiler would think that a non-member function was being defined, as opposed to the startEngine() member function of the Car class.

The line isRunning_ = true; sets the protected: data member isRunning_ to true. If Car a; a.startEngine(); has been executed, this line would set a.isRunning_ to true (even though a.isRunning_ is protected: it does exist and can be accessed by member functions of the Car class).

FAQ 2.19

What are the basics of adding a constructor to a class?

A *constructor* (a.k.a. *ctor*) is a special member function that is called whenever an object of the class is created. This gives the class developer a chance to initialize the object's member data so that the rest of the member functions can assume that they have a coherent object to work with. Syntactically constructors are member functions with the same name as the class; they are not virtual, and they have no return type.

new

Like normal member functions, constructors are declared in the class's body, which normally appears in the class's header file. For example, the header file for class Car might be file Car.hpp. Here is an example showing the declaration of some constructors in header file Car.hpp:

```
#ifndef CAR_HPP
#define CAR_HPP

class Car {
public:
   Car();                                        ──────── Declare a constructor
   Car(int initRadioFreq, int horsepower);  ──── Declare another constructor
   // ...
protected:
  bool isRunning_;
  bool radioOnAM_;
  int  radioFreq_;
  int  horsepower_;
};

#endif
```

The first constructor takes no parameters and is called whenever an object is created without parameters. For example, the first constructor is used to initialize the first two Car objects created in the following function , and the second constructor (the one that takes two parameters of type int) is used to initialize the third and fourth Car objects created in the following function f().

```
void f()
{

   Car a1;  ──────────── The first ctor is used to initialize a1 and *p1
   Car* p1 = new Car();

   Car a2(880, 200);  ──── The second ctor is used to initialize a2 and *p2
   Car* p2 = new Car(880, 200);

   // ...
}
```

Constructors are often defined in the source file associated with the class. For example, the source file associated with class Car might be file "Car.cpp". Here is an example showing the definition of the first constructor in source file Car.cpp:

```
#include "Car.hpp"  ──── Get the Car class
```

```
Car::Car()  ◄──────────── Define a constructor
: isRunning_ (false)
, radioOnAM_ (true)
, radioFreq_ (880)
, horsepower_(150)
{
  // ...
}
```

The line `Car::Car()` tells the compiler that this is the definition of a constructor of class `Car`. Thus constructors are normally of the form `X::X(/*...*/)`.

The line `: isRunning_ (false)` initializes the `protected:` data member `isRunning_` to `false`; `radioOnAM_`, `radioFreq_`, and `horsepower_` are initialized similarly. This list of initializations between the `:` and the `{` is allowed only in constructors and is called an initialization list. Since the goal of the constructor is to initialize the object to a coherent state, all of an object's member variables should be initialized in every constructor.

Since the second constructor takes parameters, it probably uses these parameters to initialize the member variables in the `Car` object. For example the two parameters might be used to initialize the radio's frequency and the car's horsepower:

```
Car::Car(int initRadioFreq, int horsepower)
: isRunning_ (false)
, radioOnAM_ (false)
, radioFreq_ (initRadioFreq)
, horsepower_(horsepower)
{
  // ...
}
```

FAQ 2.20

What are the basics of adding a destructor to a class?

Every class can optionally have a *destructor* (a.k.a. *dtor*). A destructor is a special member function that is automatically called whenever an object of the class is destroyed. This feature of C++ allows the class developer to close any files the object has opened, release any memory the object has allocated, unlock any semaphores the object has locked, and so on. In general, this gives an object a chance to clean up after itself.

Syntactically a destructor is a member function whose name is a tilde character (~) followed by the name of the class. Like constructors, destructors cannot have a return

new

type. Unlike constructors, destructors can, and often are declared with the `virtual` keyword, and a class can have only one destructor. Like all member functions, a destructor is declared in the class body, which normally appears in the class's header file. For example, the header file for class `Car` might be file `Car.hpp`.

```
#ifndef CAR_HPP
#define CAR_HPP

class Car {
public:
   virtual ~Car();  ◄─── Declaration of a destructor
   // ...
protected:
   // ...
};

#endif
```

Destructors are often defined in the source file for class `Car`, such as in file `Car.cpp`:

```
#include "Car.hpp"

Car::~Car()
{
   // ...  ◄─── Clean-up code goes here
}
```

If a class doesn't have a destructor, the compiler conceptually gives the class a destructor that does nothing. Therefore if a class doesn't need to do anything special inside its destructor, the easiest thing to do is to not even declare a destructor. In fact, in applications that follow the guidelines of this book, a destructor is needed only in a relatively small percentage of the classes.

FAQ 2.21

What are the basics of defining a class that contains a pointer to an object allocated from the heap?

Overview: (1) Try to avoid this situation. (2) If it can't be avoided, use an `auto_ptr`.

Try to avoid defining a class that contains a pointer to an object allocated from the heap. For example, consider the situation where a car contains an engine. There are two choices: the preferred way would be for the engine object to be physically embedded inside the car object, and the undesirable way would be for the car object to contain a pointer to the engine object, where the car allocates the engine object from the heap. Here is a sample `Engine` class:

```cpp
#include <iostream>
using namespace std;

class Engine {
public:
  Engine();
  virtual void start();
};

Engine::Engine()
{
  cout << "Engine constructor\n";
}

void Engine::start()
{
  cout << "Engine::start()\n";
}
```

The car class shown in the following code, class `Car`, uses the preferred approach: each `Car` object physically contains its `Engine` object. Compared to using a pointer to an `Engine` allocated from the heap, the technique shown in class `Car` is easier, safer, and faster, and it uses less memory.

```cpp
class Car {
public:
  Car();
  virtual void startEngine();
protected:
  Engine e_;   ◄──── Physically embed an Engine object inside every Car object
};

Car::Car()
 : e_ ()   ◄──────── Initialize the Engine object that's inside the Car object
{
  // Intentionally left blank
}

void Car::startEngine()
{
  e_.start();   ◄──── Call the start() member function of the Engine object
}
```

Although this is the preferred approach, sometimes it is necessary, or perhaps expedient, to allocate the inner object from the heap and have the outer object contain a pointer to the inner object. When this happens, an auto_ptr should be used:

```
#include <memory>  ◄────────────────── To get auto_ptr
using namespace std;
typedef auto_ptr<Engine> EnginePtr;

class Car {
public:
  Car();
  virtual void startEngine();
  virtual ~Car();
  Car(const Car& c);  ◄─────────────── This can be ignored for now; see FAQ 30.12
  Car& operator= (const Car& c);  ◄── This can be ignored for now; see FAQ 30.12
protected:
  EnginePtr p_;  ◄─────────────────── Every Car object contains an auto_ptr to its
                                      Engine object
};

Car::Car()
: p_ (new Engine())  ◄────────────── Allocate an Engine object for the Car object
{
  // Intentionally left blank
}

void Car::startEngine()
{
  p_->start();  ◄──────────────────── Call the start() member function of the
                                      Engine object
}
```

Logically this second example is still a *contains* or *has-a* relationship, but physically the implementation is somewhat different. Note the three extra member functions that must be declared in the second version of class Car. These extra member functions are needed because an auto_ptr is used to hold the car's Engine object.

The most important message here is that it is much less dangerous to use auto_ptr than to use a raw hardware pointer, such as Car*. Thus the following technique should not be used.

```
class Car {
public:
  Car();
  virtual void startEngine();
  virtual ~Car();
  Car(const Car& c);  ◄─────────────── This can be ignored for now; see FAQ 30.10
```

```
   Car& operator= (const Car& c);  ◄──── This can be ignored for now; see FAQ 30.10
protected:
   Engine* p_;  ◄─────────────────── Bad form: Try to avoid raw hardware pointers to
                                     allocated objects

};
```

The particular dangers of using raw hardware pointers are outlined later in the book, but for now simply use an `auto_ptr` as shown in the second example.

── **FAQ 2.22**

What are the basics of global objects?

Although C++ allows global objects to be declared outside any class, it is generally bet- ter if global objects are declared as static data members of some class. Generally a static data member is declared in the `protected:` section of the class, and, if desired, `public:` static member functions are provided to get and/or set that `protected:` static data member.

For example, consider keeping track of the number of `Car` objects that currently exist. Since it would be quite cumbersome if every single `Car` object had to correctly maintain the current number of `Car` objects, it is better to store this value in a global variable, that is, as a static data member of the `Car` class. Since external users might want to find out how many `Car` objects exist, there should be a `public:` static member function to get that number. But since it would be improper for anyone but the `Car` class to change the value of this variable, there should not be a `public:` static member function to set the number of `Car` objects. The following class illustrates the static data member and the `public:` static access member function.

```
#include <iostream>
using namespace std;

class Car {
public:
   Car();
   ~Car();
   Car(const Car& c);
   static int num();  ◄──────── Member function to access num_
protected:
   static int num_;  ◄──────── Declaration of the static data member
};
```

```
Car::Car()
{
   ++num_;
}

Car::~Car()
{
   --num_;
}

int Car::num()
{
   return num_;
}

int Car::num_ = 0;  ←——— Definition of the static data member
```

Note that static data members must be defined in a source file. It is a common C++ error to forget to define a static data member, and the symptoms are generally an error message at link time. For example, static data member Car::num_ might be defined in the file associated with class Car, such as file Car.cpp.

Unlike normal data members, it is possible to access static data members before the first object of the class is created. For example, it is possible to access static data member Car::num_ before the first Car object is created, as illustrated in the main() routine that follows:

```
int main()
{
   cout << "Before creating any cars, num() returns "
        << Car::num() << "\n";
   Car a, b, c;
   cout << "After creating three cars, num() returns "
        << Car::num() << "\n";
}
```

The output of this main() routine is:

```
Before creating any cars, num() returns 0
After creating three cars, num() returns 3
```

It is also possible to use user-defined classes to define static data members. For example, if there were some sort of registry of Car objects and if the registry were conceptually a global variable, it would be better to define the registry as a static data member of the Car class. This is done just like the static int data member shown: just replace the type int with the type of the registry, and replace the initializer "= 0;" with whatever is appropriate as the initializer for the class of the registry.

FAQ 2.23

What are the basics of throwing and catching exceptions?

Exceptions are for handling errors. If a function cannot fulfill its promises for some reason, it should throw an exception. This style of reporting errors is different from the way many other programming languages report errors—many languages use a return code or error code that the caller is supposed to explicitly test. It sometimes takes a little while before new C++ programmers become comfortable with the C++ way of reporting errors.

In the example code, function processFile() is supposed to process the specified file. The file name is specified using an object of the standard string class. If the file name is not valid (for example, if it contains illegal characters) or if the file does not exist, processFile() cannot proceed, so it throws an exception. In the case of an invalid file name, processFile() throws an object of class BadFileName; in the case of a nonexistent file, it throws an object of class FileNotFound.

Functions isValidFileName() and fileExists() represent routines that determine if a given file name is valid and exists, respectively. As shown below, isValidFileName() always returns true (meaning "yes, the filename is valid") and fileExists() always returns false (meaning "no, the file does not exist"), but in practice these routines would make system calls to determine the proper result.

```cpp
#include <iostream>
#include <string>
using namespace std;

class BadFilename { };
class FileNotFound { };

bool isValidFilename(const string& filename) throw()
{
  // Pretend this checks if filename is a valid filename
  return true;
}

bool fileExists(const string& filename) throw()
{
  // Pretend this checks if filename exists as a file
  return false;
}

void processFile(const string& filename)
throw(BadFilename, FileNotFound)
```

```
{
  if (! isValidFilename(filename))
    throw BadFilename();

  if (! fileExists(filename))
    throw FileNotFound();

  // the filename is valid and exists; process the file:
  // ...
}

void f(const string& filename) throw()
{
  try {
    processFile(filename);
    // ...
  }
  catch (BadFilename& e) {
    cout << "Invalid file name: " << filename << "\n";
  }
  catch (FileNotFound& e) {
    cout << "File not found: " << filename << "\n";
  }
}
```

try and catch are keywords. The code within the block after the try keyword is executed first. In this case, f() calls processFile(). In a real application, processFile() often succeeds (that is, it often returns normally without throwing an exception), in which case the runtime system continues processing the code in the try block, then skips the catch blocks and proceeds normally. In the case when an exception is thrown, control immediately jumps to the matching catch block. If there is no matching catch block in the caller, control immediately jumps back to the matching catch block in the caller's caller, caller's caller's caller, and so on, until it reaches the catch (...) block in main(), shown below. catch (...) is a special catch-all block: it matches all possible exceptions.

```
int main()
{
  try {
    f("input-file.txt");
    // ...
  }
  catch (...) {
    cout << "Unknown exception!\n";
  }
}
```

The `throw()` declarations after the signature of the various functions (e.g., `throw()` after the signature of function `f()` and `throw(BadFilename, FileNotFound)` after the signature of function `processFile()`) are the function's way of telling callers what it might throw. Functions that say `throw()` are effectively saying, "This function doesn't throw any exceptions." Functions that say `throw(BadFilename, FileNotFound)` are effectively saying, "This function might throw a `BadFilename` object or a `FileNotFound` object but nothing else."

FAQ 2.24

What are the basics of inheritance and dynamic binding?

new

Inheritance is a powerful tool that enables extensibility. It allows the software to capture the *is-a* or *kind-of* relationship (although as will be shown in FAQ 7.01, the phrase, "is substitutable for," more accurately captures the true meaning of inheritance).

In the following example, class `Vehicle` is defined with `= 0;` after the declaration of the `startEngine()` member function. This syntax means that the `startEngine()` member function is pure virtual and the `Vehicle` class is an abstract base class, or ABC. In practice, this means that `Vehicle` is an important class from which other classes inherit, and those other derived classes are, in general, required to provide a `startEngine()` member function.

```
class Vehicle {
public:
  virtual void startEngine() = 0;
  virtual ~Vehicle();  ◄──── Destructors of ABCs are often virtual
};

Vehicle::~Vehicle()
{
  // Intentionally left blank
}
```

The idea with ABCs is to build the bulk of the application so that it knows about the ABCs but not the derived classes. For example, the following function is aware of the ABC `Vehicle` but is not aware of any of the derived classes.

```
void f(Vehicle& v)
{
  // ...
  v.startEngine();
```

```
    // ...
}
```

If the ABCs are designed properly, a large percentage of the application will be written at that level. Then new derived classes can be added without impacting the bulk of the application. In other words, the goal is to minimize the ripple effect when adding new derived classes. For example, the following derived classes can be added without disturbing function f().

```
#include <iostream>
using namespace std;

class Car : public Vehicle {
public:
  virtual void startEngine();
};

void Car::startEngine()
{
  cout << "Starting a Car's engine\n";
}

class NuclearSubmarine: public Vehicle {
public:
  virtual void startEngine();
};

void NuclearSubmarine::startEngine()
{
  cout << "Starting a NuclearSubmarine's engine\n";
}
```

The reason these won't disturb the code in function f() (and recall, function f() represents the bulk of the application) is because of two features of C++: the *is-a* conversion and dynamic binding. The is-a conversion says that an object of a derived class, such as an object of class Car, can be passed as a base reference. For example, the following objects c and s can be passed to function f(). Thus the compiler allows a conversion from a derived class (e.g., a Car object) to a base class (e.g., a Vehicle reference).

```
int main()
{
  Car c;
  NuclearSubmarine s;
  f(c);
```

```
    f(s);
}
```

The *is-a* conversion is always safe because inheritance means "is substitutable for." That is, a Car is substitutable for a Vehicle, so it won't surprise function f() if v is in fact referring to a Car.

Dynamic binding is the flip side of the same coin. Whereas the *is-a* conversion safely converts from derived class to base class, dynamic binding safely converts from base class back to derived class. For example, the line v.startEngine() in function f() actually calls the appropriate startEngine() member function associated with the object. That is, when main() passes a NuclearSubmarine into f() (line f(s) in main()), v.startEngine() calls the startEngine() member function associated with class NuclearSubmarine. This is extremely powerful, since class NuclearSubmarine might have been written long after function f() was written and compiled and put into a library. In other words, dynamic binding allows old code (f()) to call new code (NuclearSubmarine::startEngine()) without the old code needing to be modified or even recompiled. This is the essence of extensibility: the ability to add new features to an application without significant impact to existing code. It is doable with C++, but only when the design considerations are carefully thought through ahead of time; it does not come free.

UML uses the following notation to show inheritance.

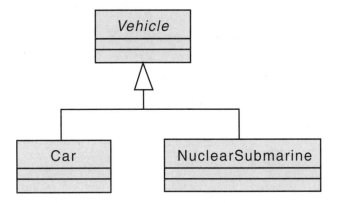

Chapter 3

Understanding the Management Perspective

FAQ 3.01

What is the purpose of this chapter?

To improve the effectiveness of developers by presenting the management perspective on common software questions.

All too often, developers live in their own world of technology and miss the "big picture." As a result, they lose credibility with decision makers by emphasizing peripheral issues, or they fail to sell a laudable idea because it was not packaged and presented effectively. Since this book aims to improve the overall effectiveness of developers, we will show how decision makers think by drawing on our own experience as managers and executives, as well as the insights we've gained from others and from work we've done as architects and developers.

FAQ 3.02

What is the core message of this chapter (and this book)?

 To increase effectiveness by being business-centric rather than technology-centric.

Technology does not exist in a vacuum. It exists in a complex milieu of customers, budgets, competitors, organizational goals, product features, time to market, and so on. In this world, there are no context-free notions of "good" and "bad" (and anyone who proclaims one technique or method as universally bad or another as universally good is hopelessly technocentric). So to make good decisions we need a context, which is defined by looking at the business objectives and using them to help define what "good" means (and what "bad" means). With the context properly defined, it is possible to evaluate technology trade-offs in a manner that always keeps the business objectives in mind.

This message is in stark contrast to what technologists typically preach. For example, technologists typically promote one design method (or inheritance model or programming language) over another using a universal notion of "good" and "bad"—they have an answer even though they don't know what the question is; one size fits all. It's as if they are saying, "I know what's good for you even though I don't understand your world."

This does not imply that different technologies don't have different trade-offs—they do. But the trade-offs can be evaluated only by looking at the business objectives and requirements. This leads to the following high-level process.

1. Examine the business objectives (*why* the application/system is being built).

2. Then examine the requirements (*what* the application/system should do).

3. Then examine all the alternate design techniques (*how* the application/system should be built).

And always make the less important decisions (such as various design techniques and ultimately the programming techniques) in light of the more important decisions (such as what the system is supposed to do and, even more important, why it is being built in the first place).

FAQ 3.03

Why are the managers in charge rather than the developers who understand technology?

Because most organizations have a culture that assumes that managers are long-term and developers are replaceable parts.

Managers are supposed to understand the goals of the organization and to ensure that the goals are achieved, often using technology in one form or another. Their job is to represent the organization, and in many cases they have a fiduciary responsibility (and personal liability) if things go wrong. In their view, developers are transient and are often more interested in technology than the welfare of the organization. This may or may not be true, and the average tenure of CIOs is probably shorter than the average tenure of developers, but what's important is the perception, not the reality.

The message is that developers can increase their influence in the organization by demonstrating that they understand the organization's business objectives and that they are committed to achieving the business objectives rather than being committed to playing around with the coolest techno-gadgets. This means making sure business issues always dominate technology issues. It also means presenting proposals in terms that managers can understand, including staffing, schedules, opportunity costs, risk, and dollars and cents. Try it some time. It works.

FAQ 3.04

How can someone manage something they don't understand?

People have been doing it for years; managers hardly ever understand what they are managing.

Should the CEO of IBM know how to configure computers? Or issue expense checks? Or control the building temperature? No. The CEO's job is to understand strategy, directions, and politics; too much knowledge about operational minutiae would indicate misfocused energies. The same sort of thinking applies to every level of management, down to the first-level supervisor. Besides, if CEOs did understand the low-level details, they'd probably drive the developers crazy micromanaging them.

So managers shouldn't try to be technology experts. But how can they manage anyway? Anyone who has ever raised children has experienced keeping control without having a clue about what they were doing or what the children were saying. Managing a software project is the same thing, only the children are older and there are books that explain their lingo.

Of course, there are good managers and bad managers. Good managers lead their teams, set realistic goals, get needed resources, mentor team members, take care of administrative issues, and communicate business objectives. In other words, good managers are worthy individuals who need all the help and support they can get. So the wise developer educates the managers and becomes a reliable source of knowledge and common sense, the trusted person. Such developers protect their managers from themselves and learn to speak their language. Manipulate your managers like your children manipulate you!

FAQ 3.05

What is the most common mistake on C++ and OO projects?

 Unnecessary complexity—the plague of OO technology.

Complexity, like risk, is a fact of life that can't be avoided. Some software systems have to be complex because the business processes they represent are complex. But unfortunately many intermediate developers try to "make things better" by adding generalization and flexibility that no one has asked for or will ever need. The customer wants a cup of tea, and the developers build a system that can boil the ocean [thanks to John Vlissides for this quip]. The result is unnecessary complexity, which increases the risk of failure. The intentions might be good but the result can be deadly.

Here are a few guidelines.

- Don't solve problems that don't need to be solved.

- Don't worry about the future until you're sure you can survive the present.

- Don't build things for the fun of it.

- The organization's health is more important than the developer's desire to play with the latest whiz-bang tool or technique.

- Don't add risk without a compelling and measurable benefit to the project.

- Don't invest in the future if your current project is in trouble.

Avoid the "death by one thousand cuts" syndrome by avoiding unnecessary complexity.

FAQ 3.06

What's the "Software Peter Principle"?

The Software Peter Principle is in operation when unwise developers "improve" and "generalize" the software until they themselves can no longer understand it, then the project slowly dies.

The Software Peter Principle can ruin projects. The insidious thing about the Software Peter Principle is that it's a silent killer—by the time the symptoms are visible, the problem has spread throughout every line of code in the project. Foolish managers deal with symptoms rather than prevention, and they think everything is okay unless there are visible bugs. Yet the problem isn't bugs, at least initially. The problem is that the project is collapsing under its own weight.

The best way to avoid this problem is to build to the skill level of the maintainers, not of the developers. If the typical maintainer won't understand the software then it's simply too complex for the organization to maintain. This means avoiding tricky, sophisticated, subtle, clever techniques unless there is a compelling reason for them. Cleverness is evil; use it only when necessary. Show concern for the long-term health of the system being developed.

FAQ 3.07

Should an organization use OO on all its projects?

No!

The organization is in some business other than OO programming, and technology is a means to an end. Developers might want to use OO because it is intellectually stimulating, but the people in charge have other goals and probably don't care what sort of technology is employed.

The message for developers is to focus presentations and justifications on achieving business goals, and make sure that OO is presented as an effective tool for achieving the desired business results rather than as a "cool" techie thing. Show why it's relevant. Above all, don't use the "it's the latest and greatest" argument as a justification: that angle has been overused for too many years and almost always turns off the listener. Also, don't use the "it will keep the developers happy" approach: most managers think that they are the people who need to be kept happy and that developers are transient, replaceable components.

FAQ 3.08

Can OO be ignored until it goes away?

 No!

Some developers fight against OO, and some managers take a "let's wait for it to go away just like (fill in the blank) did." But the fact is that OO and C++ aren't going away so everyone might as well get on board. There are lots of technical arguments for the superiority of this technology, but the best reason is nontechnical: this is the way the world is moving. Too many people have sunk too much money into building products based on OO for it to go away. And the only way to take advantage of the advances in software engineering in the last decade or two is to utilize a modern programming language such as C++.

So the reluctant developer should get on board. The trend is inevitable and there is nothing to be gained by fighting the inevitable. If management is doing the foot dragging, don't waste time with technical superiority arguments. Focus instead on the business issues, such as availability of tools, components, and people.

FAQ 3.09

What OO language is best?

 Whichever one works best for the organization.

We believe in honesty, not advocacy, and the honest answer is that there is no single answer. What is the organization's policy regarding languages? Must there be one and only one official language? What is the skill level of the staff? Are they gung-ho developers with advanced degrees in computer science/engineering or people who understand the business and have survival skills in software? Do they already have OO skills? In which language(s)? What sort of software development is being done: extending someone else's framework or building from scratch for resale? What sort of performance constraints does the software have? Is it space constrained or speed constrained? If speed, is it typically bound by I/O, network, or CPU? Regarding libraries and tools, are there licensing considerations? Are there strategic partnership relationships that affect the choice of languages? Many of these questions are nontechnical, but they are the kind of questions that need to be answered before the "which language" issue can be addressed.

Regarding the choice between C++ and Java, Java is a simpler language and thus it is generally easier to use. However C++ is more established and allows finer control over resources (for example, memory management), and this is required for some applications. Also, C++ has language features such as destructors, conversion operators and operator overloading that can be intimidating to many developers but are essential for building frameworks that hide complexity from users. Building the same framework in Java will necessarily expose some internal complexity to the developers who need to extend the framework. So C++ will always be needed, but it isn't the only answer and it isn't always the best answer.

The messages can be summarized neatly. (1) Avoid language bigotry and language wars. (2) Never, never present language trade-offs to management exclusively using technical criteria—when choosing between languages, the most important issues are typically business issues, not technical issues. (3) Don't assume that the organization wants to be on the leading edge. (4) Don't assume that the organization has a primary goal of furthering the careers of its developers.

FAQ 3.10

What is the right approach to processes and tools?

Select processes and tools based on business considerations rather than purely on technical grounds. Buy tools, don't build them. Customize existing processes; don't invent your own.

In general, the selections should be popular enough that they'll be around in five years, should be mature, should be consistent with the organization's skill levels, and should allow hiring new people who already have the necessary skills.

An important consideration is that the *process* should allow local variations. IBM's WSDDM is an example of this.

Technologists waste a lot of energy arguing the virtues and vices of the various *design notations*. As usual, business considerations should dominate technical considerations. UML is currently the most popular notation, and it is used in this book.

The emerging method of *analysis and design* from the "three amigos" (Booch, Jacobson, and Rumbaugh) associated with UML is pretty good and has been well received by the marketplace.

With respect to *design tools,* beware of "tool worship." Remember: tools don't produce designs; people produce designs. Tools capture the thoughts of the design team, but before the tool can add value, the design team first has to think some reasonably good thoughts. Some tools also generate skeleton code, but that's helpful only if the design is good. So tools are good, in that they capture and transmit ideas in a uniform manner, but underneath it all, design is much more human than mechanical.

FAQ 3.11

What is the right approach with off-the-shelf class libraries and frameworks?

 Buy, don't build.

Unless there's a compelling reason, don't roll your own class library or technical framework from scratch. There was a time when there wasn't much in the way of technical frameworks and class libraries, and back then it made sense to roll your own. But those days have passed. Note that it is still not possible to buy much in the way of industry-specific frameworks, so there is an ongoing need to build "business frameworks," but most technology-oriented frameworks are abundantly available.

For example, people using distributed objects should choose between a CORBA implementation and the latest variation of DCOM/COM+. It will be a hard decision, and it can't be analyzed in one paragraph, but the important idea is to avoid building a custom ORB unless there is some compelling reason to do so.

Chapter 4

The Architectural Perspective

What is the purpose of this chapter?

To discuss the relationship between software architecture and OO design and OO programming.

It is critical to plan for change in the software system as well as in the people who will be used to construct and maintain the software. Good architecture is the key to planning for and responding to change.

Many of the design and programming principles advocated in this book are rooted in software architecture. For example, an important architectural principle is to reduce unnecessary coupling, and this book discusses how C++ can be used to decrease coupling. Thus it is important to understand the architect's perspective and to know how to translate architectural principles into C++ constructs.

In this book, the term *software architecture* is used rather broadly to describe several activities that occur early in the development cycle, including domain analysis and defining the logical (rather than physical) organization of the system.

FAQ 4.02

Why is software architecture important?

 Because it is vital to producing good software.

Good software is correct, usable, maintainable, testable, flexible, documented, solves a meaningful problem, performs well, and has an acceptable cost of ownership. In other words, it gets the job done. It is the job of the system architect(s) to understand and balance a wide range of competing forces (business forces, management forces, and technical forces) and lay the groundwork for the rest of the team to produce good software. If the architecture is inadequate or inappropriate, everyone ends up paying a penalty.

First, every system has an architecture. Either it is explicitly defined, documented, and serves as a solid basis for ongoing system development, or it evolves haphazardly as a by-product of hundreds of ill-considered and inconsistent decisions.

Second, don't believe anyone who says that a system doesn't need an architecture or that time and money can be saved by skipping the definition of the system's architecture. Building a system without an architecture is like building an office building without blueprints—sure, the thing might get finished, but it probably won't fulfill its goals, it will probably cost more than it should, and there is a greater risk that it will collapse.

Third, software architecture techniques, OO methods, design patterns, tools, and programming languages are mature enough that there is no reason for any system to be developed without an adequate architecture.

Fourth, good software does not have to be OO software (gasp!) and does not have to be reusable (gasp again!). Too many projects have suffered from excessive worrying about reuse and not enough worrying about usability. And sometimes the concerns about what someone might want the software to possibly do someday leads to complexity that precludes it ever meeting its immediate requirements.

From an architectural perspective, the moral is to favor conservatism and to realize that common sense should prevail. This profession is tough enough; don't try to accomplish any more than is necessary and don't push the technological envelope without good reason. It is better to err on the conservative side and build a practical system. At least that way you get a chance to live and fight another day. This chapter discusses some of the important issues in making software usable, extensible, and reusable through the use of OO techniques.

FAQ 4.03

What should the architecture be based on, the problem being solved or the problem domain?

The problem domain.

new

One of the primary goals of the software architect is to build a system that will survive changes in requirements and that can be adapted to new and related problems. To achieve this goal the system architecture must have a stable base.

The specification of a single problem that is to be solved is unstable, since it depends on the whims of the customer and therefore is unsuitable as the basis for the system architecture. The problem domain is much more stable, because it is an artifact of the world in which the customer lives.

For example, every order entry system must deal with orders, customers, prices, quantities, payments, addresses, sales reports, and so on. These entities represent the problem domain and are stable across all order entry systems.

However, each particular order entry system has different parameters that reflect the customer's current requirements based on the current business situation, including different placement of fields on the screen, different colors for different fields, different currencies for multinational applications, and so on. Furthermore, some order entry systems are implemented as PC applications, others are implemented as Web-based applications, while others are implemented as Interactive Voice Response systems.

The moral for the software architect is that the system architecture should be based on the problem domain because the needs of customers change more rapidly than their world does.

FAQ 4.04

Should the software architecture be based on the policy of the problem?

No—that would be totally insane.

The policy of any single problem is unstable. Software systems based on the least stable element (the problem) are inflexible, cannot respond to changing requirements, and are doomed to become brittle.

Software should be written so that changing the requirements doesn't break the architecture. Basing the architecture on the most stable element, the *problem domain,* accomplishes this objective.

Note that software can survive problem changes only within the confines of the problem domain. It's unreasonable to expect a system that was originally designed for the problem domain of compilers to work for cellular telephones, since this would be changing the problem domain rather than just the problem.

From an architectural standpoint, the message is to usually emphasize the problem domain rather than technical infrastructure. However, there are occasional counter-examples, and this is why intimate knowledge of both technology and the problem domain is so important.

FAQ 4.05

Do customers ever change their requirements?

Ha, ha, ha! The only customers who don't change their requirements are dead customers. In all of recorded history, no customer has ever changed his/her mind less than twice (and the poor customer who only made two sets of changes was hit by a meteorite on the way to sending in the third set of changes). While it is true that some requirement changes can be avoided with foresight, it is also true that most requirement changes occur for perfectly valid reasons. Between the beginning of a project and the first release, requirements change due to changing market conditions, changing business objectives, competitive pressure, and changing technology. In the longer term (after the first release), requirements change for all the same reasons.

The message here is that changing requirements are a fact of life and the wise team plans for them rather than complaining about them.

FAQ 4.06

Are stable requirements desirable?

No—the only software that doesn't have to be changed is software no one uses.

If the job is done right the first time, people will use the software again. And since everything else in life seems to change rapidly, it is certain that the software will need to be updated, expanded, changed, or revised. The only way to have stable requirements is for the product to be so bad that no one wants to use it. Stable requirements reflect a dead product. Stable requirements are an enemy, not a friend.

The wise architect knows that change is inevitable and has the judgment needed to balance the short-term and long-term requirements in a way that the developers can implement. On the other hand, the developer needs to understand that adding nonrequested flexibility "just in case someone needs it" is not a responsible action.

What is the key to planning for change?

Understanding the problem domain.

new

Almost every OO analysis and design method promotes understanding the problem domain through some form of domain analysis. This is the process of becoming familiar with the problem domain by (among other things) interviewing domain experts, analyzing existing business processes, working with customers, and validating and refining these findings. This process produces a model of the problem domain including domain objects, services provided by these objects, and the interaction patterns of these objects.

The domain model is the extensible, flexible, reusable basis on which the software architecture should be based. The beauty of OO technology and C++ is that public inheritance (see FAQ 2.24, 7.01) can be used to reflect the fundamental, immutable properties of the problem domain and the domain model. In this way, the public inheritance relationships model the problem domain rather than depending on the fickle requirements of the even more fickle customer. Thus the architecture can and should be made to reflect the problem domain rather than the particular problem at hand.

These issues will be discussed at great length later in the book.

The key is to recognize that OO technology provides flexibility when the domain analysis is solid and the software faithfully reflects the domain analysis. Under these circumstances, changing the details of the problem creates incidental disturbances rather than fundamental disruptions.

What is a framework?

A framework is a thematic collection of software that is used to build applications.

new

A framework is a set of class hierarchies plus models of interaction and cooperation between the various objects of the various hierarchies. The framework defines a generic program structure that is suitable for building a group of related applications or systems. Usually the framework provides default behavior for common situations while allowing the default behavior to be easily overridden with application-specific behavior when necessary. That is, the framework is designed to be customized for solving a specific problem or building a specific business application.

In C++, the most important artifacts in the generic program structure are usually *abstract base classes* (ABCs) (see FAQs 2.24, 17.03). The framework also prescribes the valid interactions among the objects. In C++, the default behavior and the ability to customize the framework is usually accomplished using inheritance and dynamic binding.

FAQ 4.09

What is the "inversion of control" exhibited by frameworks?

The Hollywood model: Don't call us, we'll call you.

In traditional applications, the application programmer writes the main event loop and this "main program" reaches out and calls reusable library routines as needed. This is "piecewise reuse": the idea is to reuse little pieces of software but leave it up to the application programmer to write the main program. In this approach, the called chunks of software are the reusable assets and the main program is the "glue code" that is application specific.

Frameworks are just the opposite: the framework—not the application code—controls the flow of execution, and the framework reaches out and calls the application-specific code written by the application developer as needed. This is made possible because the framework is specially designed to call virtual functions to perform operations that are expected to be application specific. Thus, the application programmer specializes the framework by overriding these virtual functions as necessary (see FAQ 2.24).

This inversion of control is a powerful and useful concept, but it is initially quite uncomfortable for developers and their managers. For some reason, everyone emotionally equates the word "reuse" with calling little chunks of reusable code; they have a hard time seeing that frameworks (where reuse involves a big chunk of reusable code calling small chunks of application-specific code) provide higher degrees of reuse.

FAQ 4.10

What is an extensible, domain-specific framework?

A competitive advantage.

An extensible, domain-specific framework models the key abstractions of the problem domain. Domain-specific frameworks, along with the classes from general-purpose class libraries (see FAQ 28.01), are the building blocks for constructing applications/ systems for that problem domain.

An extensible, domain-specific framework should have as much *domain*-specific knowledge as possible while remaining as independent as possible from any single problem being solved. If there is not enough domain-specific knowledge, future developers must largely rediscover the problem domain. If it has too much *problem*-specific knowledge, future developers will always be fighting the problem-specific assumptions.

FAQ 4.11

What characteristics make a framework extensible yet domain-specific?

Mechanism rich, policy free.

new

In this context, *mechanism* refers to anything (information, data, procedures, processes) that is intrinsic to the problem domain; *policy* refers to anything that is likely to change or to be application specific. Examples of mechanism in order processing systems might include payment methods such as purchase orders, cash, cash on delivery, and credit cards, whereas the interest rate for late payment might be an example of policy.

So the ideal extensible, domain-specific framework is rich in the mechanism of the problem domain but free from policy within the problem. This makes it a suitable basis for a wide range of applications without forcing every organization to adopt the same policies. If it isn't mechanism rich, future developers won't get as much "oomph" (a technical term) as they might otherwise. If it isn't policy free, future developers will have to work around the obsolete policy.

Deciding what is mechanism and what is policy is an art. Within an extensible framework for order processing systems, is assuming that all transactions can be processed in a single currency an example of mechanism or policy? Clearly, this is situation specific. For some organizations this assumption is perfectly reasonable and it can be built into the mechanism of the framework. For other organizations the currency might change from transaction to transaction, in which case the decision of which currency to use is a policy decision that should not be built into the mechanism of the framework.

FAQ 4.12

What happens if the domain analysis is incorrect?

It costs money.

Once a domain analysis mistake has been discovered, randomly patching the code makes matters worse. Instead of patching code, fix the domain analysis error. Unfortunately, fixing domain analysis errors often breaks existing code.

Even though changing existing code is expensive, it is often far more expensive to continue building the software based on a faulty domain analysis. Domain analysis errors usually make software brittle.

That's why it has been said that domain-analysis errors are ten times more costly to fix than programming errors. If you must make changes, sooner is often much cheaper than later.

FAQ 4.13

How much effort should be expended to support change— that is, how much is extensibility worth?

It depends on the specific situation, but don't focus on supporting change to the point that the project won't finish on time.

An extensible product isn't worth much if it has no users. On the other hand, having lots of users but inflexible software means that enhancing and maintaining the software will be an expensive proposition. In today's rapidly changing business climate it can be deadly to have an inflexible software product. It's a delicate balancing act.

Here is a real-life example that illustrates this issue. Two organizations had similar products. One used OO technology to achieve extensibility (a new release every six months); the other shipped a new release every two years. Not only did the rapid-fire organization create four times as many sales opportunities per customer than its slower counterpart, it also used its enhanced features to become the market leader.

The only software that never changes is software that no one uses. Successful software will need to be changed. The hard decision is the judgment call as to the risk/reward ratio for investing in future extensibility. Once this decision has been made, it is important that the developer not undo the decision by gratuitously enhancing the system without authorization. Too many developers add flexibility to the software just because it can be done, paying no attention to whether it should be done.

FAQ 4.14

How does an architect make the software architecture flexible?

Intentionally.

The main message here is that flexibility is not something that comes automatically, even with OO. The other message is that it is not possible to create infinitely flexible software without introducing unmanageable complexity, so the only alternative is to rely on knowledge of the problem domain to make wise choices.

Here's a way to do it.

1. Write down the specific places where the architects and analysts think the software needs to be flexible. Make sure the list isn't too long.

2. Throw out everything on the list that a user/customer wouldn't pay real money for. Usually this means discarding all the "technical flexibility spots" such as swapping out class libraries, since customers are usually willing to pay only for things that affect the external behavior, not the internal implementation of external behavior. Again, make sure the list isn't too long.

3. Do a cost/benefit analysis on each of the remaining line items. Get the customer to add whatever survives this analysis to the "Nonfunctional Requirements Specification" or other appropriate document, just to make sure the customer realizes what's going on.

Don't try to create software that's like a rubber band—flexible in every conceivable direction. Instead, identify a few specific places where the system needs be flexible and do a good job with those places. If you get this point wrong, you'll end up with massive unnecessary complexity and your project will probably fail.

FAQ 4.15

What is the secret to achieving reuse?

Building a reuse culture.

new

Some aspects of reuse are technical (such as carrying out successful domain analysis and building extensible, domain-specific frameworks), but the real problems come from human issues. Developers need to lose the attitude that says, "I want to build my own infrastructure because it's more fun and enhances my career" and "I don't trust or want to understand someone else's work, so I'll do everything from scratch." If the human issues aren't resolved, the technology questions become immaterial.

Enlightened leadership and an appropriate reward system can sometimes overcome these problems, but sometimes the project team itself can foster the right attitude. In one case the developers decided that working together was important, and they used the word "big" to describe people and actions that contributed to reuse (as in "That is big of you") and conversely the word "small" to describe people and actions that were petty or self-centered. Thus the words "big" and "small" became an informal mechanism for the team to enforce and reinforce their culture in a reasonably nonthreatening way.

The architectural perspective is to recognize that reuse is much more than a technical question and that there are inherent limits on what is possible. There is no point in investing development effort to achieve reuse if the organizational culture will keep the reuse from actually occurring.

Part II

Object-Oriented Design

Chapters 5 through 10 cover design issues related to the use of C++ as an object-oriented programming language. An understanding of these principles is essential to using C++ effectively, particularly for large projects.

Chapter 5

Object-Oriented Fundamentals

What is the purpose of this chapter?

To explain fundamental OO concepts.

new

C++ is a huge language that can be used in many ways. The preceding chapters on management and architectural perspectives limit the ways the language is used, which makes life simpler for developers and maintainers. This chapter further limits the ways in which the language can be (mis)used.

In this book, we assume an OO approach and the C++ presentation reflects this bias. Some readers will need a refresher on OO concepts, and others need to become familiar with our terminology. Hence this chapter presents the basic OO ideas and philosophies that are used throughout the book. Don't take this to mean that all programs must use OO (they don't) or that "C++ as a better C" has no place in life (it does).

Why is the world adopting OO technology?

Because OO can handle change more effectively than its predecessors.

The former paradigm (structured analysis, design, and programming) enabled the design and construction of huge software systems. However, these systems lack the flexibility required to meet the demands placed on software in today's rapidly changing business environment. Thus, the old paradigm died from its own success: it created demand that it couldn't satisfy.

As users demanded more from software, economics dictated a better paradigm, and object-oriented technology is that better approach. This book is not just about technology; it also focuses on how to apply technology in a practical way to achieve the goals of the organization.

A cynic might note that the world is adopting OO technology whether it makes sense or not, because most of the software tools being built today assume OO orientation. The conviction of the early pioneers that OO was the best approach was a self-fulfilling prophecy.

FAQ 5.03

What are some of the benefits of using C++ for OO programming?

Large user community, multiparadigm language, performance, and legacy code access.

C++ is an object-oriented programming language with a very broad base of users. This large and thriving user community has led to high-quality compilers and other development tools for a wide range of systems. It has also led to the availability of learning aids, such as books, conferences, bulletin boards, and organizations that specialize in training and consulting. With that much support, investing in C++ is a relatively safe undertaking.

C++ is a multiparadigm language. This allows developers to choose the programming style that is right for the task at hand. For example, a traditional procedural style may be appropriate for performing a simple task such as writing the code within a small member function.

C++ software can be performance and memory efficient, provided it is designed properly. For example, well-designed, object-oriented software is normally comprehensible and therefore amenable to performance tuning. In addition, C++ has low-level—and often dangerous—facilities that allow a skilled C++ developer to obtain appropriate levels of performance.

C++ is (mostly) backward compatible with C. This is useful in very large legacy systems where the migration to OO normally occurs a few subsystems at a time rather than all at once. In particular, C++'s backward compatibility makes it relatively inexpensive to compile legacy C code with a C++ compiler, allowing the old, non-OO subsystems to coexist with the new OO subsystems. Furthermore, simply compiling the legacy C code with a C++ compiler subjects the non-OO subsystems to the relatively stronger type-safety checks of a C++ compiler. In today's quality-sensitive culture, this makes good business sense.

FAQ 5.04

What are the fundamental concepts of object-oriented technology?

Objects, classes, and inheritance.

By definition, object-oriented programming languages must provide objects, classes, and inheritance. In addition, polymorphism and dynamic binding are also required for all but the most trivial applications. Together, these five features provide the tools for fulfilling the goals of OO: abstraction, encapsulation, comprehensibility, changeability, and reusability.

An object is a software entity that combines state and behavior. A class is a programming construct that defines the common state and behavior of a group of similar objects; that is, a class has a name, and it describes the state (member data) and services (member functions) provided by objects that are instances of that class. The runtime system creates each object based on a class definition.

As an analogy, consider a home. A home is like an object since it has state (whether the lights are on, ambient temperature, and so on) and it provides services (a button that opens the garage door, a thermostat that controls the temperature, an alarm system that detects intruders, and so on). To carry the home metaphor a bit further, a blueprint for a home is like a class since a blueprint defines the characteristics of a group of similar homes.

Simple data types as `int` and `float` can be thought of as classes; variables of these types can be thought of as objects of the associated class.

Classes can be related by inheritance. In C++, inheritance facilitates polymorphism and dynamic binding. Polymorphism allows objects of one class to be used as if they were objects of another, related class. Dynamic binding ensures that the code that is executed is always consistent with the type of the object. Rather than selecting the proper code fragment by some ad hoc technique such as complex decision logic, the proper code fragment is automatically selected in a manner that is both extensible and always correct. Together, these allow old code to call new code; new classes can be added to a working system without affecting existing code.

FAQ 5.05 ———————————————————————————

Why are classes important?

 Classes are the fundamental packaging unit of OO technology.

Classes are a way to localize all the state (data) and services (typically member functions) associated with a cohesive concept. The main idea is to organize things so that when changes to the concept or abstraction occur (as is inevitable), it will be possible to go to one place to make the necessary modifications. We have seen examples in the procedural world where a simple change required modifying dozens of source code files. This shouldn't happen with a proper OO class definition, but we recall one C++ project where a simple change required modifying 46 different files. Obviously, the people responsible for this failure didn't "get it"; they may have been using C++, but they weren't using it properly. It's easy for beginners, no matter how much experience they have, to fall into this trap.

Here is the skeletal syntax for a typical class definition:

```
class ClassName {
public:
  ◄—— Public member functions declared here
protected:
  ◄—— Protected data and member functions declared here
private:
  ◄—— Private data and member functions declared here
};
```

Here is the UML representation of a class.

 FAQ 5.06 ———————————————————————————

What is an object?

 It depends on who you are.

To a programmer, an object is a region of storage with associated semantics. To a designer, an object is any identifiable component in the problem domain. In the following diagram `recRoomTV` is an object of class `TV`.

After a declaration such as `int i;`, `i` is said to be an object of type `int`. In OO/C++, an object is usually an instance of a `class`.

Here is the UML notation for an object:

```
recRoomTV :    TV
```

What are the desirable qualities of an object?

An ideal object is a service provider that is alive, responsible, and intelligent.

Each object is an independent entity with its own lifetime, internal state, and set of services. Objects should be alive, responsible, and intelligent agents. Objects are *not* simply a convenient way to package data structures and functions together. The fundamental purpose of an object is to provide services.

Ideal objects should be alive so that they can take care of themselves. They are born (constructed), live a full and productive life, and die (destroyed). Objects are expected to do something useful and maintain themselves in a coherent state. The opposite of "alive objects" is "dead data." Most data structures in procedural programs are dead in the sense that they just lie there in memory and wait for the functions to manipulate them.

Ideal objects should be responsible so that you can delegate to them. Since they are alive, they have rights and responsibilities. They have the right to look after their own affairs—programmers do not reach into their innards and manipulate them, and they are responsible for providing one or more services. This means that other objects ("users") can delegate work to them instead of having to do everything for themselves. This helps produce more modular and reusable software that consists of many objects, each of which does one thing.

Ideal objects should be intelligent so that they can provide services to their users, thus simplifying user code. For example, the knowledge of how to do some task (whether it is simple or complex) resides in only one place, inside the object. Users simply request the service; they concentrate on what needs to be done rather than how it's done. Effectively this moves complexity from the many to the few.

The benefits of moving complexity from the many to the few are all around us. As an analogy, consider how airlines might consider getting rid of all those expensive pilots and let the customers fly the airplanes for a rental fee like the car rental companies do. However, this would require, among other things, that every traveler be trained as a pilot, making air travel both more complicated and more accident prone. Instead, airlines move the intelligence regarding cockpit controls from the many to the few—from every traveler using the airlines to the pilots. The result is simpler and safer for travelers (users) and cheaper for the airlines (servers).

As a practical matter, this means that the first step for a new class is to write down its roles and responsibilities. This helps clarify why the class exists, whether or not it is needed, and what services it should provide. Defining the responsibilities of all objects prevents confusion and simplifies the design process.

FAQ 5.08

How are classes better than the three basic building blocks of procedural software?

A class is better than a C-style `struct`, better than a module, and better than a C-style function.

A class can be thought of as a C-style `struct` that is also alive and intelligent. Take away all the member functions from a class, make everything `public:`, eliminate inheritance, and remove all the static member data and functions; the result is a traditional C-style `struct`. A C-style `struct` supports multiple instances, but it is difficult to encapsulate its implementations properly. Classes support both multiple instances and encapsulation. When a C-style `struct` dreams about growing up, it dreams of being a class.

A class can be thought of as a module that also provides natural support for multiple instances and `inline` functions. Take away from a class all the non-static member data and the non-static member functions and force all remaining `static` member functions to be non-`inline`, and the result is a traditional module. Modules support encapsulation, but creating multiple instances of a module is cumbersome. Classes support both encapsulation and multiple instances. When a module dreams about growing up, it dreams of being a class.

A class can be thought of as a C-style function that can maintain state between invocations in a thread-safe manner and can also provide multiple services. If there were exactly one instance of a `class`, and all its member functions except for exactly one `public:` member function were removed, the result would be a C-style function (the object's member data would correspond to `static` data that is local to the function). C-style functions support computation, but it's cumbersome to maintain state between calls in a thread-safe manner (using `static` local data is not immediately thread safe). However, classes support computation and can maintain state between calls in a thread-safe manner (each thread can make a separate local object of the class, so there is no conflict when multiple threads are accessing their own independent data). When a C-style function dreams about growing up, it dreams of being a class.

FAQ 5.09

What is the purpose of composition?

Composition allows software to be developed by assembling existing components rather than crafting new ones.

Composition (sometimes called *aggregation*) is the process of putting an object (a part) inside another object (the composite). It models the *has-a* relationship. For example, a `FordTaurus` can be composed of, among other things, an `Engine`, `Transmission`, `InstrumentPanel`, and so on. In other words, a `FordTaurus` has an `Engine` (equivalently, an `Engine` is *part-of* a `FordTaurus`):

```
#include <iostream>
using namespace std;

class Engine {
public:
  virtual void start();
};

void Engine::start()
{
  cout << "starting Engine\n";
}

class FordTaurus {
public:
  virtual void start();
protected:
  Engine engine_;     // An Engine is part of a FordTaurus
};
```

```
void FordTaurus::start()
{
  cout << "starting FordTaurus\n";
  engine_.start();
}

int main()
{
  FordTaurus taurus;
  taurus.start();
}
```

Sometimes developers incorrectly use inheritance (kind-of) when they should use composition. For example, they might make FordTaurus inherit from Engine, which confuses kind-of with part-of.

FAQ 5.10 ——————————————————————————

What is the purpose of inheritance?

In C++, inheritance is for subtyping. It lets developers model the *kind-of* relationship.

Inheritance allows developers to make one class a kind-of another class. In an inheritance relationship, the new class is called the *derived class* and the original class from which the new class is being derived is called the *base class.* All the data structures and member functions that belong to the base class automatically become part of the derived class.

For example, suppose the class Stack has member functions push() and pop(), and there is a need for a class PrintableStack. PrintableStack is exactly like Stack except PrintableStack also provides the member function print(). Class PrintableStack can be built by inheriting from Stack—Stack would be the base class and PrintableStack would be the derived class. The member functions push() and pop() and any others that belong to Stack automatically become part of PrintableStack, so the only requirement for building PrintableStack is adding the print() member function to it.

To do something similar in C, the existing Stack source file would be modified (which is trouble if Stack is being used by other source files and they rely on the exact layout of Stack) or copied into another file that would then be tweaked. However, code copying is the least desirable form of reuse: it doubles the maintenance costs and duplicates any bugs in the original source file. Using C++ and inheritance, Stack remains unmodified, yet PrintableStack doesn't need to duplicate the code for the inherited member functions.

FAQ 5.11

What are the advantages of polymorphism and dynamic binding?

They allow old code to call new code in a substitutable fashion.

The real power of object-oriented programming isn't just inheritance; it's the ability to treat objects of derived classes as if they were objects of the base class. The mechanisms that support this are polymorphism and dynamic binding.

Polymorphism allows an object of a derived class to be passed to a function that accepts a reference or a pointer to a base class. A function that receives such objects is a polymorphic function.

When a polymorphic function invokes a member function using a base class reference or pointer, *dynamic binding* executes the code from the derived class even though the polymorphic function may be unaware that the derived class exists. The code that is executed depends on the type of the object rather than on the type of the reference or pointer. In this way, objects of a derived class can be substituted for objects of a base class without requiring any changes in the polymorphic functions that use the objects.

FAQ 5.12

How does OO help produce flexible and extensible software?

By minimizing the ripple effect of enhancements.

Even in well-designed structured systems, enhancements often require modifications to significant portions of existing design and code. OO achieves flexibility by (1) allowing the past to make use of the future, and (2) designing for comprehensibility.

The past can make use of the future when old user code (the past) can reliably and predictably call new server code (the future) without any modifications to the old user code. Inheritance, polymorphism, and dynamic binding are used to achieve this lofty goal.

Comprehensibility allows software to be understood not only by the original development team, but also by the team making the enhancements. Abstraction and specification are used to achieve this lofty goal.

This approach can be contrasted with software developed using the traditional, structured approach, where enhancements or modifications often lead to a seemingly endless cycle of random modifications (a.k.a. hacks) until the system appears to work.

FAQ 5.13

How can old code call new code?

 Through the magic of polymorphism, inheritance, and dynamic binding.

In the traditional software paradigm, it is easy for new code to call old code using sub-routine libraries. However, it is difficult for old code to call new code (unless the old code is modified so that it knows about the new code, in which case the old code is no longer old).

With object orientation, old polymorphic functions can dynamically bind to new server code. An object of a derived class can be passed to and used by an existing poly-morphic function without modifying the polymorphic function.

When compiling a polymorphic function, it is as if the compiler looks forward in time and generates code that will bind to all the classes that will ever be added. For example, a graphical drawing package might deal with squares, circles, polygons, and various other shapes. Most of the drawing package's services deal with generic shapes rather than a particular kind of shape, like a square (for example, "if a shape is selected by the mouse, the shape is dragged across the screen and placed in a new location"). Polymorphism and dynamic binding allow the drag-and-drop code to work correctly regardless of the kind of shape being manipulated. To implement this approach, class Shape would declare virtual functions for drawing and moving. The derived classes would represent the various kinds of shapes: Square, Circle, and so forth.

```cpp
#include <iostream>
using namespace std;

class Shape {
public:
  Shape(int x, int y)               throw();
  virtual ~Shape()                  throw();
  virtual void draw() const         throw() = 0;
  virtual void move(int x, int y)   throw() = 0;
protected:
  int x_, y_;
  void operator= (const Shape& s)   throw();
  Shape(const Shape& s)             throw();
};

Shape::Shape(int x, int y) throw()
: x_(x)
, y_(y)
{ }
```

```
Shape::Shape(const Shape& s) throw()
: x_(s.x_)
, y_(s.y_)
{ }

Shape::~Shape() throw()
{ }

void Shape::operator= (const Shape& s) throw()
{
  x_ = s.x_;
  y_ = s.y_;
}

void dragAndDrop(Shape& s) throw()   ←——  A polymorphic function
{
  s.move(42,24);  ←————————————————  Dynamic binding calls the "right" code
  s.draw();  ←————————————————————   (as if the compiler predicted the future)
}

class Square : public Shape {
public:
  Square(int x, int y, int width) throw();
  virtual void draw() const        throw();
  virtual void move(int x, int y) throw();
protected:
  int width_;
};

Square::Square(int x, int y, int width) throw()
: Shape(x,y)
, width_(width)
{ }

void Square::draw() const throw()
{ cout << "Square::draw\n"; }

void Square::move(int x, int y) throw()
{
  x_ = x;
  y_ = y;
  cout << "Square::move\n";
}

class Circle : public Shape {
public:
  Circle(int x, int y, int radius) throw();
  virtual void draw() const        throw();
```

```
    virtual void move(int x, int y)  throw();
protected:
    int radius_;
};

Circle::Circle(int x, int y, int radius) throw()
: Shape(x,y)
, radius_(radius)
{ }

void Circle::draw() const throw()
{ cout << "Circle::draw\n"; }

void Circle::move(int x, int y) throw()
{
    x_ = x;
    y_ = y;
    cout << "Circle::move\n";
}

int main()
{
    Square s = Square(5, 20, 3);
    Circle c = Circle(10, 15, 7);
    dragAndDrop(s);
    dragAndDrop(c);
}
```

This dragAndDrop(Shape&) function properly invokes the right member functions from class Square and Circle, even though the compiler didn't know about Square or Circle when it was compiling dragAndDrop(Shape&). Here is the output of this program.

```
Square::move
Square::draw
Circle::move
Circle::draw
```

Suppose the function dragAndDrop(Shape&) is compiled on Tuesday, and a new kind of shape—say a Hexagon—is created on Wednesday. dragAndDrop(Shape&) works with a Hexagon even though the Hexagon class didn't exist when dragAndDrop(Shape&) was compiled.

FAQ 5.14

What is an abstraction and why is it important?

An abstraction is a simplified view of an object in the user's own vocabulary.

In OO and C++, an abstraction is the simplest interface to an object that provides all the features and services the intended users expect.

An abstraction tells users everything they need to know about an object but nothing else. It is the well-defined, unambiguously specified interface. For example, on a vending machine, the abstraction is formed by the buttons and their meanings; users don't have to know about levers, internal counters, or other parts that are needed for the machine to operate. Furthermore the vending machine's price list implies a legally binding promise to users: if users put in the right amount of money, the machine promises to dispense the desired item.

The key to a good abstraction is deep knowledge of the problem domain. A good abstraction allows users to use an object in a relatively safe and predictable manner. It reduces the learning curve by providing a simple interface described in terms of the user's own vocabulary.

A good abstraction separates specification from implementation. It doesn't expose too much nor does it hide features that users need to know about. If an abstraction is good, users aren't tempted to peek at the object's implementation. The net result is simpler, more stable user code.

FAQ 5.15

Should abstractions be user-centric or developer-centric?

User-centric.

New object-oriented programmers commonly make the mistake of thinking that inheritance, objects, and so on exist to make it easier to build a class. Although this developer-centric view of OO software provides a short burst of improved productivity; it fails to produce a software development culture that has "sustainable effectiveness." In other words, a flash in the pan, then nothing.

The only way to achieve long-term success with OO is for developers to focus on their users instead of on themselves. Ironically, most developers eventually become users of their own abstractions, so they can help themselves through their efforts to help others.

Abstractions that involve technology, such as "database" or "communications link," are probably developer-centric. The best abstractions use terminology from the language of the user, such as "general ledger account" or "customer."

FAQ 5.16

What's the difference between encapsulation and abstraction?

Encapsulation protects abstractions. Encapsulation is the bodyguard; abstraction is the VIP.

Encapsulation provides the explicit boundary between an object's abstract interface (its abstraction) and its internal implementation details. Encapsulation puts the implementation details "in a capsule." Encapsulation tells users which features are stable, permanent services of the object and which features are implementation details that are subject to change without notice.

Encapsulation helps the developers of an abstraction: it provides the freedom to implement the abstraction in any way consistent with the interface. (Encapsulation tells developers exactly what users can and cannot access.) Encapsulation also helps the users of an abstraction: it provides protection by preventing dependence on volatile implementation details.

Abstraction provides business value; encapsulation "protects" these abstractions. If a developer provides a good abstraction, users won't be tempted to peek at the object's internal mechanisms. Encapsulation is simply a safety feature that reminds users not to stray over the line inadvertently.

FAQ 5.17

What are the consequences of encapsulating a bad abstraction?

Wasted money. *Lots* of wasted money.

There's nothing more frustrating than a lousy abstraction that is encapsulated. When a developer encapsulates a bad abstraction, users continually attempt to violate the abstraction's encapsulation barrier. When that happens, don't waste time trying to make it even harder for users to access the object's internals; fix the abstraction instead.

Don't think of encapsulation as a club with which the good guys (the class's authors) prevent the bad guys (the class's users) from looking inside an object. Object-oriented design and programming is not a contest between developers and users.

FAQ 5.18

What's the value of separating interface from implementation?

It's a key to eliminating the ripple effect when a change is made.

Interfaces are a company's most valuable asset. Maintaining interface consistency across implementation changes is a priority for many companies. Keeping the interface separate from the implementation allows interface consistency. It also produces software that is cheaper to design, write, debug, test, and maintain than other software.

Separating the interface from the implementation makes a system easier to understand by reducing its overall complexity. Each object needs to know only about the interfaces—not about the implementations—of the objects with which it collaborates. This is in stark contrast to most systems, in which it seems as if every source file knows about the implementation of every other source file. In one extreme case, 157 different source files had direct access to a data structure in some other source file (we're not making this up). Imagine how expensive it would be to change that data structure in response to a new customer requirement.

Separating the interface from the implementation also makes a system more flexible by reducing coupling between components. A high incidence of coupling between components is a major factor in systems becoming brittle and makes it difficult to accommodate new customer requirements in a cost-effective manner. When coupling is strong, a change to one source file affects other source files, so they require changes as well. This produces a *ripple effect* that eventually cascades through a large part of the system. Since separating the interface from the implementation reduces coupling, it also reduces ripples. The result is a more flexible software product and an organization that is better equipped to keep up with market changes.

Separating the interface from the implementation also simplifies debugging and testing. The software that provides the interface is the only software that directly touches the implementation, and therefore is the only software that can cause nonsensical, incoherent, or inconsistent behavior by the implementation. For example, if a linked list caches its length and the length counter doesn't match the number of links in the list, finding the code that caused this error is vastly simpler if only a small number of routines can directly access the nodes and the length counter.

Finally, separating the interface from the implementation encourages software reuse by reducing education costs for those who want to reuse an object. The reusers of an object need learn about only the interface rather than the (normally vastly more complicated) implementation.

FAQ 5.19

How can separating interface from implementation improve performance as well as flexibility?

new   Late life-cycle performance tuning.

Fact 1: The only objects worth tuning are the ones that create performance bottlenecks, and the only way to know which objects are the bottlenecks is to measure the behavior of a running system (profiling). Developers sometimes think they can predict where the bottlenecks will be, but studies have shown that they often guess wrong—they cannot reliably predict where the application's bottlenecks will be. Therefore, don't waste time tuning the performance of a piece of code until actual measurements have shown that it is a bottleneck.

Fact 2: The most potent means of improving performance is changing algorithms and data structures. Hand tuning the wrong algorithm or data structure has very little benefit compared to finding an algorithm or data structure that is a better match for the problem being solved. This is especially true for large problems where algorithms and data structures must be scalable.

These two facts lead to an undeniable conclusion: the most effective performance tuning occurs when the product's fundamental data structures and algorithms can be changed late in the product's life cycle. This can be accomplished only if there is adequate separation of interface from implementation.

For example, it would be expensive to change a sorted array to a binary search tree in a typical non-OO software product today, because all the places that use integer indices to access entries would need to be modified to use node pointers. In other words, the interface *is* the implementation in typical software today. The key to solving this problem is to focus on the similarity in the abstractions rather than the differences in the data structures: sorted arrays and binary trees are both containers that keep their entries in sorted order. In this light they are merely alternate implementations of the same abstraction and they should have the same interface.

The key to late life-cycle performance tuning is to hide performance differences behind a uniform interface. Thus users code to the abstraction rather than to the data structure. This allows the data structure and the algorithm to be replaced at any time.

Ultimately the key is to ask the right questions at the right time. This lofty goal is achieved by a good *software development process* (SDP). Unfortunately, many SDPs cause developers to ask the wrong questions at the wrong time, often resulting in a premature commitment to an implementation technique. Even if an SDP uses OO terminology (for example, by using the term *object diagram* rather than *data structure*), the software will be inflexible if the bulk of its code is aware of relationships that may need to change.

The first programming technique that exploited these ideas was based on abstract data types. The OO paradigm is built on top of the abstract data type technique: OO adds the ability for the user code to work with all implementations of an abstraction simultaneously. That is, among other things, OO allows the data structures to be interchanged dynamically on a case-by-case basis, which is an improvement over a statically chosen, one-size-fits-all approach.

FAQ 5.20

What is the best way to create a good interface to an abstraction?

Design the interface from the user's point of view (i.e., design the interface from the outside in). In other words, start by writing some sample user code.

Interface design decisions should be based primarily on the users' external perspective. In contrast, when the implementation is built before the interface is designed, the interface inevitably smells like the implementation. If the interface has to be explained to its users in terms of the implementation, then the implementation becomes cast in concrete.

For example, consider a member function that tells whether a particular integer is in a set-of-`int`. This is a boolean inspector: it inspects (versus mutates) the set object and it returns a boolean value. A naive name for such a member function might be `Set::isElemOf(int) const`. However, putting this name in an `if` statement shows that the name gives the wrong connotation, since the user code reads "if mySet is an element of x":

```
if (mySet.isElemOf(x)) ...
```

A much better sentence structure would be "if mySet contains x," which means the member function would be named `contains`:

```
if (mySet.contains(x)) ...
```

Note that the names of boolean inspectors should imply the meaning of the true response. For example, `File::isOpen() const` is better than `File::status() const`.

FAQ 5.21

How are `get`/`set` member functions related to poorly designed interfaces?

`Get`/`set` member functions are often used as Band-Aids to patch broken interfaces.

`Get`/`set` member functions provide users with access to an object's internal data structures. Although `get`/`set` member functions appear to encapsulate the object's implementation, all they really do is hide the name of a data member while exposing the data member's existence, as well as the relationships between the data member and all the other data members. In other words, they expose the implementation technique. Ultimately, the resultant interface makes the user code dependent on the implementation technique, and changing the implementation technique breaks user code—the ripple effect.

If a `Container` class exports information about the binary tree that implements it (for example, if it exports member functions `getLeftChild()` and `getRightChild()`), the users will be forced to think in terms of binary trees rather than containers. The result is a cluttered interface in the implementer's vocabulary instead of a simple interface defined in the user's vocabulary.

When an interface is cluttered, the resultant user code is more complicated. When an interface is defined in the implementer's vocabulary, implementation details will show through, and changing the implementation technique breaks user code. Either way, the users lose.

Please don't think that we are saying that `get` and `set` member functions are always bad. They aren't, and frameworks such as CORBA automatically provide `get` and `set` member functions for all attributes. The real issue is that a good object will always have a secret, something that it encapsulates and the interface hides, and `get` and `set` member functions can sometimes undermine the object's secrets.

FAQ 5.22

Should there be a `get` and a `set` member function for each member datum?

Not necessarily.

Some data members are a legitimate part of an object's interface. Having a `get` or `set` member function for such a datum is appropriate because the datum represents something that is part of the user's vocabulary.

One way to tell which data members are a legitimate part of an object's interface is by asking a typical user to describe the class in implementation-independent terms. The words used to describe the class form the user's vocabulary. The interface should be expressed in the user's vocabulary.

--- **FAQ 5.23**

Is the real purpose of a class to export data?

No, the real purpose of a class is to provide services.

A class is a way to abstract behavior, not just a way to encapsulate bits. A class's interface must make sense from the outside. If a user expects member functions to access an attribute, the member functions should exist. But remember: the member functions to access an attribute exist because their existence makes sense in the user's vocabulary (that is, for *outside* reasons), not because there are bits in the object (that is, not for *inside* reasons).

A class's interface should be designed from the outside in. It takes a little while for this to feel comfortable to newcomers, but it is the only right way to do the job.

This FAQ and the next one reflect a really important lesson learned from the OO modeling wars in the early 1990s: objects should reflect behaviors and services. Data modeling per se is inappropriate as an OO technique. There is still a limited place for data modeling because most object persistence schemes still end up invoking relational databases as an implementation technique, but this fact of life doesn't mean that the data model should bleed through to the user.

--- **FAQ 5.24**

Should OO be viewed as data-centric?

No, OO should be viewed as behavior-centric.

The data-centric view of OO (the wrong approach) says that objects are fundamentally buckets of bits and that the primary purpose of a class is to export attributes.

The behavior-centric view of OO (the right approach) sees objects as intelligent agents that export useful services. The behavior-centric view of OO produces more cost-effective systems that are easier to adapt to changing requirements, are easier to tune for performance, and tend to have fewer defects. The reason for these benefits is simple: behavior-centric systems move common code from a class's users into the class itself, from the many to the few. Coalescing snippets of code that show up in several users reduces maintenance costs (by reducing code bulk) and avoids duplicating defects.

Chapter 6

Specification of Observable Behavior

What is the purpose of this chapter?

To provide a practical technique that reduces the ripple effect during both development and maintenance. The technique provided in this chapter is fundamental to understanding proper inheritance as well as reducing both short-term and long-term costs, especially for large systems.

The basic idea is to unambiguously state the external behavior of each member function in some well-known location, then for other programmers to rely on this *specification* rather than digging into the code and relying on the implementation. This technique is sometimes called *programming by contract,* and it is extremely valuable whenever a software system is large enough that most programmers can't remember all the ifs, ands and buts of every member function of every class.

FAQ 6.02

Should users of a member function rely on what the code actually does or on the specification?

new   The specification!

A member function's specification unambiguously defines its externally observable behavior across all possible implementations. The specification of a member function is more than simply the member function's signature. The specification captures the essential service that the member function provides to its users in an implementation-independent fashion. This is an essential part of abstraction and encapsulation. If a class's developers do not provide a full and complete specification, then they have failed as OO programmers because they have failed to properly separate the interface from the implementation and they have forced users to look at the implementation.

Many software organizations systematically fail to observe this critical guideline. Developers in these organizations are trained to rely on what the code does instead of what it promises to do. Users of a member function must be able to rely only on the member function's specification, not on the implementation of the specification. In fact, there are only a few times when users legitimately need to look at the source code to find out what a member function actually does (such as when you are inspecting the code to ensure it fulfills its promise).

In the following example, suppose `Version1` and `Version2` represent two versions of the same class. Note that the specification (that is, the description of the behavior that other programmers are supposed to rely on) of member function `f()` did not change even though the implementation of `Version2::f()` is different from that of `Version1::f()`.

In this case, the specification says that the member function `f()` "Promises that the return value will be some even number," and presumably this captures the essential behavior of `f()`. The designer may have done this to allow some implementations to return 4, while other implementations return a random even number between 0 and 100, while other implementations return even numbers less than zero. Users who rely only on this specification won't be hurt by the new version since their code would work for any even number. On the other hand, users who rely on what the code actually does (i.e., who rely on member function `f()` always returning 4) could break since they may rely on the value being greater than zero or greater than 2 or one of a hundred other assumptions.

```
class Version1 {
public:
```

```
    int f();   // Promises that the return value will be some
               // even number
};

int Version1::f() { return 4; }

class Version2 {
public:
    int f();   // Promises that the return value will be some
               // even number
};

int Version2::f() { return -2; }
```

Never assume that a member function will always do what the code currently does. The code will change, and the specification is generally more stable than the code.

What are the advantages of relying on the specification rather than the implementation?

Time, completeness, flexibility, fixability, extensibility, understandability, and scalability.

Time: It is far easier to read the member function's specification than to reverse-engineer its actual behavior.

Completeness: If a specification is insufficient or absent, the class is broken and must be fixed. By forcing users to rely on the specification rather than the implementation, users report an insufficient specification as a serious error. Thus specifications are developed early in the development life cycle and will be maintained throughout the life cycle

Flexibility: The code of a member function may (and generally does) change. When it does, user code that relies only on the specification doesn't break, assuming the new behavior is compatible with the old specification. However, user code that depends on how the member function was implemented may break when legitimate modifications are made.

Fixability: A defect can be defined as a member function that doesn't fulfill its specification. The right course of action when specifications have been written is usually to make the member function do what it is supposed to do, rather than changing the specification to reflect the erroneous implementation. However, it is unclear how to fix the defect in organizations where specifications are not used and developers have to rely on what the code does instead of what it promises to do. When the code is rewritten to fix the defect, other defects will undoubtedly appear in other portions of the system that relied on the earlier version of code. This ripple effect results in the development team "chasing" the defect through the system as they have to make more and more modifications to the system to try and make it work.

Extensibility: Adaptable specifications give latitude to derived classes. If users rely on the code of the base class, users may break when supplied with a derived class.

Understandability: By providing accurate specifications, the system's behavior can be more easily understood. In systems that don't use complete and consistent specifications, the long-term result is an overreliance on those rare individuals, the system experts, who can understand the entire system at once. For example, to repair a certain defect, either part X or part Y must be modified. Without specification of what these parts are supposed to do, only the system expert can determine whether any other component is going to break if X or Y are changed. Specifications enable average developers to make more of these decisions. From a business perspective, this mitigates risk if the system expert is run over by a truck.

Scalability: The larger the system the more important it is to separate the specification from the implementation.

Write code to fulfill a specification, not the other way around.

FAQ 6.04

What are advertised requirements and advertised promises?

An *advertised requirement* is a condition that the user of a member function must comply with before the member function can be used. Some people use the term *precondition* instead of the term advertised requirement.

An *advertised promise* is a guarantee that a member function makes to its users. Some people use the term *postcondition* instead of the term advertised promise.

When a user fails to fulfill the advertised requirements of a member function, the member function usually fails to fulfill its advertised promises. For example, part of the advertised promise for `myStack.pop()` is that the number of elements will decrease by one. Therefore the advertised requirements for `myStack.pop()` will include `!myStack.isEmpty()` since `myStack.pop()` cannot fulfill this promise when `myStack.empty()` returns `true`.

When users fail to fulfill the advertised requirements, member functions normally throw exceptions. It is also legal, although often less desirable, for member functions to respond more severely to users who fail to fulfill the advertised requirements. For example, if `Stack::pop()` were invoked in a performance-critical path of the system, testing the advertised requirement might prove to be too expensive, in which case `Stack::pop()` might advertise, "If the `Stack isEmpty()`, arbitrarily disastrous things might happen." This is a trust issue: such a statement in the requirement makes it the user's responsibility to guarantee that the preconditions are met prior to the call. This is normally done for performance purposes, where the number of redundant tests and/or the added complexity of those tests would be prohibitively expensive.

FAQ 6.05

How are the advertised requirements and advertised promises of the member functions specified?

Through the disciplined and consistent use of comments in the class declaration. For example, each member function can have the following lines just before or just after the declaration:

- `// PURPOSE:` Tells users the overall purpose of the member function.

- `// REQUIRE:` Tells users the advertised requirements. Since these must make sense to users, the text in this section should refer only to parameters and `public:` member functions.

- `// PROMISE:` Tells users the advertised promises. Since these must make sense to users, the text in this section should refer only to parameters and `public:` member functions.

This technique is illustrated in the following example:

```
class Empty { };
class Full { };

class Stack {
public:
  Stack() throw();
    // PURPOSE: Initializes a Stack
    // REQUIRE: Nothing
    // PROMISE: size() will be zero

  unsigned size() const throw();
    // PURPOSE: Returns the number of elements on this Stack
    // REQUIRE: Nothing
    // PROMISE: Return value will be between 0 and 10
    //          inclusive
```

```
    int top() const throw(Empty);
      // PURPOSE: Returns the top element of this Stack
      // REQUIRE: size() must not be zero
      // PROMISE: Nothing

    void push(int elem) throw(Full);
      // PURPOSE: Pushes elem onto the end of this Stack
      // REQUIRE: size() must be strictly less than 10
      // PROMISE: size() will increase by 1
      // PROMISE: top() will be the same as parameter elem

    int pop() throw(Empty);
      // PURPOSE: Pops and returns the top element from this
      // REQUIRE: size() must not be zero
      // PROMISE: size() will decrease by 1
      // PROMISE: Returns the same as if top() were called at
      //             the beginning

protected:
  int data_[10];
  unsigned size_;
};

inline Stack::Stack() throw()
: size_(0)
{ }

inline unsigned Stack::size() const throw()
{ return size_; }

inline int Stack::top() const throw(Empty)
{
  if (size_ == 0)
    throw Empty();
  return data_[size_-1];
}

inline void Stack::push(int elem) throw(Full)
{
  if (size_ == 10)
    throw Full();
  data_[size_++] = elem;
}

inline int Stack::pop() throw(Empty)
{
  if (size_ == 0)
    throw Empty();
```

```
      return data_[--size_];
    }

    int main()
    {
      Stack s;
      s.push(42);
      int elem = s.pop();
    }
```

Keeping a class's specification in the header file (for example, the .hpp file) makes it easier for developers to find the specification and keep it synchronized with the code when changes are needed.

FAQ 6.06

Why are changes feared in development organizations that don't use specification?

Because no one knows what will break.

new

Changes come in three flavors.

- *Type 1:* Implementation changes that do not change the interface specification

- *Type 2:* Interface changes that are substitutable (that is, backward compatible)

- *Type 3:* Interface changes that are nonsubstitutable (that is, non-backward compatible)

Changes of type 1 and type 2 are relatively cheap compared with changes of type 3, since changes of type 1 and type 2 cannot break user code that relies only on the specification; changes of type 3 can break user code.

   In particular, there is often an enormous ripple effect when nonsubstitutable (that is, non-backward compatible) changes are made to a software application's interfaces. In some cases organizations can spend more time adjusting their old code than writing new code. This is especially true for organizations that are building large, complicated systems or applications. Because of this, it is important for developers to know what kind of changes they are making.

   With proper specification, anyone (including maintenance programmers) can easily determine whether a proposed change to an interface will break existing code that uses that interface. Read on for more details.

FAQ 6.07

How do developers determine if a proposed change will break existing code?

The specification.

Unfortunately there is often an enormous ripple effect when nonsubstitutable (that is, non-backward compatible) changes are made to a software application's interfaces. In some cases organizations can spend more time adjusting their old code than writing new code. This is especially true for organizations that are building large, complicated systems or applications.

Developers should therefore be somewhat cautious of the difference between a substitutable change and a change that will break existing user code.

With proper specification, anyone (including maintenance programmers) can easily determine whether a proposed change to an interface will break existing code that uses the interface. Ill-specified systems typically suffer from "change phobia": if anyone even contemplates changing *anything,* everyone starts sending out their résumés for fear that the system will collapse. Unfortunately, changes often *do* make the world fall apart in ill-specified systems. It's called maintenance cost and it eats software organizations alive.

FAQ 6.08

What are the properties of a substitutable (backward compatible) change in a specification?

Require no more, promise no less.

A change to an interface doesn't have to break existing code that uses the interface. If the new specification is substitutable with respect to the old specification, the user code will not break. Substitutable changes have two distinct properties. First, any user who fulfilled the old advertised requirements still fulfills the new ones (thus the new requirements must not get stronger). Second, any member function that fulfills the new advertised promises also would have fulfilled the old ones. In other words, existing user code must be adjusted if the replacement class requires users to do more and/or promises less than the original class did.

For example, Mac agrees to mow Lonnie's lawn for $10. Mac could substitute his friend, Patches, if the requirements went down (say $5) or if the promises went up (weeding the garden, for instance). However, Lonnie would be justifiably upset if Patches required more (say $20) or promised less (to mow only half the lawn, for instance).

In the following example, `Version1` and `Version2` represent subsequent versions of some class. `Version2` is substitutable for `Version1` since `Version2` requires no more and promises no less than `Version1` (in fact, `Version2` requires less and promises more).

```
class Version1 {
public:
   int f(int x);
     // REQUIRE: Parameter x must be odd
     // PROMISE: Return value will be some even number
};

class Version2 {
public:
   int f(int x);
     // REQUIRE: Parameter x can be anything
     // PROMISE: Return value will be 8
};
```

For `Version2` to be substitutable for `Version1`, *every* member function must be substitutable. That is, every member function for the new version must require no more and promise no less than the equivalent member function in the old version. If even one member function is changed such that it requires more or promises less, the entire class is not substitutable.

FAQ 6.09

How can it be shown that the implementation of a member function fulfills its specification?

The implementation requires no more than the advertised requirements of its specification and delivers no less than the advertised promises of its specification.

The implementation of a member function doesn't have to be as picky as its advertised requirements. Also, a member function can deliver more than the minimum specified by its advertised promises. In the following example, the actual behavior of `Fred::f()` is different from its advertisement but different in a way that is substitutable and thus won't surprise users.

```
class Fred {
public:
  int f(int i);
    // REQUIRE: Parameter i must be odd
    //   (if i is odd, this doesn't guarantee to fulfill its
    //    PROMISE)
    // PROMISE: Return value will be some even number
};

int Fred::f(int i)
{
  if (i % 2 == 0) {
    // This could throw an exception here, but it doesn't
    // have to
  }

  // This is allowed to return any even number,
  // but it can do something very specific if desired ...
  return 8;
}

int main()
{
  Fred fred;
  int result = fred.f(37);
  // This is allowed to assume result is even
  // (but it's not allowed to assume result is 8.)
}
```

A specification is said to be adaptable when it is vague enough that an implementation may actually require less than its advertised requirements or when an implementation may actually deliver more than its advertised promises. Adaptable specifications are common in base classes since the adaptability gives extra latitude to derived classes.

FAQ 6.10

Is it possible to keep the specification synchronized with the code?

It's challenging, but it's doable.

On projects ranging from very small (10K lines of OO/C++) to very large systems (millions of lines of OO/C++) our experience has shown that this is a solvable problem.
   Here are some guidelines.

- All developers must be trained to properly specify all classes and member functions.

- The specifications must be kept with the class declarations (usually in a header file) so that it is easy for developers and users to refer to them.

- All users must be trained to rely on specifications rather than implementations.

- Everybody must treat a specification error as a defect that must be fixed with the same urgency that code defects are fixed.

- Everybody must be trained to recognize the differences between substitutable changes and nonsubstitutable changes.

It is possible to keep the specification synchronized with the code because of the nature of specifications. Since specifications describe behavior in terms that are observable to the user, rather than in terms of the implementation, specifications tend to be relatively stable compared with the implementation. Furthermore, since all the other software components of the system are built by relying on the specification rather than the implementation (see FAQ 6.09), the specifications tend to stabilize fairly early in the product life cycle. So as a practical matter, the problem isn't keeping the specification synchronized with the code but the reverse: making sure the code is synchronized with the specification. In other words, once a lot of software has been written based on a particular specification, that specification is more stable than the underlying code that implements the specification, so the issue is making sure the code faithfully implements the specification rather than the other way around.

Remember: specifications are prescriptive rather than descriptive. Specifications prescribe what the code must do rather than describe what the code already does. If the implementation of a member function and the member function's specification disagree, and if a lot of software was already built based on the specification, it is often easier to change the implementation to be consistent with the specification rather than the other way around.

In contrast, when there is no explicit specification that programmers can rely on, the implementation ends up being the de facto specification. Once that happens any change to the implementation (including fixing bugs in some cases!) can break the user code. In those cases it is trivial to keep the specification and the implementation in sync (the implementation *is* the specification), but it makes the whole application brittle—any change anywhere can trigger dozens of other changes.

Chapter 7

Proper Inheritance

What is proper inheritance?

When the advertised behavior of the derived class is substitutable for that of the base class.

Proper inheritance and substitutable behavior can be guaranteed when the specifications of the member functions of the derived class require no more and promise no less than the specifications of the corresponding member functions in the base class(es). The derived class can also add new member functions. The specification for these new member functions can require as much or promise as little as they like, since they are not constrained by existing member functions in any base class.

   In the following example, the specification for `Derived::f()` requires no more (in fact, it imposes a weaker requirement) and promises no less (in fact, it makes a stronger promise) than the specification of `Base::f()`. This will not break users of the base class, so this is proper inheritance.

```
#include <iostream>
using namespace std;

class Base {
public:
  virtual int f(int x);
    // REQUIRE: Parameter x must be an odd number
    // PROMISE: Return value will be some even number
  virtual ~Base();
};
```

```
Base::~Base()
{ }

class Derived : public Base {
public:
  virtual int f(int x);
    // REQUIRE: Parameter x can be any integer
    // PROMISE: Return value will be 8
};

int Base::f(int x)
{
  if (x % 2 == 0)
    throw "Even!";
  return x + 1;
}

int Derived::f(int x)
{ return 8; }

void sample(Base& b)
{
  // We should pass only odd numbers, since b may actually
  // be a Base...
  int result = b.f(37);

  // We expect result to be even
  if (result % 2 == 1)
    cerr << "PANIC: call the hotline at 1-800-BAD-BUGS\n";
}

int main()
{
  Base b;       sample(b);
  Derived d;    sample(d);
}
```

Note that every member function of the derived class must have substitutable behavior with respect to the corresponding specification in the base class(es). If even one derived class member function specifies stronger requirements or weaker promises than the corresponding specification in the appropriate base class, the inheritance relationship is improper.

Finally note that this chapter deals with public inheritance. private and protected inheritance have completely different rules (see FAQ 37.01).

FAQ 7.02

What are the benefits of proper inheritance?

Substitutability and extensibility.

Substitutability: An object of a properly derived class can be freely and safely substituted for an object of its base class. For example, suppose a user defines a function `sample(Base& b)`. If class `Derived` properly inherits from class `Base`, `sample(Base& b)` will work correctly when an object of class `Derived` is passed instead of an object of class `Base`. In contrast, there is no guarantee that `sample(Base& b)` will work correctly when it is passed an object of a class that was produced by improper inheritance.

Extensibility: The properly derived class can be freely and safely used in place of its base class even if the properly derived class is created months or years after the user code was defined. It's easy to extend a system's functionality when you add properly derived classes that contain enhanced functionality. These guarantees cannot be made when improper inheritance is used.

Note that these guarantees work only when the user code relies on the specification of the base class rather than the (possibly more specific) implementation of the base class (see FAQ 6.02).

FAQ 7.03

What is improper inheritance?

A design error that creates a mess.

Improper inheritance occurs when the derived class is not substitutable with respect to its base class(es), that is, when the specification of one or more inherited member functions either requires more or promises less than the corresponding specification in the base class.

One symptom of improper inheritance is that the user code may be forced to use dynamic typing (that is, runtime type checks, capability queries, and downcasting) and to treat objects of different derived classes in different ways (for example, to avoid using some member functions on some derived classes).

Improper inheritance has a nearly unbounded cost on the code that uses base class pointers and references (recall that this is, by design, the bulk of the application; see FAQ 2.24). The initial development cost is greater, since the code that uses base class pointers and references needs to be littered with runtime type checks and complex decision logic. The long-term maintenance costs are also greater: every time a new derived class is added, all the runtime type checks in all the user code must be reanalyzed to ensure that nothing will break.

Most of the benefits of OO technology vanish when improper inheritance is employed. In C++, public inheritance should be tied closely to subtyping, which means public inheritance has a strong semantic meaning. When public inheritance is used improperly, the software usually ends up being brittle and over budget and delivered late.

FAQ 7.04

Isn't the difference between proper and improper inheritance obvious?

Apparently not.

Improper inheritance is a very common design error. This seems to be because developers base inheritance relationships on their intuition rather than the objective criteria of substitutability.

The following inheritance relationships are improper because the derived class either requires more or promises less.

- A `Stack` is not a kind-of `List` (assuming `List` provides member functions that allow insertions in the middle of the list and `Stack` does not).

- A `ListOfApples` is not a kind-of `ListOfFruit` (assuming that any type of `Fruit` can be put into a `ListOfFruit`).

The following inheritance relationships may or may not be proper inheritance depending on the specified behavior of the base class and the derived class.

- A `Circle` may not be a kind-of `Ellipse`.

- An `Ostrich` may not be a kind-of `Bird`.

- An `Integer` may not be a kind-of `RationalNumber`.

These examples are explained in Chapter 8.

FAQ 7.05

Is substitutability based on what the code does or what the specification promises the code will do?

The specification, not the implementation.

The specification of an overridden member function must require no more and promise no less than the specification of the corresponding member function in the base class. The overriden member functions must also correctly implement whatever specifications they provide. However, when the base class gives an adaptable specification, the code of the override doesn't necessarily have to do the same as the code of the base class.

In the following example, `Base::f()` provides an adaptable specification: the code is more specific than the strict minimum guaranteed by the specification. The code of the derived class isn't substitutable with respect to the implementation of the base class, but it is substitutable with respect to the specification of the base class. Since the user code, `sample(Base& b)`, relies only on the specification of `Base::f()` rather than the more specific implementation, this user code won't break when it is passed a `Derived` object. However, if the user code had relied on the implementation of `Base::f()`, it would break when passed a `Derived` object (it would also break if a legitimate, substitutable modification was made to `Base::f()`, such as returning `42`).

```
#include <iostream>
using namespace std;

class Base {
public:
  virtual int f();
    // PROMISE: Return value will be some even number
  virtual ~Base();
};

Base::~Base()
{ }

class Derived : public Base {
public:
  virtual int f();
    // PROMISE: Return value will be 8
};

int Base::f()
{
```

```
  // This is allowed to return any even number
  return 4;
}

int Derived::f()
{
  // This must return 8...
  return 8;
}

void sample(Base& b)
{
  int result = b.f();

  // This is allowed to expect that result will be even,
  // but it must not assume that result is 4
  if (result % 2 == 1)
    cerr << "PANIC: call the hotline at 1-800-BAD-BUGS\n";
}

int main()
{
  Base b;      sample(b);
  Derived d;   sample(d);
}
```

Never assume that a class will always be implemented as it is currently implemented (see FAQ 6.02).

FAQ 7.06

Is it proper to revoke (hide) an inherited `public:` member function?

No.

Never. The rest of the software was written based on the promises made by the base class (see FAQ 6.02). Since the main idea of polymorphism and dynamic binding is to pass a derived class object to a function that takes a base class pointer or reference, this "rest of the system" often works with derived class objects without knowing it (see FAQ 2.24). Everything works fine as long as the derived class objects *behave* like the base class promises they will behave. However if the derived class is not substitutable for the base class, all that code that was written based on the base class's promises (the "rest of the system") will break.

In order to be substitutable, the derived class object must support *all* the member functions of the base class. If even one of the member functions promised by the base class has been revoked (hidden) by a derived class, a large portion of the rest of the system could break.

Public inheritance requires keeping promises—and hiding or revoking promised behavior will surprise the rest of the system. Too often, programmers try to use inheritance even when it doesn't fit the constraints of substitutability. Typically this means creating a derived class, then trying to revoke (hide) whatever inherited `public:` member functions don't make sense in the derived class.

Revoking an inherited `public:` member function is evil.

Recall that this chapter covers the guidelines for `public` inheritance. `private` and `protected` inheritance are different: it is appropriate and proper to revoke (hide) inherited `public:` member functions in a `private` or `protected` derived class (see FAQ 37.01).

FAQ 7.07

What is specialization?

A major source of confusion and design errors.

Some people assume that proper inheritance can be determined by the vague concept of *specialization*. For example, if `Derived` is a special `Base`, some people assume that `Derived` can be derived properly from `Base`. While this simple rule works some of the time, it is incorrect often enough to be misleading. The guiding principle is for the derived class to behave like the base class, and specialization sometimes leads designers in the wrong direction.

One problem with the concept of specialization is that it can be ambiguous. Does it mean "better than" (`JetPlane` is a specialized `Plane`) or "more skilled" (`Doctor` is a specialized `Person`) or "subset of" (`Circle` is a specialized `Ellipse`) or "more specific" (`Unix` is a specialized `Operating System`) or "restricted" (a `List` that can only contain `Circle` objects is a specialized `List` that can contain any `Shape`)? Because of the potential ambiguity, it is hard to make a blanket statement about specialization as a reliable approach to public inheritance.

Not only is it ambiguous, but in certain cases it is completely incorrect. In particular, specialization does not imply that `Derived` must support all the operations defined by `Base`, as is necessary for proper inheritance.

Forget specialization and learn about substitutability.

FAQ 7.08

What do subsets have to do with proper inheritance?

Nothing.

Remember, the goal is to avoid breaking existing code that uses base class pointers and references. Since elements of a subset don't necessarily *behave* in a backward compatible way with respect to the superset, users might be surprised if they are passed an element of a subset, and all that code using base class pointers/references might break. It doesn't matter that intuition says otherwise; the fact remains that the whole subset notion is wrong often enough that it is not a reliable design principle. Consider the following two examples:

- The set of circles is a subset of the set of all ellipses, yet circles can't deform themselves asymmetrically, which may be a member function of class `Ellipse` (see FAQ 8.08).

- The set of ostriches is a subset of the set of all birds, yet ostriches cannot fly, which may be a member function of class `Bird` (see FAQ 8.04).

The root problem with the subsets-mean-subclasses idea is that subsets deal with values, where objects normally have mutative member functions (deform asymmetrically, fly, and so on).

Forget subsets and learn about substitutability.

Chapter 8

Detecting and Correcting Improper Inheritance

Can improper inheritance wreck a project?

You bet!

Many important projects go off track because of bad inheritance. It's a disease that can eat a project alive. We've been asked to look at numerous failed projects with very large budgets, and improper inheritance is a typical problem. Small projects can sometimes avoid the full consequences of improper inheritance if the developers communicate well and the system design is easy to follow, even if it is incorrect. Large projects don't have this luxury, and improper inheritance causes working code to break in ways that can't be fixed easily.

The problem is quite real and can be very subtle. In our training and mentoring experience, very few OO newcomers handle this topic easily.

FAQ 8.02

What's the best way to learn how to avoid improper inheritance?

 Work a few simple examples, such as those provided in this chapter. Then get lots of experience working with people who understand this issue. And ignore your intuition.

The examples use simple ideas such as birds and ostriches, rational numbers and integers, stacks and lists, apples and fruit. Real-world problems don't directly use these words, but almost every improper inheritance situation maps to one of these simple examples.

Anyone who doesn't understand the examples in this chapter will probably be hurt in the real world.

FAQ 8.03

Is intuition a reliable guide to understanding proper inheritance?

 No!

Probably the most important message in this chapter is *Don't trust your intuition*. People who are still ignorant of their ignorance are dangerous. It takes a while before intuition (or "gut feel") lines up with proper inheritance. Until then, get help from someone with battle scars. Don't be mentored by anyone with shiny new armor—be mentored by someone whose armor is old and dented.

FAQ 8.04

Is an `Ostrich` a kind-of `Bird`?

 Not if all birds can fly!

Suppose a system uses a base class `Bird` with member functions `altitude()` and `fly()`, where `fly()` promises that the bird's `altitude()` will be greater than zero.

```
class Bird {
public:

    int altitude() const;
       // PROMISE: Returns this Bird's current altitude

    virtual void fly();
       // PROMISE: altitude() will return a value > 0

    virtual ~Bird();
};

Bird::~Bird()
{ }
```

Can an `Ostrich` class inherit from `Bird`? Unfortunately, ostriches can't fly (that is, the altitude of an ostrich remains at zero when it tries to fly). Despite its intuitive appeal and regardless of how many other member functions are inheritable, deriving `Ostrich` from `Bird` causes problems. The problems stem from the inherent incompatibility of the following statements.

1. The altitude of every `Bird` will be greater than zero when it flies ("all birds can fly").

2. `Ostrich` is a kind-of `Bird`.

3. The altitude of an `Ostrich` remains zero after it flies ("ostriches cannot fly").

At least one of the statements must be false; they cannot be simultaneously satisfied. We examine the impact of invalidating each of the three statements. Note that there is no correct solution; the particular situation dictates whichever is best (or perhaps least bad).

- Invalidating statement 1 requires changing the behavior of `Bird` to remove the promise that the bird's altitude will be greater than zero when it flies. Unfortunately, this breaks existing user code that relies on the original behavior. In a small system, it might be feasible to change all the user code that is broken, but in large systems this is usually not a practical alternative.

- Invalidating statement 2 implies that the `Ostrich` class cannot inherit from the `Bird` class even though ostrich is a type of bird in the biological sense. In this case the reason is that `Bird` really means `Bird_That_Can_Fly`.

- Invalidating statement 3 means that the altitude of an `Ostrich` must be greater than zero after it flies. To make this option more palatable, one can imagine that an `Ostrich` uses some artificial means to increase its altitude (stairs, a jet-pack, plane tickets, or something like that).

There are two common traps that people typically fall into. The first is to suggest the following as a fourth alternative: create a class such as `AnyBird`, and inherit both `Bird` and `Ostrich` from that new base class. Although there is nothing wrong with this alternative, it is not a fourth alternative. This is merely a repackaging of alternative 2 since it does not try to make `Ostrich` inherit from `Bird` and does not try to make `Ostrich` substitutable for `Bird`.

The second common trap is to assume that there must be some universal right or best answer for the problem. In reality, it is critical that designers know all three of the tools that can get them out of an improper inheritance situation. In other words, when an improper inheritance situation comes up, make sure to try all three possibilities— do not dismiss any of them ahead of time. For example, although the third choice ("make the ostrich fly") seems undesirable in principle, there are times when it may be the most practical. For example, if there is enough code that has already been written based on the promise in the base class, then it will be very expensive to change the base class's promise, ruling out alternative 1. Furthermore, if it is important to be able to pass the derived class into that preexisting code, alternative 2 is ruled out, leaving only alternative 3.

If the problem is caught early enough in the software development life cycle, clearly it is still possible to weaken the base class's promises since there is not yet a lot of existing code that relies on the strong promises made by the base class. So one of the messages here is to think rather than hack. If a problem like this is detected early enough, the cost will be minimal; if it isn't caught until late in the game, the consequences can be pretty grim.

Do not confuse substitutability with subset. Even though the set of ostriches is a subset of the set of birds (every ostrich is in the set of birds), this does not imply that the behavior of `Ostrich` is substitutable for the behavior of `Bird`. The substitutability relation has to do with behavior, not subsets. When evaluating a potential inheritance relationship, the important factor is substitutable behavior, not subsets (see FAQ 7.08).

FAQ 8.05

Should an overridden virtual function throw an exception?

Only if the base class says it might.

It's appropriate for an override to throw an exception if and only if the specification of the member function in the base class says it might (there is a special case for legacy code that considers the absence of an exception specification in the base class to allow the derived class to throw whatever it wants, but this is for historical reasons only). Without such a specification in the base class, throwing an exception in an override is similar to false advertising. For example, consider a used-car salesman selling a kind-of car that blows up (that is, throws an exception) when you turn on the ignition switch. Ralph Nader would correctly say that such a vehicle isn't substitutable for a car. Code should do what the specification says it will do, or other code that relies on those promises may break.

Also, consider the Ostrich/Bird dilemma. Suppose Bird::fly() promises never to throw an exception, as follows.

```cpp
#include <iostream>
using namespace std;

class Bird {
public:
  Bird() throw();
  virtual ~Bird() throw();
  int altitude() const throw();
  virtual void fly() throw();
    // PROMISE: altitude() will return a number > 0; never
    // throws an exception
protected:
  int altitude_;
};

Bird::Bird() throw()
: altitude_(0)
{ }

Bird::~Bird() throw()
{ }

int Bird::altitude() const throw()
{ return altitude_; }

void Bird::fly() throw()
{ altitude_ = 100; }
```

Based on this promise, it is legitimate and appropriate to assume that the fly() member function will not throw an exception. For example, the following sample code is decorated with a throw(), meaning that this function promises not to throw an exception.

```cpp
void sample(Bird& bird) throw()
{
```
◄─── *Legitimate reliance on what Bird::fly() says*

```
    bird.fly();
}
```

But suppose `Ostrich::fly()` is defined to throw an exception, as follows.

```
class CannotFly { };

class Ostrich : public Bird {
public:
  virtual void fly() throw(CannotFly);
    // PROMISE: Throws an exception despite what Bird says
};

void Ostrich::fly() throw(CannotFly)
{ throw CannotFly(); }
```

Now suppose someone legitimately passes an `Ostrich` into the `sample()` code:

```
int main()
{
  Ostrich bird;
  sample(bird);  ◄——— Legitimate conversion from Ostrich to Bird
}
```

Unfortunately the program will crash in the `sample()` function, since the `fly()` member function ends up throwing an exception. One cannot blame `main()` for passing an `Ostrich` into the `sample()` function; after all, `Ostrich` inherited from `Bird` and therefore `Ostrich` is supposed to be substitutable for `Bird`. One cannot blame `sample()` for believing the promise made by `Bird::fly()`; indeed programmers are supposed to rely on the specification rather than the implementation. So the blame rests with the author of class `Ostrich`, who claimed that `Ostrich` was substitutable for `Bird` even though it didn't behave like a `Bird`.

The lesson is that improper inheritance cannot be fixed by throwing an exception if the base class prohibits the throwing of an exception. This is because the root of improper inheritance is behavior that violates a contract, and throwing an exception is part of a function's behavior. Specifically, the behavior of an overridden virtual function that throws an exception conflicts with a base class contract that prohibits the throwing of an exception.

For an exception to this guideline, see FAQ 26.12.

FAQ 8.06

Can an overridden virtual function be a no-op?

Only if the base class says it might.

It's proper for an overridden virtual function to do nothing if and only if the specification of the member function in the base class tells users that it might do nothing. Without such a specification in the base class, doing nothing is like false advertising. For example, consider a used-car salesman selling a kind-of car where applying the brakes is a no-op (that is, the brake lines have been cut). Ralph Nader would correctly say that such a vehicle isn't substitutable for a car.

Consider the `Ostrich`/`Bird` dilemma. Suppose `Bird::fly()` promises that the altitude of the `Bird` will be strictly positive.

```
#include <iostream>
using namespace std;

class Bird {
public:
  Bird() throw();
  virtual ~Bird() throw();
  int altitude() const throw();
  virtual void fly() throw();
    // PROMISE: altitude() will return a number > 0;
    // never throws an exception
protected:
  int altitude_;
};

Bird::Bird() throw()
: altitude_(0)
{ }

Bird::~Bird() throw()
{ }

int Bird::altitude() const throw()
{ return altitude_; }

void Bird::fly() throw()
{ altitude_ = 100; }
```

Based on this promise, it is appropriate and normal for users to write code such as the following.

```
void sample(Bird& bird) throw()
{
  bird.fly();

  if (bird.altitude() <= 0)
    cerr << "Error! Call the hotline at 1-800-BAD-BUGS\n";
}
```

But suppose `Ostrich::fly()` is defined as a no-op:

```
class Ostrich : public Bird {
public:
  virtual void fly() throw();
    // PROMISE: altitude() will still be zero
};

void Ostrich::fly() throw()
{
  // Does nothing despite what Bird said (bad!)
}
```

Now suppose someone legitimately passes an `Ostrich` into the `sample()` code:

```
int main()
{
  Ostrich bird;
  sample(bird);
}
```

Note that decorating the `Ostrich` class with a comment ("I can't fly") isn't good enough, since many users won't even be aware that they're dealing with an `Ostrich`.

Trying to make this safe with a `canYouFly()` query still breaks existing user code, because calls to `bird.fly()` need to be patched with a test, "If you can fly, then fly." Note also that these *capability queries* limit extensibility (see FAQ 27.07).

The lesson is that improper inheritance cannot be fixed by having the overridden function do nothing if the contract of the base class says the function will do something. This is because the root cause of improper inheritance is behavior that violates a contract and doing nothing can violate a contract. Specifically, the behavior of an overridden virtual function that does nothing conflicts with a base class contract that says the member function will do something.

FAQ 8.07

Why does C++ make it so hard to fix the Ostrich/Bird dilemma?

The problem is bad domain analysis and has nothing to do with C++.

The problem of whether or not Ostrich is substitutable for Bird is not a failure of the C++ language, nor is it a failure of object-oriented technology. It is a failure of domain analysis. The domain analysis incorrectly concluded something about the problem domain: that the altitude of all kinds-of birds is positive when they fly.

Stable OO software depends on both an accurate understanding of the problem domain and properly encoding problem domain knowledge in class relationships. If nobody on the design team understands the problem domain (in this case, birds), it should not be surprising that the design will be flawed. This underscores the critical role of the "domain expert" on OO projects.

FAQ 8.08

Should Circle inherit from Ellipse?

The answer depends on what class Ellipse promises to do. Circle can be substitutable for Ellipse only if Circle supports *all* of the member functions defined by Ellipse.

Suppose Ellipse has a setSize(x,y) member function that sets the width and height of the Ellipse.

```
#include <iostream>
using namespace std;

class Ellipse {
public:
  Ellipse(float width, float height) throw();
    // PROMISE: width() will return the same as parameter
    // width
    // PROMISE: height() will return the same as parameter
    // height
  virtual ~Ellipse() throw();
  virtual void setSize(float width, float height) throw();
    // PROMISE: width() will return the same as parameter
    // width
```

```
      // PROMISE: height() will return the same as parameter
      // height
    float width() const throw();
    float height() const throw();
protected:
    float width_, height_;
};

Ellipse::Ellipse(float width, float height) throw()
: width_(width)
, height_(height)
{ }

Ellipse::~Ellipse() throw()
{ }

void Ellipse::setSize(float width, float height) throw()
{
    width_ = width;
    height_ = height;
}

float Ellipse::width() const throw()
{ return width_; }

float Ellipse::height() const throw()
{ return height_; }
```

Now suppose someone uses an `Ellipse` and sets its width to 10 and its height to 20:

```
void sample(Ellipse& ellipse)
{
    // Set the dimensions of the Ellipse to 10 X 20
    ellipse.setSize(10, 20);

    // Legitimately rely on the promises made by Ellipse:
    if (ellipse.width() != 10 || ellipse.height() != 20)
      cerr << "Error! Call the hotline at 1-800-BAD-BUGS\n";
}
```

In this case, a derived class called `Circle` would not be substitutable for `Ellipse` because `Circle` (presumably) cannot be resized asymmetrically.

```
class Circle : public Ellipse {
public:
    Circle(float initRadius) throw();
      // PROMISE: width() will equal initRadius,
      // height() will equal initRadius
```

```
    // But what should we do with setSize(float x, float y); ?
};

Circle::Circle(float initRadius) throw()
: Ellipse(initRadius, initRadius)
{ }
```

For example, if someone legitimately passed a `Circle` in to function `sample()`, then the `Circle` would get deformed so it is no longer circular:

```
int main()
{
  Circle c(10);
  cout << "initial Circle dimensions = "
       << c.width() << "x" << c.height() << "\n";

  sample(c);
  cout << "final Circle dimensions = "
       << c.width() << "x" << c.height() << '\n';
}
```

The output of this program is

```
initial Circle dimensions: 10x10
final Circle dimensions: 10x20
```

A 10 × 20 circle is a strange-looking circle!

The lesson is that proper inheritance is based on substitutable behavior.

What can be done about the asymmetric-circle dilemma?

Admit that you can't have it all.

Despite its intuitive appeal, and regardless of how many other member functions are inheritable, deriving `Circle` from `Ellipse` causes problems. The problems stem from the inherent incompatibility of the following statements.

1. Every `Ellipse` can be stretched asymmetrically.

2. `Circle` is substitutable for `Ellipse`.

3. A `Circle` cannot be stretched asymmetrically.

At least one of those statements must be false. The options are exactly the same as with the `Ostrich` / `Bird` dilemma. Hmmm. Is there a pattern here? The three options follow.

- Invalidating statement 1 requires that either
  `Ellipse::setSize(x,y)` be removed or given an adaptable specification such as "This may or may not do something." Either way, the change may break existing code that relies on the former promises made by class `Ellipse`.

- Invalidating statement 2 prohibits passing a `Circle` as a kind-of `Ellipse`.

- Invalidating statement 3 means that `Circle` must be able to stretch asymmetrically, which is not mathematically desirable.

The basic problem is that `Ellipse` is too strong. Ellipse has such powerful member functions that `Circle` can't be substituted. The options are to weaken `Ellipse`, strengthen `Circle`, or admit that a `Circle` isn't substitutable for an `Ellipse`.

The situation occurred as a result of an inadequate domain analysis. Either the requirements for class `Ellipse` were not understood or the consequences of trying to define `Circle` as substitutable for `Ellipse` were overlooked. Remember: do not confuse substitutability with specialization. Because a circle is a specialized ellipse (circles are ellipses that have an extra symmetry constraint) does not imply that `Circle` is substitutable for `Ellipse`. The substitutability relation has to do with behaviors, not specialization. When evaluating a potential inheritance relationship, the only criterion should be substitutability. The derived class should never surprise code that expects a properly functioning base class.

Note that if `Circle::setSize(x,y)` is redefined so that it throws an exception, it would break user code unless the specification of `Ellipse::setSize(x,y)` allows exceptions to be thrown. If `Circle::setSize(x,y)` is redefined to be a no-op, it would break user code unless the specification of `Ellipse::setSize(x,y)` says, "This member function might do nothing."

There are other ways to illustrate this basic issue. `Integer` is not substitutable for `RationalNumber` if `RationalNumber` has a divide-self-by-two member function (unless the divide-self-by-two member function has a weak specification, such as "Multiplying the result by two might not give the original number").

This issue is important because it comes up so often in real-life situations. This is not about ellipses or birds or integers. This is about wasted money and failed projects. Unfortunately, the projects that are most vulnerable to improper inheritance are the larger ones with bigger budgets and more to lose.

FAQ 8.10

What is the one issue in these FAQs that doesn't seem to die?

Trying to solve the "circle deriving from ellipse" relationship by having ellipse derive *new* from circle.

We like getting e-mail. We like getting letters. We like receiving phone calls. We appreciate kind words and advice. But, please, no more talk about circles, ellipses, and how the two can be related. Many people have suggested that a "solution" to trying to derive a circle from an ellipse is to derive the ellipse from the circle. That is not a dependable solution, despite the mathematical arguments, and it misses the fundamental OO issue of substitutability that is controlled by expectations. Look at it this way: at a topology conference, everyone "knows" that a coffee cup is the same as a doughnut because their fundamental groups are the same. But when topologists have breakfast, they recognize that these two concepts are not substitutable. Most of the time they manage to eat the donut and pour coffee into the cup. So it's a question not of reality but of perception and context.

It really doesn't matter what mathematics says about circles and ellipses. The entire discussion comes down to adherence to the specification of the base class. Reality, mathematical or otherwise, is irrelevant.

`Ellipse` can be substitutable for `Circle` *if you say so up front and avoid logical impossibilities*. `Circle` can be substitutable for `Ellipse` *if you say so up front and avoid logical impossibilities*. `Ostrich` can be substitutable for `CoffeeCup` if you push it hard enough, but either `Ostrich` or `CoffeeCup` is going to have a weird interface. The point is that substitutable interfaces can be forced or they can be natural, but either way, proper inheritance requires substitutable interfaces.

FAQ 8.11

Should `Stack` inherit from `List`?

Probably not.

It is tempting to inherit `Stack` from `List` to reuse the `List` class (for example, if `List` were a linked list). However, even if `List` is an abstract class, it will normally define member functions that aren't natural for a `Stack`, and if `List` provides member functions that class `Stack` doesn't want to support, inheritance would be wrong.

For example, the `public:` interface to a typical `Stack` class might look like the following (some or all of these member functions may be `virtual`; this is a stack of integers—see FAQ 25.02 for how to make it a `template`).

```
class Empty { };
class BadPosition { };

class Stack {
public:
  void      push(int item) throw();
  // Push another item onto this
  int       pop() throw(Empty);
  // Remove the top item from this
  int       top() const throw(Empty);
  // Peek at the top item of this
  unsigned size() const throw();
  // Returns the number of items
};
```

In contrast, the `public:` interface of a typical `List` class might look like the following (some or all of these member functions may be `virtual`; this is a list of integers—see FAQ 25.02 for how to make it a `template`).

```
class List {
public:
  void      prepend(int item) throw();
  void      append(int item) throw();
  void      removeFirst() throw(Empty);
  void      removeLast() throw(Empty);
  void      insertAtPosition(int item, unsigned position)
            throw(BadPosition);
  void      removeAtPosition(unsigned position)
            throw(BadPosition,Empty);
  int&      operator[] (unsigned index)
            throw(BadPosition,Empty);
  int       operator[] (unsigned index) const
            throw(BadPosition,Empty);
  unsigned size() const throw();
  void      setSize(unsigned newSize) throw();
  unsigned countMatches(int itemToMatch) const throw();
  unsigned findPositionOfMatch(int item) const throw();
};
```

If `Stack` were to inherit from `List`, `Stack` would need to support all the member functions that are in class `List`, including member functions to access, insert, and/or remove elements at an arbitrary position within the `Stack`. If these member functions are considered inappropriate for `Stack`, then `Stack` should not inherit from `List` and should use composition instead (see FAQ 5.09).

Remember: do not confuse substitutability and code reuse. Just because `Stack` may use the bits and code from `List` does not imply that `Stack` is substitutable for `List`. The substitutability relation is governed by behavior, not code reuse. When evaluating a potential inheritance relationship, the only criterion should be substitutability.

FAQ 8.12

Is code reuse the main purpose of inheritance?

The main purpose of inheritance is to express an externally meaningful relationship that describes the *behavior* of two entities within the problem domain. This relationship is called the *is-substitutable-for* relationship, although sometimes the less accurate terms *is-a* or *kind-of* are used instead. The critical insight here is that inheritance springs out of the reality of the problem domain, not out of a technical goal within the solution domain. The most important code reuse that comes from (proper) inheritance is the reuse in large systems of existing code that trusts the new derived class to be substitutable for the base class. Reusing a snippet of code from another class can be thought of as low-level reuse.

Inheritance can result in low-level code reuse as a side effect, but low-level code reuse can also be gained from composition, sometimes more appropriately than through inheritance. Trying to achieve low-level code reuse via inheritance often results in improper inheritance. For example, deriving `Stack` from `List` is an attempt to achieve code reuse via inheritance, and it results in improper inheritance.

As suggested, composition is probably a better technique for this situation. In the following example, a `Stack` object is a composite built from a `List` object. Thus, class `Stack` is reusing the code from class `List` via composition (some or all of these member functions may be `virtual`; these classes use integers but real stacks and lists would be generic via templates; see FAQ 25-01).

```
class Empty { };
class BadPosition { };

class List {
public:
```

```
  void      prepend(int item) throw();
  void      append(int item) throw();
  int       removeFirst() throw(Empty);
  int       removeLast() throw(Empty);
  void      insertAtPosition(int item, unsigned position)
            throw(BadPosition);
  int       removeAtPosition(unsigned position)
            throw(BadPosition,Empty);
  int&      operator[] (unsigned index)
            throw(BadPosition,Empty);
  int       operator[] (unsigned index) const
            throw(BadPosition,Empty);
  unsigned size() const throw();
  void      setSize(unsigned newSize) throw();
  unsigned countMatches(int itemToMatch) const throw();
  unsigned findPositionOfMatch(int item) const throw();
protected:
  // Implementation intentionally omitted
};

class Stack {
public:
  void      push(int x)  throw();
  int       pop()         throw(Empty);
  int       top()  const throw(Empty);
  unsigned size() const throw();
protected:
  List list_;
};

void Stack::push(int x) throw()
{ list_.append(x); }

int Stack::pop() throw(Empty)
{ return list_.removeLast(); }

int Stack::top() const throw(Empty)
{ return list_[list_.size()-1]; }

unsigned Stack::size() const throw()
{ return list_.size(); }
```

Here is the UML notation for composition: In the following example, a `Stack` object is a composite built from a `List` object.

Is container-of-thing a kind-of container-of-anything?

No, even if thing is a kind-of anything.

This design error is, unfortunately, both common and disastrous.

Despite its intuitive appeal, container-of-thing is not a kind-of container-of-anything (more precisely, a container-of-thing is not *substitutable for* a container-of-anything). A container-of-anything allows anything to be inserted into it, but container-of-thing only allows things to be inserted into it. Therefore, container-of-thing is strictly less powerful than container-of-anything, and the software that is based on the promises of container-of-anything breaks when it receives a container-of-thing instead.

This is often surprising to people new to OO or the study of proper inheritance. The reason for the surprise is that people often rely on the intuitive notion of *kind of*, but the intuitive notion is inappropriate as a design principle. The reasons are that *kind of* is somewhat muddy (what *exactly* does it mean?), and also it is wrong often enough to be unreliable and therefore dangerous. Remember: the most important issue is substitutability. If intuition and substitutability are in conflict, reject intuition.

Is bag-of-apple a kind-of bag-of-fruit, assuming bag-of-fruit allows the insertion of any kind-of fruit?

NO!

This is a specific example of the general guideline presented in the previous FAQ.

In the following, `Fruit` is an ABC, and `Apple` and `Banana` are concrete kinds-of `Fruit`. The UML diagram and the code are both shown.

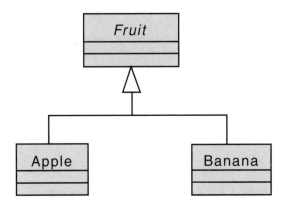

```
#include <iostream>
using namespace std;

class Fruit {
public:
  virtual void printClassName() const throw() = 0;
  virtual ~Fruit() throw();
};

Fruit::~Fruit() throw()
{ }

class Apple : public Fruit {
public:
  virtual void printClassName() const throw();
};

void Apple::printClassName() const throw()
{ cout << "Apple\n"; }

class Banana : public Fruit {
public:
  virtual void printClassName() const throw();
};

void Banana::printClassName() const throw()
{ cout << "Banana\n"; }
```

The following `BagOfFruit` class allows insertion and removal of objects of any kind-
of `Fruit`.

```
class Full  { };
class Empty { };

class BagOfFruit {
public:
  BagOfFruit() throw();
  unsigned size() const throw();
  void insert(Fruit& f) throw(Full);
  Fruit& remove() throw(Empty);
protected:
  enum      { maxSize_ = 20 };
  unsigned  size_;
  Fruit*    data_[maxSize_];
};

BagOfFruit::BagOfFruit() throw()
: size_(0) { }

unsigned BagOfFruit::size() const throw()
{ return size_; }

void BagOfFruit::insert(Fruit& f) throw(Full)
{
  if (size_ == maxSize_) throw Full();
  data_[size_++] = &f;
}

Fruit& BagOfFruit::remove() throw(Empty)
{
  if (size_ == 0) throw Empty();
  return *data_[--size_];
}
```

The following demonstrates a polymorphic function that inserts any kind of Fruit into any kind of BagOfFruit. Note that the parameter for bag.insert() is correct, since class BagOfFruit guarantees that this member function can accept any kind of Fruit.

```
void insertFruitIntoBag(BagOfFruit& bag, Fruit& fruit)
{
  bag.insert(fruit);
}
```

The following BagOfApple class claims (by inheritance) to be a kind-of BagOfFruit. However, BagOfApple is not substitutable for BagOfFruit. There are several other things wrong with this class as well; it uses a reference cast, and it hides BagOfFruit::remove() and BagOfFruit::insert(Fruit&).

```
class BagOfApple : public BagOfFruit {
public:
  BagOfApple() throw();
  void insert(Apple& a) throw(Full);
  Apple& remove() throw(Empty);
};

BagOfApple::BagOfApple() throw()
: BagOfFruit()
{ }

void BagOfApple::insert(Apple& a) throw(Full)
{ BagOfFruit::insert(a); }

Apple& BagOfApple::remove() throw(Empty)
{ return (Apple&) BagOfFruit::remove(); }
```

Because class BagOfApple inherits from class BagOfFruit, BagOfApple objects can be passed to insertFruitIntoBag(). Unfortunately, this permits nonsensical combinations of bags and fruits to be passed to insertFruitIntoBag(). For example, a banana can be inserted into a BagOfApples.

```
int main()
{
  BagOfApple bagOfApple;
  Banana banana;
  insertFruitIntoBag(bagOfApple, banana);

  cout << "Removing an Apple from bagOfApple: ";
  Apple& a2 = bagOfApple.remove();
  a2.printClassName();
}
```

The output of this program follows.

```
Removing an Apple from bagOfApple: Banana
```

The pointer (reference) cast in the remove() member function can be blamed, but the real culprit is improper inheritance. Inheritance must be evaluated using substitutability, a rigorous criterion, because intuition is often wrong.

Is parking-lot-for-cars a kind-of parking-lot-for-arbitrary-vehicles (assuming parking-lot-for-vehicles allows parking any kind-of vehicle)?

NO!

new

This is another specific example of the general guideline presented earlier.

In the following, `Vehicle` is an ABC and `Car` and `NuclearSubmarine` are concrete kinds-of `Vehicle`.

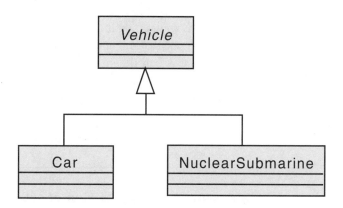

```
#include <iostream>
using namespace std;

class Vehicle {
public:
  virtual ~Vehicle();
};

Vehicle::~Vehicle()
{ }

class Car : public Vehicle {
public:
  virtual void startEngine() throw();
};
```

```
void Car::startEngine() throw()
{ cout << "starting a Car...\n"; }

class NuclearSubmarine : public Vehicle {
public:
  virtual void launchMissile();
};

void NuclearSubmarine::launchMissile() throw()
{ cout << "starting a War...\n"; }
```

If a container of `Car` was a kind-of container of `Vehicle`, someone might put a `NuclearSubmarine` inside the container of `Car`, then remove the `NuclearSubmarine` thinking it was a `Car`.

This is an egregious error. When the `startEngine()` member function is called, the `launchMissile()` may actually be executed (depending on the compiler and implementation). Thus, starting the car's engine might inadvertently start World War III! See the previous FAQ to see the user code that might cause this to happen.

The root problem is bad inheritance. A bad design can't be patched with a little extra inheritance. Throwing more inheritance at an already defective design will usually make it worse. If the design is broken, it needs to be fixed, not patched with clever coding tricks.

FAQ 8.16

Is array-of `Derived` a kind-of array-of `Base`?

No! And the compiler usually doesn't detect this error.

This is another specific example of the general guideline presented earlier. For example, suppose class `Base` has some virtual functions:

```
#include <iostream>
using namespace std;

class Base {
public:
  Base() throw();
  virtual ~Base() throw();
  virtual void f() throw();
};

Base::Base()
{ }
```

```
Base::~Base()
{ }

void Base::f() throw()
{ cout << "Base::f()\n" << flush; }
```

Suppose class `Derived` has some data, such as integer `i_`:

```
class Derived : public Base {
public:
  Derived() throw();
  virtual void f() throw();
protected:
  int i_;
};

Derived::Derived() throw()
: Base()
, i_(42)
{ }

void Derived::f() throw()
{ cout << "Derived::f()\n" << flush; }
```

Making a `Base` pointer refer to the first element in an array-of `Derived` objects is okay, provided users never perform pointer arithmetic (such as applying the subscript operator) using the `Base` pointer. Subscripting into the array using the `Base` pointer is wrong since it will use `sizeof(Base)` for the pointer arithmetic rather than `sizeof(Derived)`. Thus, subscripting into the array using the Base pointer may not refer to *any* `Derived` object:

```
void sample(Base* b) throw()
{
  cout << "b[0].f(): " << flush;
  b[0].f();
  cout << "b[1].f(): " << flush;
  b[1].f();  ◄——— Bang!
}

int main()
{
  Derived d[10];
  sample(d);
}
```

To understand what happened in function `sample()`, imagine a typical 32-bit computer that implements virtual functions in the usual way: a single virtual pointer in the object. In this case `sizeof(Base)` might be 4 (that is, one machine word for the virtual pointer), and `sizeof(Derived)` might be 8 (the `Derived` class objects have whatever size was in the `Base` plus the data from `Derived`). But since the compiler only knows that b points to `Base` in function `sample()`, it will use `sizeof(Base)` when computing subscripts. So `b[1]` will be 4 bytes after the beginning of the array, which is somewhere in the middle of object `d[0]`!

Regardless of the specifics of the machine used, it is *very* unlikely that `b[1]` will refer to the same address as `d[1]` since `sizeof(Derived)` is different than `sizeof(Base)`. So the best possible outcome would be an immediate system crash (which is extremely likely; try it!).

This underscores the advantage of using an array-like class instead of using a C++ array. The compiler would have detected the error in the preceding problem if a `vector<Derived>` had been used rather than a `Derived[]` (`vector<T>` is the standard array-like template; see FAQ 28.13). For example, attempting to pass a `vector<Derived>` to `sample(vector<Base>& a)` would have caused a compile-time error message; see FAQ 8.17. (Remember: don't use pointer casts to "cover up" error messages. When you get an error message, fix the underlying problem rather than simply trying to get the compiler to stop generating error messages).

FAQ 8.17

Does the fact that an array-of `Derived` can be passed as an array-of `Base` mean that arrays are bad?

Yes, arrays are dangerous. Use template container classes instead.

Compared to a C++ array, a template container class (see FAQs 2.15, 28.01) catches more errors at compile time, thus reducing the reliance on runtime testing. For example, if the standard template `vector<T>` had been used, the previous attempt to pass a `vector<Derived>` as a `vector<Base>` would have been caught at compile time.

```
#include <vector>
#include <iostream>
using namespace std;

void sample(vector<Base>& a) throw()
{
  cout << "a[0].f(): ";
  a[0].f();
  cout << "a[1].f(): ";
```

```
    a[1].f();
}

int main()
{
  vector<Base> b(10);
  sample(b);

  #ifdef GENERATE_ERROR
    vector<Derived> d(10);
    sample(d);  ◄───── Error caught at compile time (fortunately)
  #endif
}
```

Templates allow the compiler to distinguish between a pointer to a thing and a reference to an array-of things. In contrast, when C++ arrays were used in the previous FAQ, the compiler wasn't able to detect the error of passing an array-of Derived as if it were a kind-of array-of Base. The compiler detects this error if templates are used.

Chapter 9

Error Handling
Strategies

FAQ 9.01

Is error handling a major source of fundamental mistakes?

Yes.

new

Unfortunately, error handling is usually not considered during the design process in most systems, and instead it is allowed to evolve chaotically and in an ad hoc manner. Part of this is the old-dog-new-trick problem: many programmers' instincts about error handling are based on outdated technology, which tends to lead them in the wrong direction. The purpose of this chapter is to present a sound strategy for modern error handling.

A software application's error-handling strategy must be designed as carefully as the rest of the system. Without a careful design, error handling will be applied inconsistently and will create more problems than it solves. Typically, half of a system's code is dedicated to handling errors in one way or another, and systems that attempt to survive faults, as opposed to simply crashing, have even more to gain from good error-handling strategies.

FAQ 9.02

How should runtime errors be handled in C++?

Use C++ exceptions.

The purpose of the C++ exception-handling mechanism is to handle errors in software composed of independently developed components operating in a single process and under synchronous control.

In C++, a routine that cannot fulfill its promises should `throw` an exception. The caller that knows how to handle this unusual situation can `catch` the thrown exception. Callers can specify the types of exceptions they are willing to handle; exceptions that don't match the specified types are automatically propagated to the caller's caller. Thus intermediate callers (between the thrower and the catcher) can simply ignore the exception. Only the original thrower and the ultimate catcher need to know about the unusual situation.

This is illustrated in the following call graph. In the diagram, `main()` calls `f()`, which calls `g()`, and so forth. Typically these routines are member functions on objects, but they may also be non-member ("top-level") functions. Eventually routine `i()` detects an erroneous situation such as an invalid parameter, an invalid return value from another object, an invalid entry in a file, a network outage, or insufficient memory, and `i()` throws an exception. The thrown exception is caught by `f()`, meaning control is transferred from `i()` to `f()`. Routines `g()`, `h()`, and `i()` are removed from the runtime stack and their local variables are destructed.

The effect is to separate policy from mechanism. Objects at low levels (such as `i()`) have the mechanism to detect and throw exceptions, and objects at higher levels, such as `f()`, specify the policy of how exceptions are to be handled.

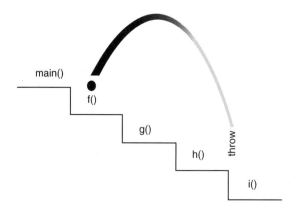

FAQ 9.03

What happens to objects in stack frames that become unwound during the `throw`/`catch` process?

They are properly destructed.

new

Local objects that reside on the stack between the `throw` and the `catch` are properly destructed in stack order; last constructed, first destructed. The result is an extension of the C++ destructor discipline, and allocated resources can be safely kept in an object whose destructor releases the resource. This resource is often memory, but it could also be files that need to be closed, semaphores that need to be unlocked, and so on. For example, a local `auto_ptr` should be used to hold the pointer to an allocated object, as shown in FAQ 2.07.

FAQ 9.04

What is an exception specification?

A specification indicating which exception objects a function expects to throw.

new

For example, in FAQ 2.23, routine `fileExists()` is decorated with the specification `throw()`, indicating that `fileExists()` never throws any exceptions, and routine `processFile()` is decorated with the specification `throw(BadfileName, FileNotFound)`, indicating that `processFile()` expects to throw `BadFileName` or `FileNotFound` (or some object derived from those classes) but nothing else.

If a function throws an exception other than those listed in the exception specification, the `unexpected()` function is called, which (by default) calls `terminate()`, which (by default) calls `abort()`. See FAQ 26.11 for how to change this default behavior.

In general, exception specifications should be used. One place where they are contraindicated, however, is where bug fixes for very large systems are shipped to customers in small binary pieces that are "patched" into the original binary. This is because exception specifications can unnecessarily increase the number of source files that must be shipped with such a bug fix. However for those systems that ship bug fixes as a complete executable, exception specifications should be used.

FAQ 9.05

What are the disadvantages of using return codes for error handling?

They don't separate exceptional logic from normal logic as well as exceptions do, they impose avoidable overhead, and they can't be used in constructors.

Return codes are a nice-guy approach; they allow the caller to do something when an error occurs but they don't *require* the caller to do anything or even notice that the error has occurred.

Return codes require an explicit `if`-check after every function call. This spreads the error-handling code into every caller of every function rather than focusing it on the relatively few routines that can actually correct the problem. Return codes therefore create a complex chain that is hard to test and maintain—everyone percolates the error information backward until finally someone is capable of handling it.

Since testing for return codes requires a conditional branch in the normal execution path, it imposes runtime costs for situations that rarely occur. When functions were hundreds of lines long, checking for return codes was a small percentage of the executable code. But with OO, where member functions often have less than ten lines of code, return codes would impose an unnecessary performance penalty.

Return codes can't be returned from constructors. Fortunately constructors can (and should) throw exceptions. So using return codes with constructors can be disastrous since return codes allow errors to remain uncorrected. For example, if a hash table can't allocate memory for its hash buckets, it might set an error flag within its object, hoping the caller will check this flag and do the right thing. Thus all the object's callers are expected to check this flag (presumably another member function that would have to be added), and all the object's member functions would also have to check the flag. This adds a lot of unnecessary decision logic as well as overhead.

FAQ 9.06

What are the advantages of `throw ... catch`?

Clarity, compiler support, and runtime support.

The most important advantage is that `throw ... catch` clearly separates normal logic from exception-handling logic. In contrast, when a function call uses return codes to signal exceptions, the caller must check the return code with control flow logic (`if`).

This mingles normal logic with exception-handling logic, increasing the complexity of both paths.

A second advantage is that `throw...catch` can transmit an arbitrarily large amount of information from the `throw` point to the `catch` point. This is because C++ allows arbitrary objects, as opposed to just simple data types, to be thrown, and these objects can carry behavior as well as data from where the error is detected to where the error is handled. In contrast return codes are almost always simple data types such as `int`.

Also, `throw...catch` allows different error handlers to be defined for different types of objects and automatically transfers control to the correct error handler.

Finally, `throw...catch` is suited for OO programming. In contrast, return codes are ill suited for OO: since many member functions tend to be short, return codes would overwhelm the routine's normal logic with error-handling logic.

FAQ 9.07

Why is it helpful to separate normal logic from exception handling logic?

The program is easier to read because normal logic doesn't get lost in the error-handling code.

Consider the following `Matrix` class.

```
#include <iostream>
#include <string>
using namespace std;

class Matrix {
public:
  Matrix() throw();
  // ...
};
```

Suppose the goal is to create a routine that will add, subtract, multiply, and divide two matrices (assuming a suitable definition for matrix division). The routine is supposed to handle any overflow condition by printing a message to `cout`, but it is supposed to report any underflow condition back to the caller. Two solutions are presented here: the first uses C++ exceptions and the second uses return codes.

The following low-level routines that perform the arithmetic would be an ideal example for operator overloading, but in an effort to keep the two solutions as similar as possible, normal named functions are used instead. The header `<stdexcept>` declares the standard C++ exceptions `overflow_error` and `underflow_error`.

```
#include <stdexcept>
using namespace std;
Matrix add(const Matrix& a, const Matrix& b)
            throw(overflow_error,underflow_error);
Matrix sub(const Matrix& a, const Matrix& b)
            throw(overflow_error,underflow_error);
Matrix mul(const Matrix& a, const Matrix& b)
            throw(overflow_error,underflow_error);
Matrix div(const Matrix& a, const Matrix& b)
            throw(overflow_error,underflow_error);
```

The routine that does the actual work, `solutionA()`, is defined as follows. As specified, the routine handles overflow errors by printing a message but doesn't handle underflow errors, instead (implicitly) passing the underflow exception back to its caller.

```
void solutionA(const Matrix& a, const Matrix& b)
                throw(underflow_error)
{
  try {
    cout << "a + b is " << add(a, b) << '\n';
    cout << "a - b is " << sub(a, b) << '\n';
    cout << "a * b is " << mul(a, b) << '\n';
    cout << "a / b is " << div(a, b) << '\n';
  }
  catch (overflow_error& e) {
    cout << "overflow: " << e.what() << '\n';
  }
}
```

Now consider the same situation using return codes. First the four arithmetic routines are declared, as before. However, this time two separate return values are needed: the `Matrix` result and the return code that indicates whether there is an error. In this case the `Matrix` result is passed by reference and the return code is returned, but these could be reversed easily. The return code has three potential values: `OK`, `OVERFLOW_ERROR`, and `UNDERFLOW_ERROR`:

```
enum ReturnCode {
  OK,
  OVERFLOW_ERROR,
  UNDERFLOW_ERROR
};

ReturnCode add(Matrix& result, const Matrix& a,
               const Matrix& b);
```

```
ReturnCode sub(Matrix& result, const Matrix& a,
               const Matrix& b);
ReturnCode mul(Matrix& result, const Matrix& a,
               const Matrix& b);
ReturnCode div(Matrix& result, const Matrix& a,
               const Matrix& b);
```

Up until this point the return code technique is not substantially more (or less) complex than the technique that uses C++ exceptions. However, the code that *uses* the arithmetic routines is much more complex when return codes are used. This routine needs to explicitly check the return code from each of the arithmetic calls. This tends to mix the normal logic with the error handling logic:

```
ReturnCode solutionB(const Matrix& a, const Matrix& b)
{
  Matrix result;
  ReturnCode rc;

  rc = add(result, a, b);
  if (rc == OK) {
    cout << "a + b is " << result << '\n';
  } else if (rc == OVERFLOW_ERROR) {
    cout << "overflow error: Matrix + Matrix\n";
    return OK;   ◄──── Overflow has been handled so return normally
  } else {
    return rc;   ◄──── Some other error such as Underflow
  }

  rc = sub(result, a, b);
  if (rc == OK) {
    cout << "a - b is " << result << '\n';
  } else if (rc == OVERFLOW_ERROR) {
    cout << "overflow error: Matrix - Matrix\n";
    return OK;
  } else {
    return rc;
  }

  rc = mul(result, a, b);
  if (rc == OK) {
    cout << "a * b is " << result << '\n';
  } else if (rc == OVERFLOW_ERROR) {
    cout << "overflow error: Matrix * Matrix\n";
    return OK;
  } else {
    return rc;
  }
```

```
    rc = div(result, a, b);
    if (rc == OK) {
      cout << "a / b is " << result << '\n';
    } else if (rc == OVERFLOW_ERROR) {
      cout << "overflow error: Matrix / Matrix\n";
      return OK;
    } else {
      return rc;
    }

    return OK;
  }
```

In this case, the normal algorithm gets lost in the code for error detection and error recovery.

FAQ 9.08

What is the hardest part of using exception handling?

 Deciding what is an error and when an exception should be thrown.

One of the hardest parts of using exception handling is deciding when to throw an exception. Without proper guidelines, programmers spend endless hours discussing "Should this function throw an exception when X happens? What about when Y happens? Or how about when Z happens?" Often these discussions go in circles with no clear resolution. Usually this happens when the programmers have not been given any guidelines for deciding what is and is not an exception. Even worse are situations where exception handling is added to the system as an afterthought, usually just before it ships, and every programmer makes up and follows a unique set of ad hoc rules.

A useful guideline is "A function should throw an exception when anything occurs that prevents it from fulfilling its promises (a.k.a. its contract)." One advantage of this approach is that it ties exception handling to the functional specification of a class and its member functions—that is, it gives a rational basis for deciding what is and what is not an exception. Obviously this means that a function's promises must be clearly defined before a decision can be made about whether something is an error (see FAQ 6.04).

Another advantage of this approach is that it clearly separates errors—things that require an exception to be thrown—from unusual cases, which should not cause an exception to be thrown. The point is that a function should not throw an exception just because something unusual happens. Specifically, if a function detects a situation that happens rarely but that doesn't prohibit the function from fulfilling its promises, then it needs to handle the case and should not throw an exception.

Although it sounds trite, exception handling is for handling errors, not for handling unusual situations. For example, assume that one of the member functions of class `Gardener` is mowing the lawn.

```
class Gardener {
public:
  void mowTheLawn();
};

int main()
{
  Gardener mac;
  mac.mowTheLawn();
}
```

Is it an error if mac the `Gardener` is asked to mow the lawn and the lawn mower runs out of gas? Or if the lawn mower breaks and cannot be fixed until a new part arrives? Or if mac has taken the day off because he is sick? Or if mac is too busy? Or if mac gets hit by lightning (a truly exceptional event)?

Ten different people will give ten different answers as to which, if any, of these are errors. The only way to be sure is to refer to the contract with mac. If the contract says that someone (not necessarily mac) will mow the lawn some time after a request is submitted, then none of the situations is an error, because mac or one of his heirs can eventually fulfill the contract. If the contract says the lawn will be mowed on the same day that the request is submitted, then running out of gas might not be an error, but mac's illness and a breakdown requiring overnight repairs are errors.

FAQ 9.09

When should a function throw an exception?

When it can't fulfill its promises.

When a function detects a problem that prevents it from fulfilling its promises, the function should throw an exception. If the function can recover from the problem so that it can still provide its user with the services it promised, then it has handled the problem and should not throw an exception.

Ideally, exceptions are rare in practice (less than 1% of the time). If an event happens much more frequently than this, perhaps it is not an error, and perhaps the exception-handling mechanism isn't the right choice.

In the following example, the gardener throws an exception if he cannot mow the lawn on the same day the user requests the lawn to be mowed. This occurs when the gardener's lawn mower runs out of gas after 5:00 P.M. (when the gas stations close).

```cpp
#include <iostream>
#include <cstdlib>
#include <stdexcept>
#include <string>
using namespace std;

// pretend this returns the current hour (0 .. 23):
int currentHourHand() throw()
{ return rand() % 24; }

class NoGas : public runtime_error {
public:
  NoGas(const string& what) throw();
};

NoGas::NoGas(const string& what)
: runtime_error (what)
{ }

class LawnMower {
public:
  LawnMower() throw();
  void mowOneRow() throw(NoGas);
  void fillErUp() throw(NoGas);
  bool empty() const throw();
protected:
  unsigned gasLeft_;
};

LawnMower::LawnMower() throw()
: gasLeft_(10)
{ }

void LawnMower::mowOneRow() throw(NoGas)
{
  if (empty()) fillErUp();
  --gasLeft_;
}

void LawnMower::fillErUp() throw(NoGas)
{
  if (currentHourHand() >= 17) {
    cout << "sorry, gas stations are closed at this hour\n";
    throw NoGas("Gas stations are closed");
```

```cpp
  }
  cout << "filling up the tank\n";
  gasLeft_ = 10;
}

bool LawnMower::empty() const throw()
{ return gasLeft_ == 0; }

class Gardener {
public:
  Gardener() throw();
  void mowTheLawn() throw(NoGas);
protected:
  LawnMower mower_;
  int       rowsInLawn_;
};

Gardener::Gardener() throw()
: mower_()
, rowsInLawn_(25)
{ }

void Gardener::mowTheLawn() throw(NoGas)
{
  for (int row = 0; row < rowsInLawn_; ++row) {
    cout << "starting to mow a row\n";
    mower_.mowOneRow();
  }
}

int main()
{
  Gardener mac;
  try {
    cout << "Mac is trying to mow the lawn\n";
    mac.mowTheLawn();
    cout << "Mac succeeded at mowing the lawn!\n";
  }
  catch (NoGas) {
    cout << "sorry, Mac ran out of gas after 5pm\n";
  }
}
```

FAQ 9.10

What is the best approach for the hierarchy of exception objects?

new   A monolithic hierarchy of exception classes works best.

Within the limited realm of exception classes, a singly rooted inheritance tree is superior to a forest of trees. This is an exception (pun intended) to the usual guideline that C++ class hierarchies should be a forest of trees.

One advantage of a monolithic hierarchy for exception classes is in catch-all situations. For example, `main()` often uses a `try` block that catches all possible exceptions. This catch-all block logs the uncaught exception and possibly restarts `main()`. This can be done via ellipses (`catch(...)`), but a monolithic hierarchy of exception classes allows `main()`'s `catch` clause to extract information from the exception object by means of member functions provided by the root class of the exception hierarchy. This allows a more detailed description of the unknown exception to be logged.

For example, suppose all exceptions are derived from the standard exception class called `exception`:

```cpp
#include <iostream>
#include <exception>
using namespace std;

int main()
{
  try {
            ◄──── The code that would normally go into main() goes here
    return 0;
  }
  catch (const exception& e) {
    // Oh No! somehow an exception leaked.
    cerr << "uncaught exception: " << e.what() << '\n';
  }
  catch (...) {
    cerr << "an exception didn't inherit from class exception!\n"
         << "contact the company at 1-800-BAD-BUGS\n";
  }
  return 1;
}
```

FAQ 9.11

How should exception classes be named?

Name the error, not the thrower.

The server should throw an exception whose class name describes the error that occurred rather than describing the code that detected the exception. In other words, the type of the exception object should embody the meaning of what went wrong.

For example, if a List class is asked to remove an element and the List is empty, the List should throw an exception such as EmptyContainer rather than an exception such as ListError.

The purpose of this advice is to enhance information hiding. For example, suppose class List is used to build class Queue; the EmptyContainer exception might be meaningful to users of Queue.

However, if List threw a ListError, users of Queue would become aware of the internal implementation details of Queue (that is, it uses a List). Since this could introduce a ripple effect (for example if the Queue found it more efficient to use a vector than to use a List, all the users of Queue might have to update their catch(ListError) blocks), the author of the Queue class would probably want to catch all these ListError exceptions and repackage them as something that doesn't expose the List detail, then throw that more generic object. So either the author of Queue has extra work to do or the users of Queue end up knowing too much about how Queue is implemented. Clearly it would have been easier if List had thrown something generic such as ContainerIsEmpty.

FAQ 9.12

Where do setjmp and longjmp belong in C++?

In your worst enemy's code.

Never use setjmp() and longjmp() in C++. Use try / catch / throw instead. The major problem with longjmp() is that it jumps out of the function without unwinding the stack, so local (auto) objects aren't destructed properly. In contrast, when C++ exceptions are used, local (auto) objects are properly destructed.

Chapter 10

Testing Strategies

What is the purpose of this chapter?

This chapter describes a systematic technique to pinpoint the root cause of a certain category of bugs.

The chapter is concerned with finding the root cause of problems, not just the symptoms. This is in contrast with most testing efforts, which focus on exposing symptoms but don't provide any formal help in locating the root cause of the problems.

This chapter also focuses on systematic techniques as opposed to *ad hoc* or luck-based debugging.

The basic idea is to bury various checks inside the objects so that the objects end up checking their own work; thus the notion of *self-testing objects*.

What are the advantages of self-testing objects?

Testing starts earlier, continues longer, requires almost no human intervention, focuses on the most commonly used paths, and adapts as the system evolves.

There is very little human effort required for objects that test themselves other than writing the behavioral self-tests and the `testInvariant()` member function. The runtime system works a lot harder because it must continually reverify the object's state and its transitions, but there is very little human (payroll-intensive) intervention.

By integrating an object's test harnesses with the object, the self-testing strategy reduces reliance on big-bang testing. In practice, self-testing detects defects earlier than they otherwise would be with traditional, big-bang testing. This is because every use of the class becomes an impromptu test harness. This reduces the cost of finding and repairing defects, and it improves the business efficiency during system integration. The effect is to change the concept of testing from an event to a life style.

By building self-testing objects, developers ensure that their objects continually adapt as the system evolves. Thus, when the objects are used in new and unforeseen ways, the objects continue to verify themselves using the same test code and against the same standards without anyone having to reverse engineer them and build new test harnesses.

Since every use of an object becomes a miniature test harness, the overall effect is to exhaustively test the most commonly used paths through an object. This is quite a different result than that provided by most unit testing approaches, since most unit testing approaches require explicit and often elaborate test harnesses to be built, and these test harnesses typically provide spotty testing at best.

Finally, since self-testing objects check their own results, traditional test harnesses for unit testing are significantly simpler to develop. For example, the test harnesses don't need to check the result of an operation, since the object already checks its own results. This means that the test harnesses don't need to start out with some specific set of tests to be run but instead can generate test scenarios on the fly by passing randomly generated values into randomly selected member functions. This can both reduce the cost of building test harnesses for unit testing and improve their coverage.

The self-testing technique is similar to the quality mandate in manufacturing. The whole is correct because every part is correct and because every combination of parts is tested.

FAQ 10.03

What are some common excuses people use for not building self-testing into their objects?

 Excuse: "The self-testing code is too trivial to worry about." Reality: If it's that simple, then it will be easy to write.

Excuse: "The self-testing code is too complex." Reality: If it's complex, then it's worth the trouble no matter how long it takes.

Excuse: "I can't afford the time to write the self-testing code." Reality: You haven't done your job until your class's internals are documented.

Excuse: "Calling the self-testing code will consume too much CPU." Reality: That's bogus. You can remove 100% of the runtime overhead by using `#ifdef`. Besides, if it's going to consume a lot of CPU, then either the self-testing checks are sophisticated or the class is very important and commonly used, both of which are arguments *in favor* of this approach, not against it.

Excuse: "The self-testing code might contain bugs, so the technique would be worthless." Reality: Also bogus. If you're not sure that you can express the promise (postcondition) and invariant of your own class correctly, then those promises and invariants should be tested. The self-testing approach provides this for free since it simultaneously tests the class's documentation (its promises and invariants) at the same time as it tests the class's implementation.

FAQ 10.04

What will happen if techniques like those presented here are not used?

The maintenance programmers are doomed to crawl for miles over broken glass.

new

Here are some facts. First, in large systems the "distance," as measured in statements executed, from where an error occurs to where it is detected by the program crashing or producing incorrect results is usually very large, sometimes millions of instructions. Second, one of the most effective techniques for reducing the time and pain associated with debugging is to minimize this distance, that is, discover the error as soon as possible after it has occurred. Third, there are usually thousands of small invariants that programs must maintain to be correct. Fourth, when programs are built using classes and objects, most of these little invariants are associated with the classes and objects.

Therefore, by collecting all these small and seemingly inconsequential invariants and attaching them to the right objects in a systematic fashion, it is possible to build a very robust system that tests itself. This, in turn, minimizes the amount of broken glass that has to be crawled through in trying to find that one fault that occurred a few million instructions ago and just caused the system to crash.

Some programmers build self-testing objects for the good of the team, others out of enlightened self-interest. Either way, self-testing objects should be built. After all, no one should have to crawl over broken glass when such a simple and obvious technique is available.

By the way, if you happen to be the developer who finds everyone else's bugs because you are methodical and they are cowboys, then you should be lobbying hard for your team to use these techniques. Either that or maybe you should just institute a policy that the cowboys on the team eat the glass you have to crawl through because they refuse to build self-testing objects.

FAQ 10.05

When is a class correct?

new   When it meets or exceeds its external agreements and abides by its internal constraints.

A class's external agreements include requirements imposed on users of the class and promises made to the users. This behavior is observable in the sense that it is expressed in terms of the class's `public:` member functions. This behavior can and should be tested. For example, just before a member function returns, the member function can check that it actually fulfilled its promises (a.k.a. postconditions; see FAQ 6.04). This is called *behavioral self-testing,* and it often involves adding checks at the bottom of the member function that check the member function's promises. These checks are normally put in an `assert()` statement or perhaps in an `#ifdef`; that way the checks can be removed if they cause too much performance degradation (see FAQ 10.06).

A class's internal constraints define the allowed states of data structures associated with objects of the class. Every object of the class must abide by these restrictions at all times. The class can and should test these class invariants (see FAQ 10.07).

FAQ 10.06

What is behavioral self-testing?

When an object checks its work before letting others see what happened.

The promises made by a member function can be encoded as a test that is executed at the end of the member function. For example, if the member function `List::removeFirst()` promises that `List::size()` will return one less than it did before, an explicit test to this effect can be made at the end of the `List::removeFirst()` member function. The code associated with behavioral self-tests can be wrapped in an `#ifdef` so that it can be easily removed or reinstalled as desired:

```
#include <stdexcept>
#include <cassert>
```

```
#include <cstdlib>
#include <string>
using namespace std;
class List;

class Node {
private:
  friend List;
  int   elem_;
  Node* next_;
  Node(int elem, Node* next) throw();
};

Node::Node(int elem, Node* next) throw()
: elem_(elem)
, next_(next)
{ }

class Empty { };

class List {
public:
  List() throw();
  bool empty() const throw();
  int  size() const throw();
  int  peekAtFirst() const throw(Empty);
  void prepend(int x) throw();
  int  removeFirst() throw(Empty);
    // REQUIRE: empty() must return false
    // PROMISE: Return value will be the initial value of peekAtFirst()
    // PROMISE: size() will be reduced by 1
  List             (const List& list) throw();  // copy constructor
  List& operator= (const List& list) throw();  // assignment operator
  ~List() throw();
protected:
  Node* first_;
};

List::List() throw()
: first_(NULL)
{ }

List::~List() throw()
{ while (first_ != NULL) removeFirst(); }

bool List::empty() const throw()
{ return first_ == NULL; }

int List::size() const throw()
{
```

```
      int ans = 0;
      for (const Node* p = first_; p != NULL; p = p->next_)
        ++ans;
      return ans;
    }

    int List::peekAtFirst() const throw(Empty)
    {
      if (empty()) throw Empty("List::peekAtFirst()");
      return first_->elem_;
    }

    void List::prepend(int x) throw()
    { first_ = new Node(x, first_); }

    int List::removeFirst() throw(Empty)
    {
      if (empty()) throw Empty("List::removeFirst()");
      #ifndef NDEBUG
        int peekAtFirstInit = peekAtFirst();
        int sizeInit = size();
      #endif

      // remove first element from the List
      int result = first_->elem_;
      Node* oldFirstNode = first_;
      first_ = first_->next_;
      delete oldFirstNode;

      #ifndef NDEBUG
        assert(result == peekAtFirstInit);
        assert(size() == sizeInit - 1);
      #endif
      return result;
    }

    int main()
    {
      List a;
      a.prepend(42);
      a.prepend(24);
      int elem = a.removeFirst();
    }
```

Naturally the assert(...) statements can be replaced by other assertion-checking techniques, if desired. The point is that the object checks its own results.

FAQ 10.07

What is a class invariant?

Stuff that's true whenever anyone else is looking.

The *class invariant* is the collection of boolean expressions that are always true for objects of the class. It is normal for a member or friend function (see FAQ 19.05) to temporarily violate the invariant, but the member or friend function must restore the invariant before returning to the user.

Here is the invariant for a `Date` class, encoded in the `protected:` `testInvariant()` member function.

```
#include <cassert>

class Date {
public:
                ←──────── The public: interface for Date goes here
protected:
  void testInvariant() const throw();
  int day_;
  int month_;
  int year_;
};

inline void Date::testInvariant() const throw()
{
  assert(day_ >= 1 && day_ <= 31);
  assert(month_ >= 1 && month_ <= 12);
}
```

The statement `assert(month_ >= 1 && month_ <= 12);` evaluates the conditional as a boolean. If `month_` is out of range, the assertion fails and the `assert()` statement causes an error message to be printed and the program to be killed. During development, the debugger often opens at this point so that the programmer can determine exactly what went wrong and why. Compiling with the symbol NDEBUG defined (for example, via the `-DNDEBUG` option on many command-line driven compilers) causes the `assert(...)` code to vanish completely.

FAQ 10.08

Why should the invariant be captured explicitly?

As maintenance documentation and to catch bugs.

The class invariant should be recorded, if for no other reason than as documentation for future maintainers. Since a developer's job isn't done until the internal constraints of the data structure have been properly documented, there is really no choice. Someone somewhere has to write down these internal constraints.

If the internal constraints of the class's data structure are to be documented, the most natural and accessible place is along with the class's code. And source code is the most unambiguous way to express this documentation since expressing it in a natural language is relatively imprecise.

Plus, if the invariant is captured in a member function, the member function can be called at strategic moments during an object's life cycle, which effectively tests the documentation as well as testing the class's member functions. In other words, this technique makes sure that the invariant is correct and makes sure that the other member functions don't violate the invariant. If desired, these calls to the invariant can be placed in an `#ifdef` or an `assert()` so they can easily be removed before the software is shipped.

In cases where a class has a nontrivial invariant, practical experience has shown that this can catch a sizeable percentage of a class's bugs.

FAQ 10.09

When should the `testInvariant()` member function be called?

At the end of constructors to make sure the invariant was established and at the end of mutator member functions to make sure the invariant was maintained.

Rule 1: Every `public:` constructor must establish the invariant. Every `public:` constructor must initialize its object so that it passes the invariant test (this means avoiding any technique that allows the object to be initialized to garbage and requiring the user to call an `init()` member function). Thus every `public:` constructor should call `testInvariant()` as the last thing it does. Normally this call should be in an `#ifdef` or an `assert()` so that it can be easily removed or reinstalled as desired.

Rule 2: Every `public:` member function must maintain the invariant. Every `public:` member function may assume that its object passes the invariant test at the beginning and must restore its object's invariant by the time it returns. Thus every `public:` member function that mutates the object should call `testInvariant()` as the last thing it does. Normally this call should also be in an `#ifdef` or an `assert()` so that it can be easily removed or reinstalled as desired.

FAQ 10.10

What can be done to ensure that an object doesn't get blown away by a wild pointer?

Empower the object to test its invariant at the beginning of every `public:` member function and every friend function (see FAQ 19.05).

Wild pointers can corrupt a sleeping object. Wild pointers are the SCUD missiles of the software world—they are undirected terrorist instruments that wreak havoc in chaotic ways. Once a wild pointer has scribbled on an object, the object also exhibits chaotic behavior, often developing wild pointers of its own. The chain reaction spreads like a virus—each wild pointer infects a few more objects. Eventually one of the wild pointers attempts to scribble on something protected by the hardware and then the system crashes.

Once this chain reaction has occurred, programmers must rely on intuition and blind luck when looking for the root cause of the problem. We call this voodoo debugging, since it is about as effective as a fortune teller reading chicken entrails—indeed, the technology of reading entrails is remarkably similar to that of reading a core dump after corruption by wild pointers.

An object can help detect wild pointers by beginning all its `public:` member functions with a call to `testInvariant()`. This ensures that the object is still in a consistent state.

```
#include <cassert>
using namespace std;

class Date {
public:
  Date() throw();
  Date& operator++ () throw();
  int month() const throw();
  int day()   const throw();
  int year()  const throw();
protected:
  void testInvariant() const throw();
  int month_;
  int day_;
  int year_;
};

inline void Date::testInvariant() const throw()
{
```

```
    assert(day_ >= 1 && day_ <= 31);
    assert(month_ >= 1 && month_ <= 12);
}

Date::Date() throw()
: month_(7)
, day_  (4)
, year_ (1776)
{
    testInvariant();  ←—— public: constructors must establish the invariant
}

int Date::month() const throw()
{
    testInvariant();  ←—— Wild pointers can corrupt a sleeping object
    return month_;
}

int Date::day() const throw()
{
    testInvariant();  ←—— Wild pointers can corrupt a sleeping object
    return day_;
}

int Date::year() const throw()
{
    testInvariant();  ←—— Wild pointers can corrupt a sleeping object
    return year_;
}

Date& Date::operator++ () throw()
{
    testInvariant();  ←—— Wild pointers can corrupt a sleeping object
    // ...  ←——————————— Put code to increment the date here
    testInvariant();  ←—— public: mutators must maintain the invariant
    return *this;
}
```

Since the assert(...) statements within the testInvariant() member function vanish when the symbol NDEBUG is defined, and since the testInvariant() member function is defined using the inline keyword, all the calls to testInvariant() will vanish when NDEBUG is defined. Normally it is not necessary to define the symbol NDEBUG until fairly late in the software development cycle, and some projects (particularly business applications that are not CPU bound) leave it on even after the software is deployed to its users.

Part III

Language Facilities

Chapters 11 through 28 cover the facilities of the C++ language and the Standard C++ Library. The material is presented in roughly the same order that the facilities appear in the C++ Standard.

Chapter 11

References

What is a reference?

A reference is an alias, an alternate name for an object. References are frequently used for passing parameters by reference (pass-by-reference; see FAQ 2.09). In the following example, function swap() receives its parameters by non-const reference since it needs to change the values of the caller's actual parameters, in this case main()'s i and j.

```
#include <iostream>
using namespace std;

void swap(int& x, int& y) throw()
{
  int temp = x;
  x = y;
  y = temp;
}

int main()
{
  int i = 5;
  int j = 7;
  cout << "before: i=" << i << ", j=" << j << '\n';
  swap(i, j);
  cout << "after:  i=" << i << ", j=" << j << '\n';
}
```

Here x and y become aliases for main()'s i and j, respectively. The effect is similar to the C-style pass-by-pointer, but without the caller having to take the address of the parameters and without the callee having to dereference pointers. That is, it would be illegal to change swap(i,j) in main() to swap(&i,&j), and it would be illegal to change x = y in swap() to *x = *y.

FAQ 11.02

What does "referent" mean?

"Referent" is a synonym for the object to which the reference refers; see FAQ 2.09. In the following example, j is the reference and i is the referent.

```
int main()
{
  int  i;
  int& j = i;
}
```

FAQ 11.03

When can a reference be attached to its referent?

A reference can be attached to its referent only at the moment the reference is initialized. Not only that, C++ requires every reference initialization to have a referent.

The following example initializes j to be an alias for i, but the initialization of k is illegal because reference k is not attached to an object.

```
int main()
{
  int  i;
  int& j = i;

  #ifdef GENERATE_ERROR
    int& k;    //ERROR: references must be initialized
  #endif
}
```

When a function receives a parameter by reference, the reference is initialized by being attached (bound) to the actual argument provided by the caller.

FAQ 11.04

What happens when a value is assigned to a reference?

The reference remains bound to the same referent, and the value of the referent is changed.

Because a reference is an alias for its referent, anything done to the reference is actually done to the referent. In particular, a reference is an lvalue (an expression that can appear on the left side of an assignment operator) for the referent. Therefore, assigning to a reference changes the referent.

Said another way, a reference *is* its referent—not a copy of the referent nor a pointer to the referent, but the referent itself.

For example, in the following function f(), the first statement changes main()'s i because the formal parameter x is an alias for i. The second statement also changes i (as well as x) because the address of i is stored in y. The third statement does not change i because z is a copy of the original value of i.

```
void f(int& x, int* y, int z) throw()
{
  x = 5;    //main()'s i changed to 5
  *y = 6;   //main()'s i changed to 6
  z = 7;    //no change to main()'s i
}

int main()
{
  int i = 4;
  f(i, &i, i);
}
```

FAQ 11.05

What is a local reference?

A local reference is a local (auto) reference variable that isn't a parameter. The following example illustrates how local references provide a temporary alias relationship. Integer reference j is an alias for integer i, so changing i to 5 changes j, and changing j changes i.

```
int main()
{
```

```
int  i;
int& j = i; //establish the alias relation between j and i
i = 5;      //assigning 5 to i, changes both i and j
j = 6;      //assigning 6 to j, changes both i and j
}
```

Local references are not as common as reference parameters. Local references are sometimes used to avoid recalculating the same location several times; they allow a function
to attach a handle to an object that would otherwise require nontrivial address computation to access. Applications that do a lot of data cacheing sometimes use local references.

FAQ 11.06

What does it mean to return a reference?

The function call expression is an lvalue to the referent.

When a function returns a reference, the function call becomes an lvalue (see FAQ
11.04) for the referent. This is normally used to allow operator expressions (such as the
subscript operator, the dereference operator, and so on) to be used as lvalues. The following example shows how returning a reference allows a subscript operator to be an
lvalue.

```
#include <iostream>
#include <stdexcept>
using namespace std;

class Array {
public:
  float& operator[] (unsigned i) throw(out_of_range);
protected:
  float data_[100];
};

inline float& Array::operator[] (unsigned i)
throw(out_of_range)
{
  if (i >= 100u)
    throw out_of_range("Array index is out of range");
  return data_[i];
}
```

```
int main()
{
  Array a;
  for (unsigned i = 0; i < 100; ++i)
    a[i] = 3.14 * i;
  for (unsigned j = 0; j < 100; ++j)
    cout << a[j] << '\n';
}
```

Returning a reference to `data_[i]` doesn't return a copy of `data_[i]`; it returns `data_[i]` itself. Therefore, anything done to the expression in the caller (`a[i]`) is actually done to `data_[i]`. In the example, the statement `a[i] = ...` actually changes `data_[i]` within object a.

C programmers should note that this allows a function call to appear on the left side of an assignment operator.

FAQ 11.07

What is the result of taking the address of a reference?

The address of a reference is the address of the referent.

Remember that the reference *is* the referent. Anything done to the reference—including taking its address—is actually done to the referent. For example, the following code will print yes since `&i` will be equal to `&j`.

```
#include <iostream>
using namespace std;

void sample(int* p, int* q)
{
  if (p == q)
    cout << "yes\n";
  else
    cout << "no\n";
}

int main()
{
  int  i = 5;
  int& j = i;
  sample(&i, &j);
}
```

FAQ 11.08

Can a reference be made to refer to a different referent?

No, it can't.

Unlike a pointer, once a reference is bound to an object, it cannot be made to refer to a different object. The alias cannot be separated from the referent.

For example, the last line of the following example changes i to 6; it does not make the reference k refer to j. Throughout its short life, k will always refer to i.

```
int main()
{
  int  i = 5;
  int  j = 6;
  int& k = i;  ◄——— Bind k so it is an alias for i
        k = j;  ◄——— Change i to 6—does NOT bind k to j
}
```

FAQ 11.09

Why use references when pointers can do everything references can do?

Because references are better than pointers for some tasks.

Using a pointer when a reference will do is like using a chain saw to trim your finger-nails—it will do the job, but you'd better be extremely careful.

In C, pointers are used for a variety of tasks because there is no other tool available for doing these tasks. Programmers learn to live with the dangers of pointers in C because there is no alternative. It's as if C gives you a chain saw and expects you to use it for building houses, shredding paper, trimming fingernails, and cutting hair.

When all that's needed is an alias for an object, a pointer is overkill, but a reference is ideal. Pointers are a powerful and valuable part of any programmer's toolbox. However, they should be used only when necessary. Don't give a chain saw to a user who just wants a manicure.

Use references when you can, use pointers when you have to. (See FAQ 11.11.)

FAQ 11.10

Aren't references just pointers in disguise?

No, they are not.

It is important to realize that references and pointers are quite different. A pointer should be thought of as a separate object with its own distinct set of operations (*p, p->blah, and so on). So creating a pointer creates a new object. In contrast, creating a reference does not create a new object; it merely creates an alternative name for an existing object. Furthermore the operations and semantics for the reference are defined by the referent; references do not have operations of their own.

In the following example, notice that assigning 0 to the reference j is very different than assigning 0 to the pointer p (the 0 pointer is the same as the NULL pointer; see FAQ 1.09).

```
int main()
{
   int  i = 5;
   int& j = i; ◄─────────── j is an alias for i
   int* p = &i; ◄─────────── p is a new object, not an alias

   j = 0; ◄─────────── Changes i
   p = 0; ◄─────────── Changes p; does not affect i
}
```

Because of their low-level nature, pointers are poor substitutes for references. Holding on to the belief that pointers and references are the same is like saying that char* and a string class are the same or that void* and long are the same—there is a way to map from one to the other but the mapping is forced and is unnatural. Furthermore, the purpose of programming in C++ is not to write C++ programs that look just like C programs.

Pointers and references are not the same, even though many compilers implement them using similar assembly language instructions. This is an implementation detail that does not change the message of this FAQ.

FAQ 11.11

When are pointers needed?

References are usually preferred over pointers when aliases are needed for existing objects, making them useful in parameter lists and as return values. Pointers are required when it might be necessary to change the binding to a different referent or to refer to a nonobject (a NULL pointer). Pointers often show up as local variables and member objects. An example of this can be seen in the class `Array` that follows.

```
class Array {
public:
   int& operator[] (int i);  ◄——— References in signatures can make interfaces intuitive
protected:
   int* data_;  ◄——————————— Pointers as member data allow reallocation
};
```

The only time a parameter or return value should be a pointer is when the function needs to accept or return a sentinel value. In this case the function can accept or return a pointer and use the NULL pointer as the sentinel value.

FAQ 11.12

Why do some people hate references?

Most of the complaints we've heard about references have come from C programmers who are new to C++, and the complaints reflect a combination of teaching old dogs new tricks and the lack of good training on what references are all about.

It often takes C programmers time to get used to references. In the beginning, C programmers typically complain that pass-by-reference doesn't require explicit syntax in the caller's source code (for example, no & in the caller code). After using C++ for a while, however, developers realize that this is information hiding, which is an asset rather than a liability.

An important goal of OO technology is to enable developers to program in the language of the problem domain rather than the language of the computer. The information hiding provided by a reference is a small step in the migration.

In C, the maxim is "No hidden mechanism." C++ intentionally discards this C maxim since it is inconsistent with the C++ goal of programming in the language of the problem domain rather than the language of the machine. The new maxim is "Pay for it only if you use it."

Write C++ code in the language of the problem domain, not the language of the machine.

FAQ 11.13

Does `int& const x` make sense?

No, it doesn't. Since a reference is always bound to the same referent, the `const` is superfluous and possibly confusing.

```
class Fred { };
void f(Fred& const a);              Wrong; should be f(Fred& a);
void g(const Fred& const a);        Wrong; should be g(const Fred& a);

void sample(Fred& a)
{
   Fred& const b = a;               Wrong; should be Fred& b = a;
   const Fred& const c = a;         Wrong; should be const Fred& c = a;
}
```

Chapter 12

New and Delete

Does `new` do more than allocate memory?

Yes, it also initializes the new object.

Assuming `Fred` is a known type, the expression `new Fred()` is a two-step operation. The first step is to allocate `sizeof(Fred)` bytes of memory using a memory allocator primitive called `operator new(size_t nbytes)` (`size_t` is a typedef for an `unsigned` integral type such as `unsigned int`). This memory allocation primitive is conceptually similar to but not interchangeable with `malloc(size_t nbytes)`. The second step is to call the appropriate constructor of the class (`Fred::Fred()` in this case).

Similarly, `delete p` is a two-step operation: it first calls the destructor on the object `*p`, then it releases the memory pointed to by p using a memory deallocation primitive. This memory deallocation primitive is called `operator delete(void* p)` and is conceptually similar to but not interchangeable with `free(void* p)`.

Why is `new` better than good old trustworthy `malloc()`?

It does more.

Object construction: In C++, `new` and `delete` create and destroy objects. In contrast, `malloc()` and `free()` merely allocate and deallocate memory.

Safety: The new operator returns a pointer of the correct type whereas the function malloc() returns a void*, which isn't type safe. The C language allows a void* to be converted to any other pointer, but this is a dangerous hole in C's type-checking system. C++ doesn't have this weakness: converting a void* to a different pointer type requires an explicit cast in C++.

Flexibility: The new operator can be overloaded by a class. For example, new Fred() can use a different memory allocation primitive than is used by new Wilma(). In contrast, malloc() cannot be overloaded on a class-by-class basis.

FAQ 12.03

Does C++ have a counterpart to realloc() that goes along with new and delete?

No; and don't use realloc() directly, since bitwise copying of an object of a user-defined class is evil.

When realloc() needs to move data during the reallocation, it uses a bitwise copy, which is disastrous for many user-defined classes (see FAQ 30.15). C++ objects know how to copy themselves using their own copy constructors and assignment operators.

Never use realloc() on objects of user-defined classes. Let the objects copy themselves. Better yet, use the vector template class rather than pointers to arrays, and the vector template will take care of reallocation automatically and correctly (see FAQ 28.13).

FAQ 12.04

Can pointers returned from new be deallocated with free()? Can pointers returned from malloc() be deallocated with delete?

No!

It is perfectly legal, moral, and wholesome to use malloc() and delete in the same program or to use new and free() in the same program. But it is illegal, immoral, and despicable to call free() on a pointer allocated via new or to call delete on a pointer allocated via malloc().

Even if it appears to work on your particular compiler on your particular machine, please don't do it. Corrupting the heap is a very subtle and disastrous thing; it's just not worth the trouble—even if the data type is a simple array of char; even if some programmers think it would be cool. Just say no.

FAQ 12.05

Does `delete p` delete the pointer p or the referent *p?

The referent *p.

If verbosity were a virtue, the syntax would be changed from `delete p` to `deleteTheThingPointedToBy p`. One could argue that the current syntax is misleading, but the same abuse of English occurs with `free(p)` from the C language: `free(p)` doesn't free p; rather it frees the memory pointed to by p.

FAQ 12.06

Should the pointer returned from `new Fred()` be checked to see if it is NULL?

new

No, `new Fred()` never ever returns NULL. Instead, if new runs out of memory during `new Fred()`, it throws an exception of type `bad_alloc` (see FAQ 9.02).

Because of this, the `if` test in the following example is considered bad form since it increases code size, increases code complexity, and increases testing costs, yet it adds no value (remember, exceptions guarantee that p will *never* be NULL).

```
#include <new>
using namespace std;

class Fred { };

void sample() throw(bad_alloc)
{
  Fred* p = new Fred();
  if (p == NULL) {  ←—— Bad Form! Shouldn't check for NULL
    // ...
  }
  // ...
}
```

```
int main()
{ sample(); }
```

C programmers please note that this behavior is very different from the way out-of-memory is handled by malloc(). To be safe, *every* call to malloc() has to be followed by an explicict if test to see if malloc() returned NULL.

FAQ 12.07

How can new be convinced to return NULL rather than throw an exception?

new

Replace new Fred() with new(nothrow) Fred(). Note that this is a step backward for the reasons already described, so this technique should not be extensively used in new C++ code. However this technique is relevant for people who have to deal with C++ software that was written before new Fred() threw exceptions.

When preexception C++ code is compiled on a modern C++ compiler, the use of exceptions may cause the application to crash. In this case, there are two basic options: update the application by making it *exception safe* (that is, make the code do something reasonable even if something such as new throws an exception), or patch the application by replacing new Fred() with new(nothrow) Fred(). Often, but not always, it is cheaper to patch it rather than make it exception safe. The following example demonstrates this technique.

```
#include <new>
using namespace std;

void sample() throw()
{
  Fred* p = new(nothrow) Fred();  ◄─── Note the nothrow
  if (p == NULL) {  ◄───────────────── This test is required!
    // ...
  }
}
```

How can new be set up to automatically flush pools of recycled objects whenever memory runs low?

Applications that do a lot of freestore allocations can sometimes improve performance by using global pools of recycled objects. For example, when a dynamically allocated Fred object is no longer needed, the programmer can say p->discard() rather than delete p, and the discard() member function adds the object to a static pool of Fred objects. Then when a Fred object is needed, the programmer says Fred::create() rather than new Fred(), and the static create() member function returns the first entry from the list (or returns new Fred() if the list is empty).

Everything works great until memory runs low, at which point the pool of Fred objects needs to be flushed to free up available memory. It would be ideal if the runtime system would automatically call some routine such as Fred::flushPool() whenever new ran low on memory, since the pool could be flushed without any functional impact. For example, if someone wants to create a Wilma object and the system runs out of memory because there are too many recycled Fred objects in the Fred pool, the goal is to have the system automatically call Fred::flushPool(), which actually deletes all the Fred objects on the recycled list. We set up the Fred class with its pool of recycled objects:

```
#include <new>
using namespace std;

class Fred {
public:
    static Fred* create() throw(bad_alloc);  ◄── Named Constructor Idiom; see FAQ 16.08
    virtual void discard() throw();  ◄──────────── p->discard() is analogous to delete p
    static bool flushPool() throw();  ◄─────────── Returns true if it freed some memory
private:
    Fred()  throw();  ◄─────────── Constructor is private: so users can't say new Fred()
    ~Fred() throw();  ◄─────────── Destructor is private: so users can't say delete p
    void init() throw();  ◄─────── Initializes (or possibly reinitializes) the object as if it was just created
    Fred* nextRecycled_;
    static Fred* headRecycled_;
};

void Fred::init() throw()
{
```

```
      // ...  ◄─────── This is where the constructor's logic should go
      nextRecycled_ = NULL;
    }

    Fred::Fred() throw()
    { init(); }

    Fred::~Fred() throw()
    {  }  ◄─────────── The destructor doesn't need to do anything with the recycled list

    Fred* Fred::headRecycled_ = NULL;

    Fred* Fred::create() throw(bad_alloc)
    {
      if (headRecycled_ == NULL)
        return new Fred();
      Fred* p = headRecycled_;
      headRecycled_ = headRecycled_->nextRecycled_;
      p->init();  ◄─── Reinitializes the object as if it were just created
      return p;
    }

    void Fred::discard() throw()
    {
      nextRecycled_ = headRecycled_;
      headRecycled_ = this;
    }

    bool Fred::flushPool() throw()
    {
      bool stuffGotDeleted = (headRecycled_ != NULL);
      while (headRecycled_ != NULL)
        delete create();
      return stuffGotDeleted;
    }
```

First, notice how users are prevented from saying new Fred() or delete p. Instead users must say Fred::create() and p->discard(), respectively. The discard() member function adds the object to the recycled pool, and the create() static member function uses the recycled pool if it isn't empty. Finally the flushPool() static member function flushes the pool of recycled Fred objects, and returns a bool indicating whether anything actually was deleted.

Next, to acomplish the larger goal of having the system automatically call Fred::flushPool() whenever new runs out of memory, a special function is created that calls Fred::flushPool() (and possibly other similar pools, such as

Wilma.::flushPool()). This special function is known as a *new handler* and is called flushAllPools() in the following example. If operator new(size_t nbytes) runs out of memory, it calls this function, which tries to delete some unneeded memory. If the new handler succeeds at freeing up some storage, it simply returns to operator new(size_t nbytes), and operator new(size_t nbytes) tries the allocation again. If the new handler is unsuccessful at freeing up storage, it avoids an infinite loop by throwing an exception:

```
#include <new>
using namespace std;

void flushAllPools() throw(bad_alloc)
{
  unsigned n = 0;
  n += Fred::flushPool();
  // Flush any other pools as well,
  // e.g., n += Wilma::flushPool();
  if (n == 0) throw bad_alloc();  // Nobody freed memory;
                                  // prevent infinite loop
}
```

The final step is to register the function flushAllPools() as the official *new handler*. This is done using the set_new_handler() function and is normally called very early in the application's execution:

```
int main()
{
  set_new_handler(flushAllPools);  ◄——— Install the "new handler"
  // ...
}
```

The rest is automatic: if someone says new Barney() and the underlying allocator (operator new(size_t nbytes)) runs out of memory, the allocator automatically calls the new handler (flushAllPools()), which flushes the Fred pool (Fred::flushPool()). If something actually was flushed, the new handler returns to operator new(size_t), which tries again. If it fails a second time, the whole process repeats. Eventually one of two things happens: either operator new(size_t) succeeds, in which case the caller who said new Barney() will never know that any of this ever happened, or flushAllPools() fails to flush anything and throws an exception (in which case the new Barney() attempt vanishes, and control goes to the appropriate catch handler; see FAQ 9.03). In either case, the users who are saying new Barney() don't know anything about the pool mechanism—it is invisible to them.

FAQ 12.09

What happens if `delete p` is called when `p` is `NULL`?

Nothing.

Calling `delete p` when p is NULL is safe and is guaranteed to do nothing. This simplifies code that uses `delete` by letting programmers say `delete p;` rather than `if (p != NULL) delete p;`. For example,

```
class Fred { };

void sample(Fred* p) throw()
{
  #if 0
    if (p != NULL)  ←——— Bad form!
      delete p;
  #else
    delete p;  ←——————— Good form!
  #endif
}

int main()
{
  sample(new Fred());
  sample(NULL);
}
```

There are two problems with the explicit `if` test: first, some people get the test backwards (e.g., they say `if (!p) delete p;` which is backward), and second, `if` tests significantly increase the cost of testing—to achieve branch point coverage, both the "if true" and the "if false" branches of every `if` need to be exercised. Thus, adding unnecessary branch points, such as `if` statements, to an application causes the creation of unnecessary test cases. Conversely, if a branch point can be removed from the software without complicating or invalidating something else, in general the expected quality of the software goes up and the testing cost goes down.

FAQ 12.10

What happens when a pointer is deleted twice?

Catastrophe.

Suppose there is a pointer variable p. The first time `delete p` is executed, the object `*p` is safely destructed and the memory pointed to by p is safely returned to the heap. The second time the same pointer is passed to `delete` without a subsequent `new` that returned that pointer, the remains of what used to be an object at `*p` are passed to the destructor (which could be disastrous), and the memory pointed to by p is handed back to the heap a second time. This is likely to corrupt the heap and its list of free memory. The following example illustrates this situation.

```
class Fred { };

int main()
{
  Fred* p1 = new Fred();
  Fred* p2 = p1;
  delete p1;
  delete p2; ⟵—— Delete the same pointer twice: DISASTER!
}
```

FAQ 12.11

How can an array of things be allocated and deallocated?

new

The best way is to be radical. Instead of trying to use an array pointer correctly, it is easier (and often more efficient) not to use explicit pointers at all but instead to use a container template such as `vector` (see FAQ 28.13). Please don't use explicit pointers unless it is necessary. Pointers are a source of a lot of errors; using a good container class library can eliminate many pointer errors.

If it is necessary or desired to use pointers anyway, the right way to allocate an array of things is with `p = new Fred[n]`. When the array is deallocated, the `[]` must appear just after the `delete` keyword, such as `delete[] p;`. Here is an example.

```
class Fred { };

int main()
{
  Fred* p = new Fred[100]; ⟵—— Allocate an array of Fred
  delete[] p; ⟵———————— [] is required when deallocating the array
}
```

The purpose of the syntactic difference between `delete p` and `delete[] p` is to distinguish deleting a thing from deleting an array of things. This is because there is no syntactic difference between the type "pointer to a thing" (`Fred*`) and the type "pointer to the first element of an array of things" (Fred*). This is a feature that C++ inherited from C.

After all this, recall that the real solution is to not use pointers at all but instead to use a good container class library. For example, when an array of things is needed, use a container class that implements an array of things, such as the standard template vector (see FAQ 28.13).

FAQ 12.12

What if delete p (not delete[] p) is used to delete an array allocated via new Fred[n]?

Catastrophe.

It is the programmer's responsibility—not the compiler's—to verify that the connection between new[] and delete[] is correct. If it is wrong, don't expect either a compiler error message or a clean runtime exception. Expect a disaster. Worse, the disaster might not show up during testing; it might not show up until after the software is in the field.

For example, some implementations immediately corrupt the heap when the [] is omitted when deleting an array of objects; other implementations fail to destruct all but the first object in the array. The latter could cause memory leaks if the destructors release memory, cause deadlock if the destructors unlock semaphores, compromise system integrity in other ways, or trigger some combination of any or all of these.

Remember that this headache can be instantly eliminated if container classes, such as vector, are used instead of raw pointers. Please use raw pointers only when it's absolutely necessary.

FAQ 12.13

Can the [] of delete[] p be dropped when p points to an array of some built-in type such as char?

No; there is no reason to do this and it risks an avoidable disaster.

Some programmers tragically think that the [] in the delete[] p exists only so that the compiler will call the appropriate number of destructors. Following this reasoning, they assume that the [] are optional when the array is of some built-in type such as an array of char:

```
#include <new>
using namespace std;

void sample(int n) throw(bad_alloc)
{
  char* p = new char[n];
  // ...
  delete p;  ◄─── ERROR! Should be delete[] p;
}

int main()
{ sample(10); }
```

The delete p; line above is wrong, and it can cause a disaster at runtime. In particular, the underlying deallocation primitive called for delete p; is operator delete(void*), but the deallocation primitive called for delete[] p; is operator delete[](void*). The default behavior for the latter is to call the former, but users are allowed to replace the latter with a different behavior. For example, someone might replace operator new[](size_t) (the allocation primitive called for new char[n]) and operator delete[](void*) with a separate heap from operator new(size_t) and operator delete(void*). If that happens, the delete p; line sends the pointer to the wrong heap, which could result in a disaster at runtime.

Remember: use container classes rather than raw pointers. This example could use the standard string class or perhaps something like the standard vector template.

FAQ 12.14

How is an object constructed at a predetermined position in memory?

With the placement syntax of the new operator, also known as *placement new*.

Objects are normally created on the stack, on the heap, or in static memory. These correspond to automatic allocation, dynamic allocation, and static allocation, respectively. But these normal techniques don't allow the programmer to specify the exact address at which the object will live.

Occasionally an object's desired location is known before the object is created, such as when the hardware uses a piece of storage as a way of communicating with the software. In these cases, *placement new* can be used.

The following example places an object of class Fred at the hexadecimal address 0xFEEDBABE and passes (42, 42) to the Fred constructor.

```
#include "Fred.hpp"  ◄──────  Pretend this defines class Fred
#include <new>
using namespace std;

void sample()
{
  void* place = (void*) 0xFEEDBABE;
  Fred* p = new(place) Fred(42, 42);
  // ...
}
```

The storage pointed to by `place` must be large enough to hold `sizeof(Fred)` bytes and must be properly aligned to hold a `Fred object`. The returned pointer p is numerically the same as `place`, but p is a `Fred*` rather than a `void*`.

FAQ 12.15

How can class `Fred` guarantee that `Fred` objects are created only with `new` and not on the stack?

The class can make all of its constructors `private:` or `protected:` and can provide `static create()` member functions. The copy constructor should also be made `private:` or `protected:`, even if it doesn't need to be defined otherwise (see FAQ 30.06). The `static` (or `friend`) `create()` functions then create the object using `new` and return a pointer to the allocated object. Here's an example.

```
#include <new>
#include <memory>
using namespace std;

class Fred;  // Forward declaration
typedef  auto_ptr<Fred>  FredPtr;

class Fred {
public:
  static FredPtr create()              throw(bad_alloc);
  static FredPtr create(int i)         throw(bad_alloc);
  static FredPtr create(const Fred& x) throw(bad_alloc);
  virtual void goBowling();
private:
  Fred(int i=10)       throw();
  Fred(const Fred& x) throw();
  int i_;
};
```

```
FredPtr Fred::create()                  throw(bad_alloc)
                                        { return new Fred(); }
FredPtr Fred::create(int i)             throw(bad_alloc)
                                        { return new Fred(i); }
FredPtr Fred::create(const Fred& x) throw(bad_alloc)
                                        { return new Fred(x); }
Fred::Fred(int i)         throw() : i_(i)     { }
Fred::Fred(const Fred& x) throw() : i_(x.i_) { }

void sample()
{
  FredPtr p(Fred::create(5));
  p->goBowling();
}
```

Note that derived classes can't be instantiated since all of the constructors are private:. Derived classes could be instantiated only if some of the constructors were protected:.

_____ **FAQ 12.16**

How are objects created by placement new destroyed?

By explicitly calling the object's destructor. This is about the only time a destructor is called explicitly (see FAQ 20.10). For example, if p is a Fred* that was returned from placement new, *p can be destructed as follows.

```
#include <new>
using namespace std;

class Fred {
public:
  Fred(int i, int j) throw();
  virtual ~Fred() throw();
};

Fred* construct(void* place) throw()
{
  Fred* p = new(place) Fred(42, 42);
  return p;
}

void destruct(Fred* p) throw()
{
  p->~Fred();   ◄——— Do this only with placement new
}
```

```
void sample() throw()
{
  void* place = (void*) 0xFEEDBABE;
  Fred* p = construct(place);
  // ...
  destruct(p);
}
```

Caution: Do not explicitly call the destructor of an object that will later be automatically destroyed, such as an object on the stack, an object on the heap that will be deleted, or a static object. The only time a destructor should be called explicitly is when the programmer is in total control of the storage allocation and lifetime of the object—in other words, only with objects initialized by the placement new syntax.

FAQ 12.17

In p = new Fred(), does the Fred memory "leak" if the Fred constructor throws an exception?

new   No, the system straightens things out automatically.

If an exception occurs in the Fred constructor during p = new Fred(), the sizeof(Fred) bytes that were allocated are automatically released back to the heap. This is because new Fred() is a two-step process.

1. sizeof(Fred) bytes of memory are allocated using the memory allocation primitive void* operator new(size_t nbytes). This primitive is similar in spirit to malloc(size_t nbytes) (however operator new(size_t) and malloc(size_t) are not interchangeable; the two memory allocation primitives may not even use the same heap!). Recall that size_t is a typedef for some unsigned integral type such as unsigned int. Many system headers cause this typedef to be defined.

2. A Fred object is constructed in the returned memory location by calling the Fred constructor. Thus the pointer returned from the first step is passed as the constructor's this parameter. The call to the constructor is conceptually wrapped in a try block so that the memory can be released if the constructor throws an exception.

Thus the compiler generates code that looks something like that shown in following function sample().

```
#include <new>
using namespace std;

class Fred {
public:
  Fred() throw();
  virtual ~Fred() throw();
};

void sample() throw(bad_alloc)
{
  // Original code:  Fred* p = new Fred();
  Fred* p = (Fred*) operator new(sizeof(Fred));  ◄──── Step 1: Allocate memory
  try {
    new(p) Fred();  ◄─────── Step 2: Construct the object (see FAQ 12.14)
  }
  catch (...) {
    operator delete(p);  ◄──── Deallocate the memory
    throw;  ◄─────── Rethrow the exception the constructor threw
  }
}
```

The statement new(p) Fred(); is called the placement new syntax (see FAQ 12.14).
The effect is to call the Fred constructor, passing the pointer p as the constructor's
this parameter.

_____ **FAQ 12.18**

Is it legal (and moral) for a member function to say `delete this`?

Yes, but be careful.

Programmers usually have a hard time emotionally accepting that this is valid, probably because it seems as if the member function is inside the object and deleting the
object during a member function seems strange. But with care, this technique can be
perfectly safe. Here is how we define "with care."

1. The this object must have been allocated via new (see FAQ 12.15), not
   by new[] (see FAQ 12.11) nor by placement new (see FAQ 12.14) nor by
   a local object on the stack nor by a global nor by a member of another
   object. It has to have been allocated by plain, ordinary new.

2. The member function that contains delete this; must be the last
   member function that is invoked on the this object.

3. The remainder of the member function after the delete this; line must not touch any piece of the this object, including calling any other member functions or touching any data members.

4. No other piece of code should even examine the this pointer itself after the delete this; line. No one may examine it, compare it with another pointer, compare it with NULL, print it, cast it, do anything with it.

5. Make sure no one else does a delete on the object. For example, if the object is still being held by an auto_ptr (which would be a good thing!), the release() member function must be called on the auto_ptr; otherwise the auto_ptr will delete the object again, which would be a disaster. For example:

```
#include <iostream>
using namespace std;

class Fred {
public:
  Fred();
  virtual ~Fred();
  virtual void discard() throw();
};

void Fred::discard() throw()
{ delete this; }
```

FAQ 12.19

After p = new Fred[n], how does the compiler know that there are n objects to be destructed during delete[] p?

Warning: This FAQ is quite low level. The only people who really need to worry about this level of detail are those in extremely performance sensitive situations where CPU cycles are at a premium. Of course it also might be interesting to those who are just plain curious . . .

Whenever someone says Fred* p = new Fred[n], the runtime system is required to store the number of objects, n, in a place that can be retrieved knowing only the pointer, p. The compiler can use any technique it wants to use, but there are two popular ones.

1. The code generated by p = new Fred[n] might store the number n in a static associative array, where the pointer p is used as the lookup key and

the number n is the associated value. For example, using the standard map template (see FAQ 28.14), this associative array might be map<void*, size_t>. The code generated by delete[] p would look up the pointer in the associative array, would extract the associated size_t, then would remove the entry from the associative array.

2. The code generated by p = new Fred[n] might allocate an extra sizeof(size_t) bytes of memory (possibly plus some alignment bytes) and put the value n just before the first Fred object. Then delete[] p would find n by looking at the fixed offset before the first Fred object (that is, before *p) and would deallocate the memory starting at the beginning of the allocation (that is, the block of memory beginning the fixed offset before *p).

Neither technique is perfect. Here are a few of the tradeoffs.

1. The associative array technique is slower but safer: if someone forgets the [] when deallocating an array of things, (a) the entry in the associative array would be a leak, and (b) only the first object in the array would be destructed. This may or may not be a serious problem, but at least it *might* not crash the application.

2. The overallocation technique is faster but more dangerous: if someone says delete p where they should have said delete[] p, the address that is passed to operator delete(void* p) would not be a valid heap allocation—it would be at least sizeof(size_t) bytes *after* a valid heap allocation. This would probably corrupt the heap. Bang, you're dead.

Chapter 13

Inline Functions

What is the purpose of `inline` functions?

In some cases, `inline` functions make a compute-bound application run faster.

In a broad sense, the idea behind `inline` functions is to insert the code of a called function at the point where the function is called. If done carefully, this can improve the application's performance in exchange for increased compile time and possibly (but not always) an increase in the size of the generated binary executables. As usual, the devil is in the details. Read the fine print; it does make a difference.

It is useful to distinguish between "`inline`," a keyword qualifier that is simply a request to the compiler, and "inlined," which refers to actual inline expansion of the function. The expansion is more important than the request, because the costs and benefits are associated with the expansion.

Fortunately C++ programmers normally don't need to worry whether an `inline` function actually is inlined, since the C++ language guarantees that the semantics of a function cannot be changed by the compiler just because it is or isn't inlined. This is an important guarantee that changes the way compilers might optimize code otherwise.

C programmers may notice a similarity between `inline` functions and `#define` macros. But don't push that analogy too far, as they are different in some important ways. For example, since `inline` functions are part of the language, it is generally possible to step through them in a debugger, whereas macros are notoriously difficult to debug. Also, macro parameters that have side effects can cause surprises if the parameter appears more than once (or not at all) in the body of the macro, whereas `inline` functions don't have these problems. Finally, macros are always expanded, but `inline` functions aren't always inlined.

FAQ 13.02

What is the connection between the keyword "`inline`" and "inlined" functions?

new

Fans of *Alice's Adventures in Wonderland* will appreciate that a function decorated with the keyword `inline` may not be inlined, but an inlined function may not have been specified as `inline`, while the only sure way to be inlined is to not exist at all!

A function can be decorated with the `inline` keyword either in the class definition or in its own definition if the definition physically occurs before the function is invoked. The compiler does not promise that an `inline` function will be inlined, and the details of when/when not are compiler-dependent. For example, many compilers won't actually inline recursive and/or very long `inline` functions. So an `inline` function may not be inlined.

On the other hand, any function that is defined within the class body will be treated implicitly as an `inline` function with or without the explicit `inline` keyword. Again, there is no guarantee that it will be inlined, but the compiler will try anyway. So some functions are inlined without the `inline` keyword.

Finally, compiler-generated default constructors, copy constructors, destructors, and assignment operators are treated as `inline`, and often (but not always) they end up being inlined because they usually don't do anything tricky. These are the functions that are usually inlined, and they don't even explicitly appear in the code.

FAQ 13.03

Are there any special rules about inlining?

Yes. Here are a few rules about inlining.

1. Any source file that contains usage of an `inline` function must contain the function's definition.

2. An `inline` function must be identically defined everywhere. The easy way to do this is to define it once, preferably in the class header file, and

include the definition as needed. The hard way is to carefully redefine the function everywhere and learn the one-definition rule (see FAQ 13.04). But even the easy way has a potential glitch, so read FAQ 13.04 regardless.

3. `main()` cannot be `inline`.

But these are just language rules that tell *how* to do `inline` functions. To find out *when* to do `inline` functions, read the rest of this chapter.

FAQ 13.04

What is the one-definition rule (ODR)?

The ODR says that C++ constructs must be identically defined in every compilation unit in which they are used.

For example, if source file `foo.cpp` and source file `bar.cpp` are in the same program and class `Fred` appears in both source files, then class `Fred` has to be identically defined in the two source files. Similarly, the definition of an `inline` function must be the same in the two source files.

Here's what "identically defined" means. With respect to the ODR, two definitions contained in different source files are said to be identically defined if and only if they are token-for-token identical and the tokens have the same meaning in both source files. The last clause is important: it warns that merely including the same definition in two places isn't good enough to prevent ODR problems, because the tokens (such as `typedefs`) can have different meanings in the different locations. Note that "identically defined" does not mean character-by-character equivalence. For example, two definitions can have different whitespace or different comments yet still be "identical."

FAQ 13.05

What are some performance considerations with `inline` functions?

Here are some important facts about inlined functions.

1. They might improve performance, or they might make it worse (see FAQ 13.06).

2. They might cause the size of the executable to increase, or they might make it smaller (see FAQ 13.07).

3. When they are nontrivial, they probably will complicate the development effort if employed too early in the development cycle. Provisions to use them can be made early but the final decision should be made later (see FAQ 13.08).

4. When they are provided to third-party programmers, they can make it difficult to maintain binary compatibility between releases of the software (see FAQ 13.09).

The only dangerous idea about inlining is the attitude that says, "Fast is good, slow is bad; inlining is faster, so everything should be inlined." If only life were that simple.

FAQ 13.06

Do inlined functions improve performance?

Inlined functions sometimes improve overall performance, but there are other cases where they make it worse.

It is reasonable to define functions as `inline` when they are on the critical path of a CPU-bound application. For example, if a program is network bound (spending most of the time waiting for the network) or I/O bound (spending most of the time waiting for the disk), inlining might not make a significant impact in the application's performance since processor performance might not be relevant. Even in cases when the program is CPU bound, there is no point in worrying about optimizing a function unless it is on a critical execution path, that is, unless it is taking up a major portion of the time consumed by the program.

In cases where processor optimization is relevant, `inline` functions can speed up processing in three ways:

1. Eliminating the overhead associated with the function call instruction

2. Eliminating the overhead associated with pushing and popping parameters

3. Allowing the compiler to optimize the code outside the function call more efficiently

The first point is worth pursuing only in very exceptional circumstances because the overhead of the call instruction itself is normally quite small. However, the call instruction can have some expensive side effects that can be eliminated when the call is inlined. For example, if the called routine is not inlined, accessing the called routine's executable code can cause a *page fault* (a page fault happens in virtual memory operating systems when some chunk of the application is temporarily stored on disk rather than in memory). In extreme cases, this can cause a situation called *thrashing,* a situation in which most of the time is spent handling page faults. Even when a page fault does not occur (that is, when the executable code of the called routine is already in memory), the code of the called routine might not be in the processor's cache, a situation called a *cache miss.* Cache misses can be expensive on certain CPU-bound applications.

The second point can be important, because value semantics can have considerable overhead. A function with many formal parameters, whether they use value semantics or not, can do quite a bit of stack pushing and popping. Even if the parameter is a simple built-in type such as `int` or `char`, there is some nontrivial overhead. For example, parameters of built-in types are often located in one of the processor's registers, so the caller has to move the parameter out of the register onto the stack, and the called routine often pulls it back off the stack into a register, and when the call is finished, the caller pulls it back off the stack into its original register. All that can normally be eliminated if the call is inlined.

The third point, also known as *procedural integration,* is typically the major source of improvement. By letting the compiler see more code at once (by integrating the called procedure into the calling code), optimizer can often do a better job: it can often generate more efficient code.

But performance can be lost as well as gained. Sometimes inlined functions lead to larger binary files that cause thrashing on virtual memory operating systems (see FAQ 13.07). But there are other times where the paging performance is actually improved, because inlining can provide locality of reference and a smaller working set as well as, paradoxically, smaller executables.

FAQ 13.07

Do inlined functions increase the size of the executable code?

Sometimes yes, sometimes no.

When large functions are inlined, the executable generally grows larger. However when small functions are inlined, the executable can actually become smaller, since the amount of executable code needed to call a function, including pushing all the registers and parameters, can be larger than the amount of code that would have been generated had the call been inlined.

Consider the following example. With optimization turned on, the size of the generated code was 33% smaller when the member functions were inlined compared to when they were not inlined.

```
class Stack {
public:
  Stack()                 throw();
  void push(int elem) throw();
  int  pop()              throw();
  int  top()    const  throw();
  bool full()   const  throw();
  bool empty()  const  throw();
protected:
  enum      { dataMax_ = 10 };
  unsigned  len_;
  int       data_[dataMax_];
};

inline      Stack::Stack()             throw() : len_(0) { }
inline void Stack::push(int elem) throw()
                                       { data_[len_++] = elem;      }
inline int  Stack::pop()               throw()
                                       { return data_[--len_];      }
inline int  Stack::top()     const  throw()
                                       { return data_[len_-1];      }
inline bool Stack::full()    const  throw()
                                       { return len_ == dataMax_; }
inline bool Stack::empty()   const  throw()
                                       { return len_ == 0;          }

int main()
{
  Stack s;
  s.push(0); s.push(1); s.push(2); s.push(3); s.push(4);
  s.push(5); s.push(6); s.push(7); s.push(8); s.push(9);
  s.pop();   s.pop();   s.pop();   s.pop();   s.pop();
  s.pop();   s.pop();   s.pop();   s.pop();   s.pop();
}
```

FAQ 13.08

Why shouldn't the inlining decision be made when the code is first written?

Except for trivial access member functions, the information for making intelligent inlining decisions usually comes from profiling actual code, not from the developer's intuition.

Intuition is a crummy guide when it comes to performance. There are so many issues to consider that vary with the compiler, operating system, hardware, and system configuration that very few programmers can anticipate exactly where the bottlenecks will occur. Chapter 33, "High-Performance Software," discusses this in more detail.

But even if the bottlenecks are known ahead of time, using `inline` on nontrivial functions early in the development cycle can add significant frustrations to the edit-compile-debug cycle. Since `inline` functions normally are defined in header files, when an `inline` function is changed the compiler will normally recompile every source file (for example, every .cpp file) that includes that function. This often means recompiling the world, which can take a long, long time on a medium or large project.

FAQ 13.09

What happens when a programmer uses an inlined function obtained from a third party?

It makes it harder for that third party to maintain binary compatibility between releases of the third party's software.

The code of an inlined function is copied into the user's executables. So subsequent changes to the inlined function require recompilation of the user's code, which can be painful or even politically impossible if there is a vendor-customer relationship.

For example, vendors who want to provide their customers with binary-compatible releases of a library must avoid changing any `inline` functions that are accessible to their customers. Typically this is done by considering the implementation of any `inline` functions that have been shipped to customers to be "frozen"—frozen code can never, ever change. Recall that the compiler-synthesized construction, assignment, and destruction routines are implicitly `inline` (see FAQ 13.02), so achieving binary compatibility requires these routines to be explicitly defined as non-`inline`. For example, if the compiler defines them as `inline`, and if the class layout ever changes, they will change from release to release. This includes relatively innocuous changes to the class layout, such as adding or removing a `private:` data member.

Another, more subtle, problem is the potential breakdown of information hiding. For example, users of an `inline` function must have a copy of the source code, and that copy gets bound into their program. Think about that for a second. Maybe they haven't read this book, and maybe they don't understand the importance of respecting interfaces. Maybe they rely on the implementation rather than the specification; giving them the code opens up that opportunity. If so, the implementation techniques are turned into concrete. This makes life harder.

FAQ 13.10

Is there an easy way to swap between `inline` and non-`inline` code?

new   Yes, with a little macro magic.

Most projects should turn off inlining during development. That is, they use a compiler option that causes the compiler to not inline any `inline` functions. This can make the code easier to debug, but it still doesn't help the edit-compile-debug problem mentioned in FAQ 13.08. For example, turning off inline expansion via a compiler option does not improve compile-time performance—the compiler still has to parse the body of every `inline` function in a header every time a source file is compiled that includes the header. Furthermore, depending on the compiler, turning off inline expansion may increase code bulk—the compiler may create duplicate `static` copies of each `inline` function seen by the compiler during every compilation unit. Finally, and probably most important, turning off inline expansion doesn't help the "recompile the world" problem (see FAQ 13.08) since the `inline` functions are still in the `include` files.

Although macros are evil, this is one of the areas where they can be used to bypass the compile-time overhead mentioned in FAQ 13.08. The strategy is straightforward. First, define all `inline` functions outside the class body in a separate file (call this the `.inl` file or `.ipp` file). Then, in the `.inl` file, change the keyword `inline` to the preprocessor symbol `INLINE`. Finally, conditionally `#include` the `.inl` file from either the bottom of the `.hpp` file or from the `.cpp` file, depending on whether or not `INLINE` should become `inline` or nothing.

In the following example, `inline.hpp` defines a macro `INLINE` to be either the keyword `inline` or nothing, depending on whether the `USE_INLINE` symbol is `#defined`. For example, if the compiler supports the `-D` option as a way to `#define` a symbol, compiling with `-DUSE_INLINE` causes `INLINE` to become `inline`. Here is file `inline.hpp`.

```
#ifndef INLINE_HPP
#define INLINE_HPP

#ifdef USE_INLINE
  #define INLINE   inline
#else
  #define INLINE   /*nothing*/
#endif

#endif
```

File Fred.hpp defines class Fred with two member functions, f() and g(). If the symbol USE_INLINE is #defined, file Fred.inl is #included from Fred.hpp. Here is file Fred.hpp.

```
#ifndef FRED_HPP
#define FRED_HPP

#include "inline.hpp"

class Fred {
public:
  void f() throw();   ◄───────────── No code in the class body
  void g() throw();
};

#ifdef USE_INLINE   ◄───────────── #ifdef means "if defined"
  #include "Fred.inl"
#endif

#endif
```

File Fred.inl defines Fred::f() preceded with the symbol INLINE. Note that Fred.inl does not #include "Fred.hpp". Here is file Fred.inl.

```
#include <iostream>
using namespace std;

INLINE void Fred::f() throw()  ◄─── Uses INLINE, not inline
{ cout << "Fred::f() is optionally inlined\n"; }
```

File Fred.cpp defines Fred::g() as non-inline. If the symbol USE_INLINE is *not* #defined, file Fred.inl is #included from Fred.cpp. Here is file Fred.cpp.

```
#include "Fred.hpp"
using namespace std;

#ifndef USE_INLINE  ◄───────────── #ifndef means "if not defined"
  #include "Fred.inl"
#endif

void Fred::g() throw()
{ cout << "Fred::g() is never inlined\n"; }
```

It is important to note that users of Fred don't have to be aware of the .inl file. For example, if file UserCode.cpp uses a Fred object, it won't need to change due to the INLINE magic. Here is a sample file that uses a Fred object, file UserCode.cpp.

```
#include "Fred.hpp"

int main()
{
  Fred x;
  x.f();
  x.g();
}
```

This strategy can be easily modified to allow class-specific inlining. Simply replace the line #include "inline.hpp" with the contents of that file, then change USE_INLINE to USE_INLINE_Fred and INLINE to INLINE_Fred throughout.

Chapter 14

Const Correctness

How should pointer declarations be read?

Pointer declarations should be read right to left.

If `Fred` is some type, then

- `Fred*` is a pointer to a `Fred` (the `*` is pronounced "pointer to a").
- `const Fred*` is a pointer to a `Fred` that cannot be changed via that pointer.
- `Fred* const` is a `const` pointer to a `Fred`. The `Fred` object can be changed via the pointer, but the pointer itself cannot be changed.
- `const Fred* const` is a `const` pointer to a `Fred` that cannot be changed via that pointer.

References are similar: read them right to left.

- `Fred&` is a reference to a `Fred` (the `&` is pronounced "reference to a").
- `const Fred&` is a reference to a `Fred` that cannot be changed via that reference.

Note that `Fred& const` and `const Fred& const` are not included in the second list. This is because references are inherently immutable: you can never rebind the reference so that it refers to a different object.

FAQ 14.02

How can C++ programmers avoid making unexpected changes to objects?

With proper use of the keyword `const`, the C++ compiler detects many unexpected changes to objects and flags these violations with error messages at compile time. This is often called *const correctness*. For example, function `f()` uses the `const` keyword to restrict itself so that it won't be able to change the caller's `string` object:

```
#include <string>
using namespace std;
void f(const string& s) throw();   // Parameter is received
                                   // by reference-to-const
```

If `f()` changes its passed `string` anyway, the compiler flags it as an error at compile time:

```
void f(const string& s) throw()
{
  #ifdef GENERATE_ERROR
    s += "foo";  ◄──────────────── Error: The string cannot be mutated via s
  #endif
}
```

In contrast, function `g()` declares its intent to *change* the caller's `string` object by its lack of the `const` keyword in the appropriate place:

```
void g(string& s) throw();   // Parameter is received by
                             // reference-to-non-const
```

For example, it is legal and appropriate for `g()` to modify the caller's `string` object:

```
void g(string& s) throw()
{
  s += "foo";  // OK: Modifies the caller's string object
}
```

Also it would be legal and appropriate for `g()` to pass its parameter to `f()`, since the called function, `f()`, is at least as restrictive as the caller, `g()` (in this case, the called function is actually *more* restrictive):

```
void g(string& s) throw()
{
  f(s);          // OK (though it doesn't happen to modify
                 // caller's string object)
```

```
    s += "foo";  // OK: Modifies the caller's string object
}
```

However, it would be illegal for the opposite to occur. That is, if f() passed its parameter to g(), the compiler would give an error message since the called function, g(), is less restrictive than the caller, f():

```
void f(const string& s) throw()
{
  #ifdef GENERATE_ERROR
    g(s); ←——————————————— Error: The const string& cannot be passed as a string&
  #endif
}
```

FAQ 14.03

Does `const` imply runtime overhead?

No, there is no runtime overhead. All tests for `const`ness are done at compile time. Neither runtime space nor speed is degraded.

FAQ 14.04

Does `const` allow the compiler to generate more efficient code?

Occasionally, but that's not the purpose of `const`. The purpose of `const` is correctness, not optimization. That is, `const` helps the compiler find bugs, but it does not (normally) help the compiler generate more efficient code.

Declaring the `const`ness of a parameter or variable is just another form of type safety; therefore, `const` correctness can be considered an extension of C++'s type system. Type safety provides some degree of semantic integrity by promising that, for instance, something declared as a `string` cannot be used as an `int`. However, `const` correctness guarantees even tighter semantic correctness by making sure that data that is not intended to be changed cannot be changed. With `const` correctness, it is easier to reason about the correctness of the software. This is helpful during software inspection.

It is almost as if `const string` and `string` are of different, but related, classes. Because type safety helps produce correct software (especially in large systems and applications), `const` correctness is a worthy goal.

FAQ 14.05

Is `const` correctness tedious?

It is no more tedious than declaring the type of a variable.

In C++, `const` correctness is simply another form of type information. In theory, expressing any type information is unnecessary, given enough programmer discipline and testing. In practice, developers often leave a lot of interesting information about their code in their heads where it cannot be exploited or verified by the compiler. For instance, when programmers write a function such as the following `print()` function, they know implicitly that they are passing by reference merely to avoid the overhead of passing by value; there is no intention of changing the `string` during the `print()` operation.

```
#include <string>
using namespace std;

void print(string& s);   // Does not change s ◄─── Wrong way to docu-
                                                     ment the restriction
```

If this information is documented only by comments in the code or in a separate manual, it is easy for these comments to become inconsistent with the code; the compiler can't read comments or manuals. The most cost-effective way to document this information is with the five-letter word `const`:

```
void print(const string& s); ◄─── Right way to document the restriction
```

This form of documentation is succinct, in one place, and can be verified and exploited by the compiler.

FAQ 14.06

Why should `const` correctness be done sooner rather than later?

Adding constraints later can be difficult and expensive. If a function was not originally restricted with respect to changing a by-reference parameter, adding the restriction (that is, changing a parameter from `string&` to `const string&`) can cause a ripple through the system. For instance, suppose `f()` calls `g()`, and `g()` calls `h()`:

```
#include <string>
#include <iostream>
using namespace std;

void f(string& s) throw();
void g(string& s) throw();
void h(string& s) throw();

int main()
{
  string s;
  f(s);
}

void f(string& s) throw()
{ g(s); }

void g(string& s) throw()
{ h(s); }

void h(string& s) throw()
{ cout << s << '\n'; }
```

Changing f(string& s) to f(const string& s) causes error messages until g(string&) is changed to g(const string&). But this change causes error messages until h(string&) is changed to h(const string&), and so on. The ripple effect is magnificent—and expensive.

The moral is that const correctness should be installed from the very beginning.

FAQ 14.07

What's the difference between an inspector and a mutator?

An inspector is a member function that returns information about an object's state without changing the object's abstract state (that is, calling an inspector does not cause an observable change in the behavior of any of the object's member functions). A mutator changes the state of an object in a way that is observable to outsiders: it changes the object's abstract state. Here is an example.

```
class Stack {
public:
  int pop();              //Mutator
  int numElems() const;   //Inspector
};
```

The pop () member function is a mutator because it changes the Stack by removing the top element. The numElems () member function is an inspector because it simply counts the number of elements in the Stack without making any observable changes to the Stack. The const decoration after numElems () indicates that numElems () promises not to change the Stack object.

Only inspectors may be called on a reference-to-const or pointer-to-const:

```
void sample(const Stack& s) throw()
{
  s.numElems();   // OK: A const Stack can be inspected

  #ifdef GENERATE_ERROR
    s.pop();       // Error: A const Stack cannot be mutated
  #endif
}
```

FAQ 14.08

When should a member function be declared as const?

 There are two ways to look at it. When looking at the member function from the inside out, the answer is "whenever the member function wants to guarantee that it won't make any observable changes to its this object." When looking at the member function from the outside in, the answer is "whenever a caller needs to invoke the member function via a reference-to-const or pointer-to-const." Hopefully these two approaches end up agreeing with each other. If not, then the application may have a serious design flaw, or perhaps it needs to be *const overloaded* (that is, two member functions with the same name and the same parameters, but one is a const member function and the other is not).

The compiler won't allow a const member function to change *this or to invoke a non-const member function for this object:

```
#include <stdexcept>
using namespace std;

class Stack {
public:
  Stack() throw();
  void push(int elem) throw(runtime_error);
  // Throws exception if numElems() is 10
  int  pop()          throw(runtime_error);
  // Throws exception if numElems() is 0
```

```
    int  numElems() const throw();
protected:
  int numElems_;
  int data_[10];
};

int Stack::numElems() const throw()
{
  #ifdef GENERATE_ERROR
    ++numElems_;     //ERROR: Can't modify *this
    pop();           //ERROR: pop() isn't a const member function
  #endif
  return numElems_;
}
```

Although not fleshed out in this example, member functions push() and pop() may throw exceptions in certain circumstances. In this case they throw runtime_error, which is the standard exception class that is thrown for errors that are detectable only at runtime.

Does const apply to the object's bitwise state or its abstract state?

The const keyword should refer to the object's abstract state.

The const modifier is a part of the class's public: interface; therefore, it means what the designer of the public: interface wants it to mean. As an interface designer, the most useful strategy is to tie const to the object's abstract state rather than to its bitwise state. For example, in some circumstances a member function changes its object's bitwise state, yet the change doesn't cause any observable change to any of the object's public: member functions (that is, the abstract state is not changed). In this case, the member function should still be const since it never changes the *meaning* of the object (see FAQ 14.12). It is even more common for a member function to change an object's abstract state even though it doesn't change the object's bitwise state.

For example, the following MyString class stores its string data on the heap, pointed to by the member datum data_. (The name bad_alloc is the standard exception class that is thrown when memory is exhausted, and the name out_of_range is the standard exception class that is thrown when a parameter is out of range.)

```
#include <new>
#include <stdexcept>
#include <iostream>
using namespace std;

class MyString {
public:
  MyString(const char* s) throw(bad_alloc);
 ~MyString() throw();
  MyString(const MyString& s) throw(bad_alloc);
  MyString& operator= (const MyString& s) throw(bad_alloc);
  unsigned size() const throw();
  char& operator[] (unsigned index)         throw(out_of_range);
  char  operator[] (unsigned index) const throw(out_of_range);
  void toUpper() throw();  //capitalizes the string
protected:
  unsigned len_;
  char* data_;
};

int main()
{
  MyString s = "xyz";
  for (unsigned i = 0; i < s.size(); ++i)
    cout << "Character #" << i << " is " << s[i] << '\n';
  s.toUpper();
}
```

The abstract state of the MyString object s is represented by values returned by s[i], where i ranges from 0 to s.size()-1, inclusive. The bitwise state of a MyString is represented by the bits of s itself (that is, by s.len_ and the pointer s.data_).

Even though s.toUpper() doesn't change s.len_ or the pointer s.data_, MyString::toUpper() is a non-const member function because it changes the abstract state (the state from the user's perspective). In other words, toUpper() doesn't change the bitwise state of the object, but it does change the meaning of the object; therefore it is a non-const member function.

FAQ 14.10

When should const not be used in declaring formal parameters?

Do not use const for formal parameter types that are passed by value, because a const on a pass-by-value parameter affects (constrains) only the code inside the function; it does not affect the caller. For example, replace f(const Fred x) with either f(const Fred& x) or f(Fred x).

As a special case of this rule, it is inappropriate to use Fred* const in a formal parameter list. For example, replace f(Fred* const p) with f(Fred* p), and replace g(const Fred* const p) with g(const Fred* p).

Finally, do not use Fred& const in any context. The construct is nonsensical because a reference can never be rebound to a different object. (See FAQ 14.01.)

FAQ 14.11

When should `const` not be used in declaring a function return type?

A function that returns its result by value should generally avoid const in the return type. For example, replace const Fred f() with either Fred f() or const Fred& f(). Using const Fred f() can be confusing to users, especially in the idiomatic case of copying the return result into a local.

The exception to this rule is when users apply a const-overloaded member function directly to the temporary returned from the function. An example follows.

```
#include <iostream>
using namespace std;

class Fred {
public:
  void wilma()       throw() { cout << "Fred::wilma()\n"; }
  void wilma() const throw() { cout << "Fred::wilma() const\n"; }
};

      Fred f() throw() { cout << "f(): "; return Fred(); }
const Fred g() throw() { cout << "g(): "; return Fred(); }

int main()
{
  f().wilma();  ◄──── Calls the non-const version of the wilma() member function
  g().wilma();  ◄──── Calls the const version of the wilma() member function
}
```

Because f() returns a non-const Fred, f().wilma() invokes the non-const version of Fred::wilma(). In contrast, g() returns a const Fred, so `g().wilma()` invokes the `const` version of `Fred::wilma()`. Thus, the output of this program is as follows.

```
f(): Fred::wilma()
g(): Fred::wilma() const
```

How can a "nonobservable" data member be updated within a `const` member function?

Preferably the data member should be declared with the `mutable` keyword. If that cannot be done, `const_cast` can be used.

A small percentage of inspectors need to make nonobservable changes to data members. For example, an object whose storage is physically located in a database might want to cache its last lookup in hopes of improving the performance of its next lookup. In this case there are two critical issues: (1) if someone changes the database, the cached value must somehow be either changed or marked as invalid (*cache coherency*); (2) the `const` lookup member function needs to make a change to the cached value. In cases like this, changes to the cache are not observable to users of the object (the object does not change its abstract state; see FAQ 14.09).

The easiest way to implement a nonobservable change is to declare the cache using the `mutable` keyword. The `mutable` keyword tells the compiler that `const` member functions are allowed to change the data member.

```
int readFromDatabase() throw()
{ return 42; }  ◀───────  Pretend this reads from the database

class Fred {
public:
  int get() const throw();
private:
  mutable int cache_;
  mutable bool cacheOk_;
};

int Fred::get() const throw()
{
  if (! cacheOk_) {
    cache_ = readFromDatabase();
    cacheOk_ = true;
```

```
   }
   return cache_;
}

int main()
{
   Fred f;
   int x = f.get();       ◄──── Access the database the first time it's called
   int y = f.get();       ◄──── Uses the cache; no database calls
   int z = f.get();       ◄──── Uses the cache; no database calls
}
```

The second alternative is to cast away the constness of the this pointer using the const_cast keyword. In the following example, self is equal to this (that is, they point to the same object), but self is a Fred* rather than a const Fred* so self can be used to modify the this object.

```
class Fred2 {
public:
   int get() const throw();
private:
   int cache_;
   bool cacheOk_;
};

int Fred2::get() const throw()
{
   if (! cacheOk_) {
      Fred2* self = const_cast<Fred2*>(this);
      self->cache_ = readFromDatabase();
      self->cacheOk_ = true;
   }
   return cache_;
}
```

─── **FAQ 14.13**

Can an object legally be changed even though there is a const reference (pointer) to it?

Yes, due to aliasing.

The const part restricts the reference (pointer); it does not restrict the object. Many programmers erroneously think that the object on the other end of a const reference (pointer) cannot change. For example, if const int& i refers to the same int as int& j, j can change the int even though i cannot. This is called aliasing, and it can confuse programmers who are unaware of it.

```cpp
#include <iostream>
using namespace std;

void sample(const int& i, int& j) throw()
{
  int orig = i;
  j++;  ◄─── Incrementing j can change the int called i
  if (i != orig)
    cout << "The value of i is different!\n";
}

int main()
{
  int x = 3;
  sample(x, x);
}
```

There is no rule in C++ that prohibits this sort of thing. In fact, it is considered a feature of the language that programmers can have several pointers or references refer to the same object (plus it could not be figured out in some cases, e.g., if there are intermediate functions between main() and sample(const int&,int&) and if these functions are defined in different source files and are compiled on different days of the week). The fact that one of those references or pointers is restricted from changing the underlying object is a restriction on the reference (or pointer), not on the object.

FAQ 14.14

Does const_cast mean lost optimization opportunities?

No, the compiler doesn't lose optimization opportunities because of const_cast.

Some programmers are afraid to use const_cast because they're concerned that it will take away the compiler's ability to optimize the code. For example, if the compiler cached data members of an object in registers, then called a const member function, in theory it would need to reload only those registers that represent mutable data members. However in practice this kind of optimization cannot occur, with or without `const_cast`.

The reason the optimization cannot occur is that it would require the compiler to prove that there are no non-`const` references or pointers that point to the object (the aliasing problem; see FAQ 14.13), and in many cases this cannot be proved.

Chapter 15

Namespaces

What is the purpose of this chapter?

This chapter covers the basic material on namespaces.

new

The purpose of namespaces is to reduce the number of name clashes that occur with multiple, independently developed libraries. In the early days of C++, this was not as big a problem because there weren't as many C++ libraries as there are today. This situation changed about the time that the standard template library was formalized, and today the large number of class libraries and frameworks on the market accentuates the need for a mechanism to resolve name conflicts.

The original goal for namespaces was to have an elegant solution that could be explained to the typical developer in ten minutes and that could be implemented by a compiler-writer in two weeks. The problem was a bit more difficult than anticipated, and, like almost every other feature in C++, it has some dark corners that most people should avoid. But the basic ideas of namespaces are technically sound and within the grasp of any professional developer.

FAQ 15.02

What is a namespace?

new A namespace is a declarative region that can be used to package names, improve program readability, and reduce name clashes in the global namespace. It is an elegant alternative to using prefixes to indicate the sources of names.

At the most basic level, the syntax for namespaces is shown in the following example.

```
namespace MySubsystem {
  class Fred {  ◄───── Class MySubsystem::Fred
    // ...
  };

  class Wilma {  ◄───── Class MySubsystem::Wilma
    // ...
  };

  void funct()  ◄───── Function MySubsystem::funct()
  {
    // ...
  }

  // Other declarations for MySubsystem go in here
}
```

Namespaces facilitate building large systems by partitioning names into logical groupings.

Namespaces are "open" and can be added to at different places. For most situations, this incremental approach is probably a better alternative than trying to specify all of the names in one location, and this approach is used heavily in the standard library. However the incremental approach must be used carefully, because the effect is as if the compiler made a single pass and knew about only the names that were part of the namespace the last time the namespace was explicitly introduced into the source file.

Namespaces can be nested if desired. Java has a concept similar to namespaces called *packages*.

UML expresses namespaces as shown below (they are called *packages* in UML):

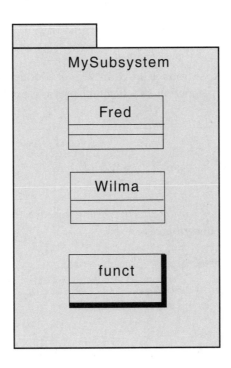

How can code outside a namespace use names declared within that namespace?

One way to use a declaration from a namespace is, for every occurrence, to use the scope operator : : to prefix the name declared in the namespace with the name of the namespace. For example,

```
namespace People {
   int fred = 2;
   int wilma = 3;
}

void f() throw()
{
```

```
    int i = People::fred + People::wilma;
  }
```

Another approach is to to introduce the equivalent of a local name with what is known as a *using declaration*. The function f() from the previous example could be written as

```
  void f2() throw()
  {
    using People::fred;      // Use People's fred
    int i = fred + People::wilma;
  }
```

Another approach is called a *using directive*. Using this idea, the function f() from the previous example could be written as

```
  void f3() throw()
  {
    using namespace People;   // Declare all names from People
    int i = fred + wilma;
  }
```

Note that a using directive does not declare any variables; it merely makes names available.

Finally, notice that the global namespace can be thought of as the namespace without an identifier (i.e., ::fred refers to fred in the global namespace).

FAQ 15.04

What happens if two namespaces contain the same name?

Suppose two different namespaces have their own versions of class string. Both namespaces can be introduced into the same code fragment without conflict, as long as there are no unqualified references to string. However, if there are unqualified references to string, the compiler issues an error because the unqualified name string is ambiguous. This is illustrated in the following example.

```
  namespace A {
    int x = 1;
    int z = 2;
  }

  namespace B {
    int y = 3;
```

```
    int z = 4;
}

void doSomethingWith(int i) throw();

void sample() throw()
{
    using namespace A;   ←──────── OK: Introduces A::x and A::z
    using namespace B;   ←──────── OK: Introduces B::y and B::z

    doSomethingWith( x );  ←──────── OK: Unqualified x unambiguously resolves to A::x
    doSomethingWith( y );  ←──────── OK: Unqualified y unambiguously resolves to B::y

    doSomethingWith( A::z );  ←──── OK: The A:: qualifications makes this unambiguous
    doSomethingWith( B::z );  ←──── OK: The B:: qualifications makes this unambiguous

    #ifdef GENERATE_ERROR
      doSomethingWith( z );  ←──── Error: Ambiguous: A::z or B::z?
    #endif
}

main()
{ sample(); }
```

FAQ 15.05

What are some of the rules for using namespaces?

The following example due to Stroustrup (*C++ Programming Language*, Third Edition, 1997) illustrates some of the basic ideas.

```
namespace X {
    int i, j, k;
}

int k;

void f1() throw()
{
    int i = 0;
    using namespace X;   // make names from X accessible
    i++;                 // local i
    j++;                 // X::j
    k++;                 // error: X::k or global k?
    ::k++;               // the global k
    X::k++;              // X's k
}
```

```
void f2() throw()
{
  int i = 0;
  using X::i;           // Error: i declared twice in f2()
  using X::j;
  using X::k;           // Hides global k
  i++;
  j++;                  // X::j
  k++;                  // X::k
}
```

FAQ 15.06

What is name lookup?

Name lookup, sometimes known as Koenig lookup, is a clever solution to a difficult problem. Consider the problem of printing a `string` in the following example.

```
#include <iostream>
#include <string>

void sample() throw()
{
  std::string s = "hello world";
  std::cout << s;  ←——————————— How does the compiler find the proper <<?
}
```

The `operator<<` that's needed is a non-member function that takes a `string` as a parameter and is packaged with the `string` class. How is the compiler supposed to find the proper operator? One approach is to make all the names in the entire standard namespace accessible without qualification (e.g., `using namespace std;`), but this is an ugly solution that is discussed in FAQ 15.09. An equally ugly alternative is to change `sample()` to the following:

```
void sample2() throw()
{
  std::string s = "hello world";
  std::operator<< (std::cout, s);  ←——Ugly
}
```

Koenig lookup is a better alternative. It recognizes that non-member functions associated with a parameter class such as `string` can be thought of as part of an extended `public:` interface, and there is no harm in having the compiler automatically look for such functions in the same namespace as the parameter class. This is the technique known as name lookup, and it allows the example above to work "as is." The trick is that a class parameter, in this case `string`, somehow identifies a namespace, in this case `std`, and then all the non-member functions that refer to that parameter class are automatically made available. It's a pretty slick idea that usually simplifies life.

FAQ 15.07

What are the tradeoffs between the various techniques for using names from a namespace, particularly the standard namespace?

Relying solely on the scope operator leads to programs that are hard to read, particularly for frequently used classes such as `string`. Clutter is not desirable in programs that have to be maintained.

The *using declaration* is probably the best solution for most cases, because the developer specifically declares what is intended. But this can be tedious, particularly when pulling names from the standard library.

The *using directive* is less desirable than the using declaration because it pollutes the global namespace unnecessarily and opens the door for later code breakage. This is because compiler writers and class library providers can add names to the standard namespace, which means that programs that utilize `using namespace std;` can suddenly fail to compile even though the user has not changed anything.

Despite this, we utilize `using namespace std;` throughout this book to allow our examples to compile and to allow the reader who has not read this chapter yet to muddle through, but this practice has little to recommend it.

FAQ 15.08

Can namespaces break code?

Namespaces can cause code to suddenly not compile without changes by the programmer. The easiest way this can occur is discussed in FAQ 15.09, but that situation involves the conscious use of using directives, so there shouldn't have been any surprises at the consequences. Here's an example that's a little more insidious.

Start with a header that declares a namespace `MySubsystem` and a class `Fred` in that namespace. For example, the following might be in file `MySubsystem.hpp`:

```
#ifndef MY_SUBSYSTEM_HPP
#define MY_SUBSYSTEM_HPP

namespace MySubsystem {
  class Fred { };
}

#endif
```

Now suppose some user code creates a normal function f() that takes a parameter of type MySubsystem::Fred:

```
#include "MySubsystem.hpp"

void f(MySubsystem::Fred& x) throw();

int main()
{
  MySubsystem::Fred x;
  f(x);  // Uses the global f() that takes
         // MySubsystem::Fred& as a parameter
}
```

Now suppose a revision of MySubsystem.hpp adds a function f(Fred& x) to namespace MySubsystem:

```
#ifndef MY_SUBSYSTEM_HPP
#define MY_SUBSYSTEM_HPP

// This is a revision of the original header
namespace MySubsystem {
  class Fred { };
  void f(Fred& x) throw();
}

#endif
```

Suddenly, there is ambiguity as to which f(x) is needed, and the code will not compile.

There are even more exotic examples, but the main point is that there are several ways ambiguity can creep in, and the programmer has to resolve the conflicts manually. This is not a severe problem because the compiler flags it and it is relatively easy to fix.

FAQ 15.09

Do namespaces have any other applications?

Namespaces have cleaned up some old problems in two other ways. First, unnamed namespaces are preferable to the use of static global members and reduce the number of meanings that can be placed on the word "static." Second, using declarations are now the preferred alternative to access declarations that were used to work around some knotty problems with private inheritance.

FAQ 15.10

How do namespaces solve the problem of long identifiers?

There is a simple macro-like solution for the long namespace name problem—

```
namespace CWLN = CompanyWithLongName;
```

—which allows the use of either the short or the long form of the name. This solution is known as *namespace aliases*.

Chapter 16

Using Static

What is the purpose of this chapter?

This chapter explores the issues related to the situation that occurs when a class contains static data members and/or static member functions.

What are static class members?

Static class members are data and functions that are associated with the class itself, rather than with the objects of the class.

In the following example, class Fred has a *static data member* x_ and an *instance data member* y_. There is only one copy of Fred::x_ regardless of how many Fred objects are created (including *no* Fred objects), but there is one y_ per Fred object. Thus x_ is said to be associated with the class and y_ is said to be associated with an individual object of the class. Similarly class Fred has a static member function f() and an instance member function g().

```
class Fred {
public:
   static void f() throw();      ◄──── Member function associated with the class
          void g() throw();      ◄──────────── Member function associated with an individual object of the class
```

```
protected:
   static int x_;  ←——————— Data member associated with the class
   int y_;  ←——————— Data member associated with an individual object of the class
};
```

Everything except instance data members must be defined somewhere, such as in the Fred.cpp source file:

```
#include "Fred.hpp"

void Fred::f() throw()  ←——— The static keyword is not used at the function's definition
{ /*...*/ }

void Fred::g() throw()
{ /*...*/ }

int Fred::x_ = 3;  ←——————— Static data members must be explicitly defined in
                             exactly one source file
```

Static data members are often referred to as *class data,* and static member functions are often referred to as *class services* or *class methods.*

FAQ 16.03

What is an analogy for static data members?

Static data members are like data located in the factory rather than in the objects produced by the factory.

In Detroit, there's a big sign with a running total of the number of cars produced during the current year. But that information isn't under the hood of any given car; all the car knows is a serial number indicating its ordinal number. The total number of cars produced is therefore factory data.

In the following example, class Car is the factory that is used to produce Car objects. Every car has a serial number (serial_). The factory keeps count of the number of cars that have been built via num_, which is a class (or static) datum; serial_ is an object (or instance) datum. The constructors of class Car are responsible for incrementing the number of cars that have been built; for simplicity this number is used as the serial number.

```
#include <iostream>
using namespace std;
```

```
class Car {
public:

  Car() throw();  ←─────────────────── Increments Car::num_
  Car(const Car& c) throw();  ←─────── Increments Car::num_

  // No need for an explicit assignment operator or destructor
  // since these don't create new Car objects (but see FAQ 30.06).

  static int num_;  ←──────────────── Class data

private:
  int serial_;  ←──────────────────── Object data
};

Car::Car() throw()
: serial_(num_)
{
  cout << "Car ctor\n";
  ++num_;
}

Car::Car(const Car& c) throw()
: serial_(num_)
{
  cout << "Car copy\n";
  ++num_;
}

int Car::num_ = 0;  ←─────────────── Class data is automatically initialized, often before main()
```

Just as a factory exists before it produces its first object, class (`static`) data can be accessed before the first object is instantiated as well as after the last object has been destroyed.

```
int main()
{
  cout << "Car::num_ = " << Car::num_ << '\n';
  {
    Car a;
    cout << "Car::num_ = " << Car::num_ << '\n';
    Car b;
    cout << "Car::num_ = " << Car::num_ << '\n';
    Car c = a;
    cout << "Car::num_ = " << Car::num_ << '\n';
  }
```

```
    cout << "Car::num_ = " << Car::num_ << '\n';
}
```

The output is

```
Car::num_ = 0
Car ctor
Car::num_ = 1
Car ctor
Car::num_ = 2
Car copy
Car::num_ = 3
Car::num_ = 3
```

Note: See the next FAQ regarding `inline` functions that access static data members.

FAQ 16.04

Can `inline` functions safely access static data members?

No!

Static data members should normally be accessed by non-`inline` functions only (and then only from non-`inline` functions that are defined in the same source file as the static data member's definition). In some cases `inline` functions can access static member data, but the programmer needs to think through the issues fairly carefully—they're somewhat tricky.

Suppose class `Fred` contains two static data members: `Fred::i_` is of type `int` and `Fred::s_` is of class `string`, the standard string class. The data member `Fred::i_` is initialized before any code starts running, so `Fred::i_` *can* be accessed from an `inline` function. However if an `inline` function accesses `Fred::s_`, and if the `inline` function is called from another compilation unit, the `inline` function might access `Fred::s_` before it has been initialized (that is, before the constructor of `Fred::s_` has run). This would be a disaster.

Static data members are guaranteed to be initialized before the first call to any non-`inline` function within the same source file as the static data's definition. In the following example, file `Fred.cpp` defines both static data member `Fred::s_` and member function `Fred::f()`. This means that `Fred::s_` will be initialized before `Fred::f()` is called. But if someone calls `inline` function `Fred::g()` before calling `Fred::f()`, accessing `Fred::s_` could be a disaster since `Fred::s_` might not be initialized yet.

Here is file `Fred.hpp`.

```
#include <string>
#include <iostream>
using namespace std;

class Fred {
public:
  static void f() throw();
  static string g() throw();
private:
  static string s_;
};

inline string Fred::g() throw()
{ cout << s_; return s_; }
```
← EVIL: Fred::s_ might not be initialized yet

Here is file `Fred.cpp`.

```
#include "Fred.hpp"

string Fred::s_ = "Hello";

void Fred::f() throw()
{ cout << s_; }
```
← GOOD: Fred::s_ is guaranteed to be initialized

Here is an example showing how the above code could possibly fail (this code is assumed to be in a different source file, such as `main.cpp`).

```
#include "Fred.hpp"

int main()
{ Fred::g(); }
```

Note that some—but not all—compilers will initialize static data member `Fred::s_` before `main()` begins. Thus this code is doubly evil since it will subtly fail on some compilers and accidentally work on others. In fact, its success or failure might even depend on the order that object files are passed to the linker, and some visual environments hide the linker so well that many programmers don't even know the order in which object files are passed to the linker.

To make matters worse, the following source file, say `even-worse.cpp`, calls `inline` function `Fred::g()`—therefore accessing `Fred::s_`—during static initialization. Many compilers will cause this to happen before `main()` begins, so this is even more likely to cause a problem (but again, the problem will depend randomly on things like the link order, the compiler, the version number, the phase of the moon, etc.).

```
#include "Fred.hpp"

string x = Fred::g();
```

FAQ 16.05

What is an analogy for static member functions?

Static member functions are like services attached to the factory rather than services attached to the objects produced by the factory.

```
#include <cstdlib>
#include <iostream>
using namespace std;

class Car {
public:

  Car() throw();
  Car(const Car& c) throw();
  // No need for an explicit assignment operator or destructor
  // since these don't create new Car objects.

  static int num() throw();  ◄──────── Class service
  int odometer() const throw();  ◄──── Object service
  void drive() throw();  ◄──────────── Object service: You drive a Car, not a factory

private:
  static int num_;  ◄──────────────── Class data
  int       miles_;  ◄─────────────── Object data
};

Car::Car() throw()
: miles_(0)
{
  cout << "Car ctor\n";
  ++num_;
}

Car::Car(const Car& c) throw()
: miles_(c.miles_)
{
  cout << "Car copy\n";
  ++num_;
}

int Car::num() throw()  ◄──────── Should be in same source file as num_; see FAQ 16.04
{ return num_; }

int Car::odometer() const throw()
{ return miles_; }
```

```
void Car::drive() throw()
{ ++miles_; }

int Car::num_ = 0;
```
← *Class data is automatically initialized, often before main()*

Some services make sense only when applied to an object.

```
void fiddleWithObject(Car& car) throw()
{
  while (rand() % 10 != 0)
    car.drive();
  cout << "car.odometer() = " << car.odometer() << '\n';
}
```

Some services make sense only when applied to the factory.

```
void fiddleWithClass() throw()
{
  cout << "Car::num() returns " << Car::num() << '\n';

  #ifdef GENERATE_ERROR
    Car::drive();
    Car::odometer();
  #endif
}
```
Car::drive(); ← *ERROR: Can't drive a factory*
Car::odometer(); ← *ERROR: Factories don't have odometers*

Since the factory exists before it produces its first object, the factory can provide services before instantiating an object. That is, `fiddleWithClass()` can be called before the first `Car` object is created and/or after the last `Car` object is destructed:

```
int main()
{
  fiddleWithClass();

  {
    Car a;
    fiddleWithClass();
    fiddleWithObject(a);
  }

  fiddleWithClass();
}
```

FAQ 16.06

How is a static data member similar to a global variable?

A static data member is like a global variable with a funny name that does not need to be `public:`.

If a class has a static data member, there is only one copy of that datum even if there are many instances of the class. This is like a global variable. The difference is that a static data member has a funny (scoped) name (it doesn't pollute the global namespace) and it needn't be `public:` (static data members can be `private:`, `protected:`, or `public:`).

These factors allow classes to be the logical packaging device; source files are reduced to mere buckets of bits and code. There is no need to use source files for hiding data (for instance, there is no need to use file-scope static data to hide data in a source file) since the data can now be hidden in a class. This distinction allows the physical packaging of software to be different from the logical packaging. For example, physical packaging may be optimized based on page fault analysis or on compile-time performance or for maintainability, and so forth.

Global data is rarely used any more. Normally objects and instance data work fine, but when true global data is required, the right choice is normally to use static member data (that is, class-scope static data members) or to put the data in an unnamed namespace.

FAQ 16.07

How is a static member function similar to a friend function?

A static member function is like a friend function with a funny name that needn't be `public:`.

Static member functions and top-level (C-like) friend functions are similar in that neither has an implicit `this` parameter, and both have direct access to the class's `private:` and `protected:` parts.

Except for overloaded operators, most friend functions end up actually being static member functions, because static member functions have a scoped name (they don't pollute the global namespace) and they don't have to be `public:`—they can also be `private:` or `protected:`.

What is the named constructor idiom?

An idiom that allows a specific name for an operation that is similar to a constructor.

Occasionally, classes have a large suite of overloaded constructors. Because all constructors for a class have the same name, it can be confusing to select between the various overloaded constructors. When this happens, the named constructor idiom may be appropriate.

For example, consider a complex number class, Complex, that supports construction using either polar coordinates (magnitude, angle) or rectangular coordinates (real part, imaginary part). Unfortunately, these constructors are very similar; both constructors take two floats. Should Complex(2,1) be interpreted as specifying polar form ("2 at angle 1") or as specifying rectangular form ("2 plus 1 times the imaginary constant")?

Many potential solutions exist to resolve this ambiguity. A boolean flag could indicate which is intended, or an extra dummy parameter on one of the constructors could be used to avoid runtime overhead by making the selection at compile time rather than at runtime. Another solution is to use the named constructor idiom, which is a way of using static member functions to provide alternative constructors for a class. Usually, the named constructor idiom results in user code that is more direct and readable:

```cpp
#include <cmath>
#include <iostream>
using namespace std;

class Complex {
public:
  Complex(float real=0.0) throw();
  static Complex rect(float real, float imag) throw();   ←⎱ The so-called
  static Complex polar(float mag,  float ang) throw();   ←⎰ named constructors
private:
  Complex(float real, float imag) throw();
  float real_, imag_;
};

inline Complex::Complex(float real) throw()
: real_(real)
, imag_(0)
{ }

inline Complex::Complex(float real, float imag) throw()
: real_(real)
```

```
, imag_(imag)
{ }

inline Complex Complex::rect(float real, float imag) throw()
{ return Complex(real, imag); }

inline Complex Complex::polar(float mag,  float ang) throw()
{ return Complex(mag*cos(ang), mag*sin(ang)); }
```

Both `rect()` and `polar()` are static member functions that operate like constructors. Users explicitly call whichever version they want.

```
int main()
{
  Complex a;  ◄──────────────────  real part=0, imag part=0
  Complex b = 3.14;  ◄──────────  real part=3.14, imag part=0
  Complex c = Complex::rect(3,2);  ◄──── real part=3, imag part=2
  Complex d = Complex::polar(3,2);  ◄──── magnitude=3, angle=2 radians
}
```

FAQ 16.09

How should static member functions be called?

Explicitly name the class using `::`.

For documentation purposes, calls to static member functions should be coded as `Classname::staticMember()` rather than as `object.staticMember()` or `ptr->staticMember()`. The `::` is a reminder that the member function is statically bound (see FAQ 21.09) and that the member function is attached to the class rather than to an individual object of the class.

Calling a static member function `Classname::f()` from another member function of class `Classname` is an exception to this rule. In this case, the call can be simply `f()`, since the meaning is usually clear in this context. For example, when `Classname::f()` is a `protected: static` member function of the class, simply write `f()` rather than `Classname::f()`.

Why might a class with static data members get linker errors?

Static data members must be explicitly defined in exactly one source file.

Here's an example of a header file, such as `Fred.hpp`.

```
class Fred {
public:
   static int x_;  ◄─── Declare (not define) static member Fred::x_
};
```

The linker generates an error ("`Fred::x_` is not defined") unless (exactly) one of the source files defines `Fred::x_`. This definition is normally done in the class's source file, such as file `Fred.cpp`:

```
#include "Fred.hpp"
int Fred::x_ = 42;  ◄─── Define static member Fred::x_
```

Note that the explicit initializer (= 42 in the example) is optional. That is, the line could be changed to

```
int Fred::x_;  ◄─── Initialize Fred::x_ to 0
```

Note that even when the static data member is `private:` or `protected:`, it must still be explicitly defined as shown in one of the two examples.

How is a `const` static data member initialized?

A `const` static data member is declared in the class and is normally defined (and initialized) in a source file, such as a `.cpp` file. But in some cases it can be initialized in the class body proper. For example, integral types, such as `int`, `unsigned long`, `char`, and so on, are special: they can be initialized where they are declared in the class body proper.

Here is a sample header file, `Fred.hpp`.

```
#include <string>
using namespace std;
```

```
class Barney { };

class Fred {
public:
  // ...
private:
  static const int i_ = 42;        Integral data types can be initialized in
  static const char c_ = 'z';      the class body proper

  static const float x_;           Nonintegral data types must be defined in
  static const string s_;          the source file, not in the class body proper
  static const Barney b_;
};
```

Here is corresponding source file, `Fred.cpp`.

```
#include "Fred.hpp"

const float Fred::x_ = 3.14;
const string Fred::s_ = "Hello";
const Barney Fred::b_;
```

Another common style is to use anonymous (unnamed) enums. This style is no longer needed, but it is typical in older C++ code. For example, the `static const int i_ = 42` from the previous example can be replaced by enum { i_ = 42 }, as shown in the following example.

```
class Fred {
public:
  // ...
private:
  enum { i_ = 42 };              Older style
  // static const int i_ = 42;   Newer style
};
```

In either case, the constant is called `Fred::i_`, and it can be `private:`, `protected:`, or `public:`.

FAQ 16.12

What is the right strategy for implementing a function that needs to maintain state between calls?

Turn the function into a functionoid. Do *not* create a function with local static data.

In C, it was common to create a function that maintained state between calls by means of local, static data inside the function body. Since this is unsafe in a multithreaded environment, in C++ such a function should be implemented as a *functionoid*, which is a fancy name for a class that has one major member function. The local static data from the original C-like function should become nonstatic member data of the functionoid class. The benefit is to allow different callers to have different values for the datum that used to be static. For example, every calling function that wants its own copy of the function's state can simply create its own distinct functionoid object.

Viewing a function with local static data as a global functionoid object makes it clear why the static data is expensive to model (global variables aren't fun!). For example, consider the `rand()` function, which remembers some state between calls:

```
int rand() throw()
{
   static unsigned long current = 1001;  ◄─── Bad form: Local static data
   current = current * 22695477UL + 1;
   return int(current >> 12) & 0x7fff;
}
```

The static variable `current` introduces subtle dependencies between users of the function. Any change in the calling pattern can alter the behavior of this routine. Such routines are notorious in shared-memory, multithreaded environments.

A better way to do this is with a class. Every user function that wants a pseudorandom stream of numbers can create its own object of this class.

```
#include <iostream>
using namespace std;

class RandomSequence {  ◄─────────────── Good form: Functionoid
public:
   RandomSequence(int initialSeed=1001) throw();
   int next() throw();
protected:
   unsigned long current_;
};
```

```
RandomSequence::RandomSequence(int initialSeed) throw()
  : current_(initialSeed) { }

int RandomSequence::next() throw()
{
  current_ = current_ * 22695477UL + 1;
  return int(current_ >> 12) & 0x7fff;
}
```

The user gets a sequence of random numbers by using the member function next().

```
void printRandomSequence() throw()
{
  RandomSequence rand;
  for (int i = 0; i < 10; ++i)
    cout << rand.next() << ' ';
}

int main()
{ printRandomSequence(); }
```

Before, there was a global rand() function with a single state variable. Now there is a local rand object and as many state variables as there are user functions that want an independent pseudorandom sequence. The dependencies among callers (and especially among the various threads) are eliminated at the source. There is no more shared static data.

Another reason to create a functionoid object is when a function performs several distinct operations. In C, such a function would often accept a what-to-do parameter that selected the operation to be performed. In C++, such a multioperation function should be implemented as an object. Each distinct operation performed by the original function should become a distinct member function on the object. Such an object is also called a functionoid.

FAQ 16.13

How can the function call operator help with functionoids?

The *function call operator* lets users pretend that the functionoid is a function.

In the previous example, class RandomSequence is a functionoid. Unlike a standard function, RandomSequence can maintain state between calls without sharing that state between all of its callers.

Functionoids often use the function call operator (operator()()) rather than a named member function such as next(). In the following code, next() has been replaced by operator()() in class RandomSequence.

```
#include <iostream>
using namespace std;

class RandomSequence {
public:
  RandomSequence(int initialSeed=1001) throw();
  int operator()() throw();  ◄────── The name of the member function is operator()
protected:
  unsigned long current_;
};

RandomSequence::RandomSequence(int initialSeed) throw()
: current_(initialSeed) { }

int RandomSequence::operator()() throw()
{
  current_ = current_ * 22695477UL + 1;
  return int(current_ >> 12) & 0x7fff;
}
```

Given an object of class RandomSequence called rand, users can now use rand() instead of rand.next():

```
int main()
{
  RandomSequence rand;
  for (int i = 0; i < 10; ++i)
    cout << rand() << ' ';
}
```

FAQ 16.14

Is it safe to be ignorant of the static initialization order problem?

No, ignorance of the *static initialization order* problem can result in application crashes.

The static initialization order problem has to do with the lifetimes of class-scope static objects and file-scope or namespace-scope objects. These objects are constructed near the beginning of the application's execution (often before `main()` begins) and are destructed after `main()` finishes. The nightmare scenario occurs when there is an order dependency between initializations across different compilation units (that is, different .cpp files). This can be both dangerous and subtle.

For example, suppose a constructor of class `Fred` uses a static data member of class `Wilma`, and a user creates a global `Fred` object. If the static objects in the user's source file are initialized before those in the source file containing `Fred`'s static data member, `Fred`'s constructor will access a `Wilma` object before it is constructed.

Although this description sounds uncommon, it actually shows up quite often in practice, especially with factory objects whose constructor registers something in a "registry" object. For example, `Wilma` is actually a `map` (a registry object) and `Fred` is a "factory" object whose constructor registers something in the `map`.

In the following example, the order of the global `Fred` and the static data member have been arranged to simulate this disaster.

```
#include <iostream>
using namespace std;

class Wilma {
public:
  Wilma()  throw();
  void f() throw();
};

inline Wilma::Wilma()  throw() { cout << "Wilma ctor\n"; }
inline void Wilma::f() throw() { cout << "Wilma used\n"; }

class Fred {
public:
  Fred() throw();
protected:
  static Wilma wilma_;
};

inline Fred::Fred() throw()
{
  cout << "Fred ctor\n";
  wilma_.f();
}

Fred x;
Wilma Fred::wilma_;

int main()
{ }
```

The (annotated) output from this program shows that the Wilma object is used before it is initialized. This is a disaster.

```
Fred ctor
Wilma used  ◄────── The static object is used
Wilma ctor  ◄────── The static object is constructed
```

FAQ 16.15

What is a simple and robust solution to the static initialization order problem?

A very simple and fairly robust solution is to change the static data member into a static member function that returns a reference to a dynamically allocated object. This provides *construct on first use* semantics, which is desirable in many situations.

The following code shows how to apply this technique to the example from the previous FAQ. The static data member Wilma Fred::wilma_ has been changed to a static member function, Wilma& Fred::wilma(), and all uses of Fred::wilma_ have been changed to Fred::wilma(). Class Wilma is not shown since it is unchanged from the example in the previous FAQ.

```
class Fred {
public:
  Fred() throw();
protected:
  static Wilma& wilma() throw();  ◄──── Used to be static Wilma wilma_;
};

inline Fred::Fred() throw()
{
  cout << "Fred ctor\n";
  wilma().f();  ◄──────────────────── Used to be wilma_.f()
}

Fred x;

Wilma& Fred::wilma() throw()  ◄────────── Used to be Wilma Fred::wilma_;
{
  static Wilma* p = new Wilma();  ◄──── Don't forget the "static"!
  return *p;
}
```

In the static member function `Fred::wilma()`, pointer p is `static`, so the new `Wilma()` object is allocated only the first time that `Fred::wilma()` is called. All subsequent calls simply return a reference to the same `Wilma` object.

As shown in the (annotated) output from this program, the `Wilma` object is initialized before it is used. This is good.

```
Fred ctor
Wilma ctor ◄──── The static object is constructed
Wilma used ◄──── The static object is used
```

FAQ 16.16

What if the static object's destructor has important side effects that must eventually occur?

new

One limitation of the technique described in the previous FAQ is that it abandons the static `Wilma` object on the heap—the `Wilma` object is never destructed. If the `Wilma` object's destructor has important side effects that should eventually happen, then the implementation of `Fred::wilma()` needs to be changed so that it simply returns a local static object by reference.

The following code shows how to apply this technique to the example from the previous FAQ. The local static pointer `static Wilma* p = new Wilma();` has been changed to simply `static Wilma w;`, and the `return` statement simply returns the local static object w. Class `Wilma` is not shown since it is unchanged from the example in the previous FAQ.

```
class Fred {
public:
  Fred() throw();
protected:
  static Wilma& wilma() throw(); ◄──── Same as in the previous FAQ
};

inline Fred::Fred() throw()
{
  cout << "Fred ctor\n";
  wilma().f(); ◄──────────────────── Same as in the previous FAQ
}

Fred x;
```

```
Wilma& Fred::wilma() throw()
{
   static Wilma w;   ◄──────────  Used to be static Wilma* p = new Wilma();
   return w;
}
```

Since the local static object w is static, it is initialized only the first time control flows over its declaration, that is, the first time Fred::wilma() is called. This is the same construct on first use semantics as was described in the previous FAQ, which is normally quite desirable.

Unfortunately, this solution has its own problems. Remember why this solution was proposed in the first place: the Wilma object's destructor has important side effects that need to eventually occur. Although this second solution guarantees that they will occur (assuming the Fred::wilma() function is called at least once), it introduces a new problem that the previous solution did not have: a static *deinitialization* order problem. In particular, if some static object's destructor calls Fred::wilma(), Murphy's Law says that that call will occur *after* the static Wilma object has been destructed. If that may occur, the best solution is the nifty counter technique, which is described in the next FAQ.

FAQ 16.17

What if the static object's destructor has important side effects that must eventually occur *and* the static object must be accessed by another static object's destructor?

new

This is the most restrictive of all scenarios since it means that the construction must occur before the object is first used, and it must be destructed after its last use. The solution is called the *nifty counter technique*. What happens is that a static counter is created (the nifty counter) along with a static object in each source file whose constructor increments this nifty counter and whose destructor decrements the nifty counter. When the nifty counter is incremented from zero, the static object is initialized, and when the nifty counter is decremented to zero, the static object is destructed.

The following code shows how to apply this technique to the example from the previous FAQ. The static data member is back, but this time it is a static pointer. Nested class Fred::Init has a static counter (the nifty counter) called count_, which is incremented by Fred::Init's constructor and decremented by Fred::Init's destructor. The Fred::wilma_ object is created when the nifty counter is incremented from zero and is destructed when the counter is decremented back to zero. Class `Wilma` is not shown since it is unchanged from the example in the previous FAQ.

Here is the header file `Fred.hpp`.

```
class Fred {
public:
  Fred() throw();
protected:
  class Init;              ◄──────────── This declares nested class Fred::Init
  friend Init;             ◄──────────── So Fred::Init can access Fred::wilma_
  static Wilma* wilma_;    ◄──────────── This is now a static pointer
};

class Fred::Init {
public:
  Init()  throw() { if (count_++ == 0) wilma_ = new Wilma(); }
  ~Init() throw() { if (--count_ == 0) delete wilma_; }
private:
  static unsigned count_;
};

static Fred::Init fredInit;  ◄────── The key: a static Fred::Init object defined in
                                     the header file

inline Fred::Fred() throw()
{
  cout << "Fred ctor\n";
  wilma_->f();  ◄──────────────────── This is now safe
}
```

Here is the source file `"Fred.cpp"`:

```
#include "Fred.hpp"

unsigned Fred::Init::count_ = 0;
Wilma* Fred::wilma_ = NULL;
```

Every source file that includes header file `Fred.hpp` ends up with its own static `Fred::Init` object called `fredInit`. Since this static object appears very early in the source file, it is initialized before most other static objects in the source file (in particular, it is guaranteed to be initialized before any static object in the source file could call `Fred::Fred()`, since the call to any member function of class `Fred` can occur only after the header of class `Fred` has been `#included`).

Of all the source files that include header file `Fred.hpp`, one of them, say `foo.cpp`, is initialized first. During the static initialization of `foo.cpp`, the nifty counter `Fred::Init::count_` is incremented from zero, and the `Fred::wilma_` object is created. Since the `Fred::wilma_` object is initialized before any calls to any member functions of class `Fred` can be made, it is guaranteed to be constructed before it is used.

The static deinitialization situation is similar but opposite. Of all the source files that include `Fred.hpp`, one of them, say `foo.cpp`, is the last one to be deinitialized. Since deinitialization occurs in bottom to top order, the static `Fred::Init` object in file `foo.cpp` is one of the last things that is destructed (certainly it is destructed after any static object could call any member function of class `Fred`). Therefore the `Fred::wilma_` object is destructed just after the last static object could possibly use it: it will not be used after it has been destructed.

Unfortunately the nifty counter technique also has problems. Although it never allows an object to be used either before construction or after destruction, it does force a small amount of static initialization code into every source file that includes header file `Fred.hpp`. This means that a large percentage of the application needs to be paged into memory during startup, which can significantly degrade startup performance, especially if there are a lot of source files that include headers that use the nifty counter technique.

FAQ 16.18

What are some criteria for choosing between all these various techniques?

Here are the pros and cons of each of the three techniques that were presented.

new

- *Construct on first use with new:* Users access the static object via a non-`inline` access function. The access function has a local static pointer and allocates the object via `new`. Pro: The technique is easy to remember, simple to use, efficient during startup, safe during startup, and safe during shutdown. Con: The static object is abandoned on the heap—if the static object's destructor has important side effects that must occur, this technique cannot be used. (See FAQ 16.15.)

- *Construct on first use with a local static object:* Users access the static object via a non-`inline` access function. The access function has a local static object. Pro: The technique is easy to remember, simple to use, efficient during startup, and safe during startup, and it eventually destructs the object. Con: The technique is not safe during shutdown—if a static object's destructor calls the access function, the static object could be accessed after it is destroyed, which would be a disaster. (See FAQ 16.16.)

- *Nifty counter:* The static object is constructed when the nifty counter is incremented from 0 and is destructed when the nifty counter is decremented to 0. Pro: The technique is simple to use, safe during startup, and safe during shutdown, and it eventually destructs the object. Con: Potential performance problem during startup and shutdown. (See FAQ 16.17.)

In our experience, a significant percentage of static objects that should be constructed before they are first used are registry objects (for example, a map object that will be populated during static initialization by other static objects). In most of these cases, the first technique is sufficient since the map object rarely has to be destructed—it can be abandoned on the heap. This is good news because the first technique is easy to use, easy to remember, is fast, and is safe during both startup and shutdown.

Chapter 17

Derived Classes

What is the purpose of this chapter?

This chapter discusses derived classes and inheritance at the programming language
level. Part II discusses the same information on a design level and should be read before
this chapter. This chapter dwells only on public, single, nonvirtual inheritance, which is
the most prevalent form. Chapter 38 discusses some of the other types of inheritance.

new

How does C++ express inheritance?

Here is a typical C++ inheritance declaration.

new

```
#include <iostream>
using namespace std;

class Vehicle {
public:
  virtual void startEngine() throw() = 0;
  virtual ~Vehicle() throw();
};

Vehicle::~Vehicle() throw()
{ }
```

```
class V8Engine {
public:
  void start() throw();
};

void V8Engine::start() throw()
{ cout << "starting V8Engine\n"; }

class Car : public Vehicle {
public:
  virtual void startEngine() throw();
protected:
  V8Engine engine_;
};

void Car::startEngine() throw()
{ engine_.start(); }
```

This relationship can be described in several equivalent ways.

- Car is a kind-of Vehicle.

- Car is derived from Vehicle.

- Car is a subclass of Vehicle.

- Car is a child class of Vehicle (not common in the C++ community).

- Vehicle is the base class of Car.

- Vehicle is the parent class of Car (not common in the C++ community).

- Vehicle is the super-class of Car (not common in the C++ community).

As a consequence of the kind-of relationship, a Car object can be treated as a Vehicle object. For example, since function f(Vehicle&) accepts any kind-of Vehicle, it can be passed a Car or an object of any other class derived from Vehicle:

```
void f(Vehicle& v) throw()
{ v.startEngine(); }

int main()
{
  Car c;
  f(c);
}
```

UML uses the following notation to show inheritance.

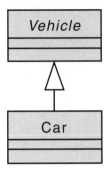

What is a concrete derived class?

A concrete derived class is a derived class that has no pure virtual functions.

Because an abstract class cannot be instantiated directly, one or more derived classes are normally defined as implementations of the abstraction provided by the abstract class. A concrete derived class simply provides definitions for all its inherited pure virtual functions. If a definition for one of the inherited pure virtual functions is forgotten, any attempt to instantiate the class results in the compiler issuing an error message.

Abstract base class Base has two pure virtual member functions f() and g(), and derived class Derived provides a definition for f() but not for g(). Therefore Derived is also abstract:

```
class Base {
public:
  virtual void f() throw() = 0;
  virtual void g() throw() = 0;
};

class Derived : public Base {
public:
  virtual void f() throw();
};

void Derived::f() throw()
{ }
```

If `Derived2` were derived from `Derived` and `Derived2` had to be concrete, `Derived2` would have to provide a definition for `g()`, but it wouldn't be required to override `Derived::f()`. This is shown in the following example.

```
class Derived2 : public Derived {
public:
  virtual void g() throw();
};

void Derived2::g() throw()
{ }

void sample() throw()
{ Derived2 x; }  ◄─── OK: Derived2 is a concrete class
```

FAQ 17.04

Why can't a derived class access the `private:` members of its base class?

A derived class can't access the `private:` members of its base class because the base class intentionally hides some of its implementation details from its derived classes.

Suppose class `Fred` contains a member datum or member function that is likely to change. Unless derived classes need to access this member, the base class `Fred` would be wise to declare the member as `private:`. This reduces the ripple effect of changes in the base class. For example, the `private:` member can be removed or modified without fear of breaking derived classes. That is, the derived classes are protected from rewrites whenever the semantics or even existence of the `private:` member change.

For example, class `Wilma` below can access `publ_` and `prot_`, but cannot access `priv_`.

```
#include <iostream>
using namespace std;

class Fred {
public:
  Fred() throw();
  int publ_;
protected:
  int prot_;
private:
```

```
    int priv_;
};

Fred::Fred() throw()
: publ_(1)
, prot_(2)
, priv_(3)
{ }

class Wilma : public Fred {
public:
  void printem() const throw();
};

void Wilma::printem() const throw()
{
  cout << publ_ << '\n';  ◄——— OK: Derived can access base's public: stuff
  cout << prot_ << '\n';  ◄——— OK: Derived can access base's protected: stuff

  #ifdef GENERATE_ERROR
    cout << priv_ << '\n';  ◄——— Error: Derived cannot access base's private: stuff
  #endif
}

int main()
{
  Wilma a;
  a.printem();
}
```

The designer of a base class gives derived classes access to implementation details by declaring them as `protected:`.

FAQ 17.05

How can a base class protect derived classes so that changes to the base class will not affect them?

The easiest solution is to define a `protected:` interface in addition to the `public:` interface.

A class hierarchy is more resilient to changes if it has two distinct interfaces for two distinct sets of users.

- Its public: interface serves unrelated classes.

- Its protected: interface serves derived classes.

Both interfaces must be fully specified. For instance, the actual raw data of a class could be private: with a set of protected: inline member functions for accessing this data. These inline member functions define an interface between the derived classes and the raw bits of the base class. Then the private: data of the base class could be changed within reasonable bounds without affecting the derived classes. It would still be necessary to recompile the derived classes after a change to the base class, though the source code of the derived class would not need to be changed unless the protected: interface is modified in a nonbackward compatible manner.

For example, suppose class Base has an int data member. Base can ensure that derived classes do not rely on the specific data structure by making the data structure private: (in this case, a simple int) and defining inline protected: members for accessing these data. Derived class Derived accesses the value using these protected: inline member functions.

```
class Base {
public:
  Base() throw();
protected:
  void storeValue(int value) throw();
  int  retrieveValue() const throw();
private:
  int value_;
};

inline Base::Base()                        throw() : value_(37) { }
inline void Base::storeValue(int value) throw() { value_ = value; }
inline int  Base::retrieveValue() const throw() { return value_; }

class Derived : public Base {
public:
  void f(int i) throw();
};

void Derived::f(int i) throw() { storeValue(i); }

int main()
{
  Derived d;
  d.f(42);
}
```

Can a derived class pointer be converted into a pointer to its public base class?

Such conversions are possible and don't even require a pointer cast.

A publicly derived class is a kind-of its base class. By implication, the upward conversion is perfectly safe, and is quite common. For example, a pointer to a Car is in fact already pointing at a Vehicle, since a Car is a kind-of a Vehicle.

```
class Vehicle { };
class Car : public Vehicle { };

void f(Vehicle* v) throw();

void g(Car* c) throw()
{
  f(c);   //Perfectly safe; no cast needed
}
```

How can a class Y be a kind-of another class X as well as getting the bits of X?

This is easy: use public inheritance.

Here is the C++ syntax for public inheritance.

```
class X              { /*bits and/or code go here*/ };
class Y : public X { /*more bits and/or code go here*/ };
```

This does two distinct things. First, it provides the kind-of relationship: Y is a kind-of X, therefore Y supports the same services as X (Y might add some new member functions as well). Second, it shares bits and code: Y inherits X's bits (data structures) and code (algorithms).

FAQ 17.08

How can a class Y get the bits of an existing class X without making Y a kind-of X?

There are three alternatives. The preferred solution is normal composition, also known as *has-a*. But in some cases private inheritance should be used, and in a few cases, protected inheritance should be used.

Here is the class X that will be used in each of the three following examples.

```
class X {
public:
  void f() throw();
  void g() throw();
private:
  int a_;
  float b_;
};
```

Here is the C++ syntax for composition (that is, Y has-a X). This is the preferred solution.

```
class Y1 {
public:
  void f() throw();
protected:
  X x_;  ←──────────── Composition: Y1 is not a kind-of X
};

void Y1::f() throw()
{ x_.f(); }  ←──────────── Y1 calls member functions in X ("reuse")
```

Here is the C++ syntax for private inheritance, which is semantically the same as has-a but with an increased ripple effect (changes to the `protected:` part of X can break the private derived class Y2). This is the second of the three alternatives.

```
class Y2 : private X {  ←──── Private inheritance: Y2 is not a kind-of X
public:
  using X::f;  ←──────────── Same semantics as above: Calls to Y2::f() end up in X::f()
};
```

Here is the C++ syntax for protected inheritance, which is semantically the same as has-a but with an even greater ripple effect than private inheritance (changes to the `protected:` part of X can break the protected derived class Y3 and can also break any classes derived from Y3). This is the last of the three alternatives.

```
class Y3 : protected X {  ◄——— Protected inheritance: Y3 is not a kind-of X
public:
  using X::f;  ◄——————————— Same semantics as above: Calls to Y3::f() end up in X::f()
};
```

In all three cases, a Y object has a X object, and users of Y are unaware of any relationship between Y and X. For example, user code will not break if the relationship between Y and X changes—or even is eliminated. See FAQ 37.01 for more information on private and protected inheritance.

FAQ 17.09

How can a class Y be a kind-of another class X without inheriting the bits of X?

It's doable, but C++ has to be outfoxed.

The only mechanism provided by C++ that defines the kind-of relationship also forces inheriting the bits of the base class. If the base class's data structures are inappropriate for certain derived classes, it's necessary to outfox C++ by deferring the definition of the bits to the lower levels of the class hierarchy.

One way to do this is to define an ABC that possesses no (or few) internal data structures, then define the data structures in the concrete derived classes. In this way, the derived classes define the kind-of relationship, but they don't have any bits imposed on them by the base class. For example, both X and Y would inherit from this common ABC, but they would not inherit from each other. Strictly speaking, this does not achieve the original goal (Y is not a kind-of X), but it is normally close enough. The reason is that the bulk of the system can (hopefully) be written to use the ABC rather than X or Y directly, and inheritance allows both X and Y to be passed into the bulk of the system.

Chapter 18

Access Control

What is the purpose of this chapter?

This chapter presents the three types of access control in C++ classes. Access controls allow the programmer to declare a class's members as `public:`, `protected:`, and/or `private:`.

How are `private:`, `protected:`, and `public:` different?

The situation is similar to personal secrets (shared only with friends), family secrets (shared with friends and children), and nonsecrets (shared with anybody), respectively.

A `private:` member of a class is accessible only by members and friends of the class.

A `protected:` member of a class is accessible by members and friends of the class and by members and friends of derived classes, provided they access the base member via a pointer or a reference to their own derived class.

A `public:` member of a class is accessible by everyone.

There is no difference between the access rules for data members and member functions. "Members and friends of class X" include member functions of class X, friend functions of class X, and member functions of friend classes of class X.

FAQ 18.03

Why can't subclasses access the `private:` parts of their base class?

The base class encapsulation has to protect itself from being undermined.

Suppose a subclass could access the `private:` portion of its base class. Would it make sense if just anyone could take away the option for the base class developer to change internal mechanisms in the future because they had subclassed a base class and locked in on its implementation? That would not be in anyone's best interests. So there is a need for ways to distinguish between

- Mechanisms and services that are available to everyone, the `public:` interface

- Mechanisms and services that are available only to subclasses, the `protected:` interface

- Mechanisms and services that are reserved for change without concern for breaking user code, the `private:` interface

Note that this is not a security issue. Developers can always look at the header files to see what is going on. The key notion is that the designer makes different promises to different audiences, and access controls provide a way to do that.

Also, notice that a subclass can access the `protected:` portion of its base class only when it acts specifically as a subclass. It cannot access the `protected:` portion of an object of its base class that is freestanding or of a different derived class.

FAQ 18.04

What's the difference between the keywords `struct` and `class`?

The difference is mostly perception.

From a pure language perspective, the major difference between the keywords `struct` and `class` is the default access level assigned to members and base classes. The default access level assigned to members and base classes of a `struct` is `public:`, while the default access level for members and base classes of a `class` is `private:`. Regardless, it is best to put an explicit `public`, `private`, or `protected` in the base class specifications, and it is usually best for the class to start with an explicit `public:`. With that approach, these defaults are of little consequence in practice.

The perception, however, is very different. A `struct` is perceived as an open bucket of bits. Most `struct`s have very few member functions (often they have only a constructor), and they are often entirely `public:`.

FAQ 18.05

When should a data member be `protected:` rather than `private:`?

Some authors discourage `protected:` data in all cases on the grounds that it creates a stronger coupling with the derived class. For example, if a derived class were written by a customer or some other third party, changing the `protected:` data could break the derived class's code. In these situations, it is far better to create a `protected:` access function to the `private:` data rather than to allow direct access to `protected:` data by derived classes.

However, one size does not fit all. Although there are situations when third parties create derived classes, there are also many situations when they do not. From a practical standpoint, an organization often has a very well-defined notion of which classes will be inherited from by third parties, which classes will be inherited from internally, and which classes will not be inherited from at all. Those who erroneously believe that inheritance is for code reuse will be alarmed at that last statement, but when proper inheritance is practiced, inheritance is planned and prepared for ahead of time; it is not normally something programmers stumble into. (See FAQs 7.01, 8.12.)

FAQ 18.06

Why is `private:` the default access level for a class?

The default assumption makes small programs easier to read. For example, when a member function is defined within the class body proper (a practice that we are not advocating), it is easier to understand the code if the data appears before the code. Note that the compiler finds the class's data member independent of whether it appears before or after the usage, but human readers don't usually do a two-pass scan. Since the data is often `private:`, the default access level makes it a tiny bit easier when functions are defined within the class body proper. For example, this is particularly valuable for textbook examples that define member functions within their class to save presentation space.

But typical development efforts separate a lot of the implementation into a distinct file, such as a `.cpp` file. Thus, the problem with the member function coming before the data doesn't exist, and there is more reason to put the `public:` portion first. This lets the human reader see the interface portion of the class without having to wade through irrelevant implementation detail.

Different authors take different approaches to this issue, but we probably all subscribe to the same guiding principle. Any differences are due to our audiences and presentation style rather than philosophies.

Chapter 19

Friend Classes and Friend Functions

What is a friend?

A friend is an entity to which a class grants access authority.

new

Friends can be functions, other classes, or individual member functions of other classes. Friend classes are used when two or more classes are designed to work together and need access to each other's implementation in ways that the rest of the world shouldn't be allowed to have. In other words, they help keep private things private. For instance, it may be desirable for class `DatabaseCursor` to have more privilege to the internals of class `Database` than `main()` has.

In the early days of OO, people had all sorts of strange ideas. Some people thought that the class was the fundamental unit that had to be encapsulated and concluded that friendship was evil. Experience has shown that some abstractions require more than one class, and that the abstraction needs the encapsulation barriers more than the component classes. As long as they are used properly, friends enhance the encapsulation of abstractions.

Friend classes normally imply that one abstraction (a database with multiple cursors, for example) is implemented using several distinct classes (`Database` and `DatabaseCursor`). Using several classes to implement one abstraction is especially useful when the various classes have different lifetimes or different cardinalities. For example, it is likely that there are an arbitrary number of `DatabaseCursor` objects for any given `Database` object.

```cpp
#include <stdexcept>
#include <string>
using namespace std;

class BTree { /*...*/ };
class Cache { /*...*/ };
class DatabaseCursor;

class Database {
public:
  unsigned numRecords() const throw();
protected:
  friend DatabaseCursor;   // Grant access to DatabaseCursor
  BTree btree_;
  Cache cache_;
};

class DatabaseCursor {
public:
  string getCurrentRecord() const throw(out_of_range);
  void   changeCurrentRecord(const string& record)
                                      throw(out_of_range);
  void   goToNextRecord() throw(out_of_range);
protected:
  Database* db_;  ←—— The Database to which this cursor object is attached
                  ←—— Pointers into the BTree and/or Cache go here
};
```

It would be a bad idea to force class `Database` and class `DatabaseCursor` into one class by moving the member functions of `DatabaseCursor` into class `Database` (so we would now have `Database::getCurrentRecord()`). This would impose a one-cursor-per-database policy and would cause `Database` to manage both the data and a current position within that data.

The UML diagram for this friendship relationship follows.

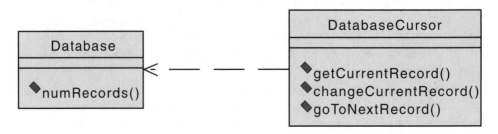

FAQ 19.02

What's a good mental model for friend classes?

A secret handshake or other technique to exchange information with a confidant in such a way that normal people are unable to access the same secrets. Friend classes prevent users (the normal people) from seeing the information being exchanged through the secret codes that connect the various objects (confidants).

The overall effect is to *keep private things private.*

The alternative to granting special access privileges between the classes would be for the classes to declare `public:` member functions that allow *anyone* to manipulate the class's `private:` members. For instance, in the `DatabaseCursor` example, class `Database` would need to provide `public:` member functions to manipulate its cache, B-tree, file system, and so on. Although the implementation bits would be encapsulated, the implementation technique would be exposed. Subsequent changes to the implementation technique would break users' code.

In the traditional software realm, friendship is called tight cohesion, and is, within limits, considered good.

FAQ 19.03

What are some advantages of using friend classes?

Friend classes are useful when a class wants to hide features from users that are needed only by another, tightly coupled class. Compared to making a member `public:`, it is sometimes better to make the member `private:`, which eliminates potential misuse by unknown users, and grant friendship status to the tightly cohesive class, thereby keeping implementation details hidden from the rest of the world.

Friend classes also arise when a member function on a class needs to maintain state between calls and when multiple copies of this state must exist. Under these circumstances, the member function becomes a friend class, and the multiple copies of the state become multiple objects of the friend class.

FAQ 19.04 ———————————————————————————

Do friends violate the encapsulation barrier?

Not necessarily.

If the encapsulation barrier is narrowly defined as the suite of member functions on a class, then friends violate the encapsulation barrier. However, this is a naive view of encapsulation, and applying it consistently actually degrades the overall encapsulation of a system. For example, if another entity needs to be part of the same abstraction, this naive approach suggests that the first class should expose its implementation technique via an unnecessarily large suite of get/set member functions.

The enlightened view is that the encapsulation barrier encapsulates an abstraction, not just a class. For example, the earlier example of a database with multiple cursors illustrates an abstraction that is too rich to be implemented by a single class. In cases like this, friend classes are a valuable way of hiding the (possibly complex) interrelationships between the various pieces of the abstraction.

Friends don't violate the encapsulation barrier; they are *part of* the encapsulation barrier.

FAQ 19.05 ———————————————————————————

What is a friend function?

A friend function is a nonmember function that has been granted access to a class's non-`public:` members. This improves an interface without breaking encapsulation.

For example, the syntax most objects use for printing is cout << x, where x is the object being printed and cout is the output stream (ostream) on which the object is being printed. This printing service is provided by operator<<, which needs to be a friend function of the class of x rather than a member function of the class of x, because the ostream needs to be on the left side of the << operator and the object being printed on the right side. In general, binary operators can be member functions only if the member function is attached to the left hand argument of the operator.

```
#include <iostream>
#include <cstdlib>
using namespace std;

class MyString {
public:
```

```
    MyString(const char* s="")  throw();
   ~MyString()                  throw();
    MyString(const MyString& s) throw();
    MyString& operator= (const MyString& s) throw();
    friend ostream& operator<< (ostream& o, const MyString& s) throw();
  protected:
    char* s_;
  };

  MyString::MyString(const char* s) throw()
  : s_(strdup(s)) { }

  MyString::~MyString() throw()
  { free(s_); }

  ostream& operator<< (ostream& o, const MyString& s) throw()
  { return o << s.s_; }

  int main()
  {
    MyString s = "fred";
    cout << s << "\n";
  }
```

FAQ 19.06

When should a function be implemented as a friend function rather than a member function?

Whenever it improves readability of user code.

Generally, member functions are used rather than friend functions. However if a friend function would make the code that uses the class more readable, a friend function should be used.

It is important that the decision be based not on the readability of the code within the class but rather on the readability of the code that uses the class. There isn't that much difference between the internal implementation details within a friend function and those within a member function. But even more important is the economics of the situation. It's more important to focus on the many users of the class than it is to worry about the class itself.

The point of friend functions is that they allow the syntax for the user code to be intuitive while still maintaining the class's encapsulation barrier. This can lead to easier-to-use classes, which reduces education costs and improves the quality of the user code—intuitive interfaces are abused less often.

FAQ 19.07

What are some guidelines to make sure friend functions are used properly?

Friend functions should be part of the class's `public:` interface, and their code should be owned by the class's owner.

Guideline 1: Friend functions should make the user's code easier to understand. Look at some sample syntax of how a user would use the class with the friend function, and compare it with the moral equivalent of the sample syntax if the friend function were changed into a member function. The friend function version should be used if and only if it results in more intuitive user code (see FAQ 19.06).

Guideline 2: Friend functions should be used only for operations that are part of the `public:` interface of a class. They should not be used every time someone wants to do something tricky with the class. If a user has a function that needs to access the innards of your class (for example, because the class's current `public:` interface isn't powerful enough), fix the problem (the interface) rather than patching the symptoms. Don't grant friendship to everyone.

Guideline 3: A friend function or class should be under the political and technical authority of the same team that owns the class itself. Granting friendship status to a function or class under the political authority of a team other than the one implementing the class results in a scheduling headache—changes that involve coordinating multiple participants who may not always be in a position to handle the requested modifications in a timely manner is a nightmare.

FAQ 19.08

What does it mean that friendship isn't transitive?

A friend of a friend isn't (necessarily) a friend.

Friendship is personal; it is explicitly granted to a particular, named individual. All friends of a class are declared explicitly in the body of the class. This clearly identifies the entities that need to be updated when the `private:` part of a class is changed.

In the following code, `operator<<` is a friend of `BinaryTree`, which is a friend of `BinaryTreeNode`, but this does not make `operator<<` a friend of `BinaryTreeNode`.

```
#include <iostream>
using namespace std;

class BinaryTreeNode;  ◄────── Predeclare class BinaryTreeNode

class BinaryTree {
public:
  friend ostream& operator<< (ostream&, const BinaryTree&) throw();
       ◄──────────────────────── operator<< can access BinaryTree
protected:
  BinaryTreeNode* root_;
};

class BinaryTreeNode {
public:
  // Public interface for BinaryTreeNode goes here
private:
  friend BinaryTree;  ◄────── BinaryTree can access BinaryTreeNode
  BinaryTreeNode* left_;
  BinaryTreeNode* right_;
};

ostream& operator<< (ostream& ostr, const BinaryTree& bt) throw()
{
  // This code can access bt.root_ (it's a friend of BinaryTree),
  // but not bt.root_->left_ (it's not a friend of BinaryTreeNode).
  return ostr;
}
```

If operator<< needs to access BinaryTreeNode::left_ or BinaryTreeNode::right_, it must be made a friend of BinaryTreeNode as well:

```
class BinaryTreeNode {
public:
  // Public interface for BinaryTreeNode goes here
private:
  friend BinaryTree;  ◄────── BinaryTree can access BinaryTreeNode
  friend ostream& operator<< (ostream&, const BinaryTree&) throw();
       ◄──────────────────────── operator<< can access BinaryTreeNode
  BinaryTreeNode* left_;
  BinaryTreeNode* right_;
};
```

Note that the compiler doesn't care where a friend declaration appears within a class, so the placement is normally done to make the code easily readable by other programmers (see FAQ 19.12). In the example, normal users might be somewhat confused by the friendship relationship between BinaryTreeNode and operator<<, so it has been moved out of the public: section (the public: section is where normal users look to find out how to use a class).

FAQ 19.09

What does it mean that friendship isn't inherited?

Just because someone trusts you does not automatically mean they will trust your children.

Suppose class Fred grants friendship privileges to another class Base and class Derived is derived from class Base. Derived does not automatically have friendship privileges to access the innards of Fred just because its base class is a friend of Fred. This rule improves encapsulation. Without this rule, anyone could automatically gain friendship (and access to internals) by deriving from a known friend.

```
class Base;

class Fred {
  friend Base;
};

class Base {
  //Member functions of Base are friends of Fred
};

class Derived : public Base {
  //Member functions of Derived are not friends of Fred
};
```

In the following example, an EggCarton is not supposed to have more than a dozen eggs (numEggs_ <= 12). Class EggCartonFiller is trusted not to violate the semantics of an EggCarton, so EggCarton makes EggCartonFiller a friend. This friendship allows EggCartonFiller::addAnEgg() to access EggCarton::numEggs_.

```
class EggCartonFiller;    // Tell the compiler that
                          // "EggCartonFiller" is a class

class EggCarton {
public:
```

```
    EggCarton() throw();    // Creates an empty carton
  private:
    friend EggCartonFiller;
    int numEggs_;           // numEggs_ can't exceed a dozen
};

EggCarton::EggCarton()
: numEggs_(0) { }

class EggCartonFiller {
public:
  void addAnEgg(EggCarton& carton) throw();
};

void EggCartonFiller::addAnEgg(EggCarton& carton) throw()
{
  if (carton.numEggs_ < 12)
    ++ carton.numEggs_;
}
```

If friendship were inherited, anyone could create a class derived from `EggCartonFiller` and possibly violate the semantics of an `EggCarton`.

```
class SubversiveFiller : public EggCartonFiller {
public:
  void violateEncapsulation(EggCarton& carton) throw();
};

void SubversiveFiller::violateEncapsulation(EggCarton& carton) throw()
{
  #ifdef GENERATE_ERROR
    carton.numEggs_ = 13;  ◄──── Compile-time error: Can't access carton.numEggs_
  #endif
}
```

FAQ 19.10

What does it mean that friends aren't virtual?

Friend functions don't bind dynamically. However there is a simple one-line idiom that enables the functionality of a virtual function (that is, dynamic binding) with the syntax of a friend function. This idiom is called the *virtual friend function idiom*.

The virtual friend function idiom provides the effect of friend functions that bind dynamically; it is used when the syntax of a friend function is desired but the operation must be dynamically bound.

Simply put, use a friend function that calls a `protected:` virtual member function. For example, suppose class `Shape` is an abstract base class (ABC), and a `Shape` is printed via `cout << aShape`, where `aShape` is a `Shape&`, which refers to an object of a derived class, such as `Circle`. To use the virtual friend function idiom, `operator<<` would be a friend of `Shape` and would call a `protected:` pure virtual member function such as `print(ostream&) const`.

```cpp
#include <iostream>
using namespace std;

class Shape {
public:
  virtual ~Shape() throw();
  friend ostream& operator<< (ostream& ostr, const Shape& s)
                             throw();
protected:
  virtual void print(ostream& ostr) const throw() = 0;
};

inline ostream& operator<< (ostream& ostr, const Shape& s)
                           throw()
{
  s.print(ostr);    ◄─────── The friend calls a protected: virtual
  return ostr;
}

Shape::~Shape() throw()
{ }
```

Because `print()` is virtual, the right implementation will always be invoked. Because `print()` is pure virtual, concrete derived classes are required to provide a definition—`Shape` doesn't have enough knowledge about itself to print itself.

```cpp
class Circle : public Shape {
public:
  Circle() throw();
protected:
  virtual void print(ostream& ostr) const throw();
                       ◄─────── Derived classes override the member, not the friend
  float radius_;
};

Circle::Circle() throw()
: radius_(42) { }

void Circle::print(ostream& ostr) const throw()
{ ostr << "Circle of radius " << radius_; }
```

Because `print()` is `protected:`, users must use the official syntax provided by `operator<<` (this avoids cluttering the interface with two ways of doing the same thing).

```
void userCode(Shape& s)
{ cout << s << '\n'; }  ◄─── Users use the friend, not the member

int main()
{
  Circle c;
  userCode(c);
}
```

The output is

```
Circle of radius 42
```

Note that there is only one `operator<<` for the entire `Shape` hierarchy. Derived classes provide a definition for `print(ostream&) const`, but they do not declare or define `operator<<`.

What qualities suggest a friend function rather than a member function?

The three P's of friendship: position, promotion, or perception.

Position: Use a friend function when the object being operated on can't appear as the leftmost argument. For example, the syntax to print an object n is usually `cout << n`, where `cout` can be replaced by any `ostream`. Notice that n is not the leftmost argument and therefore `operator<<` cannot be a member of n's class. If `operator<<` needs access to n's internal state, it must be a friend of n's class.

```
#include <iostream>
using namespace std;

class Fraction {
public:
  Fraction(int num=0, int denom=1) throw();
  friend ostream& operator<< (ostream& o, const Fraction& n)
                                throw();
protected:
```

```
    int num_, denom_;
};

Fraction::Fraction(int num, int denom) throw()
: num_    (num)
, denom_  (denom)
{ }

ostream& operator<< (ostream& o, const Fraction& n) throw()
{ return o << n.num_ << '/' << n.denom_; }

int main()
{
  Fraction n = Fraction(3,8);     // "3/8"
  cout << "n is " << n << '\n';
}
```

Promotion: Use a friend function to allow promotion of the leftmost argument. For example, the Fraction class might want to support 5*n, where n is a Fraction object. This may require promoting the leftmost argument from an int to a Fraction, where this is implemented by passing a single int parameter to Fraction's constructor—Fraction(5). The operator* needs to be a friend because C++ never automatically promotes the this object in a member function invocation.

```
#include <iostream>
using namespace std;

class Fraction {
public:
  Fraction(int num=0, int denom=1) throw();
  friend Fraction operator* (const Fraction& a,
                             const Fraction& b) throw();
protected:
  int num_, denom_;
};

Fraction::Fraction(int num, int denom) throw()
: num_(num), denom_(denom) { }

Fraction operator* (const Fraction& a, const Fraction& b)
                    throw()
{ return Fraction(a.num_*b.num_, a.denom_*b.denom_); }

int main()
{
  Fraction x = Fraction(3,8);        // "3/8"
  Fraction y = 5*x;
}
```

Perception: Use a friend function when it leads to a user syntax that is more intuitive. For example, two possible syntaxes for computing the square of a fraction n are n.square() and square(n) (for example, 1/2 squared is 1/4). If the operation is constructive (if n is unchanged), square(n) may be preferred because n.square() might be incorrectly perceived as squaring n itself.

```cpp
#include <iostream>
using namespace std;

class Fraction {
public:
  Fraction(int num=0, int denom=1) throw();
  friend Fraction square(const Fraction& n) throw();
protected:
  int num_, denom_;
};

Fraction::Fraction(int num, int denom) throw()
: num_(num), denom_(denom) { }

Fraction square(const Fraction& n) throw()
{ return Fraction(n.num_*n.num_, n.denom_*n.denom_); }

int main()
{
  Fraction x = Fraction(3,8);          // "3/8"
  Fraction y = square(x);
}
```

Of the three P's for choosing between friend functions and member functions, perception is the most subjective. In many cases involving perception, a static member function such as Fraction::square(n) is better than a friend function.

FAQ 19.12

Should friend functions be declared in the private:, protected:, or public: section of a class?

For documentation purposes, they should be declared in the public: section of a class. The compiler ignores the access level (private:, protected:, or public:) where friend functions are declared. However, for documentation purposes, they should normally be declared in the public: part of the class since friend functions are inherently `public`: (most friend functions are non-member functions and are therefore conceptually declared outside the class).

For an exception to this guideline, see FAQ 19.08.

FAQ 19.13

What is a private class?

A private class is a class created only for implementation purposes and is hidden from normal users. Typically, all its constructors (and often all its other members as well) are `private`: and it declares another class as its `friend`. Because the private class lacks `public`: constructors or member functions, only the designated `friends` and other instances of the private class can create or use instances of the private class.

For example, the `Node` class associated with a linked list class might be so specialized that no other class would benefit from reusing it. In this case the `Node` class can be a private class and can declare the linked list class as a `friend`. In the following code, class `Node` is nested inside class `List`. Although not strictly part of the private class concept, this technique has the further benefit of reducing the number of names in the outer namespace (nesting `Node` inside `List` removes the name `Node` from the namespace that `List` is in).

```
#include <new>
#include <cstdlib>
using namespace std;

class List {
public:
  List()                              throw();
  List(const List& a)                 throw(bad_alloc);
  ~List()                             throw();
  List& operator= (const List& a)  throw(bad_alloc);
  void prepend(int e)                 throw(bad_alloc);
  bool isEmpty() const                throw();
  void clear()                        throw();
private:
  class Node;  ◄──── The private class is called List::Node
  Node* first_;
};

class List::Node {
private: ◄─────── List::Node has no public: members
```

```
  friend List; ◄──── List::Node declares List as its friend
  Node(int e, Node* next=NULL) throw();
  Node* next_;
  int   elem_;
};
```

```
List::Node::Node(int e, Node* next) throw() : next_(next), elem_(e) { }
List::List()                    throw()     : first_(NULL) { }
List::List(const List& a)  throw(bad_alloc) : first_(NULL) { *this = a; }
List::~List()                   throw()     { clear(); }
void List::prepend(int e)  throw(bad_alloc) { first_ =
                                                new Node(e, first_); }
bool List::isEmpty() const throw()          { return first_ == NULL; }
```

```
int main()
{
  List a;
  a.prepend(4);
  a.prepend(3);
  a.prepend(2);
  List b;
  b = a;
}
```

FAQ 19.14

How are objects of a class printed?

Objects of a class are normally printed via a friend function called operator<<.
Here is an example of such a friend function.

```
#include <iostream>
using namespace std;

class Fred {
public:
  friend ostream& operator<< (ostream& ostr, const Fred& x) throw();
protected:
  int i_;
};

ostream& operator<< (ostream& ostr, const Fred& x) throw()
{
  ostr << x.i_;
```

```
    return ostr;
  }
```

The function `operator<<` is a friend rather than a member, so the `Fred` parameter appears on the right side of the `<<`.

FAQ 19.15

How do objects of a class receive stream input?

Objects of a class normally receive stream input via a friend function called `operator>>`. Here is an example of such a friend function.

```
#include <iostream>
using namespace std;

class Fred {
public:
  friend istream& operator>> (istream& istr, Fred& x) throw();
protected:
  int i_;
};

istream& operator>> (istream& istr, Fred& x) throw()
{
  istr >> x.i_;
  return istr;
}
```

The `Fred` argument of `operator>>` is passed by reference (as opposed to `const` reference). This allows `operator>>` to change the caller's `Fred`, which is, of course, the whole point of stream input.

Chapter 20

Constructors and Destructors

What is the purpose of a constructor?

The constructor turns a pile of incoherent, arbitrary bits into a living object. It initializes the object's internal data members, but it may also allocate resources (memory, files, semaphores, sockets, and so on). The word "ctor" is shorthand for the word "constructor."

The constructors for class X are member functions named X. Here is an example.

```
class Battery {
public:
  Battery(int initialCharge) throw();
  void drain() throw();
protected:
  int charge_;
};

Battery::Battery(int initialCharge) throw()
: charge_(initialCharge) { }

void Battery::drain() throw()
{
```

```
      charge_ -= 5;
      if (charge_ < 0)
        charge_ = 0;
    }

    int main()
    {
      Battery yourDiscountBattery(20); //A Battery object
      Battery myNameBrandBattery(30);  //Another Battery object
    }
```

There can be more than one constructor for a class. Each constructor has the same name, so the compiler uses their signatures to uniquely identify them.

FAQ 20.02 ─────────────────────────────

What is C++'s constructor discipline?

A constructor is automatically called at the moment an object is created.

Descartes said, "I think, therefore I am." The C++ variation of Descartes' statement is "I am, therefore I can think." In other words, every object that exists ("I am") has been initialized by one of the class's constructors ("I can think"). Except for pathological cases, by the time an object is accessible, it has already been initialized by its constructor.

The developers of a class provide a set of constructors that define how objects of that class can be initialized. When users create objects of that class, they must provide arguments that match the signature of one of the class's constructors. Constructors enhance encapsulation since they force users to create objects in one of the officially supported ways. Users cannot initialize an object's state directly, because this might place the object in an incoherent or illegal state.

In the example from the previous FAQ, the constructor for class `Battery` is the member function `Battery::Battery(int initialCharge)`. This constructor initializes the `protected:` data member `charge_` to the value passed as the parameter to the constructor. The constructor is called twice in `main()`, once when `yourDiscountBattery` is created and once when `myNameBrandBattery` is created.

FAQ 20.03

What is the purpose of a destructor?

The destructor is the last member function ever called for an object. The destructor's typical purpose is to release resources that the object is holding. The word "dtor" is shorthand for the word "destructor."

A class can have at most one destructor. For a class named X, the destructor is a member function named ~X().

Just as a constructor turns a pile of incoherent, arbitrary bits into a living object, a destructor turns a living object into a pile of incoherent, arbitrary bits. A destructor blows an object to bits.

FAQ 20.04

What is C++'s destructor discipline?

If the class of an object has a destructor, C++ guarantees that the destructor is called when the object dies. A local (auto) object dies at the close of the block ({...}) in which it was created (that is, when it is conceptually popped from the runtime stack). An unbound temporary object dies at the end of the outermost expression in which the temporary was generated (often this is at the next ;). A member object dies when its containing object dies. An array element dies when its array dies. An object allocated via new (dynamically) dies when the object is deleted. With a static object, death occurs sometime after main() finishes.

Everything but dynamically allocated objects (that is, local objects, temporary objects, member objects, static objects, and array elements) are destructed in the reverse order of construction: first constructed is last destructed. In the following example, b's destructor is executed first, then a's destructor.

```
void sample() throw()
{
  Fred a;
  Fred b;
  // ...
}
```

Warning: Do not use longjmp with C++ because it subverts the guarantee that destructors will be called.

FAQ 20.05

What happens when a destructor is executed?

The destructor automatically calls the destructors for all member objects and all immediate nonvirtual base classes. First, the destructor's body ({ . . . }) is executed, then the destructors for member objects are called in the reverse order that the member objects appear in the class body, then the destructors for immediate base classes are called (in the reverse order they appear in the class declaration). Virtual base classes are special— their destructors are called at the end of the most derived class's destructor (only).

For example, suppose lock(int) and unlock(int) provide the primitives to manage mutual exclusion. The C++ interface to these primitives would be a Lock class, whose constructor calls lock(int) and whose destructor calls unlock(int).

```cpp
#include <iostream>
using namespace std;

void lock(int i) throw()
{
  cout << "pretend we acquire lock #" << i << '\n';
  //In reality, this would manipulate semaphore #i
  // (or use some other mutual exclusion primitive)
}


void unlock(int i) throw()
{
  cout << "pretend we release lock #" << i << '\n';
  //In reality, this would manipulate semaphore #i
  // (or use some other mutual exclusion primitive)
}


class Lock {
public:
  Lock(int lockNum) throw();
  ~Lock()                throw();
protected:
  int lockNum_;
private:
  // These are never defined (copying a Lock is senseless)
  Lock(const Lock&);
  Lock& operator= (const Lock&);
};
```

```
inline Lock::Lock(int lockNum) throw()
: lockNum_(lockNum) { lock(lockNum_); }

inline Lock::~Lock() throw()
{ unlock(lockNum_); }

void multiThreadedFunction() throw()
{
  cout << "no mutual exclusion here\n";
  {
    Lock lock(42);    //Pretend this is Critical section (42)
    cout << "lock provides mutual exclusion here\n";
  }

  cout << "no mutual exclusion here\n";
}
```

A whimsical developer might rename class Lock to class Critical, so that if the user code declared an object named section, Lock lock(42) would then become Critical section(42). But regardless of the names of the class and its object, the important point is that there is no need to explicitly unlock the semaphore. This eliminates a potential (and dangerous!) source of errors.

FAQ 20.06

What is the purpose of a copy constructor?

It initializes an object by copying the state from another object of the same class.

Whenever an object is copied, another object (the copy) is created, so a constructor is called (see FAQ 20.02). This constructor is called the copy constructor. If the class of the object being copied is X, the copy constructor's signature is usually X::X(const X&).

One way to pronounce X(const X&) is *X-X-ref* (pretend the const is silent). The first X refers to the name of the member function, and the X-ref refers to the type of the parameter. Some people prefer the shorthand X-X-ref to the phrase copy constructor.

In the following example, the copy constructor is MyString:: MyString(const MyString&). Notice how it initializes the new MyString object to be a copy of the source MyString object.

```
#include <new>
#include <cstring>
using namespace std;
```

```
class MyString {
public:
  MyString(const char* s) throw(bad_alloc);        ←—ctor to promote a const char*
  MyString(const MyString& source) throw(bad_alloc);  ←—Copy constructor
  ~MyString() throw();  ←————————————————————————————————Destructor
  MyString& operator= (const MyString& s)
                       throw(bad_alloc);  ←——————————— Assignment operator
protected:
  unsigned len_;    // ORDER DEPENDENCY; see FAQ 22.10
  char*    data_;
};

MyString::MyString(const char* s) throw(bad_alloc)
: len_(strlen(s))
, data_(new char[len_+1])
{ memcpy(data_, s, len_+1); }

MyString::MyString(const MyString& source) throw(bad_alloc)
: len_(source.len_)
, data_(new char[source.len_+1])
{ memcpy(data_, source.data_, len_+1); }

MyString::~MyString() throw()
{ delete[] data_; }

int main()
{
  MyString a = "xyzzy"; //Calls MyString::MyString(const char*)
  MyString b = a;        //Calls MyString::MyString(const MyString&)
}
```

FAQ 20.07

When is a copy constructor invoked?

When an object is passed by value, returned by value, or explicitly copied. Here is an example showing all three situations.

```
#include <iostream>
using namespace std;

class X {
public:
```

```
   X()            throw();
   X(const X&) throw();
};

X::X()           throw() { cout << "default constructor\n"; }
X::X(const X&) throw() { cout << "copy constructor\n";      }

X userCode(X b) throw()  ◄───── Pass by value: Copy main()'s a to b
{
   X c = b;  ◄──────────────── Explicit copy: Copy from b to c
   return c;
}  ◄──────────────────────── Return by value: Copy from c to main()'s d

int main()
{
   X a;
   cout << "calling userCode()\n";
   X d = userCode(a);
   cout << "back in main()\n";
}
```

The (annotated) output of this program is

```
default constructor ◄──────── main()'s a
calling userCode()
copy constructor ◄─────────── userCode()'s b
copy constructor ◄─────────── userCode()'s c
copy constructor ◄─────────── main()'s d
back in main()
```

Note that pass-by-value calls the copy constructor if the caller supplies another object of the same class. Supplying something else may invoke a different constructor. Similar comments apply to return-by-value.

FAQ 20.08

What is the "default constructor"?

It's the constructor that can be called with no arguments.

For a class Fred, the default constructor is often simply Fred::Fred(), since certainly that can be called (and in this case, must be called) with no arguments. However it is possible (and even likely) for a default constructor to take arguments, provided they are given default values.

```
class Fred {
public:
  Fred(int i=3, int j=5) throw();  ◄──────── Default constructor:
                                              Can be called with no args

  // ...
};
```

In either case, the default constructor is called when an object is created without any initializers. For example, object x is created by calling Fred::Fred(int,int) with defaulted arguments (3,5).

```
void sample() throw()
{
  Fred x;  ◄─────────────────────── Calls the default constructor
  Fred y(3,5);  ◄────────────────── Same effect as with object x
  // ...
}
```

Similarly the default constructor (in this case, including the defaulted parameters) is called for each element of an array. For example, each element of array a and vector b (see FAQ 28.13) is initialized by calling Fred::Fred(int,int) and passing the defaulted arguments (3,5). However, vectors are more powerful than arrays, since vectors can use something other than the default constructor when initializing the array elements (an especially important feature for those classes that don't have a default constructor). For example, the 10 elements of vector c are initialized with Fred(7,9) rather than the default choice of Fred(3,5):

```
#include <new>
#include <vector>
using namespace std;

void sample2() throw(bad_alloc)
{
  Fred a[10];  ◄────────────────────── Arrays use the contained object's default ctor
  vector<Fred> b(10);  ◄────────────── vector can use the contained object's default ctor
  vector<Fred> c(10, Fred(7,9));  ◄─── vector doesn't have to use the default ctor
}
```

Note that adding an empty pair of parentheses after a declaration is not the same as calling the default constructor. In the following example, x is an object of class Fred, but y is declared to be a function that returns a Fred by value; y is *not* a Fred object.

```
void sample3() throw()
{
  Fred x;    ←──────────── Creates an object
  Fred y();  ←──────────── Declares a function; does not create a Fred object
  // ...
}
```

Should one constructor call another constructor as a primitive?

No. Even though it is possible, it won't do what the programmer wants.

Dragons be here: if a constructor of class `Fred` calls another constructor of class `Fred`, the compiler actually initializes a temporary local object of class `Fred`. It does *not* use the call to initialize the `this` object.

Both constructors can be combined by using a default parameter or their common code can be shared in a `private: init()` member function, but one constructor should not directly call another constructor. Here is an example of an `init()` function.

```
class Fred {
public:
  Fred(int x)   throw();
  Fred(float y) throw();
  Fred(char* z) throw();
  // ...
private:
  void init(int x, float y, char* z) throw();
  // ...
};

inline Fred::Fred(int x)   throw() { init(x, 0.3, NULL); }
inline Fred::Fred(float y) throw() { init(-1, y, "foo"); }
inline Fred::Fred(char* z) throw() { init(-2, 5.2, z);   }

void Fred::init(int x, float y, char* z) throw()
{
  // ...
}
```

FAQ 20.10

Does the destructor for a derived class need to explicitly call the destructor of its base class?

No. The runtime system calls the destructor for the base class after the destructor for the derived class finishes executing.

Never call a destructor explicitly. The only exception to this is the fairly esoteric case of destructing an object that was initialized by the placement new operator (see FAQ 12.14).

FAQ 20.11

How can a local object be destructed before the end of its function?

The most important message is to *not* explicitly call a local object's destructor. The language guarantees that the object's destructor will be called again at the close of the scope in which the local was created (see FAQ 20.04). So if the destructor is called explicitly, it will be called again at the close of the scope, which can have disastrous results. Bang; you're dead.

The easiest way to make sure a local object is destructed before the end of its scope is to insert a pair of braces (that is, a new scope) so that the object will be destructed at the right time. For example, suppose the (desirable) side effect of destructing a local `File` object is to close the `File`. Now suppose a local `File` object needs to be closed before the end of the scope (i.e., the `}`) of its function. In this case simply add an extra pair of braces to scope the lifetime of the object:

```
void sample()
{
  // ...

    {  ←————————————— Added to limit the scope of File x
      File x;
      // ...  ←——————— This code will execute while File x is still open
      // ...
    }  ←——————————————— File x will close here

  // ...  ←——————————— This code will execute after File x is closed
}
```

In cases where this extra pair of braces cannot be added, add an extra member function that causes the destructor's desirable side effects to occur. This member function should mark the object so that the destructor, which will inevitably be called at the close of the object's scope, will be able to tell if the side effects have already happened. For example, a `close()` member function could be added to the `File` class, and that member function could be called where the file should be closed:

```
void sample()
{
  // ...

  File x;
  // ...  ←——————— This code will execute while File x is still open

  x.close();  ←——— File x will close here

  // ...  ←——————— This code will execute after File x is closed
}
```

The `close()` member function could mark the object so the destructor knows not to reclose the file, such as setting the underlying file handle to some invalid value such as `-1`. To avoid duplication of code in the destructor and the `close()` member function, the destructor could simply call the `close()` member function, and the `close()` member function could check to see if the file handle is in the "already closed" state.

```
#include <iostream>
#include <stdexcept>
using namespace std;

int openFile(const char* name) throw()
{
  // Normally this code would actually open the named file.
  // For this example, we pretend everything is handle 42.
  int handle = 42;
  cout << "opening " << name << " as #" << handle << '\n';
  return handle;
}

void closeFile(int handle) throw()
{
  // Normally this code would actually close the file
  cout << "closing file #" << handle << '\n';
}

class File {
public:
```

```
      File(const char* name) throw();
      ~File() throw();
      void close() throw();
  protected:
      enum { closed_ = -1 }; ←——— File::closed_ is a constant
      int handle_;
  private:
      // These are never defined; copy semantics are ill defined
      File(const File&);
      File& operator= (const File&);
  };

  inline void File::close()
  {
      if (handle_ != closed_) closeFile(handle_);
      handle_ = closed_;
  }

  inline File::File(const char* name) throw()
  : handle_( openFile(name) ) { }

  inline File::~File() throw()
  { close(); }

  void userCode(bool throwIt) throw(runtime_error)
  {
      File x("sample.txt");
      cout << "after open, before throw-or-close\n";
      if (throwIt)
          throw runtime_error("note that the file still gets closed!");
      x.close();
      cout << "after close\n";
  }

  int main()
  {
      cout << "====== without throwing an exception ======\n";
      userCode(false);

      cout << "====== with throwing an exception ========\n";
      try {
          userCode(true);
      }
      catch (exception& e) {
          cout << "exception caught; " << e.what() << '\n';
      }
  }
```

The output of this program follows.

```
====== without throwing an exception ======
opening sample.txt as #42
after open, before throw-or-close
closing file #42
after close
====== with throwing an exception ========
opening sample.txt as #42
after open, before throw-or-close
closing file #42
exception caught; note that the file still gets closed!
```

It is important to note that `closeFile()` is called exactly once per open file, whether or not an exception is thrown or the `x.close()` instruction is reached. Even if `x.close()` were explicitly called twice, the underlying file would only be closed once.

FAQ 20.12

What is a good way to provide intuitive, multiple constructors for a class?

Use the named constructor idiom.

Constructors always have the same name as the class, so the only way to differentiate between the various constructors of a class is by the parameter list. If there are numerous overloaded constructors, the differences can become somewhat subtle and subject to error.

With the *named constructor idiom,* all the constructors are declared as `private:` or `protected:`, and the class provides `public: static` member functions that return an object. These `static` member functions are the so-called named constructors. In general there is one such `static` member function for each different way to construct an object.

For example, consider a `Point` class that represents a position on a plane. There are two different constructors corresponding to the two common ways to specify a point on a plane: rectangular coordinates (X and Y) and polar coordinates (radius and angle). Unfortunately the parameters for these two coordinate systems are the same (two numbers), so the overloaded constructors would be ambiguous. For example, if someone created a point using `Point(5.7, 1.2)`, the compiler wouldn't know which coordinate system (that is, which constructor) to use.

One way to solve this ambiguity is to use the named constructor idiom:

```
#include <cmath> // To get sin() and cos()
#include <iostream>
using namespace std;

class Point {
public:
  static Point rectangular(float x, float y) throw();
  // Rectangular coordinates
  static Point polar(float radius, float angle) throw();
  // Polar coordinates
  // These static members are the so-called named constructors
  // ...
private:
  Point(float x, float y) throw();  // Rectangular coordinates
  float x_, y_;
};

inline Point::Point(float x, float y) throw()
: x_(x), y_(y) { }

inline Point Point::rectangular(float x, float y) throw()
{ return Point(x, y); }

inline Point Point::polar(float radius, float angle) throw()
{ return Point(radius*cos(angle), radius*sin(angle)); }
```

Now the users of `Point` have a clear and unambiguous syntax for creating `Point`s in either coordinate system:

```
int main()
{
  Point a = Point::rectangular(5.7, 1.2); // Obviously rectangular
  Point b = Point::polar(5.7, 1.2);       // Obviously polar
}
```

Note that the constructor(s) must be in the `protected:` section, not the `private:` section, if the class will have derived classes.

The Named Constructor Idiom can also be used to make sure objects are always created via new. In this case the `public: static` member functions (the named constructors) should allocate the object via new and should return a pointer to the allocated object.

FAQ 20.13

When the constructor of a base class calls a virtual function, why isn't the override called?

C++ is ensuring that member objects are initialized before they are used.

Objects of a derived class mature during construction. While the base class's constructor is executing, the object is merely a base class object. Later, when the derived class's constructor begins executing, the object matures into a derived class object. If a virtual function is invoked while the object is still immature, the immature version of the virtual function is called. It may sound confusing, but it's the only sensible way to do it without having across-the-board reference semantics.

For example, suppose class `Derived` overrides an inherited virtual function `f()`, and `Base::Base()` calls `f()`. Since the object is a `Base` during the execution of `Base::Base()`, `Base::f()` is invoked. If C++ allowed `Base::Base()` to call `Derived::f()`, `Derived::f()` might invoke member functions on a member object that had not yet been constructed!

```
#include <iostream>
using namespace std;

class MemberObject {
public:
  MemberObject()       throw();
  void doSomething() throw();
};

MemberObject::MemberObject()       throw()
{ cout << "MemberObject ctor\n"; }
void MemberObject::doSomething() throw()
{ cout << "MemberObject used\n"; }

class Base {
public:
  Base()               throw();
  virtual void f() throw();
};

Base::Base()   throw() { cout << "Base ctor\n"; f(); }
void Base::f() throw() { cout << "Base::f()\n"; }

class Derived : public Base {
public:
```

```
    Derived()          throw();
    virtual void f() throw();
protected:
    MemberObject m_;
};

Derived::Derived() throw()
: Base(), m_() { cout << "Derived ctor\n"; }
void Derived::f()   throw()
{ cout << "Derived::f()\n"; m_.doSomething(); }

int main()
{
    Derived d;
    cout << "====\n";
    d.f();
}
```

The output of this program follows.

```
Base ctor
Base::f()
MemberObject ctor
Derived ctor
====
Derived::f()
MemberObject used
```

If C++ allowed `Base::Base()` to call `Derived::f()`, `m_.fred()` would be called before `m_` was constructed.

C++ programmers need to be aware that Java does things quite differently, and therefore Java has a completely different problem. In Java, the derived class's override *does* get called when the base class's constructor invokes a method. This means that the derived class's override cannot assume that the derived class's constructor was run before the member function is called, so member variables that the derived class's constructor sets to some non-null state may in fact still be null when the override is called.

Neither the C++ approach nor the Java approach is a clear winner in terms of being intuitive and lacking surprises. So the most important point is to understand the differences and be prepared for a learning curve when moving between the two languages.

FAQ 20.14

When a base class destructor calls a virtual function, why isn't the override called?

C++ is helping ensure that member objects are not used after destruction.

Just as an object of a derived class matures into a derived class object during construction, it reverts back into a base class object during destruction.

Extending the example from the previous FAQ, if `Base::~Base()` calls `f()`, `Base::f()` is invoked (rather than `Derived::f()`) because the object has already reverted to a mere `Base`.

This is the right thing to do. If `Base::~Base()` could call `Derived::f()`, the destructed `MemberObject` would be used, leading to unpredictable results.

Many people don't think that this rule is intuitively obvious, either. Once again, it is an issue of reference semantics versus value semantics, and C++ was designed to maximize compatibility with C. And once again, Java does things differently, which causes its own set of problems.

FAQ 20.15

What is the purpose of placement `new`?

It's a way to pass parameters to the allocator rather than just to the constructor.

Allocating an object from the heap, such as `new Fred(5,7)`, is a two-step process: first an appropriately sized and aligned block of uninitialized memory is allocated from the heap, then the constructor is called with the `this` pointer pointing to that block of memory. Parameters are often passed to the constructor (for example, the above example passes `(5,7)`), but occasionally parameters also must be passed to the allocation step. For example, if there was a special allocator that used a particular pool of memory, it might be necessary to pass a reference to that pool of memory to the allocation step, that is, to new itself: `new(myPool) Fred(5,7)`.

Another common reason to pass a parameter for the allocation step is to pass a pointer to a particular preallocated region of memory. For example, if pointer p is a `void*` that points to a pile of memory that is at least `sizeof(Fred)` bytes long and is appropriately aligned, one could say `new(p) Fred(5,7)`. This would construct a Fred object at the location pointed to by p (that is, it would pass p as the `this` pointer to Fred's constructor) and would ultimately return a Fred* that would point to the same location that void* p points to. For example,

```
#include <new>        // Must #include this to use placement new
using namespace std;
#include "Fred.hpp" // Declaration of class Fred

void sample() throw()
{
  char memory[sizeof(Fred)];   // Line 1
  void* p = memory;            // Line 2
  Fred* f = new(p) Fred();     // Line 3 (be careful here!)
  // The pointers f and p will be equal
  // ...
}
```

Line 1 creates an array of sizeof(Fred) bytes of memory, which is big enough to hold a Fred object. Line 2 creates a pointer p that points to the first byte of this memory (experienced C programmers will note that this step is unnecessary; it's there only to make the code more obvious). Line 3 essentially calls the constructor Fred::Fred(). The this pointer in the Fred constructor is equal to p. The returned pointer f is equal to p.

Passing a void* pointer with the placement new syntax should be used only when it is essential to place an object at a particular location. For example, when writing an operating system, the placement new syntax could be used to place a Clock object at a particular memory-mapped I/O timer device. Neither the compiler nor the runtime system make any attempt to check whether the passed pointer points to a region of memory that is big enough and is properly aligned for the object being created. For example, if Fred objects need to be aligned on a 4-byte boundary but the supplied pointer p isn't properly aligned, it could be a serious (and subtle) disaster. You have been warned.

Also, the programmer takes sole responsibility to deallocate the object when the placement new syntax is used. This is done by explicitly calling the destructor, which is one of the few times a destructor should be called explicitly:

```
void sample2() throw()
{
  char memory[sizeof(Fred)];
  void* p = memory;
  Fred* f = new(p) Fred();
  // ...
  f->~Fred();  ◄──────  Explicitly call the destructor for the placed object
}
```

Chapter 21

Virtual Functions

What is the purpose of this chapter?

This chapter describes the syntax and semantics of virtual functions, which are the way C++ does dynamic binding. Part II discusses dynamic binding and should be read before this chapter. Dynamic binding is an important concept, and most member functions should be virtual unless there is some compelling performance reason not to make them virtual or unless the programmer intentionally makes the member function a *leaf* (also known as *final*) member function (see FAQ 33.10).

new

What is a virtual member function?

A virtual member function is a member function preceded by the keyword `virtual` or a member function with the same signature as a virtual function declared in a base class.

In this context, `virtual` means "overridable." More specifically, the keyword `virtual` means that the runtime system automatically invokes the proper member function when it is overridden by a derived class (dynamic binding).

A member function should be made virtual when there will be derived classes that will need to provide their own implementation for the member function. This doesn't require as much clairvoyance as it seems to imply. Normally the virtual functions represent specifically architected places where extensibility is supposed to take place.

Overriding a virtual member function is also straightforward: simply declare the member function in the derived class and define a new implementation for that member function.

FAQ 21.03

How much does it cost to call a virtual function compared to calling a normal function?

In theory, the overhead of dynamic binding is highly dependent on the compiler, operating system, and machine. In practice, almost all compilers do it the same way, and the overhead is very small.

A virtual function call typically costs 10% to 20% more than a nonvirtual function call. The overhead is smaller if there are several parameters, since the dynamic binding part of a virtual function call has constant cost. In practice, the overhead for the linkage of a function call is usually a very small percentage of the cost of the work that gets done, so the cost for a virtual function call is about the same as the cost for a normal function call.

For example, if a system or application spends 5% of its CPU utilization performing the linkage for function calls, and 25% of those calls are converted to virtual function calls, the additional overhead will be 10% of 25% of 5%, or around one-tenth of one percent overall.

If you can afford a normal function call, you can almost always afford a virtual function call.

FAQ 21.04

How does C++ perform static typing while supporting dynamic binding?

Static typing ensures that all declarations, definitions, and uses of a virtual function are consistent while dynamic binding provides the "plumbing" so that the right implementation is called at runtime.

Given a reference (or pointer) to an object, there are two distinct types in question: the static type of the reference and the dynamic type of the referent (that is, the object being referred to). In other words, the object may be an instance of a class that is derived from the class of the reference. Nonvirtual (statically bound) member functions are selected based on the (statically known) type of the reference. Virtual (dynamically bound) member functions are selected based on the (dynamically known) type of the referent.

The legality of the call is checked based on the (statically known) type of the reference or pointer. This is safe because the referent must be "at least as derived as" the type of the reference. This provides the following type safety guarantee: if the class of the reference has the indicated member function, then the class of the referent will as well.

FAQ 21.05

Can destructors be virtual?

Yes, many destructors should be virtual.

Virtual destructors are extremely valuable when some derived classes have specified cleanup code. A practical, easy-to-remember guideline: if a class has any virtual functions, it should have a virtual destructor. The rationale for this is that if a class has no virtual functions, chances are the class designer wasn't planning on the class being used as a base class, so a virtual destructor is unnecessary.

Furthermore, on most compilers there is no additional per-object space cost after the first virtual function, so there is very little reason not to make the destructor virtual if the class already has at least one virtual function.

Note that this guideline is not precise enough for every circumstance, but the precise rule is much harder to remember. Here is the more precise rule: if any derived class (or any data member and/or base class of any derived class, or any base class of any data member of any data member of any derived class, or any data member of any base class of any data member of any derived class and all other recursive combinations of base classes and data members) has (or will ever have) a nontrivial destructor, and if any code anywhere deletes (or will ever delete) that derived class object via a base class pointer, then the base class's destructor needs to be virtual.

FAQ 21.06

What is the purpose of a virtual destructor?

A virtual destructor causes the compiler to use dynamic binding when calling the destructor.

A destructor is called whenever an object is deleted, but there are some cases when the user code doesn't know *which* destructor should be called. For example, in the following situation, while compiling `unawareOfDerived(Base*)`, the compiler doesn't even know that `Derived` exists, much less that the pointer `base` may actually be pointing at a `Derived`.

```
#include <iostream>
using namespace std;

class Base {
public:
  ~Base() throw();  ◄────── Should be virtual but is not
};

Base::~Base() throw()
{ cout << "Base destructor\n"; }

void unawareOfDerived(Base* base)
{ delete base; }

class Derived : public Base {
public:
  ~Derived() throw();
};

Derived::~Derived() throw()
{ cout << "Derived destructor\n"; }

int main()
{
  Base* base = new Derived();
  unawareOfDerived(base);
}
```

Because `Base::~Base()` is nonvirtual, only `Base::~Base()` is executed and the `Derived` destructor will not run. This could be a very serious error, especially if the `Derived` destructor is supposed to release some precious resource such as closing a shared file or unlocking a semaphore.

The solution is to put the `virtual` keyword in front of `Base`'s destructor. Once that is done, the compiler dynamically binds to the destructor, and thus the right destructor is always called:

```
class Base {
public:
  virtual ~Base();
};
```

What is a virtual constructor?

The `virtual` keyword cannot be applied to a constructor since a constructor turns raw bits into a living object, and until there is a living object against which to invoke a member function, the member function cannot possibly work correctly. Instead of thinking of constructors as normal member functions on the object, imagine that they are static member functions (see FAQ 16.05) that create objects.

Even though constructors cannot actually be `virtual`, a very simple idiom can be used to have the same effect. This idiom, called the *virtual constructor idiom*, allows the creation of an object without specifying the object's exact type. For example, a base class can have a virtual `clone() const` member function (for creating a new object of the same class and for copying the state of the object, just like the copy constructor would do) or a virtual `createSimilar() const` member function (for creating a new object of the same class, just as the default constructor would do).

Following is an example of this idiom (the return type is an `auto_ptr` to help prevent memory leaks and wild pointers; see FAQ 32.01).

```cpp
#include <new>
#include <memory>
#include <iostream>
using namespace std;

class Shape;
typedef auto_ptr<Shape>   ShapePtr;

class Shape {
public:
            Shape()                              throw();
  virtual ~Shape()                               throw();
  virtual void draw() const                      throw() = 0;
  virtual ShapePtr clone() const                 throw(bad_alloc) = 0;
  virtual ShapePtr createSimilar() const throw(bad_alloc) = 0;
};

Shape::Shape()  throw() { }
Shape::~Shape() throw() { }

class Circle : public Shape {
public:
  Circle(int radius=0)                           throw();
```

```
  virtual void draw() const            throw();
  virtual ShapePtr clone() const       throw(bad_alloc);
  virtual ShapePtr createSimilar() const throw(bad_alloc);
protected:
  int radius_;
};

Circle::Circle(int radius) throw()
: Shape(), radius_(radius) { }

void Circle::draw() const throw()
{ cout << "Circle: radius=" << radius_ << '\n'; }

ShapePtr Circle::createSimilar() const throw(bad_alloc)
{ return new Circle(); }

ShapePtr Circle::clone() const throw(bad_alloc)
{ return new Circle(*this); }
```

In `Circle::createSimilar() const` and `Circle::clone() const`, the kind-of relationship allows the conversion from a `Circle*` to a `Shape*`, then the `Shape*` is converted to an `auto_ptr<Shape>` (that is, to a `ShapePtr`) by the `auto_ptr`'s constructor. In `Circle::clone() const`, the expression `new Circle(*this)` calls `Circle`'s copy constructor, since `*this` has type `const Circle&` inside a `const` member function of class `Circle`.

Users can use `clone` and/or `createSimilar` as if they were virtual constructors. An example follows.

```
void userCode(ShapePtr s) throw()
{
  cout << "userCode() number 1: ";
  s->draw();

  ShapePtr copy = s->clone();
  cout << "userCode() number 2: ";
  copy->draw();

  ShapePtr similar = s->createSimilar();
  cout << "userCode() number 3: ";
  similar->draw();
}  ◄────── copy and similar are automatically deleted here (see FAQ 2.07)

int main()
{
  ShapePtr c(new Circle(42));
  cout << "main() number 1: ";
  c->draw();
```

```
    userCode(c);
      ◄─────── Because of auto_ptr's copy semantics, c will be NULL here (see FAQ 2.11)
}
```

The output of this program follows.

```
main() number 1: Circle: radius=42
userCode() number 1: Circle: radius=42
userCode() number 2: Circle: radius=42
userCode() number 3: Circle: radius=0
```

FAQ 21.08

What syntax should be used when a constructor or destructor calls a virtual function in its object?

Use the scope operator, ::.

new

For example, if a constructor or a destructor of class `Base` calls a virtual function `this->f()`, it should call it using `Base::f()` rather than merely `f()`.

In our experience, this guideline reduces the probability that misunderstandings will introduce subtle defects, since it forces developers to explicitly state what the compiler is obliged to do anyway. In particular, when a constructor invokes a virtual member function that is attached to `this` object, the language guarantees that the member function that is invoked is the one associated with the class of the constructor, even if the object being constructed will eventually be an object of a derived class that has its own version of the virtual function. An analogous statement can be made for calling a virtual function from a destructor.

```
#include <iostream>
using namespace std;

class Base {
public:
  Base() throw();
  virtual void f() throw();
  virtual ~Base() throw();
};

Base::Base() throw()
{
  cout << " Base::Base() calling f()\n";
  f();  ◄─────── For clarity, this should be written Base::f();
}
```

```
void Base::f() throw()
{ cout << "  Base::f()\n"; }

Base::~Base()
{ }

class Derived : public Base {
public:
  Derived() throw();
  virtual void f() throw();
};

Derived::Derived() throw()
: Base()
{
  cout << " Derived::Derived() calling f()\n";
  f();   ◄──────── For clarity, this should be written Derived::f();
}

void Derived::f() throw()
{ cout << "  Derived::f()\n"; }

int main()
{
  cout << "Creating a Derived:\n";
  Derived d;
}
```

The initialization list of `Derived::Derived()` calls `Base::Base()`, even if `Base()` isn't explicitly specified in the initialization list. During `Base::Base()`, the object is merely a `Base` object, even though it will eventually be a `Derived` object (see FAQ 20.14). This is why `Base::f()` is called from the body of `Base::Base()`. During the body of `Derived::Derived()`, however, `Derived::f()` is called. The output of this program is as follows.

```
Creating a Derived:
 Base::Base() calling f()
  Base::f()
 Derived::Derived() calling f()
  Derived::f()
```

Since developers are often somewhat surprised by this language feature, we recommend that such calls should be explicitly qualified with the scope operator, `::`.

FAQ 21.09

Should the scope operator : : be used when invoking virtual member functions?

Only from derived classes, constructors, or destructors.

The purpose of the scope operator is to bypass the dynamic binding mechanism. Because dynamic binding is so important to users, user code should generally avoid using : :. For example, the following prints Base::f() even though the object is really a Derived.

```
#include <iostream>
using namespace std;

class Base {
public:
  virtual void f() throw();
  virtual ~Base()  throw();
};

void Base::f() throw() { cout << "Base::f()\n"; }
Base::~Base()  throw() { }

class Derived : public Base {
public:
  virtual void f() throw();
};

void Derived::f() throw() { cout << "Derived::f()\n"; }

int main()
{
  Derived d;
  d.Base::f(); ◄——— Legal but dubious
  d.f(); ◄——————— Generally this is better for nonstatic member functions called from user code
}
```

FAQ 21.10

What is a pure virtual member function?

A pure virtual member function is a member function that the base class forces derived classes to provide. Normally these member functions have no implementation; but see FAQ 21.11.

A pure virtual member function specifies that a member function will exist on every object of a concrete derived class even though the member function is not (normally) defined in the base class. This is because the syntax for specifying a pure virtual member function forces derived classes to implement the member function if the derived classes intend to be instantiated (that is, if they intend to be concrete).

For example, all objects of classes derived from `Shape` will have the member function `draw()`. However, because `Shape` is an abstract concept, it does not contain enough information to implement `draw()`. Thus `draw()` should be a pure virtual member function in `Shape`.

```
class Shape {
public:
  virtual void draw() = 0;
};
```

This pure virtual function makes `Shape` an abstract base class (ABC). Imagine that the "= 0" is like saying "the code for this function is at the NULL pointer."

Pure virtual member functions allow users to write code against an interface for which there are several functionally different variants. This means that semantically different objects can be passed to a function if these objects are all under the umbrella of the same abstract base class.

FAQ 21.11

Can a pure virtual function be defined in the same class that declares it?

Yes, but new C++ programmers don't usually understand what it means, so this practice should be avoided if the organization rotates developers.

If the goal is to create a member function that will be invoked only by derived classes (such as sharing common code in the abstract base class), create a `protected:` non-virtual function instead of using this feature. If the goal is to make something that may be callable from user code, create a distinctly named member function so that users aren't forced to use the scope operator, `::`.

The exception to this guideline is a pure virtual destructor in an ABC (see FAQ 21.13).

How should a virtual destructor be defined when it has no code?

It should normally be defined as an `inline` virtual function. An example follows.

```cpp
#include <iostream>
using namespace std;

class Base {
public:
  virtual void f() throw();
  virtual void g() throw();
  virtual ~Base()  throw();
};

void Base::f() throw() { cout << "Base::f()\n"; }
void Base::g() throw() { cout << "Base::g()\n"; }
inline Base::~Base()  throw() { }

class Derived : public Base {
public:
  virtual void f() throw();
};

void Derived::f() throw() { cout << "Derived::f()\n";  }

int main()
{
  Base b;  ◄──────  OK: Base is not an ABC
  b.f();
  b.g();

  Derived d;
  d.f();
  d.g();
}
```

The reason `Base::~Base()` is inline is to avoid an unnecessary function call when `Derived::~Derived()` automatically calls `Base::~Base()` (see FAQ 20.05). In this case, `Derived::~Derived()` is synthesized by the compiler.

FAQ 21.13

Can an ABC have a pure virtual destructor?

Yes, provided the ABC (abstract base class) gives an explicit definition elsewhere. An example follows.

```
class Base {
public:
  Base() throw();
  virtual ~Base() throw() = 0;
};

inline Base::Base()  throw() { }
inline Base::~Base() throw() { }  ◄——— Defined even though pure virtual

class Derived : public Base {
public:
  Derived() throw();
};

Derived::Derived() throw() : Base() { }

int main()
{ Derived d; }
```

Leaving out a definition for `Base::~Base()` will cause a linker error, because `Derived::~Derived()` automatically calls `Base::~Base()` (see FAQ 20.05). In this case, `Derived::~Derived()` is synthesized by the compiler.

Depending on the compiler, there may be a marginal performance benefit in using a pure virtual destructor with an explicit inline definition versus the inline virtual technique that was described in the previous FAQ. Calls to inline virtual functions can be inlined if the compiler is able to statically bind to the class. However, the compiler may also make an outlined copy of an inline virtual function (for any other cases where it isn't able to statically bind to the call). Although in theory destructors of ABCs don't have these limitations, in practice not all compilers produce optimal code when using the inline virtual technique.

FAQ 21.14

How can the compiler be kept from generating duplicate out-lined copies of inline virtual functions?

If a class has one or more virtual functions (either inherited or first-declared in that class), then the class should have at least one non-inline virtual function.

Many compilers use the location of the first non-inline virtual function to determine the source file that will house the class's magical stuff (the virtual table, out-lined copies of inline virtual functions, and so on). If all of the class's virtual functions are defined inline, these compilers may put a static copy of a class's magical stuff in every source file that includes the class's header file.

  Note that this advice is fairly sensitive to the compiler. Some compilers won't generate copies of the magical stuff even if all the virtual functions in a class are inline. But even in these compilers, it doesn't cost much to ensure that at least one of the class's virtual functions is non-inline.

FAQ 21.15

Should a class with virtual functions have at least one non-inline virtual function?

It is a good idea.

If the base class has a virtual destructor, the destructor in the derived class will also be virtual, and, unless specified otherwise, will be inline.

  The safest bet is to give every derived class at least one non-inline virtual function (assuming the base class has a virtual destructor). To show how subtle this can be, consider this trivial example.

```
class Base {
public:
   virtual ~Base() throw();
};

class Derived : public Base {
   // ...
};
```

```
int main()
{ }
```

Even though no `Base` or `Derived` objects are created, the preceding example will fail to link on many systems. The reason is that the only virtual function in class `Derived` is inline (`Derived::~Derived()` is a synthesized inline virtual function), so the compiler puts a `static` copy of `Derived::~Derived()` into the current source file. Since this `static` copy of `Derived::~Derived()` invokes `Base::~Base()` (see FAQ 20.05) the linker will need a definition of `Base::~Base()`.

Adding a non-inline virtual function to a derived class (for example, `thisDoesNothing()`) eliminates the linker errors for that derived class, because the compiler puts the (only) copy of the magical stuff into the source file that defines the non-inline virtual function.

```
class Derived2 : public Base {
public:
  //...
private:
  virtual void thisDoesNothing() throw();
};

// This goes in exactly one source file, such as Derived2.cpp
void Derived2::thisDoesNothing() throw()
{ }
```

Chapter 22

Initialization Lists

What are constructor initialization lists?

Constructor initialization lists are the best way to initialize member objects.

All member objects are initialized before the body of the constructor begins executing. Constructor initialization lists allow the class to exercise control over the construction of the member objects before the execution of the constructor.

Here is an example of using an initialization list.

```
#include <new>
#include <string>
using namespace std;

class Person {
public:
  Person(const string& name) throw(bad_alloc);
  // ...
protected:
  string name_;
};

Person::Person(const string& name) throw(bad_alloc)
: name_(name) ◄──── The initialization list copies name into name_
{
        ◄──────────── Note: No assignment here since the init list copies name into name_
}
```

```
int main()
{
  Person fred("Fred Flintstone");
  // ...
}
```

FAQ 22.02

What will happen if constructor initialization lists are not used?

new

Initialization lists are usually a performance issue, although there are cases when initialization lists impact correctness (see FAQ 22.03 and 22.04). In some cases the code of a constructor can be three times slower if initialization lists are not used. For example, consider the following Person class.

```
#include <new>
#include <string>
using namespace std;

class Person {
public:
  Person(const string& name, const string& suffix) throw(bad_alloc);
  // ...
private:
  string name_;
};
```

The following implementation of the constructor initializes member object name_ using an initialization list. From a performance perspective, it is important to note that the result of the + operator is constructed directly inside member object name_. A temporary object is not needed in this case, and most compilers do not produce an extra temporary object. This typically requires one allocation of memory from the heap and one copy of the data from each string.

```
Person::Person(const string& name, const string& suffix)
throw(bad_alloc)
: name_(name + suffix)   ◄──── Good: Use initialization rather than assignment
{ }
```

In contrast, the following constructor sets up member object name_ using assignment. In this case the default constructor (see FAQ 20.08) may have allocated a small amount of memory (many string classes store a `'\0'` byte even in cases when the string is empty); then that memory is immediately discarded in the assignment operator. In addition, the compiler will probably have to create a temporary object, and this temporary object is passed into the `name_` object's assignment operator; then the temporary is destructed at the `;` . That's inefficient. All together, this constructor might make three calls to the memory allocation routines (two allocations, one deallocation) and might copy the string's data twice (once into the temporary and once into `name_`).

```
Person::Person(const string& name, const string& suffix)
throw(bad_alloc)
{ name_ = name + suffix; }  ◀────Inefficient: Assignment used rather than initialization
```

Conclusion: All other things being equal, code will run faster with initialization lists than with assignment.

What's the guideline for using initialization lists in constructor definitions?

As a general rule, all member objects and base classes should explicitly appear in the initialization list of a constructor. In addition to being more efficient than default initialization followed by assignment, using the initialization list makes the code clearer since it takes advantage of something that the compiler is going to do anyway.

Note that there is no performance gain in using initialization lists with member objects of built-in types, but there is no loss either, so initialization lists should be used for symmetry.

For an exception to this guideline, see FAQ 22.11.

Is it normal for constructors to have nothing inside their body?

Yes, this happens frequently.

The body of a constructor is the `{...}` part. A constructor should initialize its member objects in the initialization list, often leaving little or nothing to do inside the

constructor's body. When the constructor body is empty, it can be left empty, perhaps
(`{ }`), or decorated with a comment such as

```
// Intentionally left blank.
```

An example follows (`Fract` is a fraction class).

```
#include <iostream>
using namespace std;

class Fract {
public:
  Fract(int numerator=0, int denominator=1) throw();
  int numerator()   const throw();
  int denominator() const throw();
  friend Fract operator+ (const Fract& a, const Fract& b) throw();
  friend Fract operator- (const Fract& a, const Fract& b) throw();
  friend Fract operator* (const Fract& a, const Fract& b) throw();
  friend Fract operator/ (const Fract& a, const Fract& b) throw();
  friend ostream& operator<< (ostream& ostr, const Fract& a) throw();
protected:
  int num_;   //numerator
  int den_;   //denominator
};

Fract::Fract(int numerator, int denominator)
: num_(numerator)
, den_(denominator)
{ }

int Fract::numerator()   const throw() { return num_; }
int Fract::denominator() const throw() { return den_; }

ostream& operator<< (ostream& ostr, const Fract& a) throw()
{ return ostr << a.num_ << '/' << a.den_; }

int main()
{
  Fract a;                  cout << "a = " << a << endl;
  Fract b = 5;              cout << "b = " << b << endl;
  Fract c = Fract(22,7);    cout << "c = " << c << endl;
}
```

The output of this program follows.

```
a = 0/1
b = 5/1
c = 22/7
```

Notice that the initialization list resides in the constructor's definition and not its declaration (in this case, the declaration and the definition are separate).

FAQ 22.05

How is a `const` data member initialized?

Nonstatic `const` data members are declared in the class body with a `const` prefix, and their state must be initialized in the constructor's initialization list. The value used to initialize the `const` data member can be a literal value, a parameter passed to the constructor, or the result of some expression. After initialization, the state of a `const` data member within a particular object cannot change, but each object can initialize its `const` data member to a different value.

In the following example, `i_` is a non-`const` member variable and `j_` is a `const` member variable.

```
class Fred {
public:
  Fred(int i)         throw();
  Fred(int i, int j) throw();
protected:
  int i_;
  const int j_;
};

Fred::Fred(int i) throw()
: i_(i)
, j_(10)  ◄─────── Initialize const member j_ with a literal value
{ }

Fred::Fred(int i, int j) throw()
: i_(i)
, j_(j)  ◄─────── Initialize const member j_ with a constructor parameter
{ }

int main()
{
  Fred a(5);       //a.j_ will always be 10
  Fred b(5,15);    //b.j_ will always be 15
  Fred c(5,20);    //c.j_ will always be 20
}
```

FAQ 22.06

How is a reference data member initialized?

It must be initialized in the initialization list of each constructor. An example follows.

```
class Fred {
public:
  Fred(int& i) throw();
protected:
  int& i_;
};

Fred::Fred(int& i) throw()
: i_(i)  ←——— References must be initialized in the initialization list
{ }

int main()
{
  int x;
  Fred a(x);    //a.i_ will always be an alias for x
}
```

Be sure to avoid binding a reference data member to an object passed to the constructor by value (for example, if parameter i were passed by value), since the reference (i_) would refer to a temporary variable allocated on the stack. This would create a dangling reference since value parameters disappear as soon as the function (the constructor in this case) returns.

Depending on the phase of the moon, a dangling reference might crash the program.

FAQ 22.07

Are initializers executed in the same order in which they appear in the initialization list?

 Not necessarily.

C++ constructs objects by initializing the subobjects of immediate base classes in the order the base classes appear in the class declaration, then initializing member objects in the order they appear in the class body layout. It uses this ordering so that it can guarantee that base class subobjects and member objects are destructed in the opposite order from which they are constructed. Member objects are destructed in the reverse order of the class body layout, then subobjects of immediate base classes are destructed in the reverse order they appear in the base class list in the class declaration. The order of the initialization list is irrelevant.

The following example demonstrates the fact that initialization order is tied to the order of the class layout rather than to the order of the initialization list. First, class Noisy prints a message during its constructor and destructor.

```
#include <iostream>
#include <string>
using namespace std;

class Noisy {
public:
  Noisy(const string& msg) throw();
 ~Noisy() throw();
protected:
  string msg_;
};

Noisy::Noisy(const string& msg) throw()
: msg_(msg)
{ cout << "construct " << msg_ << "\n"; }

Noisy::~Noisy() throw()
{ cout << "destruct "  << msg_ << "\n"; }
```

Now class Fred inherits from Noisy and also has two member objects of class Noisy.

```
class Fred : public Noisy {
public:
  Fred() throw();
protected:
  Noisy a_;
  Noisy b_;
};
```

The constructor of class Fred lists its three Noisy objects in a different order than the one in which they are actually initialized. The important thing to notice is that the compiler ignores the order in which members show up in the initialization list:

```
Fred::Fred() throw()
: b_("b_")
, a_("a_")
, Noisy("base")
{ }

int main()
{ Fred x; }
```

The constructor's initialization list order is (b_, a_, base-class), but the class body layout order is the opposite: (base-class, a_, b_). The output of this program demonstrates that the initialization list's order is ignored:

```
construct base
construct a_
construct b_
destruct b_
destruct a_
destruct base
```

Even though the order of initializers in a constructor's initialization list is irrelevant, see the next FAQ for a recommendation.

FAQ 22.08

How should initializers be ordered in a constructor's initialization list?

Immediate base classes (left to right), then member objects (top to bottom).

In other words, the order of the initialization list should mimic the order in which initializations take place. This guideline discourages a particularly subtle class of order dependency errors by giving an obvious, visual clue. For example, the following contains a hideous error.

```cpp
#include <iostream>
using namespace std;

class Y {
public:
  Y()       throw();
  void f() throw();
};

Y::Y()       throw() { cout << "Y ctor\n"; }
void Y::f() throw() { cout << "Y used\n"; }

class X {
public:
  X(Y& y) throw();
};

X::X(Y& y) throw() { y.f(); }
```

```
class Z {
public:
  Z() throw();
protected:
  X x_;
  Y y_;
};

Z::Z() throw()
: y_()
, x_(y_)  ◄──── Bad form: Should have listed x_ before y_
{ }

int main()
{ Z z; }
```

The output of this program follows.

```
Y used
Y ctor
```

Note that y_ is used (Y::f()) before it is initialized (Y::Y()). If the guideline espoused by this FAQ was employed, the error would be more obvious: the initialization list of Z::Z() would have read x_(y_), y_(), visually indicating that y_ was being used before being initialized.

Not all compilers issue diagnostic messages for these cases.

FAQ 22.09

Is it moral for one member object to be initialized using another member object in the constructor's initialization list?

Yes, but exercise great caution.

In a constructor's initialization list, it is best to avoid using one member object from the this object in the initialization expression of a subsequent initializer for the this object. This guideline prevents subtle order dependency errors if someone reorganizes the layout of member objects within the class (see the previous FAQ).

Because of this guideline, the constructor that follows uses s.len_ + 1 rather than len_ + 1, even though they are otherwise equivalent. This avoids an unnecessary order dependency.

```
#include <new>
using namespace std;
```

```
class MyString {
public:
  MyString()                                throw(bad_alloc);
 ~MyString()                                throw();
  MyString(const MyString& s)               throw(bad_alloc);
                                            // Copy constructor
  MyString& operator= (const MyString& s)  throw(bad_alloc);
                                            // Assignment
protected:
  unsigned len_;
  char*    data_;
};

MyString::MyString() throw(bad_alloc)
: len_(0)
, data_(new char[1])
{ data_[0] = '\0'; }

MyString::~MyString() throw()
{ delete[] data_; }

MyString::MyString(const MyString& s) throw(bad_alloc)
: len_ ( s.len_                )
, data_( new char[s.len_+1] )  ⟵ Not new char[len_+1]
{ memcpy(data_, s.data_, len_+1); }

int main()
{
  MyString a;       // Default ctor; zero length String ("")
  MyString b = a;   // Copy constructor
}
```

An unnecessary order dependency on the class layout of len_ and data_ would have been introduced if the constructor's initialization of data_ had used len_+1 rather than s.len_+1. However using len_ within a constructor body ({...}) is okay. No order dependency is introduced since the entire initialization list is guaranteed to finish before the constructor body begins executing.

FAQ 22.10

What if one member object has to be initialized using another member object?

Comment the declaration of the affected data members with the comment //ORDER DEPENDENCY.

If a constructor initializes a member object of the this object using another member object of the this object, rearranging the data members in the class body could break the constructor (see FAQ 22.08). This important maintenance constraint should be documented in the class body. For example, in the constructor that follows, the initializer for data_ uses len_ to avoid a redundant call to strlen(s), thus introducing an order dependency in the class body.

```
#include <new>
using namespace std;

class MyString {
public:
  MyString(const char* s)                 throw(bad_alloc);
                                          // Promote const char*
  MyString(const MyString& s)             throw(bad_alloc);
                                          // Copy constructor
  MyString& operator= (const MyString&) throw(bad_alloc);
                                          // Assignment
 ~MyString()                             throw();
protected:
  unsigned len_;     // ORDER DEPENDENCY
  char*    data_;    // ORDER DEPENDENCY
};

MyString::MyString(const char* s) throw(bad_alloc)
: len_ ( strlen(s)        )
, data_( new char[len_+1] )
{ memcpy(data_, s, len_+1); }

MyString::~MyString() throw()
{ delete[] data_; }

int main()
{ MyString s = "xyzzy"; }
```

Note that the //ORDER DEPENDENCY comment is attached to the affected data members in the class body, not to the constructor initialization list. This is because the order of member objects in the class body is critical; the order of initializers in the constructor initialization list is irrelevant (see FAQ 22.07).

FAQ 22.11

Are there exceptions to the rule "Initialize all member objects in an initialization list"?

Yes, to facilitate argument screening.

Arguments to constructors sometimes need to be checked (or screened) before they can be used to initialize a member object. When it becomes difficult to squeeze the resultant if (...) throw ... logic into the initialization list, it may be more convenient to initialize the member object via its default constructor, then modify its state in the constructor body ({ ... }) via assignment or some other mutative member function.

This situation is usually limited to classes that are built directly on built-in types (int, char*, and so forth), because constructors for user-defined (class) types normally check their own arguments.

For example, in the preceding FAQ, MyString::MyString(const char*) passed its parameter to strlen(const char*) without verifying that the pointer was non-NULL. This test can be implemented by using assignment in the constructor.

```
#include <new>
#include <cstdlib>
#include <stdexcept>
using namespace std;

class MyString {
public:
  MyString(const char* s) throw(bad_alloc, runtime_error);
  MyString(const MyString& s) throw(bad_alloc);
  MyString& operator= (const MyString& s) throw(bad_alloc);
  ~MyString() throw();
protected:
  unsigned len_;
  char*    data_;
};

MyString::MyString(const char* s)
throw(bad_alloc, runtime_error)
// No initialization list due to argument screening
{
```

```
    if (s == NULL)
       throw runtime_error("NULL pointer in MyString ctor");
    len_ = strlen(s);
    data_ = new char[len_+1];
    memcpy(data_, s, len_+1);
}

MyString::~MyString() throw()
{ delete[] data_; }

int main()
{ MyString s = "xyzzy"; }
```

Using assignment rather than initialization tends to remove order dependencies. For example, `MyString::MyString(const char*)` no longer introduces an order dependency in the member data of class `MyString`. However, doing this may introduce performance penalties if the member objects are user-defined (class) types.

_____ **FAQ 22.12**

How can an array of objects be initialized with specific initializers?

Why use arrays in the first place? Why not use containers, particularly from the standard library? If arrays are a must, and if the elements require specific initializers, the answer is the { . . . } initializer syntax.

```
#include <iostream>
using namespace std;

class Stack {
public:
   Stack(int maxLen=5) throw();
   Stack(const Stack& s) throw();
   // ...
};

Stack::Stack(int maxLen) throw()
{ cout << "Stack: maxLen=" << maxLen << '\n'; }

Stack::Stack(const Stack& s) throw()
{ cout << "Stack: copy ctor\n"; }

int main()
```

```
{
    // 'a' will be constructed with maxLen=7:
    Stack a(7);

    // All 4 stacks in 'b' will be constructed with maxLen=5
    Stack b[4];

    // c[0] will copy from a, c[1] maxLen=8, c[2] maxLen=7,
    // c[3] will be constructed without arguments (maxLen=5):
    Stack c[4] = { a, Stack(8), 7 };
}
```

The (annotated) output of this program follows.

```
Stack: maxLen=7  ◄──────  This is a
Stack: maxLen=5  ◄──────  This is b[0]
Stack: maxLen=5  ◄──────  This is b[1]
Stack: maxLen=5  ◄──────  This is b[2]
Stack: maxLen=5  ◄──────  This is b[3]
Stack: copy ctor ◄──────  This is c[0]
Stack: maxLen=8  ◄──────  This is c[1]
Stack: maxLen=7  ◄──────  This is c[2]
Stack: maxLen=5  ◄──────  This is c[3]
```

Chapter 23

Operator Overloading

Are overloaded operators like normal functions?

Yes, overloaded operators are syntactic sugar for normal functions.

Operator overloading allows existing C++ operators to be redefined so that they work on objects of user defined classes. Overloaded operators are syntactic sugar for equivalent function calls. They form a pleasant facade that doesn't add anything fundamental to the language (but they can improve understandability and reduce maintenance costs).

For example, consider the class `Number` that supports the member functions `add()` and `mul()`. Using named functions (that is, `add()` and `mul()`) makes `sample()` unnecessarily difficult to read, write, and maintain.

```
#include <stdexcept>
using namespace std;

class Number {
public:
  friend Number add(Number a, Number b) throw(range_error);
  friend Number mul(Number a, Number b) throw(range_error);
};

Number sample(Number a, Number b, Number c)
throw(range_error)
{ return add(add(mul(a,b), mul(b,c)), mul(c,a)); }
```

The syntax is clearer if operators + and * work for class `Number` in the same way they work for the built-in numeric types.

```
inline Number operator+ (Number a, Number b) throw(range_error)
{ return add(a, b); }

inline Number operator* (Number a, Number b) throw(range_error)
{ return mul(a, b); }

Number sample2(Number a, Number b, Number c) throw(range_error)
{ return a*b + b*c + c*a; }
```

FAQ 23.02

When should operator overloading be used?

When it makes sense to users.

The goal of operator overloading should be to improve the readability of code that uses a class. However, it should be used only in ways that are semantically familiar to users. For instance, it would be nonintuitive to use `operator+` for subtraction.

The ultimate goal is to reduce both the learning curve and the defect rate for users of a class. Another related goal is to enable users to program in the language of the problem domain rather than in the language of the machine.

Here are a few examples of operator overloading that are intuitive.

- `myString + yourString` might concatenate two string objects.

- `myDate++` might increment a `Date` object.

- `a * b` might multiply two `Number` objects.

- `a[i]` might access an element of an `Array` object.

- `x = *p` might dereference a "smart pointer" (see FAQ 31.09) that acts as if it points to a disk record. The actual implementation could use a database lookup to get the value of record `x`.

While it is true that operator overloading can be overutilized (by trying to define everything as an operator), it can also be underutilized. For some reason, some developers hate to implement overloaded operators in their classes. They don't do it even in places where it should be done. One reason some developers don't do it is because they're not used to it—they don't do it every day, so they're not comfortable with it. Another reason they don't do it is because Java doesn't have operator overloading (as if that were a reason to not do something in C++). And another reason they don't do it is because they think that it makes their code ugly by adding all those member functions with funny operator names.

Our response to these concerns (in particular the last one) is go back to two of the central tenets of this book: "Design classes from the outside in" and "Think of your users, not yourself" when designing interfaces. In particular, if overload operators make sense to the users of the library/class or *their* code will be easier to understand and maintain, then the developer should define overloaded operators.

FAQ 23.03

What operators can't be overloaded?

The only C++ operators that can't be overloaded are dot (`.`), `.*`, arithmetic if (`?:`), size (`sizeof`), `typeid`, and `::`.

Here's an example of an array-like class without operator overloading.

```
class Array {
public:
  int& elem(unsigned i) throw(out_of_range);
protected:
  int data_[100];
};

inline int& Array::elem(unsigned i) throw(out_of_range)
{ return data_[i]; }

void sample()
{
  Array a;
  a.elem(10) = 42;
  a.elem(12) = 10;
  a.elem(12) += a.elem(10);
}
```

The member function `elem(unsigned)` returns a reference to the `i`th element of the `Array`. A better solution, one whose user syntax is more intuitive, would replace `elem` with `operator[]`:

```
class Array2 {
public:
  int& operator[] (unsigned i) throw(out_of_range);
```

```
protected:
  int data_[100];
};

inline int& Array2::operator[] (unsigned i) throw(out_of_range)
{ return data_[i]; }

void sample2()
{
  Array2 a;
  a[10] = 42;
  a[12] = 10;
  a[12] += a[10];
}

int main()
{
  sample();
  sample2();
}
```

FAQ 23.04

Is the goal of operator overloading to make the class easier to understand?

The goal is to help the *users* of a class rather than the *developer* of a class. There may be lots of users of a class, so this is an example of leverage: the good of the many outweighs the good of the few.

When programmers think only about themselves and the class they are writing, operator overloading seems to make matters worse. For example, class `Array2` in the previous FAQ has more symbols and clutter than the `Array` version that didn't have operator overloading. However when programmers think about the overall complexity of the application, they see that operator overloading can help. For example, all the code written by all the users of `Array2` will probably be a lot easier to understand than the equivalent code written using class `Array` (compare `sample2()` with `sample()` in the previous FAQ).

Why do subscript operators usually come in pairs?

They usually occur in pairs so that users can access elements of a `const` object.

Classes that have a subscript operator often have a pair of subscript operators: a `const` version and a non-`const` version. The `const` version normally returns the element by value or by `const` reference, and the non-`const` version normally returns the element by non-`const` reference. The code for the two versions is normally quite similar if not identical.

For example, the following class has two subscript operators. It represents an `Array` of `Fred` objects. Class `out_of_range` is the standard exception class that is thrown if an argument is out of bounds.

```
#include <stdexcept>
using namespace std;

class Fred { };

class Array {
public:
  Fred&       operator[] (unsigned i)       throw(out_of_range);
  const Fred& operator[] (unsigned i) const throw(out_of_range);
protected:
  enum { capacity_ = 100 };
  Fred data_[capacity_];
};

Fred& Array::operator[] (unsigned i) throw(out_of_range)
{
  if (i >= capacity_) throw out_of_range("Array::operator[]");
  return data_[i];
}

const Fred& Array::operator[] (unsigned i) const throw(out_of_range)
{
  if (i >= capacity_) throw out_of_range("Array::operator[] const");
  return data_[i];
}
```

When a user accesses an element of an `Array` via a reference-to-non-const (for example, via `Array& a`; see a[3] in the following code), the compiler generates a call to the non-const subscript operator. Similarly, when a user accesses an element of an Array via a reference-to-const (for example, via const Array& b; see b[3] below), the compiler generates a call to the const subscript operator. Since the non-const subscript operator returns the element by non-const reference, things like a[3] can appear on the left side of an assignment operator. Conversely, since the const subscript operator returns the element by const reference, things like b[3] cannot appear on the left side of an assignment operator:

```
void sample(Array& a, const Array& b)
{
  Fred x, y;
  x = a[3];  ◄─────── OK: Get a[3]
  a[3] = y;  ◄─────── OK: Change a[3]

  x = b[3];  ◄─────── OK: Get b[3]
  #ifdef GENERATE_ERROR
    b[3] = y;  ◄─────── Error: b[3] cannot be changed
  #endif
}


int main()
{
  Array a, b;
  sample(a, b);
}
```

FAQ 23.06

What is the most important consideration for operators such as +=, +, and =?

Respect the user's intuition and expectations.

In classes that define +=, +, and =, the expressions a += b and a = a + b should generally have the same observable behavior. Similar comments can be made for the other identities of the built-in types. For example, if the class of a defines both a += operator that can be passed an int and the prefix ++ operator, then a += 1 and ++a should have the same observable behavior.

Similarly if the class of p defines a subscript operator and a + operator that can take i on the right side, and a dereference operator, then p[i] and *(p+i) should be equivalent.

One way to enforce these rules is to implement constructive binary operators using the corresponding mutative operators. This also simplifies maintenance. For example, the code below implements + using +=.

```
class Fred {
public:
  friend Fred operator+ (const Fred& a, const Fred& b) throw();
  Fred& operator+= (const Fred& b) throw();
};

Fred operator+ (const Fred& a, const Fred& b) throw()
{
  Fred result = a;
  result += b;
  return result;
}
```

Note that it is sometimes possible to implement `operator+` more efficiently by not using `operator+=` and similarly for the other operators (`operator-=`, `operator*=`, and so on).

FAQ 23.07

How are the prefix and postfix versions of `operator++` distinguished?

They are distinguished by a dummy parameter.

The postfix version, `i++`, is called `operator++` and has a dummy parameter of type `int`. The prefix version, `++i`, is also called `operator++`, but it has no dummy parameters. Here's an example.

```
#include <iostream>
using namespace std;

class Fred {
public:
  void operator++ ()     throw();
  void operator++ (int) throw();
};

void Fred::operator++ ()     throw() { cout << "prefix: ++i\n"; }
void Fred::operator++ (int) throw() { cout << "postfix: i++\n"; }
```

```
int main()
{
  Fred i;
  ++i;
  i++;
}
```

The output is

```
prefix: ++i
postfix: i++
```

The two versions of `operator--` are similar: the prefix version takes no parameters and the postfix version takes a single parameter of type `int`.

FAQ 23.08

What should the prefix and postfix versions of operator++ return?

`++i` should return a reference to i; `i++` should return either `void` or a copy of the original state of i.

The prefix version, `operator++()`, should return `*this`, normally by reference. For example, if the class of the object is `Fred`, `Fred::operator++()` should normally return `*this` as a `Fred&`. It is also valid, but not as desirable, if it returns `void`.

The postfix version, `Fred::operator++(int)`, should return either nothing (`void`) or a copy of the original state of the object, `*this`. In any event, it should not return a `Fred&` because that would confuse users. For example, if `i++` returned `*this` by reference, the value returned from `i++` would be the same as the value returned from `++i`. That would be counterintuitive.

It is often easiest if `Fred::operator++(int)` is implemented in terms of `Fred::operator++()`:

```
#include <iostream>
using namespace std;

class Fred {
public:
  Fred& operator++ ()    throw();
  Fred operator++ (int) throw();
};
```

```
Fred& Fred::operator++ () throw()
{
  cout << "do the increment here\n";
  return *this;  ←——— The prefix version returns the new value of *this
}

Fred Fred::operator++ (int) throw()
{
  Fred old = *this;
  ++(*this);  ←——— The postfix version calls the prefix version
  return old;  ←——— The postfix version returns the old value of *this
}

int main()
{
  Fred i;
  ++i;  ←——— Call the prefix version
  i++;  ←——— Call the postfix version
}
```

Note that users should avoid i++ in their code unless the old state of i is needed. In particular, simple statements such as i++; (where the result of i++ is ignored) should generally be replaced by ++i;. This is because i++ may cause more overhead than ++i for user-defined (classes) types. For example, calling i++ may create an unnecessary copy of i. Of course, if the old value of i is needed, such as in j = i++, the postfix version is beneficial.

The two versions of operator-- are similar: the prefix version should return *this by reference, and the postfix version should return either the old state of *this or void.

FAQ 23.09

How can a `Matrix`-like class have a subscript operator that takes more than one subscript?

It should use operator() rather than operator[].

When multiple subscripts are needed, the cleanest approach is to use operator() rather than operator[]. The reason is that operator[] always takes exactly one parameter, but operator() can take any number of parameters. In the case of a rectangular Matrix-like class, an element can be accessed using an (i,j) pair of subscripts. For example,

```
#include <stdexcept>
using namespace std;

class Matrix {
public:
  double& operator() (unsigned row, unsigned col)
    throw(out_of_range);
  double  operator() (unsigned row, unsigned col) const
    throw(out_of_range);
private:
  enum { rows_ = 100, cols_ = 100 };
  double data_[rows_ * cols_];
};

inline double& Matrix::operator() (unsigned row, unsigned col)
throw(out_of_range)
{
  if (row >= rows_ || col >= cols_)
    throw out_of_range("Matrix::operator()");
  return data_[cols_*row + col];
}

inline double Matrix::operator() (unsigned row, unsigned col) const
throw(out_of_range)
{
  if (row >= rows_ || col >= cols_)
    throw out_of_range("Matrix::operator()");
  return data_[cols_*row + col];
}
```

To access an element of a Matrix object, users use m(i,j) rather than m[i][j] or m[i,j]:

```
int main()
{
  Matrix m;
  m(5,8) = 106.15;  ◄——— Set element (5,8)
  cout << m(5,8);   ◄——— Get element (5,8)
}
```

FAQ 23.10

Can a ** operator serve as an exponentiation operator?

No, it can't.

The names, precedence, associativity, and arity (number of arguments) of operators are predefined by the language. There is no ** operator in the C++ language, and it is not possible to add the ** operator to the C++ language.

In fact, the expression x ** y is already syntactically legal C++. It means, x * (*y) (that is, y is treated like a pointer that is dereferenced). If C++ allowed users to provide new meaning to **, the compiler's lexical analyzer (the lowest-level operation in the compiler) would need to be contextually dependent on the semantic analyzer (the highest-level operation in the compiler). This would probably introduce ambiguities and break existing code.

Operator overloading is merely syntactic sugar for function calls. Although syntactic sugar is sweet, it is not fundamentally necessary. Raising a number to a power is best performed by overloading pow(base, exponent), a double precision version of which can be found in the <cmath> header file.

Another candidate for an exponentiation operator is operator^, but it has neither the proper precedence nor the proper associativity.

Don't force-fit the semantics of an overloaded operator.

Chapter 24

Assignment Operators

What should assignment operators return?

Assignment operators should generally return *this by reference. This means that they adhere to the same convention used by the built-in types by allowing assignment to be used as an expression rather than simply as a statement. This allows assignment to be cascaded into larger expressions. An example follows.

```
#include <iostream>
using namespace std;

class Fred {
public:
  Fred(int i=3) throw();
  Fred& operator= (const Fred& x) throw();
  friend int operator== (const Fred& a, const Fred& b) throw();
protected:
  int i_;
};

Fred::Fred(int i) throw()
: i_(i) { }

Fred& Fred::operator= (const Fred& x) throw()
{ i_ = x.i_; return *this; }

int operator== (const Fred& a, const Fred& b) throw()
{ return a.i_ == b.i_; }
```

```
int main()
{
  Fred x, y, z;
  x = y = 5;  ◄─────────── Result of y = 5 used as an expression
  if ((z = x) == y)  ◄───── Result of z = x used as an expression
    cout << "z (which was assigned from x) is equal to y\n";
}
```

FAQ 24.02

What is wrong with an object being assigned to itself?

Nothing, unless the programmer who developed the class failed to implement the assignment operator correctly.

Assigning an object to itself is called *self-assignment*.

No one intentionally assigns an object to itself (a = a). However, since two different pointers or references could refer to the same object (aliasing), a statement like a = b could assign an object to itself. If that happens, and if the object doesn't properly handle it, a disaster could occur, especially if remote ownership is involved (see FAQ 30.08). An example follows.

```
#include <new>
using namespace std;

class Wilma { };

class Fred {
public:
  Fred()                  throw(bad_alloc);
  Fred(const Fred& f) throw(bad_alloc);
 ~Fred()                  throw();
  Fred& operator= (const Fred& f) throw(bad_alloc);
  //...
private:
  Wilma* p_;
};

Fred::Fred()                  throw(bad_alloc)
: p_(new Wilma())       { }
Fred::Fred(const Fred& f) throw(bad_alloc)
: p_(new Wilma(*f.p_)) { }
Fred::~Fred()                  throw()
{ delete p_; }
Fred& Fred::operator= (const Fred& f) throw(bad_alloc)
{
```

```
                        ◄─────────── BAD FORM: Forgot to check for self-assignment!
  delete p_; ◄─────────── BAD FORM: Delete the old before allocating the new!
  p_ = new Wilma(*f.p_);
  return *this;
}

void sample(Fred& a, Fred& b) throw(bad_alloc)
{ a = b; }

int main()
{
  Fred x;
  sample(x, x);
}
```

Even though the code of `sample()` doesn't appear to be assigning an object with itself, the two references `a` and `b` could (and in this case, do) refer to the same object. Unfortunately, the assignment operator fails to check for self-assignment, which means that the statement `delete p_` deletes both `this->p_` and `f.p_`. Yet the next line uses the deleted object `*f.p_`, meaning that the program is using a dangling reference. Depending on the contents of class `Wilma`, this could be a disaster.

FAQ 24.03

What should be done about self-assignment?

The programmer who creates the class needs to make sure self-assessment is harmless. The simplest way to make sure that self-assignment is harmless is to perform an `if` test such as the one shown in the following example.

```
#include <new>
using namespace std;

Fred& Fred::operator= (const Fred& f) throw(bad_alloc)
{
  if (this == &f) ◄─────── GOOD FORM: Check for self-assignment
    return *this;
  // ...
}
```

Self-assignment can also be rendered harmless by efficiency considerations. For example, the following assignment operator replaces the allocated memory only if the old allocation is too small to handle the new state. In this class, self-assignment would automatically be handled since it would skip the allocate/deallocate steps:

```
#include <new>
#include <iostream>
#include <cstring>
using namespace std;

class String {
public:
  String()                               throw(bad_alloc);
  String(const char* s)                  throw(bad_alloc);
  String(const String& s)                throw(bad_alloc);
 ~String()                               throw();
  String& operator= (const String& s) throw(bad_alloc);
protected:
  unsigned len_;
  char*    data_;
};

String& String::operator= (const String& s) throw(bad_alloc)
{
  if (s.len_ > len_) { ◄——— Makes self-assignment harmless; no need to explictly test
    char* newData = new char[s.len_+1];
    delete[] data_;
    data_ = newData;
  }
  memcpy(data_, s.data_, s.len_+1);
  len_ = s.len_;
  return *this;
}
```

The goal is to make self-assignment harmless, not to make it fast. It doesn't make sense to optimize self-assignment since self-assignment is rare. For example, when self-assignment actually occurs, the assignment operator would unnecessarily call memcpy(). Although that call could be removed by an extra if test, the extra if test would put more overhead on the normal path in an attempt to optimize the pathological case. So in this case the right trade-off is to avoid the extra if test and put up with an unnecessary memcpy() in the case of self-assignment.

FAQ 24.04

Should an assignment operator throw an exception after partially assigning an object?

The assignment operator should either completely succeed or leave the object unchanged and throw an exception.

This gives callers some strong assurances: if the assignment operator returns normally (as opposed to throwing an exception), the caller is assured that the assignment was completely successful; if the assignment operator throws an exception, the caller is assured that the object was left in a consistent state.

Sometimes achieving this goal means that the object's new state must be copied into some temporary variables; then, after all potential error conditions are bypassed, the state can be copied into the this object.

In any event, it would be a mortal sin to leave the object in a corrupt state when an exception is thrown. For example, if an exception is thrown while evaluating new Wilma(*f.p_) (that is, either an out-of-memory exception or an exception in Wilma's copy constructor), this->p_ will be a *dangling pointer*—it will point to memory that has already been deleted.

```
#include <new>
using namespace std;

class Wilma { };

class Fred {
public:
  Fred()                       throw(bad_alloc);
  Fred(const Fred& f)          throw(bad_alloc);
  ~Fred()                      throw();
  Fred& operator= (const Fred& f) throw(bad_alloc);
  //...
private:
  Wilma* p_;
};

Fred::Fred()                 throw(bad_alloc)  : p_(new Wilma()) { }
Fred::Fred(const Fred& f)    throw(bad_alloc)  : p_(new Wilma(*f.p_)) { }
Fred::~Fred()                throw()           { delete p_; }

Fred& Fred::operator= (const Fred& f) throw(bad_alloc)
{
  if (this == &f) ◄──────── Check for self-assignment: GOOD FORM!
    return *this;
  delete p_; ◄──────── Delete the old before allocating the new: BAD FORM!
  p_ = new Wilma(*f.p_);
  return *this;
}
```

The easiest way to solve this problem is simply to reverse the order of the new and delete lines. That is, to allocate the new Wilma(*f.p_) first, storing the result into a temporary `Wilma*`, then to do the `delete p_` line, and finally to copy the temporary pointer into `p_`:

```
Fred& Fred::operator= (const Fred& f) throw(bad_alloc)
{
   if (this == &f)  ◄─────── Check for self-assignment: GOOD FORM!
      return *this;
   Wilma* p2 = new Wilma(*f.p_);
   delete p_;  ◄─────── Allocate the new before deleting the old: GOOD FORM!
   p_ = p2;
   return *this;
}
```

Note that reversing the order of the `new` and `delete` statements has the beneficial side effect of making self-assignment harmless even without the explicit `if` test at the beginning of the assignment operator. That is, if the initial `if` test is removed and someone does a self-assignment, the only thing that happens is an extra copy of a `Wilma` object. Since making an extra copy of a `Wilma` object shouldn't generally cause problems (especially since the caller was expecting a copy to be made during assignment anyway), the `if` test can be removed, thus simplifying the code and improving the performance in the normal (non-self-assignment) case. Remember: the goal is to make self-assignment harmless, not to make it fast. Never optimize the pathological case (self-assignment) at the expense of the normal case (non-self-assignment). (See FAQ 24.03.)

The modified assignment operator follows.

```
Fred& Fred::operator= (const Fred& f) throw(bad_alloc)
{
   // Self assignment is handled by order of first three lines:
   Wilma* p2 = new Wilma(*f.p_);
   delete p_;
   p_ = p2;
   return *this;
}
```

FAQ 24.05

How should the assignment operator be declared in an ABC?

The assignment operator of an ABC should generally be `protected:`.

By default, assignment operators for all classes are `public:`. For ABCs, this default should usually be changed to `protected:` so that attempts to assign incompatible objects are trapped as compile-time errors. An example follows.

```
class Position { };  ◄──────  The position of the Shape

class Shape {
public:
  // ...
protected:
  Position p_;
};

class Square : public Shape { /*...*/ };
class Circle : public Shape { /*...*/ };

void sample(Shape& a, Shape& b)
{ a = b; }  ◄──────────────── Nonsensical, but (unfortunately) legal since Shape::operator=() is public:

int main()
{
  Square a;
  Circle b;
  sample(a, b);
}
```

Instead, the assignment operator for an ABC should be `protected:`, as shown in the following code.

```
class Shape {
public:
  // ...
protected:
  void operator= (const Shape& s) throw();
  Position p_;
};

inline void Shape::operator= (const Shape& s) throw()
{ p_ = s.p_; }
```

Note that the `protected:` assignment operator assigns the internal state of one Shape to another Shape. If it didn't assign the Shape's p_ member object, each derived class would have to define an explicit assignment operator in order to do what the base class's assignment operator should have done in the first place.

Also note that the `protected:` assignment operator can return void instead of the usual *this (see FAQ 24.07).

FAQ 24.06

When should a user-defined assignment operator mimic the assignment operator that the compiler would generate automatically?

When an ABC defines an assignment operator merely to make it `protected:`.

When a `protected:` assignment operator contains the same code that the compiler would have synthesized automatically, its only purpose is to prevent users from assigning to an object of the class. This is common with abstract base classes. Here's an example.

```
class Position { };

class Shape {
public:
  virtual void draw() const throw() = 0;
  virtual ~Shape() throw();
protected:
  Position pos_;
  void operator= (const Shape& s) throw();
};

inline void Shape::operator= (const Shape& s) throw()
{ pos_ = s.pos_; }

Shape::~Shape() throw()
{ }
```

Note that such an assignment operator does not automatically trigger the Law of the Big Three (see FAQ 30.13).

FAQ 24.07

What should be returned by `private:` and `protected:` assignment operators?

Either return a reference to the `this` object, or make the return type `void`.

Assignment operators that are `private:` or `protected:` needn't return `*this` because such operators have very few users, and therefore the advantage of returning `*this` is limited.

Assignment operators are often declared as `private:` to prevent users from assigning objects of the class (see FAQ 30.13). They are often left undefined to prevent being accidentally called by a member function or a friend function.

Assignment operators are often declared as `protected:` in abstract base classes to ensure that assignment doesn't occur when the destination is a reference to an abstract class (for example, assigning a circle to a square when both are referenced by a `Shape&`; see FAQ 24.05).

FAQ 24.08

Are there techniques that increase the likelihood that the compiler-synthesized assignment operator will be right?

Following a few simple rules helps the compiler to synthesize assignment operators that do the right thing. Without an assignment operator discipline, developers will need to provide an explicit assignment operator for too many classes, because the compiler-synthesized version will be incorrect an unnecessarily large percentage of the time.

The following FAQs provide guidelines for an assignment operator discipline that we have found to be effective and practical.

FAQ 24.09

How should the assignment operator in a derived class behave?

An assignment operator in a derived class should call the assignment operator in its direct base classes (to assign those member objects that are declared in the base class), then call the assignment operators of its member objects (to change those member objects that are declared in the derived class). These assignments should normally be in the same order that the base classes and member objects appear in the class's definition. An example follows.

```
class Base {
public:
  Base& operator= (const Base& b) throw();
protected:
  int i_;
};
```

```
Base& Base::operator= (const Base& b) throw()
{
  i_ = b.i_;
  return *this;
}

class Derived : public Base {
public:
  Derived& operator= (const Derived& d) throw();
protected:
  int j_;
};

Derived& Derived::operator= (const Derived& d) throw()
{
  Base::operator= (d);
  j_ = d.j_;
  return *this;
}
```

Typically, a `Derived::operator=` shouldn't access the member objects defined in a base class; instead it should call its base class's assignment operator. Nor should a `Base::operator=` access member objects defined in a derived class (that is, it usually shouldn't call a virtual routine, like `copyState()`, to copy the derived class's state).

If a `Base::operator=` tried to copy a derived class's state via a virtual function, the compiler-synthesized assignment operators in the derived classes would be invalidated. This requires defining an explicit assignment operator in an unnecessarily large percentage of the derived classes. This added work often negates any common code that is shared in the base class's assignment operator.

For example, suppose `Base` defines `Base::operator= (const Base& b)`, and this assignment operator calls virtual function `copyFrom(const Base&)`. If the derived class `Derived` overrides `copyFrom(const Base&)` to change the entire abstract state of the `Derived` object, then the compiler-synthesized implementation of `Derived::operator= (const Derived&)` is likely to be unacceptable: the compiler-synthesized `Derived::operator= (const Derived&)` would call `Base::operator= (const Base&)`, which would call back to `Derived::copyFrom(const Base&)`; after returning, the `Derived` state would be assigned a second time by `Derived::operator= (const Derived&)`.

At best, this is a waste of CPU cycles because it reassigns the `Derived` member objects. At worst, this is semantically incorrect, because special changes made during `Derived::copyFrom(const Base&)` may get wiped out when the `Derived` member objects are subsequently assigned by `Derived::operator= (const Derived&)`.

Can an ABC's assignment operator be `virtual`?

An ABC's assignment operator can be virtual only if all derived classes of the ABC will be assignment compatible with all other derived classes and if the developer is willing to put up with a bit of extra work. This doesn't happen that often, but here's how to do it.

Classes derived from a base class are assignment compatible if and only if there's an isomorphism between the abstract states of the classes. For example, the abstract class `Stack` has concrete derived classes `StackBasedOnList` and `StackBasedOnArray`. These concrete derived classes have the same abstract state space as well as the same set of services and the same semantics. Thus, any `Stack` object can, in principle, be assigned to any other `Stack` object, whether or not they are instances of the same concrete class.

If all classes derived from an ABC are assignment compatible with all other derived classes from that ABC, there are two choices: when a user has a reference to the ABC, either prevent assignment or make it work correctly.

It is easiest on the class implementer to prevent assignment when the user has a reference to the base class. This is done by making the base class's assignment operator `protected:`. The disadvantage of this approach is that it restricts users from assigning arbitrary pairs of objects referred to by `Stack` references (that is, by `Stack&`).

The other choice is to make assignment work correctly when the user has a reference to the base class. This is done by making the base class's assignment operator `public:` and `virtual`. This approach allows any arbitrary `Stack&` to be assigned with any other `Stack&`, even if the two `Stack` objects are of different derived classes. The base class version of the assignment operator must be overridden in each derived class, and these overrides should copy the entire abstract state of the other `Stack` into the `this` object.

```
class Stack {
public:
  virtual ~Stack()                           throw();
  virtual void   push(int elem)      throw() = 0;
  virtual int    pop()               throw() = 0;
  virtual int    getElem(int n) const throw() = 0;
  virtual Stack& operator= (const Stack& s) throw();
protected:
  int n_;
};

Stack::~Stack() throw()
{ }
```

```
Stack& Stack::operator= (const Stack& s) throw()
{ n_ = s.n_; return *this; }

void userCode(Stack& s, Stack& s2)
{ s = s2; }
```

The overridden assignment operator and the overloaded assignment operator in a derived class, such as the StackArray class that follows, are often different.

```
class StackArray : public Stack {
public:
  StackArray()                            throw();
  virtual void push(int x)                throw();
  virtual int  pop()                      throw();
  virtual int  getElem(int n) const  throw();
  virtual StackArray& operator= (const Stack& s) throw();
                                              //override
  StackArray& operator= (const StackArray& s)   throw();
                                              //overload
protected:
  int data_[10];
};

StackArray::StackArray()                throw()
: Stack() { }
void StackArray::push(int x)            throw()
{ data_[n_++] = x; }
int StackArray::pop()                   throw()
{ return data_[--n_]; }
int StackArray::getElem(int n) const throw()
{ return data_[n]; }

// Override:
StackArray& StackArray::operator= (const Stack& s) throw()
{
  Stack::operator= (s);
  for (int i = 0; i < n_; ++i)
    data_[i] = s.getElem(i);
  return *this;
}

// Overload:
StackArray& StackArray::operator= (const StackArray& s) throw()
{
  Stack::operator= (s);
  for (int i = 0; i < n_; ++i)
    data_[i] = s.data_[i];
  return *this;
}
```

```
int main()
{
  StackArray s, s2;
  userCode(s, s2);
}
```

Note that the override (`StackArray::operator= (const Stack&)`) returns a
`StackArray&` rather than a mere `Stack&`. This is called a *covariant return type.*

FAQ 24.11

What should a derived class do if a base class's assignment operator is `virtual`?

The developer should probably override the base class's assignment operator and also
provide an overloaded assignment operator. For example, when base class B declares
`B::operator= (const B&)` to be virtual, a publicly derived class D should provide
both the override (`D::operator= (const B&)`) and the overload (`D::
operator= (const D&)`).

```
#include <iostream>
using namespace std;

class B {
public:
  virtual ~B() throw();
  virtual B& operator= (const B& b) throw();
};

B::~B() throw()
{ }

B& B::operator= (const B& b) throw()
{ cout << "B::operator=(const B&)\n"; return *this; }

class D : public B {
public:
  virtual D& operator= (const B& b) throw();  // override
  D& operator= (const D& d) throw();          // overload
};

D& D::operator= (const B& b) throw()  // override
{ cout << "D::operator=(const B&)\n"; return *this; }
```

```
D& D::operator= (const D& d) throw()  // overload
{ cout << "D::operator=(const D&)\n"; return *this; }
```

Because the compiler resolves which override to call based on the static type of the parameters, the first assignment in the following example is the only one that calls the assignment operator that takes a D; all the others end up calling the assignment operator that takes a B. Because b in `sample()` is actually of class D, and because the base class's assignment operator is `virtual`, all four assignments call one of the assignment operators from the derived class.

```
void sample(D& d, B& b, D& d2, B& b2) throw()
{
  cout << "d = d2:  ";  d = d2;
  cout << "d = b2:  ";  d = b2;
  cout << "b = b2:  ";  b = b2;
  cout << "b = d2:  ";  b = d2;
}

int main()
{
  D d, b, d2, b2;
  sample(d, b, d2, b2);
}
```

The output is

```
d = d2:   D::operator=(const D&)
d = b2:   D::operator=(const B&)
b = b2:   D::operator=(const B&)
b = d2:   D::operator=(const B&)
```

The last two calls resolve to the override (D::operator= (const B&)) because the actual class of b in `sample()` is D. If b had actually been a B, the last two calls would have resolved to B::operator= (const B&). Naturally, these calls could also resolve to some other override if the object's actual class had been some other derived class that provided an override.

Note that D::operator= (const B& b) does not detect that its parameter b is of class D.

FAQ 24.12

Should the assignment operator be implemented by using placement `new` and the copy constructor?

It's a well-known trap!

new

It is tempting to avoid duplicate code for the assignment operator for class X by trying something like this.

```
#include <new>
using namespace std;

X& X::operator= (const X& rhs)
{
  if (this != &rhs) {
    this->~X();
    new(this) X(rhs);
  }
  return *this;
}
```

There are many problems with this approach. `rhs` will be sliced whenever it is not of type X, and the dtor-new-ctor sequence does not bode well for performance. Worst of all, consider what this does to future classes derived from X, even if `operator=()` isn't declared `virtual` in a base class of X (which introduces issues of its own).

It's good to minimize duplicate code, but the smart way to do it is to put common code into a `private:` member function that can be used by both the copy ctor and assignment operator. That's a safe way to reuse code; the approach in the example should be avoided.

Chapter 25

Templates

What is the purpose of templates?

Templates share source code among structurally similar families of classes and functions.

Many data structures and algorithms can be defined independently of the type of data they manipulate. A template allows the separation of the type-dependent part from the type-independent part. The result is a significant amount of code sharing.

A template is like a cookie cutter: all the cookies it creates have the same basic shape, though they might be made from different kinds of dough. A class template describes how to build classes that implement the same data structure and algorithm, and a function template describes how to build functions that implement the same algorithm.

In other languages, these facilities are sometimes called *parameterized types* or *genericity.*

Prior to templates, macros were used as a means of implementing generics. But the results were so poor that templates have superceded them.

FAQ 25.02

What are the syntax and semantics for a class template?

The syntax of a class template is the keyword `template`, some template parameters, then something that looks a lot like a class. But semantically a class template is not a class: it is a cookie cutter to create a family of classes.

Consider a container class (see FAQ 2.15). In practice, the C++ source code for a container that holds `int`s is structurally very similar to the C++ source code for a container that holds `string`s. The resulting binary machine code is probably quite different, since, for example, copying an `int` requires different machine instructions than does copying a `string`. Trying to make the binary machine code the same might impose runtime overhead to generalize, for example, the copying operations for `int` and `string` and might also increase the complexity of the container.

Class templates give programmers another option: capturing the source code similarity without imposing extra runtime performance overhead. That is, the compiler generates special purpose code for containers of `int`, containers of `string`, and any others that are needed.

For example, if someone desired a container that acted like an array, in practice they would probably use the standard class template `vector<T>`. However, for illustration purposes we will create a class template `Array<T>` that acts like a safe array of T.

```
template<class T> ◄──────── T is a type in the declaration that follows
class Array {
public:
  Array(unsigned size=10);
  Array(const Array<T>& a);                    //copy constructor
  Array<T>& operator= (const Array<T>& a); //assignment
 ~Array() throw();
  unsigned size() const throw();
  const T& operator[] (unsigned i) const throw(out_of_range);
  T&        operator[] (unsigned i)       throw(out_of_range);
protected:
  unsigned  size_;
  T*        arr_;
};

template<class T> inline Array<T>::Array(unsigned size)
: size_(size)
, arr_(new T[size])
{ }
```

```
template<class T> inline Array<T>::~Array() throw()
{ delete[] arr_;   }

template<class T> inline unsigned Array<T>::size() const throw()
{ return size_; }

template<class T> inline const T& Array<T>::operator[] (unsigned i)
const
throw(out_of_range)
{
   if (i >= size_) throw out_of_range("Array<T>::operator[]"));
   return arr_[i];
}

template<class T> inline T& Array<T>::operator[] (unsigned i)
throw(out_of_range)
{
   if (i >= size_) throw out_of_range("Array<T>::operator[] const");
   return arr_[i];
}
```

The `template<class T>` part indicates that `T` represents a yet unspecified type in the class template definition. Note that the keyword `class` doesn't imply that `T` must be a user-defined type; it might be a built-in type such as `int` or `float`.

The C++ Standard defines the term *instantiated class* to mean the instantiation of a class template, but we will use the term *instantiation of a class template* instead, since most C++ programmers think of an instantiated class as an object rather than another class. When it doesn't matter whether it is a class template or a function template, we will drop the qualifying adjective and refer to the *instantiation of a template.*

```
#include <string>
#include "Array.hpp"
using namespace std;

int main()
{
   Array<int>    ai;   ai[5] = 42;
   Array<float>  af;   af[5] = 42.0;
   Array<char>   ac;   ac[5] = 'x';
   Array<string> as;   as[5] = "xyz";
}
```

Normally the compiler creates an instantiation of a class template when the name of a class template is followed by a particular sequence of template arguments. In this case, the only template argument is a type. The compiler generates code for the instantiated template by replacing the template argument T with the type that is supplied, such as int.

FAQ 25.03

How can a template class be specialized to handle special cases?

Use explicit specialization.

Sometimes a programmer wants the compiler to bypass the class template when creating an instantiation of a class template for a particular type and use a specialized class template instead. For example, suppose that an array of bits is needed. The natural thing to do is create an Array<bool> using the template class from FAQ 25.02.

```
#include "Array.hpp"

int main()
{
  Array<bool> ab;
  ab[5] = true;
}
```

If the previously defined Array template were used to generate the code for this class, it would end up creating an array of bool which would, at best, be optimized to be an array of bytes. Clearly a bit array would be more space-efficient than a byte array. This more space-efficient implementation can be created by defining class Array<bool> as an explicit specialization of the class template Array. Notice how class Array<bool> uses a bit array rather than a byte array.

```
#include <new>
using namespace std;

template<class T> class Array;

template<>
class Array<bool> {
public:
  typedef  unsigned char  Byte;

  class BitRef {
  public:
```

```
      BitRef(Byte& byte, unsigned bit) throw();
      operator bool() throw();
      BitRef& operator= (bool b) throw();
    private:
      Byte& byte_;
      unsigned bit_;
    };

    Array(unsigned size=10) throw(bad_alloc);
    Array(const Array<bool>& a) throw(bad_alloc);
    Array<bool>& operator= (const Array<bool>& a) throw(bad_alloc);
    ~Array() throw();
    unsigned size() const throw();
    bool   operator[] (unsigned i) const throw();
    BitRef operator[] (unsigned i)       throw();
  protected:
    unsigned size_;
    Byte*    arr_;
};

template<> inline Array<bool>::Array(unsigned size) throw(bad_alloc)
: size_(size)
, arr_ (new Byte[(size+7u)/8u])
{ memset(arr_, '\0', (size+7u)/8u); }

template<> inline Array<bool>::~Array() throw()
{ delete[] arr_; }

template<> inline unsigned Array<bool>::size() const throw()
{ return size_; }

template<> inline bool Array<bool>::operator[] (unsigned i) const
throw()
{ return (arr_[i/8u] >> (i&7u)) & 1u; }

template<> inline Array<bool>::BitRef Array<bool>::operator[]
(unsigned i)
throw()
{ return BitRef(arr_[i/8u], i&7u); }

template<> inline Array<bool>::BitRef::BitRef(Byte& byte, unsigned
bit) throw()
: byte_(byte)
, bit_(bit)
{ }

template<> inline Array<bool>::BitRef::operator bool() throw()
{ return (byte_ >> bit_) & 1u; }
```

```
template<>
inline Array<bool>::BitRef& Array<bool>::BitRef::operator= (bool b)
throw()
{
  if (b) byte_ |=  (1u << bit_);
  else   byte_ &= ~(1u << bit_);
  return *this;
}
```

`Array<bool>` is an explicit specialization of the class template `Array`, and `Array<bool>` will be used instead of `Array` whenever an `Array<bool>` is needed.

```
int main()
{
  Array<int>   ai;  ai[5] = 42;   ←———— Uses the generic class template
  Array<float> af;  af[5] = 42.0; ←———— Uses the generic class template
  Array<char>  ac;  ac[5] = 'x';  ←———— Uses the generic class template
  Array<bool>  ab;  ab[5] = true; ←———— Uses explicit specialization, not
                                         the generic class template
}
```

Explicit specializations are often used to take advantage of special properties of the type `T` and achieve space and/or speed benefits that could not be achieved using the generic class template.

It is normally best to define the explicit specialization (for example, `Array<bool>`) in the same header that defines the template itself (for example, the same header that defines `Array<T>`). That way the compiler is guaranteed to see the explicit specialization before any uses of the specialization occur.

FAQ 25.04

What are the syntax and semantics for a function template?

The syntax of a function template is the keyword `template`, some template parameters, then something that looks a lot like a function. But semantically a function template is not a function: it is a cookie cutter to create a family of functions.

Consider a function that swaps its two integer arguments. Just as with `Array` in the preceding example, repeating the code for `swap()` for swapping `float`, `char`, `string`, and so on, will become tedious. A single function template is the solution.

```
template<class T>
void swap(T& x, T& y)
{
  T temp = x;
  x = y;
  y = temp;
}
```

Every time `swap()` appears with a new combination of parameter types, the compiler creates yet another instantiation of the function template. Here is an example.

```
#include <string>
using namespace std;

int main()
{
  int    i, j;  /*...*/  swap(i,j);  //swap(int&,    int&)
  char   a, b;  /*...*/  swap(a,b);  //swap(char&,   char&)
  float  c, d;  /*...*/  swap(c,d);  //swap(float&, float&)
  string s, t;  /*...*/  swap(s,t);  //swap(string&,string&)
}
```

As with class templates, a programmer can get the compiler to bypass the function template when creating a template function: the programmer simply needs to manually create a specialized template function.

_____ **FAQ 25.05**

Should a template use `memcpy()` to copy objects of its template argument?

No.

An object should be bitwise copied only when it is known that the class of the object will forever be amenable to bitwise copy. But the class of a template argument can't be known. Here is an example.

```
#include <cstring>
#include <new>
using namespace std;

template<class T>
class Array {
```

```
public:
  Array(unsigned len=10);
  Array(const Array<T>& a);                    // copy constructor
  Array<T>& operator= (const Array<T>& a);   // assignment
 ~Array() throw();
  unsigned len() const throw();
  const T& operator[] (unsigned i) const throw();
  T&       operator[] (unsigned i)       throw();
protected:
  unsigned  len_;
  T*        arr_;
};

template<class T> inline
Array<T>::Array(unsigned len)
: len_(len), arr_(new T[len]) { }

template<class T> inline
Array<T>::~Array() throw()
{ delete[] arr_;  }

template<class T> inline
unsigned Array<T>::len() const throw()
{ return len_; }

template<class T> inline
const T& Array<T>::operator[] (unsigned i) const throw()
{ return arr_[i]; }

template<class T> inline
T& Array<T>::operator[] (unsigned i) throw()
{ return arr_[i]; }

template<class T>
Array<T>::Array(const Array<T>& a)
: len_(a.len_)
, arr_(new T[a.len_])
{
  #if 1
    for (unsigned i = 0; i < len_; ++i)   ◀── Good: The T objects copy themselves
      arr_[i] = a.arr_[i];
  #else
    memcpy(arr_, a.arr_, len_*sizeof(T));  ◀── Bad: Manipulates the T objects
  #endif
}

template<class T>
Array<T>& Array<T>::operator= (const Array<T>& a)
```

```
  {
    if (len_ != a.len_) {  ◄──────── Makes self-assignment harmless (see FAQ 24.03)
      T* arr2 = new T[a.len_];
      delete[] arr_;
      arr_ = arr2;
      len_ = a.len_;
    }

    #if 1
      // GOOD FORM: lets the T objects copy themselves
      for (unsigned i = 0; i < len_; ++i)  ◄──────── Good: The T objects copy themselves
        arr_[i] = a.arr_[i];
    #else
      // BAD FORM: manipulates the bits of the T objects
      memcpy(arr_, a.arr_, len_*sizeof(T));  ◄──────── Bad: Manipulates the T objects
    #endif

    return *this;
  }
```

If a template uses memcpy() to copy some T objects, the template must have a big, fat, juicy comment warning potential users that a class with nontrivial copy semantics might destroy the world. For example, if memcpy() were used in the example class template, and if someone created an Array<string>, it is likely that the memcpy() would create dangling references and/or wild pointers, and they would probably crash the application (see FAQ 32.01).

Finally, notice that the member functions that create T objects (that is, the constructors and the assignment operator) do *not* have *exception specifications* (see FAQ 9.04). This is because the T object's constructor may throw arbitrary exceptions, and any restrictions placed on these template member functions would be wrong for some particular type T.

FAQ 25.06

Why does the compiler complain about >> when one template is used inside another?

Maximal munch.

In the following example, a is a list of vector of int (list and vector are standard container classes; see FAQ 28.13).

```
#include <list>
#include <vector>
using namespace std;

int main()
{
  list< vector<int> >  a;
  // ...
}
```

If the declaration had been written without any spaces between the two > symbols, such as `list<vector<int>>`, the compiler would have interpreted the two > symbols as a single right-shift operator.

Here are the details. The compiler's tokenizer (something the compiler does to figure out what a program means) has a rule called the maximal munch rule: "Read characters out of the source file until adding one more character causes the current token to stop making sense." For example, the keyword `int` is one token rather than three separate tokens, `i`, `n`, and `t`. Therefore, if the tokenizer encounters two > symbols together with no whitespace between them, the maximal munch combines them into one token: `>>`.

Chapter 26

Exception Tactics

What belongs in a `try` block?

Code that may `throw` an exception from which this function might be able to recover.

If the code called from a `try` block cannot `throw` an exception, then there is no need for the `try` block. Similarly, if the code called from a `try` block can `throw` exceptions but this function cannot recover from the exceptions, then there is no point in catching the exception and no point in putting the code in a `try` block.

Simply put, a function shouldn't worry about things that it can't fix. The important message here is that `try...catch` is not like old-fashioned error codes. Programmers who don't realize the differences put a `try` block around every call to every routine that could `throw` an exception. This is not wise.

When should a function `catch` an exception?

When it knows what to do with it.

There is no point having a function catch an exception if it doesn't know what to do with it. If every function had an explicit `try` and `catch` for every function it calls, two of the benefits of C++ exceptions (reduced coding and testing costs) would be lost. Errors are commonly handled several (often many) stack frames above where they are detected. Intermediate stack frames normally ignore exceptions they can't handle.

Most object-oriented systems designate some objects as controllers. Controllers typically define the policy of the system, and, because of this, they are often the objects that are best suited for implementing the system's exception-handling policy.

FAQ 26.03

Should a `catch` block fully recover from an error?

If possible. But sometimes the best that can be done is some cleanup and a rethrow.

If a function can completely recover from the error, then it can either continue with normal processing or restart the `try` block (put the `try` block in a loop, for example).

If a function can affect a partial, local recovery from the error, the `catch` clause can propagate the exception to the calling function either by throwing the same exception object (`throw;`) or by throwing a different exception object.

The worst thing to do is to leave the system in an ill-defined state by affecting a partial, local recovery from the error and then returning to normal processing. Here is an example of acceptable ways to handle the problem.

The first step is to define some exception classes. For this example, two exception classes are needed: `BadFileName` for file names that are invalid and `AccessViolation` for file names that are valid but which refer to files that cannot be accessed by the current user (for example, insufficient privileges). Since all exception classes should inherit from a very small number of base classes (see FAQ 9.10), these exception classes inherit from the standard exception class `runtime_error`:

```
#include <stdexcept>
#include <iostream>
#include <string>
using namespace std;

class BadFileName : public runtime_error {
public:
  BadFileName(const string& filename) throw();
};

BadFileName::BadFileName(const string& filename) throw()
: runtime_error("bad file name: " + filename) { }

class AccessViolation : public runtime_error {
public:
  AccessViolation(const string& filename) throw();
};
```

```
AccessViolation::AccessViolation(const string& filename) throw()
: runtime_error("access violation on file " + filename) { }
```

The next step is to define a `File` class that pretends to check the file name and access privileges. The code for this actually uses hard-coded names: the name `BadName.txt` represents a bad file name, and the name `NoAccess.txt` represents a file that cannot be accessed. In reality this member function would call some system routines to determine whether the file name was good or bad and whether the file was accessible or not.

```
class File {
public:
  File(const string& filename) throw(BadFileName, AccessViolation);
};

File::File(const string& filename) throw(BadFileName, AccessViolation)
{
  cout << "File::File(): Opening " << filename << "\n";
  if (filename == "NoAccess.txt")
    throw AccessViolation();
  if (filename == "BadName.txt")
    throw BadFileName();
  cout << "  Successfully opened\n";
}
```

The next step is to declare some functions that catch and partially recover from these exceptions.

```
void first(const string& filename) throw();
void second(const string& filename) throw(BadFileName);

int main()
{
  first("GoodFile.txt");
  first("BadName.txt");
  first("NoAccess.txt");
}

void first(const string& filename) throw()
{
  try {
    second(filename);
  }
  catch (BadFileName& e) {
    cout << "  first(): " << e.what() << ": Finish recovery\n";
  }
```

```
    }

void second(const string& filename) throw(BadFileName)
{
  try {
    File x(filename);
  }
  catch (BadFileName& e) {
    cout << "  second(): " << e.what() << ": Partial recovery\n";
    throw;  ←——— Rethrow the BadFileName exception
  }
  catch (AccessViolation& e) {
    cout << "  second(): " << e.what() << ": Full recovery\n";
  }
}
```

The output of the program is as follows.

```
File::File(): Opening GoodFile.txt
  Successfully opened
File::File(): Opening BadName.txt
  second(): bad file name: BadName.txt: Partial recovery
  first(): bad file name: BadName.txt: Finish recovery
File::File(): Opening NoAccess.txt
  first(): access violation on file NoAccess.txt: Full recovery
```

FAQ 26.04

How should a constructor handle a failure?

It should throw an exception.

Some authors suggest that constructors should not throw exceptions. In general this is wrong. For example, constructors cannot return an error code, so attempting to use error codes is inappropriate.

Besides, a failed constructor usually indicates that the object did not achieve a self-consistent state (for example, it may not have been able to allocate sufficient memory, the appropriate file may not have existed, and so on). It is error-prone to let these objects continue to live. For example, if some other member function of the object used a nonexistent resource, it would be an error.

If a constructor experiences an error and the programmer cannot throw an exception, another alternative is to mark the object as a zombie (see FAQ 26.05).

FAQ 26.05

What are zombie objects (and why should they be avoided)?

Zombie objects are C++'s version of the living dead—objects that aren't quite alive but aren't quite dead either.

When an environment doesn't support `throw` or when a programmer decides to avoid throwing exceptions from constructors (see FAQ 26.04), an object that can't finish its constructor can set an internal status flag to indicate that the object is unusable. Then the class provides a query (inspector) member function so that users can see whether the object is usable or a zombie.

The zombie object technique has the unfortunate side effect of allowing objects to survive even though their constructor failed. This means that all member functions must first check to make sure the object isn't a zombie before using the data inside the object and that all users of an object must check to make sure the object is usable after creating the object.

In general, the zombie technique is inferior to throwing an exception.

FAQ 26.06

What should an object do if one of its member objects could throw an exception during its constructor?

Nothing, but the object and its member objects should be designed to manage their own destruction.

First some background. When the constructor of a member object throws an exception, member objects that have already been constructed are destructed. For example, if an object has member objects `x_` and `y_`, and if `x_`'s constructor succeeds (doesn't `throw`) and `y_`'s constructor `throws` an exception, then `x_`'s destructor is invoked. However the object that has member objects `x_` and `y_` was not fully constructed, so the object's destructor is not called.

The easiest way to make things work correctly is to ensure that the destructor for each member object manages its own destruction and does not rely on the composite's destructor to do anything important (since the composite's destructor is not executed). So `x_`'s destructor must completely handle the destruction of `x_` without relying on any help from the composite's destructor. This is illustrated in the following example.

```
#include <iostream>
#include <stdexcept>
using namespace std;

class X {
public:
  X() throw();
 ~X() throw();
};

X::X()  throw() { cout << "X ctor\n"; }
X::~X() throw() { cout << "X dtor\n"; }

class Y {
public:
  Y() throw(runtime_error);
};

Y::Y() throw(runtime_error)
{
  cout << "Y ctor throwing\n";
  throw runtime_error("thrown from Y ctor");
}

class A {
public:
  A() throw(int);
 ~A() throw();
protected:
  X x_;
  Y y_;
};

A::A() throw(int)
: x_()
, y_()          The exception is throw from here
{ cout << "A ctor\n"; }

A::~A() throw()
{ cout << "A dtor\n"; }

int main()
{
  try {
    A a;
    cout << "never gets here\n";
  }
  catch (exception& e) {
```

```
        cout << "main caught: " << e.what() << endl;
    }
}
```

The output follows.

```
X ctor
Y ctor throwing
X dtor
main caught: thrown from Y ctor
```

Because `A::~A()` was never invoked, it had better not do something important to `x_`, because those important things won't happen if `y_`'s constructor throws an exception.

Rule of thumb: Every member object should manage its own destruction.

Note that C++ also allows programmers to put a `try` block inside a constructor's initialization list. This can be used when the rule-of-thumb is not applied.

Should destructors throw exceptions when they fail?

No.

If a destructor is invoked during the stack-unwinding process initiated by the throwing of another exception, and that destructor throws an exception, `terminate()` is invoked, which kills the program.

Should destructors call routines that may throw exceptions?

Yes, provided the destructor catches whatever the routines might throw.

If a destructor is called while unwinding the stack caused by another exception, and that destructor calls a routine `f()` that throws an exception, the destructor must catch the second (nested) exception; otherwise the exception-handling mechanism calls the `terminate()` function. In plain English: if the destructor calls something that might `throw` an exception, the destructor should `catch` all possible exceptions.

```
#include <iostream>
#include <stdexcept>
```

```
using namespace std;

void fred() throw(runtime_error)
{
  cout << "fred() throwing\n";
  throw runtime_error("thrown from fred()");
}

class X {
public:
  ~X() throw();
};

X::~X() throw()
{
  try {
    fred();
  }
  catch (exception& e) {
    cout << "handling fred()'s exception: " << e.what() << '\n';
  }
}

int main()
{
  try {
    X x;
    cout << "main() throwing\n";
    throw logic_error("thrown from main()");
  }
  catch (exception& e) {
    cout << "handling main()'s exception: " << e.what() << '\n';
  }
}
```

X::~X() is called as a result of the exception thrown by main(). But X::~X() calls
fred(), which also throws an exception. Fortunately X::~X() catches the exception
thrown by fred(); otherwise terminate() would be called at the end of
X::~X().

The output is

```
main() throwing
fred() throwing
handling fred()'s exception: thrown from fred()
handling main()'s exception: thrown from main()
```

Should resource deallocation primitives signal failure by throwing an exception?

No.

Examples of resource deallocation primitives include overloads of `operator delete`, closing files, unlocking semaphores, and so on.

Because these are commonly called from destructors, they should signal failure by some means other than throwing an exception. The alternatives range from printing a diagnostic error message in a log file to halting the system, and the best choice depends on the circumstances. This reduces the number of cases in which `terminate()` is inadvertently called.

What should the `terminate()` function do?

Log the error, release all known systemwide resources, and call `abort()`.

The `terminate` function is called when the exception-handling system encounters an error from which it can't recover. This happens when `main()` fails to catch an exception and when a destructor called by the exception handler throws an exception. It is also the default behavior of the `unexpected` function. The `set_terminate()` function can be used to change the behavior of `terminate()`.

The `terminate` function must not return, nor may it `throw` an exception. The best approach is to log the catastrophe (flush the file after logging the error, because `abort()` doesn't close open files), release any known systemwide resources (things that other applications depend on), and call `abort()`.

C'est la vie.

What should the `unexpected()` function do?

Log the error and call `terminate()`.

new

When a function has an exception specifier and the function throws an exception that doesn't match anything in its exception specifier list (Murphy's Law), the exception-handling mechanism calls unexpected(). By default, the unexpected() function silently calls the terminate() function, which is terminal. The behavior of unexpected() can and probably should be changed by using the set_unexpected() function:

```
#include <cstdlib>
#include <iostream>
using namespace std;

class Fred    { };
class Wilma   { };

void sample() throw(Fred)
{
  switch (rand() % 3) {
    case 0:
      cout << "throwing a Fred; ";
      throw Fred();
    case 1:
      cout << "throwing a Wilma; ";
      throw Wilma();  ←——— Danger
    default:
      cout << "returning normally; ";
  }
}
```

Note that the preceding user code expected to throw a Fred but never expected to throw a Wilma (see the exception specification immediately following the signature of sample()). In practice, this happens accidentally, such as when sample() calls a function that calls a function that calls a function that throws a Wilma. In any case, sample() is erroneous; either it must catch the Wilma or it must broaden its exception specification list to tell its users that it may throw a Wilma.

```
#include <exception>

void myUnexpected() throw()
{
  cout << "unexpected exception!" << endl;
  terminate();   // Good night Nurse!
}

int main()
{
  // Without this, the program would silently crash:
  set_unexpected(myUnexpected);
```

```
for (int i = 0; i < 10; ++i) {
  try {
    cout << "trying: ";
    sample();
    cout << "no exception thrown\n";
  }
  catch (Fred) {
    cout << "caught a Fred\n";
  }
  catch (Wilma) {
    cout << "caught a Wilma\n";
  }
  catch (...) {
    cout << "this should never happen\n";
  }
}
}
```

Saving the most recently thrown exception in a global variable can enhance the technique. That way the error message in `myUnexpected()` can be more intelligent, especially if all exceptions inherit from a common base class that provides some identification services. Obviously, access to such global variables must be serialized in multi-threaded environments.

If a program is crashing silently before `main()` begins, it may be getting an unexpected exception during static initialization. In this case, it is necessary to set the unexpected function (`set_unexpected(myUnexpected);`) inside a constructor of a static object, but even then there are no guarantees since the static object may not get constructed (and therefore `myUnexpected()` function may not be registered) before the error occurs.

FAQ 26.12

Under what circumstances can an overridden virtual member function throw exceptions other than those listed by the specification of the member function in the base class?

new

When the exception is an object of a class that is publicly derived from one of the classes mentioned in the exception specification of the base class's member function. This ensures that users of the base class won't be surprised.

Suppose class `Base` has member function `f()` that promises to throw only objects of class X. If class `Derived` overrides `f()` and throws an object of unrelated class Y, user code will break, because users will get an unexpected exception. However, Derived::f() can throw an X2 if X2 is derived from X due to the is-a conversion that allows a derived class reference to automatically be converted to a base class reference.

```cpp
#include <cstdlib>
#include <iostream>
using namespace std;

class X { };
class Y { };
class X2 : public X { };

class Base {
public:
  virtual void f() throw(X);
    //PROMISE: may throw 'X', but never throws anything else
  virtual ~Base() throw();
};

Base::~Base() throw()
{ }

void userCode(Base& base) throw()
{
  try {
    base.f();
    cout << "OK: base.f() didn't throw anything\n";
  }
  catch (X& x) {
    cout << "OK: base.f() threw an X\n";
  }
  catch (...) {
    cout << "huh? base.f() threw something other than X!\n";
  }
}

class Derived : public Base {
public:
  virtual void f() throw(X, X2, Y);
    //PROMISE:
    //   may throw X  ◄──── OK: Users are expecting this
    //   may throw X2 ◄──── OK: X2 is derived from X
    //   may throw Y  ◄──── Bad form: Violates the promise of Base
};

void Base::f() throw(X)
{ if (rand() % 2 == 0) throw X(); }

void Derived::f() throw(X, X2, Y)
```

```
{
  int r = rand() % 4;
  if (r == 0) throw X();  ◀——— OK: Base users are expecting X
  if (r == 1) throw X2();  ◀——— OK: Base users are expecting X
  if (r == 2) throw Y();  ◀——— Bad: Base users don't expect Y
}

int main()
{
  Base    b;
  Derived d;
  cout << "using 'Base'\n";
  for (int i = 0; i < 10; ++i)
    userCode(b);
  cout << "using 'Derived'\n";
  for (int j = 0; j < 10; ++j)
    userCode(d);
}
```

The overridden member function in the derived class has a weaker promise than that made by the base class: `Base` promised not to throw a `Y`, and `Derived` broke this promise.

Weakening a promise breaks user code.

FAQ 26.13

How might the exception-handling mechanism cause a program to silently crash?

Of the zillion reasons a program might silently crash, we'll point out two that are related to the C++ exception-handling mechanism.

Possibility 87642: If an exception is thrown but not caught, `terminate()` is called, which calls `abort()` by default. The solution is to wrap `main()` in a `try` block that has a `catch(...)` clause (see FAQ 9.10). If that doesn't work, look for a constructor of a file-scope static object that might throw an exception. Another way to handle this problem is to replace the `terminate` function with one that prints an appropriate message before it calls `abort()`.

Possibility 253375: If an exception is thrown that didn't match anything on the exception specification list, `unexpected()` is called, which calls `terminate()` by default, which calls `abort()` by default. The solution is to replace the behavior of `unexpected()` with a function that prints an appropriate message (see FAQ 26.11).

Chapter 27

Types and RTTI

What is the purpose of this chapter?

This chapter explores static and dynamic type checking, both of which are allowed in C++. Its main theme is that static type checking is always a good idea, while the impulse to use dynamic type checking should be carefully controlled. In those cases, such as persistence, where some form of dynamic type checking might be required, runtime type identification (RTTI) should be used.

new

What is static type checking?

Static type checking, sometimes known as *static typing*, is when the compiler checks the type correctness of operations at compile time. For example, the compiler checks the parameter types of function arguments and checks that a member function invocation is guaranteed to work at runtime, then it flags improper matches as errors at compile time.

In object-oriented programs, the most common symptom of a type mismatch is the attempt to invoke a member function via a reference to an object, where the reference's type and/or the object's type does not support the member function. For example, if class X has member function f() but not member function g() and x is an instance of class X, then x.f() is legal and x.g() is illegal.

```
class X {
public:
  void f() throw();
};

void X::f() throw()
{ }

int main()
{
  X x;
  x.f();    //OK

  #ifdef GENERATE_ERROR
    //The following error is caught at compile time
    //There is no need for runtime checks
    x.g();
  #endif
}
```

Fortunately, C++ catches errors like this at compile time.

FAQ 27.03

What is dynamic type checking?

Dynamic type checking, sometimes known as *dynamic typing,* is the determination of type correctness at runtime.

With dynamic type checking, user code determines whether an object supports a particular member function at runtime rather than at compile time. Dynamic type checking is often accompanied by downcasts (see FAQ 27.11) and can unnecessarily increase the cost of C++ software. *Runtime type identification* (RTTI) is one kind of dynamic type checking that is supported directly by C++.

The following example demonstrates the wrong way to do things. Pretend that the various escape sequences toggle italics on the various kinds of printers.

```
#include <iostream>
using namespace std;

// pretend this is the escape character
const char* const esc = "ESC";

enum Type { EPSON, PROPRINTER, STAR };
```

```cpp
class Printer {
public:
  virtual ~Printer() throw();
  virtual Type type() const throw() = 0;
};

Printer::~Printer() throw()
{ }

class EpsonPrinter : public Printer {
public:
  virtual Type type() const throw();
  void italicsEpson(const char* s) throw();
};

Type EpsonPrinter::type() const throw()
{ return EPSON; }

void EpsonPrinter::italicsEpson(const char* s) throw()
{ cout << esc << "i+" << s << esc << "i-"; }

class ProprinterPrinter : public Printer {
public:
  virtual Type type() const throw();
  void italicsProprinter(const char* s) throw();
};

Type ProprinterPrinter::type() const throw()
{ return PROPRINTER; }

void ProprinterPrinter::italicsProprinter(const char* s) throw()
{ cout << esc << "[i" << s << esc << "[n"; }

class StarPrinter : public Printer {
public:
  virtual Type type() const throw();
  void italicsStar(const char* s) throw();
};

Type StarPrinter::type() const throw()
{ return STAR; }

void StarPrinter::italicsStar(const char* s) throw()
{ cout << esc << "x" << s << esc << "y"; }

void printUsingItalics(Printer& p, const char* s) throw()
{
  switch (p.type()) {
```

```
        case EPSON:
          ((EpsonPrinter&) p).italicsEpson(s);
          break;
        case PROPRINTER:
          ((ProprinterPrinter&) p).italicsProprinter(s);
          break;
        case STAR:
          ((StarPrinter&) p).italicsStar(s);
          break;
        default:
          cerr << "Call tech support at 1-800-BAD-BUGS\n";
      }
    }
```

Although the example uses classes and virtual functions, it is not the best use of OO technology. The type() member function is used in basically the same way that procedural code uses tagged unions (that is, tag fields that indicate which piece of the union is currently being used). This approach is subject to error and is nonextensible compared to the proper use of classes and virtual functions, shown later in this chapter. For example, adding a new kind of printer requires changes to the printUsingItalics() function and probably to other functions as well. This is a ripple effect that is typical with non-OO (and bad OO!) software.

FAQ 27.04 ────────────────────────────────────

What is the basic problem with dynamic type checking?

The basic problem with dynamic type checking is that it uses code to find code, creating extensibility problems later.

With dynamic type checking, code has to be written to check the type of an object to see if it supports a particular set of member functions (this is the code that is doing the finding). Accessing the member functions may require a down cast to the appropriate pointer type (this is the code that is being searched for).

When the user code uses code to find server code, the user code is more complex and fragile. OO programming is supposed to encapsulate complexity, and the inappropriate use of dynamic type checking can undo this benefit. Often dynamic type-checking tests require the user code to know the server's inheritance hierarchy, in which case changing the server's inheritance hierarchy breaks the user code. This is unfortunate, considering that one of the main goals of object-oriented technology is to reduce maintenance costs.

Dynamic type checking also requires a runtime check to ensure that the object supports the requested member function. This is usually implemented using control flow, such as an `if` or `switch` statement. These runtime tests are frequently avoidable if the design exploits the static type-checking capabilities of the C++ compiler.

Finally, it is much more expensive to catch an error at runtime than it is to find the same error at compile time. Don't use dynamic type checking without a good reason.

FAQ 27.05

How can dynamic type checking be avoided?

Design. Design. Design.

Circumstances sometimes require the use of dynamic type checking, but unfortunately, dynamic type checking is often used when it is not required. Often dynamic type checking is used because the programmer does not have enough expertise or does not take the time to produce a good object-oriented design. When dynamic type checking seems attractive, try revising the design instead. After the design has been revisited and dynamic type checking still seems desirable, use it. But be aware of the additional coding, testing, and maintenance costs.

FAQ 27.06

Are there better alternatives to dynamic type checking?

One alternative to dynamic type checking and down casts is dynamic binding and virtual functions. To use this alternative technique, member functions that show up only in the derived classes are generalized and moved up to the base class. Effectively this means that the class selection and down cast is performed automatically and safely by C++. Furthermore, this approach produces extensible software because it automatically extends itself whenever a new derived class is created—as if an extra `case` or `else if` magically appeared in the dynamic type-checking technique.

The following example is a rework of the code from FAQ 27.03. Compared to the old class hierarchy, the `italicsXXX()` member functions from the derived classes are generalized and moved into the base class as virtual member function `italics()`. This results in a substantial simplification of the user code `printUsingItalics()`. Instead of selecting the printer type based on a `type()` member function and using control flow logic to figure out what to do, the user code simply invokes the new `italics()` member function.

```
class Printer {
public:
  virtual ~Printer() throw();
  virtual void italics(const char* s) throw() = 0;
};

Printer::~Printer() throw()
{ }

class EpsonPrinter : public Printer {
public:
  virtual void italics(const char* s) throw();
};

void EpsonPrinter::italics(const char* s) throw()
{ cout << esc << "i+" << s << esc << "i-"; }

class ProprinterPrinter : public Printer {
public:
  virtual void italics(const char* s) throw();
};

void ProprinterPrinter::italics(const char* s) throw()
{ cout << esc << "[i" << s << esc << "[n"; }

class StarPrinter : public Printer {
public:
  virtual void italics(const char* s) throw();
};

void StarPrinter::italics(const char* s) throw()
{ cout << esc << "x" << s << esc << "y"; }

void printUsingItalics(Printer& p, const char* s) throw()
{ p.italics(s); }
```

From a broader standpoint, complexity is moved from the user code to the server code, from the many to the few. This is normally the right trade-off. Furthermore, adding a new kind of `Printer` doesn't require existing code to be modified—reducing the ripple effect when compared to FAQ 27.03.

FAQ 27.07

What is a capability query?

A capability query is an inspector member function (see FAQ 14.07) that allows users to determine whether an object supports some other member function. Capability queries invite inflexibility.

The *benefit* of capability queries is that they allow a class designer to avoid thinking about how users will use the objects, instead forcing the user code to explicitly test the classes and objects to see what capabilities they support.

The *problem* with capability queries is that they allow a class designer to avoid thinking about how users will use the objects, instead forcing the user code to explicitly test the classes and objects to see what capabilities they support.

Capability queries export complexity from the server to the users, from the few to the many. User code often needs explicit control flow to select operations based on the results of a capability query—user code uses code to find code (see FAQ 27.04). This impacts existing user code when new derived classes are added.

Capability queries are not normally recommended.

FAQ 27.08

What is an alternative to dynamic type checking with containers?

Templates offer a viable alternative when working with containers.

In the past, some container classes were designed assuming the existence of some kind of master base class. This has been called the *based object approach*. In particular, it was common to encounter container classes that inserted or extracted elements that were pointers to a single base class, typically called `Object`.

Applying the based object approach to containers makes it hard to mix two or more class libraries. For example, it may not be possible to put an object from one library into a container from another library, since the master base classes from the two libraries normally won't match exactly.

In general, this approach can and should be avoided through the use of templates or design patterns. The particular problem of extensible container classes has been elegantly solved in the standard C++ container classes by using templates and iterators.

Note that Java always inherits all classes from class `Object`. But since there is exactly one `Object` class in Java, as opposed to one per library vendor in C++, it isn't as big a problem in Java. The important point is that Java and C++ are very different in some fundamental ways. Syntactically they appear to be quite similar, but semantically there are some fundamental differences. Therefore just because a technique works in one language (say the based object approach works in Java) does not mean the same approach works or should be made to work in a different language (see FAQ 28.08).

FAQ 27.09

Are there cases where dynamic type checking is necessary?

Yes, particularly with persistent heterogeneous objects.

A program can't have static knowledge about things that existed before the execution of the program. If objects from several classes were previously stored in a database, the program that peels the objects off the disk drive's platter (or, equivalently, slurps them from a coaxial cable) cannot know the types of the objects because it didn't create them.

In these cases, the objects may need to be queried about their types, especially if the persistent objects are highly heterogeneous. To whatever extent possible, use the maxim "Ask once, then remember." In other words, try to avoid asking an object its type (or its capabilities) every time it is used. This is especially true if the queries require reasoning about the objects in a nonextensible manner (that is, control flow logic that uses code to find code; see FAQ 27.04).

Note that it is normally possible to avoid the type queries if the objects are known to be of the same class (homogeneous) or at least known to be derived from some common ABC that has a fairly rich set of member functions.

FAQ 27.10

Given a pointer to an ABC, how can the class of the referent be found?

This is an idea that should be avoided.

The typical reason for trying to find an object's class is to use an algorithm that depends on the object's class. If the algorithm varies depending on the derived class, then the algorithm should be a virtual member function in the class hierarchy. If the algorithm is structurally the same for all derived classes but has little pieces that differ depending on the derived class, then the little pieces should be virtual member functions in the class hierarchy. This technique lets derived classes select the ideal algorithm or algorithm fragments without any additional branch points in the software (see FAQ 27.04).

For example, finding the minimal distance to a mouse click requires different algorithms for circles, squares, lines, and so forth. One might be tempted to write non-OO code such as the following (pretend `Position`, `Shape`, `Circle`, and so forth, are classes).

```
int dist_BAD_FORM(Shape& s, Position mouse) throw()
{
  Circle* cp = dynamic_cast<Circle*>(&s);
  Square* sp = dynamic_cast<Square*>(&s);
  Line*   lp = dynamic_cast<Line*>(&s);

  if (cp != NULL) {
    //find the distance from mouse to the Circle, *cp
  } else if (sp != NULL) {
    //find the distance from mouse to the Square, *sp
  } else if (lp != NULL) {
    //find the distance from mouse to the Line, *lp
  }
}
```

One problem with this non-OO technique is that adding a new derived class requires working user code to be modified by adding a new `else if` section. Besides the obvious concern that changing working user code may break it, in large systems it is difficult to find all the places that need to be changed, and in very large systems there is typically a scheduling problem coordinating the changes in diverse teams of developers. In one organization the ripple effect was so bad that it took nine months to add a new gizmo to the system (this was mainly due to a scheduling concern since the entire system was huge—in excess of 10 million lines of non-OO code). After a proper OO design of selected subsystems, the same sorts of additions are now routinely done by a single person in a single day.[1]

A proper OO design would move the function `dist()` into the `Shape` rather than moving the `Shape` into the function `dist()`.

```
class Position { };

class Shape {
public:
  virtual ~Shape() throw();
```

---

1. "Lessons Learned from the OS/400 OO Project," *Communications of the ACM.* 1995; 38(10):54–64.

```
    virtual void draw() const throw() = 0;
    virtual int  dist(Position mouse) const throw() = 0;
};

Shape::~Shape() throw()
{ }

class Circle : public Shape {
public:
  virtual void draw() const throw();
  virtual int dist(Position mouse) const throw();
};

void Circle::draw() const throw()
{ /*draw a Circle*/ }

int Circle::dist(Position mouse) const throw()
{ /*find the distance from mouse to this Circle*/ }

class Square : public Shape {
public:
  virtual void draw() const throw();
  virtual int dist(Position mouse) const throw();
};

void Square::draw() const throw()
{ /*draw a Square*/ }

int Square::dist(Position mouse) const throw()
{ /*find the distance from mouse to this Square*/ }
```

The OO solution greatly reduces the amount of code that needs to be modified when a new class is added. A little extra design work pays large dividends.

FAQ 27.11

What is a downcast?

A downcast is the conversion of a `Base*` to a `Derived*`, where class `Derived` is publicly derived from class `Base`. A downcast is used when the client code thinks (or hopes!) that a `Base*` points to an object of class `Derived` or a class derived from `Derived` and it needs to access a member function that is provided by `Derived` but not by `Base`.

For example, suppose class `LiquidAsset` is derived from class `Asset`, and `LiquidAsset` is a derived class that is liquidatable but `Asset` itself is not liquidatable. A downcast from an `Asset*` to a `LiquidAsset*` allows the liquidation.

```cpp
#include <iostream>
using namespace std;

class Asset {
public:
  virtual ~Asset() throw();
  virtual bool isLiquidatable() const throw();
};

Asset::~Asset() throw()
{ }

bool Asset::isLiquidatable() const throw()
{ return false; }

class LiquidAsset : public Asset {
public:
  LiquidAsset(int value=100) throw();
  int  getValue() const throw();
  void setValue(int value) throw();
  virtual bool isLiquidatable() const throw();
protected:
  int value_;     //value of this asset
};

LiquidAsset::LiquidAsset(int value) throw()   : value_(value) { }
int LiquidAsset::getValue() const throw()             { return value_;    }
void LiquidAsset::setValue(int value) throw()     { value_ = value;  }
bool LiquidAsset::isLiquidatable() const throw() { return true;      }

int tryToLiquidate(Asset& asset) throw()
{
  int value;
  if (asset.isLiquidatable()) {
    LiquidAsset& liquidAsset = (LiquidAsset&) asset;
    value = liquidAsset.getValue();
    liquidAsset.setValue(0);
    cout << "Liquidated $" << value << '\n';
  } else {
    value = 0;
    cout << "Sorry, couldn't liquidate this asset\n";
  }
  return value;
}
```

```
int main()
{
  Asset        a;
  LiquidAsset b;

  tryToLiquidate(a);
  tryToLiquidate(b);
}
```

The output of this program follows.

```
Sorry, couldn't liquidate this asset
Liquidated $100
```

Although dynamic_cast (see FAQ 27.17) can eliminate the unsafe casts, it cannot eliminate the nonextensible control flow logic. See FAQ 27.12 for a better alternative.

FAQ 27.12

What is an alternative to using downcasts?

Move the user code into the object in the form of virtual functions.

An if-downcast pair can often be replaced by a virtual function call. The key insight is to replace the capability query with a service request. A service request is a virtual function that the client can use to politely ask an object to perform some action (such as "Try to liquidate yourself").

To help find the segments of code that will need to be moved into the service requests, look for those segments of code that use capability queries and depend on the type of the class. Segments of code that depend on the type of the class should be moved into the hierarchy as virtual functions; segments of code that don't depend on the type of the class can remain user code or can be nonvirtual member functions in the base class.

In the previous FAQ, the service request in the user code included the entire tryToLiquidate operation (this entire operation depended on the derived class). To apply this guideline, move the code for this operation into the class hierarchy as a virtual function.

```
#include <iostream>
using namespace std;

class Asset {
public:
```

```
  virtual ~Asset() throw();
  virtual int tryToLiquidate() throw();
};

Asset::~Asset() throw()
{ }

int Asset::tryToLiquidate() throw()
{
  cout << "Sorry, couldn't liquidate this asset\n";
  return 0;
}

class LiquidAsset : public Asset {
public:
  LiquidAsset(int value=100) throw();
  virtual int tryToLiquidate() throw();
protected:
  int value_;     //value of this asset
};

LiquidAsset::LiquidAsset(int value) throw()
: value_(value) { }

int LiquidAsset::tryToLiquidate() throw()
{
  int value = value_;
  value_ = 0;
  cout << "Liquidated $" << value << '\n';
  return value;
}

int sample(Asset& asset)
{ return asset.tryToLiquidate(); }

int main()
{
  Asset        a;
  LiquidAsset b;

  sample(a);
  sample(b);
}
```

The output of this program follows.

```
Sorry, couldn't liquidate this asset
Liquidated $100
```

In the previous FAQ, the downcast was explicit and was therefore subject to human error. In the revised solution, the conversion from `Asset*` to `LiquidAsset*` is implicitly part of the virtual function call mechanism. `LiquidAsset::tryToLiquidate()` does not need to downcast the `this` pointer into a `LiquidAsset*`.

Think of a virtual function call as an extensible `if`-downcast pair that always down casts to the right type.

FAQ 27.13

Why are downcasts dangerous?

Downcasts override the help a compiler can give and rely solely on the knowledge of the programmer.

A downcast from a base class pointer to a derived class pointer instructs the compiler to blindly reinterpret the bits of the pointer. But if you've guessed wrong about the object's class, you're in big trouble—the coerced pointer can create havoc. Learn about type-safe downcasting with RTTI (see FAQ 27.16) instead, but more important, avoid downcasts entirely.

FAQ 27.14

Should the inheritance graph of C++ hierarchies be tall or short?

The inheritance graph should be a forest of short trees.

When the inheritance graph is too tall, downcasts are common. This is because the type of the pointer is often sufficiently different from the type of the object that the desired member function is available only by downcasting the pointer. Also, the deeper the graph, the less likely that the inheritance relationships are proper. A tall graph is frequently a sign of an uninformed attempt at code reuse. Remember: inheritance is *not* for code reuse (see FAQ 8.12).

The type-safe philosophy espoused in this book discourages the unnecessary use of downcasting, even if downcasts are checked first.

FAQ 27.15

Should the inheritance graph of C++ hierarchies be monolithic or a forest?

The inheritance graph should be a forest.

The inheritance hierarchy of well-designed C++ software is normally a forest of little trees rather than a large, monolithic tree. Monolithic trees usually result in excessive use of downcasting. The type-safe philosophy espoused in this book discourages the use of downcasting.

FAQ 27.16

What is Runtime Type Identification (RTTI)?

RTTI is the official way in standard C++ to discover the type of an object and to con- vert the type of a pointer or reference (that is, dynamic typing). The need came from practical experience with C++. RTTI replaces many homegrown versions with a solid, consistent approach. It has many features and capabilities; this chapter discusses `dynamic_cast<T>()`, `static_cast<T>()`, and `typeid()`. Other features, such as `const_cast()` and `reinterpret_cast()`, and issues related to multiple/private/protected/virtual inheritance are not discussed.

FAQ 27.17

What is the purpose of `dynamic_cast<T>()`?

It's a way to see if an object supports a given interface at runtime. It can be a bit compli- cated, so this simplified FAQ covers only the normal situations that occur repeatedly.

Very loosely speaking, `dynamic_cast<T>(x)` is like the old-style cast `(T)x`, meaning that it casts the value of `x` to the type `T` (`T` is normally either a pointer or a reference to some class). `dynamic_cast<T>(x)` has several important advantages over the old-style cast. It never performs an invalid conversion since it checks that the cast is legal at runtime, and the syntax is more obvious and explicit than the old-style cast, thus appropriately calling attention to the conversion.

If `p` is a pointer, `dynamic_cast<Fred*>(p)` converts `p` to a `Fred*` like `(Fred*)p`, but if the conversion is not valid, it returns `NULL`. If `r` is a reference, dynamic_cast<Fred&>(r) converts r to a Fred& just like (Fred&)r, but if the conversion is not valid, an exception of type bad_cast is thrown. A conversion is valid if the object pointed to by p (or referred to by r) is either a Fred or a publicly derived class of Fred. Here is some sample syntax.

```
#include <iostream>
using namespace std;

class Shape {
public:
  virtual ~Shape() throw();
  // ...
};

Shape::~Shape() throw() { }

class Circle : public Shape { /*...*/ };
class Square : public Shape { /*...*/ };

void sample(Shape* p) throw()
{
  Circle* cp = dynamic_cast<Circle*>(p);
  if (cp != NULL) {
    cout << "The object is a Circle\n";
  } else {
    cout << "The object is not a Circle\n";
  }
}

int main()
{
  Circle c;
  Square s;
  sample(&c);
  sample(&s);
}
```

When dynamic_cast<T>(p) is being used to perform a downcast, p's type must designate a class with at least one virtual function (or be NULL). However, this restriction does not apply to potential recipients of the cast, such as cp in the example.

FAQ 27.18

Is `dynamic_cast<T>()` a panacea?

No, like everything else, `dynamic_cast<T>()` can be misused.

It's a horrible design error, but some programmers (mis)use `dynamic_cast<T>()` in huge `if` / `then` / `else` blocks to determine an object's type and then take the appropriate action. This situation screams out for virtual functions and dynamic binding, not the extensibility-killing misuse of RTTI (see FAQ 27.03).

Also, watch out for performance hits due to this implementation technique. It is all too easy to think of `dynamic_cast<T>()` as a constant-time operation, when in fact it may take linear time and chew up CPU cycles if the inheritance hierarchies are deep or if the advice about huge `if` blocks has been ignored.

FAQ 27.19

What does `static_cast<T>()` do?

It tells the compiler, "Trust me."

Sometimes the programmer knows the type of an object and has to or wants to let the compiler in on the secret. `static_cast<T>()` is the standard C++ way to do this at compile time. There are situations where either the knowledge to make the cast exists only in the programmer's mind or the runtime system cannot do the job because of technical reasons. Here is some sample syntax.

```
Target* tg = static_cast<Target*>(src);  // just do it
```

The C++ `static_cast<T>()` is better than C-style casting because it stands out in the code and explicitly states the programmer's understanding and intentions. It also understands and respects `const` and access controls.

FAQ 27.20

What does `typeid()` do?

It determines the precise type of an object at runtime.

Given a reference or pointer as input, `typeid()` returns a reference to a standard library class called `type_info`. `type_info` has a `name()` member function that returns the name of the parameter's type in an implementation-specific format. This name represents the precise, lowest-level type of the object. If the value of the pointer is `NULL`, `typeid()` throws a `bad_typeid` exception.

Note that `dynamic_cast<T>(p)` and `static_cast<T>(p)` are template functions, where `T` is the template parameter and `p` is the function parameter, but `typeid()` is not a template function.

`typeid()` and `dynamic_cast<T>()` are two sides of the same coin. They both take a base class pointer or reference that may refer to a derived class object. But `typeid()` returns a class name whereas `dynamic_cast<T>()` is passed a class name. `typeid()` is used to discover the object's exact class, but it doesn't convert the pointer; `dynamic_cast<T>()` converts the pointer but doesn't determine the object's exact class—the pointer may be converted to some intermediate base class rather than to the object's exact class.

The character representation of the class name from `name()` is stored in system memory and must not be `deleted` by the programmer.

FAQ 27.21

Are there any hidden costs for type-safe downcasts?

Yes, type-safe downcasts have five hidden costs.

Although type-safe downcasts never cast a pointer to an incorrect type, they have five hidden costs. They increase coding cost, maintenance cost, testing cost, runtime CPU cost, and extensibility cost.

1. *Coding cost:* Type-safe downcasts move complexity from the server code into the user code, from the few to the many.

2. *Maintenance cost:* Moving code from the server code to the user code increases the overall software bulk.

3. *Testing cost:* A test harness must be devised to exercise every `if`, including the `if`s used to test the type safety of the downcasts.

4. *Runtime CPU cost:* Additional code must be executed to test the type safety of the downcasts. This is not a constant time cost, by the way, since it may be necessary to search an entire inheritance hierarchy.

5. *Extensibility cost:* The additional control flow code needs to be modified when new derived classes are added.

The underlying cause for these costs lies with the style of programming implied by type-safe downcasts rather than with the downcasts themselves. Embracing the more extensible style of programming that does not use unnecessary downcasts is part of using C++ properly.

Chapter 28

Containers

What are container classes and what are the most common mistakes made with container classes?

Containers are objects that hold other objects (see FAQ 2.15). For example, a linked list of `string` objects is a container—users can add numerous *elements* (or *element objects*) to the list, and in this case all the elements are of type `string`. The closest that the core C++ language comes to container classes is the array—but see FAQ 28.02 to find out why C++ arrays should not be used.

Unfortunately programmers' instincts tend to lead them in the wrong direction with containers. This may be because of past experience with other programming languages or it may be for some other reason, but whatever the reason the result is the same: programmers tend to make common and serious mistakes with containers that lead to bugs. Here are a few common mistakes.

- Using arrays rather than safe container classes (the "Grandma used arrays" fiasco; see FAQ 28.02)

- Rolling your own container classes from scratch (the "not invented here" fiasco; see FAQ 28.03)

- Containers of pointers (the "random object ownership" fiasco; see FAQ 28.04)

- Containers of `char*` (the "string contents vs. string address" fiasco; see FAQ 28.06)

- Containers of `auto_ptr<T>` (the "transfer of object ownership" fiasco; see FAQ 28.07)

- Inheriting everything from `Object` (the "based object" fiasco; see FAQ 28.08)

- Selecting incompatible vendors for container classes (the "best of breed" fiasco; see FAQ 28.10)

FAQ 28.02

Are arrays good or evil?

new

Arrays are evil. They have their place in some specialized applications, but they should be avoided.

The most common mistake with container classes is failing to use them and substituting arrays instead. Unfortunately, this is not only a fairly common mistake, it's also a very dangerous mistake. Arrays simply aren't safe. They're pointers in disguise, and pointers aren't safe. Yes, Grandma used pointers and survived, but given the relative size and complexity of today's software systems and given all the other things that need to be handled, raw pointers or arrays generally aren't worth the risk. Instead pointers and arrays should be wrapped inside a safe interface—a container class.

Avoid using arrays and pointers. Use container classes instead.

FAQ 28.03

Should application development organizations create their own container classes?

No. Too many application development organizations roll their own container classes from scratch. This is often motivated by the "not invented here" (NIH) syndrome, which is lethal to any kind of reuse.

The problems with application development organizations rolling their own container classes include the following.

- *Increased development costs:* It's normally far cheaper to pay for a class library than to pay yourself to write your own.

- *Increased long-term costs:* Building your own means increasing your maintenance costs, which is usually the last thing you want to do.

- *Degraded quality:* Application developers are not usually experts in the intricacies of data structures, so they often do a mediocre job with container classes—reinventing the wheel is bad enough, but usually they reinvent a flat tire.

- *Lack of flexibility and versatility:* It is hard for an in-house development team to compete with the well-funded software houses in developing software that is flexible enough to meet the needs of the whole industry. This flexibility may be very important later in the life cycle.

- *Loss of focus:* Application developers should focus on getting the application done on time and within budget, not on plumbing.

- *Missed opportunities for standardization:* It makes sense for the containers to be as standardized as the basic language types for both training and maintenance considerations.

FAQ 28.04

What are some common mistakes with containers of pointers?

Lifetime errors caused by ownership confusion.

Be careful about containers of pointers. A container of pointers contains pointers to the objects that are inserted into the container, whereas a container of values contains copies of the objects that are inserted into the container. The main purpose of a container of pointers is to hold on to the identities of certain objects, but the main purpose of a container of values is to hold on to the state of certain objects.

Containers of pointers allow objects to be inserted without copying, allow the contained objects to be distinguished by identity rather than merely by state or value, and allow objects of classes within an inheritance lattice to be inserted without slicing (a.k.a. chopped copies). However, containers of pointers can create a difficult relationship between the user of the container and the container. For example, if a pointer to an object is in some container and someone else deletes the object, the container ends up with a dangling reference (see FAQ 24.04). In some cases this means that an object needs to know all the containers that point to it, which sometimes requires each object to maintain a container of container pointers. Sometimes users can't even change an object without informing all the containers that point to the object. For example, if a user changes an object's state and a container's order semantics depend on the object's state, the innocent change might subtly break the container's invariant. This becomes very messy and complex.

FAQ 28.05

Does this mean that containers of pointers should be avoided?

The rule of thumb is to use containers of values when you can, use containers of pointers when you must.

Containers of pointers must be used when the identity of the contained objects matters, in addition to their state. For example, containers of pointers must be used when the same instance must be "in" several containers at the same time.

Another reason containers of pointers are used is when the cost to copy an object into and out of a container is too large, but in this case judicious use of reference counting (see FAQ 31.09) and copy on write (see FAQ 31.10) can reduce the copying cost significantly.

FAQ 28.06

Surely good old-fashioned `char*` is an exception, right?

Wrong!

For example, if a container of `char*` is used when the goal is to have a container of strings, lookup requests may fail since the container will be looking for a particular pointer rather than for the contents of the string. To make matters worse, if a string buffer is used to build the string `foo` and that is inserted into the container and the string buffer is later changed to `junk`, the container will appear to contain `junk` rather than `foo`.

If a string is desired, a string class should be used and `char*` should be avoided. Every compiler vendor has a string class, and there is a standard C++ string class called `string`.

Can `auto_ptr<T>` simplify ownership problems with containers of pointers?

No, `auto_ptr<T>` usually makes things worse!

Generally speaking, `auto_ptr<T>` should not be used inside container classes. For example, if a `List` of `Fred` pointers is desired, it is usually bad to use a `List<auto_ptr<Fred> >`. The reason is that copying an `auto_ptr<T>` makes changes to the original, in addition to the obvious changes to the copy. In particular, the ownership of the referent is transferred to the copy, so the original will be `NULL`. For example, if someone retrieved a copy of an element in the `List`, that would copy the `auto_ptr<T>`, which would transfer ownership of the referent to the copy and the `auto_ptr<T>` in the `List` would be `NULL`.

Can a Java-like `Object` class simplify containers in C++?

No, that usually makes things worse!

new

Java is not C++. C++ is not Java. Just because something works well in Java doesn't mean it will work well in C++ or vice versa. Java has automatic garbage collection, C++ has destructors (FAQ 2.20); Java has a ubiquitous base class `Object`, C++ has templates (FAQ 2.15). For a lot of reasons, Java's container classes all take `Object` pointers, and they work well. It's possible to do the same thing in C++, but in C++ this technique tends to be more complex and expensive than using templates. For example, when `Fred` objects are inserted into a list of `Object*`, the only thing that is known about them is that they are some kind of `Object`. When these objects are accessed from the list, the programmer has to carefully find out what the objects really are and typically has to downcast the `Object*` before anything useful can be done with the objects. This is another form of dynamic type checking, and it can be expensive to write, test, and maintain (see FAQ 27.03).

Forcing things to inherit from a common base class such as `Object` is called the based object approach. See the next FAQ for more details on these heterogeneous containers.

FAQ 28.09

What's the difference between a homogeneous and a heterogeneous container?

The elements of a homogeneous container are all of the same type; the elements of a heterogeneous container can be of different types.

Containers come in many shades of gray. Generally speaking, the more heterogeneous the element types are, the less type safe the container is. For example, the ultimate heterogeneous container is a container of `void*` in which the various elements could point to objects of any type. Even though this seems to optimize flexibility, in practice such containers are nearly worthless. In particular, putting things into such a container is easy (any object of any type can be inserted), but when an element is removed, the user of the container knows nothing about the element's type.

A more useful form of heterogeneous container is one that requires its elements to point to objects derived from some specific base class, often an ABC. This base class typically has all or nearly all the member functions provided by the actual objects referenced by the container. For example, one might have a list of `Shape*` where the actual referents might be objects of class `Square`, `Circle`, `Hexagon`, and so on.

Note that the based object approach (see the previous FAQ) is another form of heterogeneous container.

FAQ 28.10

Is it a good idea to use a "best of breed" approach when selecting container classes?

 Not usually.

For small projects, it's often desirable to select each component using a *best of breed approach*. That is, select the best of breed in category *X*, the best of breed in category *Y*, and so on.

But for large, mission-critical projects, it is very important to reduce the overall system complexity, and selecting the very best container classes could actually make things worse (see also FAQ 39.08). Most vendors' GUI frameworks are designed to work very well with the vendor's container classes. In some cases, this increases the integration costs of mixing container classes from one vendor and GUI classes from another. Database, network, and other infrastructure frameworks are similar: it is often difficult and/or risky to mix libraries and frameworks classes from different vendors.

When this mix-and-match problem occurs, the low-cost, low-risk approach is often to select the container classes that "go with" the rest of the infrastructure. Usually that means that the container classes are less than ideal, often frustrating programmers who don't see the big picture. But remember: the goal is to reduce the overall system complexity, and container classes are only one piece.

FAQ 28.11

Should all projects use C++'s standardized containers?

Not always, because of big picture issues. We hope that someday the software industry will fully embrace standardized containers, but until then, be prepared to make decisions that will be uncomfortable.

new

When compared to other container classes, C++'s standardized containers have several benefits.

- They are standardized and are therefore portable.

- They are fast—very, very fast.

However in large and/or mission-critical applications, integration issues often dominate. When this happens, it may be better in the overall scheme of things to use a vendor's proprietary container classes (see FAQ 28.10). Programmers who have not worked on large and/or mission-critical projects where integration issues became a problem do not understand this and usually argue in favor of the portability or performance of the standardized container classes.

For example, in some cases a particular vendor's library is considered essential to the project's success, and the library might be (shouldn't be, but in the real world it might be) tightly integrated with the container classes from the same vendor. In such a case, the cost and risk of integrating standard containers might not be worth the benefit. It's a dilemma of local versus global optimization.

Of course there are some cases where performance or portability is more important than integration. In these cases the standardized C++ container classes should be considered, even if integrating them with the other third-party libraries requires some invention.

FAQ 28.12

What are the C++ standardized container classes?

The C++ container classes are a part of what was formerly known as the standard template library (STL). They include the following container classes.

- vector<Value> (see FAQ 28.13).

- list<Value> (see FAQ 28.13).

- deque<Value> (see FAQ 28.13).

- set<Value> (see FAQ 28.14).

- multiset<Value> (see FAQ 28.14).

- map<Key,Value> (see FAQ 28.14).

- multimap<Key,Value> (see FAQ 28.14).

FAQ 28.13

What are the best applications for the standardized C++ sequence container classes?

Operations that make sense for a linear sequence of objects.

The sequence container classes store their objects in a linear sequence. They include the following container classes.

- vector<T>

- list<T>

- deque<T>

They all expand themselves to allow an arbitrary number of elements to be inserted, and all provide numerous operations. The biggest difference between them is related to performance. For example, vector<T> has very fast array-like access to random elements and very fast insertions and removals at the end; list<T> is not as fast to access a random element, but it is faster when inserting in the middle or at the beginning; deque<T> is like vector<T> except that it also has very fast insertion and removal of elements at the beginning.

Some of the operations that can be performed on a sequence follow. In the following descriptions, `first` and `toofar` represent iterators within a container, and "the range [`first`, `toofar`)" means all the elements starting at `first` up to but not including the element at `toofar`.

Selected nonmutating sequence operations:

- `for_each(first, toofar, function)` applies the function to each element in the range [`first`, `toofar`).

- `find(first, toofar, const T& value)` finds the first element that is equal to `value` in the range [`first`, `toofar`), returning the corresponding iterator (or `toofar` if nothing matched). `find_if()` is similar, but it takes a predicate to determine if the element matches.

- `adjacent_find(first, toofar)` finds the first adjacent pair of elements that are equal in the range [`first`, `toofar`), returning the corresponding iterator (or `toofar` if nothing matched). An optional binary predicate can be given to determine if an adjacent pair matches.

- `count(first, toofar, const T& value, result)` counts the number of elements in the range [`first`, `toofar`) that are equal to `value` and stores that number in the by-reference parameter `result`. `count_if()` is similar, but it takes a predicate to determine if the element matches.

- `mismatch(first, toofar, first2)` finds the first mismatch between the two sequences. The elements from sequence 1 are in the range [`first`, `toofar`), and the corresponding elements from sequence 2 start at `first2`. An optional binary predicate can be used to determine if elements match.

- `equal(first, toofar, first2)` checks two sequences for element-by-element equality. It returns true if and only if the elements of sequence 1 in the range [`first`, `toofar`) match the corresponding elements of sequence 2 starting at `first2`. An optional binary predicate can be used to determine if elements match.

- `search(first, toofar, first2, toofar2)` finds a subsequence within a sequence. An optional binary predicate can be given to determine if an adjacent pair matches.

Selected mutating sequence operations:

- `copy(first, toofar, dest)` copies elements from the range [`first`, `toofar`) into the sequence starting at `dest`. `copy_backward()` is similar, but it copies elements from right to left, which is especially useful when sliding a sequence a few slots to the right (that is, when the source and destination ranges overlap).

- `swap_ranges(first, toofar, first2)` swaps the contents of the elements from range [`first`, `toofar`) with the corresponding elements from sequence 2 starting at `first2`.

- `swap(a, b)` swaps the values of the elements or the entire sequences.

- `transform(first, toofar, dest, unaryOp)` calls `unaryOp()` on each element in the range [`first`, `toofar`) and copies the results into sequence 2 starting at `dest`.

- `transform(first, toofar, first2, dest, binaryOp)` calls `binaryOp()`, passing an element from sequence 1 in the range [`first`, `toofar`) and the corresponding element from sequence 2 starting at `first2`, and copies the results into sequence 3 starting at `dest`.

- `replace(first, toofar, const T& oldValue, const T& newValue)` replaces all elements equal to `oldValue` in the range [`first`, `toofar`) with `newValue`. `replace_if()` is simliar, but it takes a predicate to determine if the element matches. `replace_copy()` and `replace_copy_if()` are similar except that the original sequence is unchanged, and the results are copied to a second sequence.

- `fill(first, toofar, const T& value)` fills the range [`first`, `toofar`) with copies of `value`. `fill_n()` is similar, but it takes a starting iterator and a number.

- `generate(first, toofar, generator)` fills the range [`first`, `toofar`) with the results of successively calling `generator()`. `generate_n()` is similar, but it takes a starting iterator and a number.

- `remove(first, toofar, const T& value)` removes those elements from the range [`first`, `toofar`) that are equal to `value`. `remove_if()` is similar, but it takes a predicate to determine if the element matches. `remove_copy()` and `remove_copy_if()` are similar except that the original sequence is unchanged, and the results are copied to a second sequence.

- `unique(first, toofar)` removes successive duplicates from the range [`first`, `toofar`). An optional binary predicate can be given to determine if an adjacent pair matches. `unique_copy()` is similar except that the original sequence is unchanged, and the results are copied to a second sequence.

- `reverse(first, toofar)` reverses the elements of the range [`first,toofar`]. `reverse_copy()` is similar except that the original sequence is unchanged, and the results are copied to a second sequence.

- `rotate(first, middle, toofar)` rotates the range [`first, toofar`] around the iterator `middle`. `rotate_copy()` is similar except that the original sequence is unchanged, and the results are copied to a second sequence.

- `random_shuffle(first, toofar)` randomly shuffles the elements in the range [`first,toofar`].

- `partition(first, toofar, unaryOp)` partitions the range [`first,toofar`] by moving elements where `unaryOp()` returns `true` to the left, the others to the right. `stable_partition()` is similar, but it preserves the relative order of the elements within each group.

Selected sorting and related operations:

- All the operations in this section take an optional binary predicate used to compare two elements.

- `sort(first, toofar)` sorts the elements in the range [`first, toofar`].

- `stable_sort(first, toofar)` sorts the elements in the range [`first,toofar`] and never reverses two elements that compare as equal.

- `binary_search(first, toofar, const T& value)` looks for `value` in the sorted sequence range [`first,toofar`] and returns `true` or `false` based on whether `value` was found.

- `includes(first, toofar, first2, toofar2)` checks if the first multiset [`first,toofar`] is a subset of the second multiset [`first2, toofar2`].

- `set_union(first, toofar, first2, toofar2, dest)` copies into `dest` the union of the first set [`first,toofar`] and the second set [`first2,toofar2`].

- `set_intersection(first, toofar, first2, toofar2, dest)` copies into `dest` the intersection of the first set [`first, toofar`] and the second set [`first2,toofar2`].

- set_difference(first, toofar, first2, toofar2, dest) copies into dest the difference between the first set [first, toofar) and the second set [first2, toofar2).

- min_element(first, toofar) finds the minimum element within the range [first, toofar). max_element() is analogous.

FAQ 28.14

What are the best situations for the standardized C++ associative container classes?

  Operations that make sense for keyed containers of objects.

The associative container classes store their objects so that the keys are in a sorted order based on a comparison object or function. They include the following container classes.

- set<T>

- multiset<T>

- map<Key,Value>

- multimap<Key,Value>

They all expand to allow an arbitrary number of elements to be inserted, and all provide numerous operations. set<T> and multiset<T> allow the insertion, lookup, and removal of keys, with multiset<T> allowing multiple copies of the same key value (some libraries use the term "bag" for this). map<Key,Value> and multimap<Key,Value> allow values to be inserted, looked up, and removed by their key, with multiset<T> allowing multiple values associated with the same key value.

Here are some selected ways to use the standard map<Key,Value> class.

```
#include <string>
#include <map>
#include <iostream>
using namespace std;

typedef  map<string,int>   AgeMap;   ←— A typedef can make the rest easier to read

int main()
{
```

```
AgeMap age;

// The subscript operator is used to access an element in the map
age["Fred"] = 42;
age["Barney"] = 38;
int n = age["Fred"];
int numElements = age.size();

// Removing an element from the map
age.erase("Barney");

// Iterators are used to loop through all the elements within the map
for (AgeMap::iterator p = age.begin(); p != age.end(); ++p)
  cout << "age of " << p->first << " is " << p->second << "\n";

// Iterators can be used to check if an entry is in the map
AgeMap::const_iterator q = age.find("Fred");
if (q == age.end())
  cout << "Fred isn't in the map\n";
else
  cout << "Fred is in the map; his age is " << q->second << "\n";
}
```

Part IV

Topics

Chapters 29 through 39 present programming guidelines for writing robust C++ programs, ways to avoid common C++ errors, and information on how C++ works with other technologies. It concludes with a discussion of the learning curve, training, and mentoring.

Chapter 29

Mixing Overloading with Inheritance

What is the difference between overloaded functions and overridden functions?

Overloading has the same scope, same name, different signatures, and `virtual` is not required. Overriding has different scopes, same name, same signatures, and `virtual` is required.

The term *signature* designates the combination of a function's name, the types and order of its parameters, and, if the function is a nonstatic member function, its `const` and/or `volatile` qualifiers.

Overloading occurs when two or more functions are in the same scope (for example, both in the same class or both at namespace scope) and have the same name but different signatures. Overriding occurs when a class and one of its derived classes both define a member function with the same signature and the member function is declared to be virtual in the base class.

In the following example, `Base::f(int)` and `Base::f(float)` overload each other, while `Derived::g()` overrides `Base::g()`.

```
#include <iostream>
using namespace std;
```

```
class Base {
public:
  virtual ~Base()          throw();
  virtual void f(int x)    throw();
  virtual void f(float x)  throw();
  virtual void g()         throw();
};

Base::~Base() throw()
  { }
void Base::f(int x) throw()
  { cout << "Base::f(int)\n"; }
void Base::f(float x) throw()
  { cout << "Base::f(float)\n"; }
void Base::g() throw()
  { cout << "Base::g()\n"; }

class Derived : public Base {
public:
  virtual void g() throw();
};

void Derived::g() throw()
  { cout << "Derived::g()\n"; }

int main()
{
  Derived d;
  Base* bp = &d;   // OK: Derived is kind-of Base
  bp->f(42);
  bp->f(3.14f);
  bp->g();
}
```

The output of this program follows.

```
Base::f(int)
Base::f(float)
Derived::g()
```

FAQ 29.02

What is the hiding rule?

A rule in C++ that tends to confuse new C++ developers.

The hiding rule says that an entity in an inner scope hides things with the same name in an outer scope. And since a class is a scope, this means that a member of a derived class hides a member of a base class that has the same name as the derived class member. Confused? Don't give up; this is really important stuff.

There are two common situations when the hiding rule confuses people. First, when a base class and a derived class declare member functions with different signatures but with the same name, then the base class member function is hidden. Second, when a base class declares a nonvirtual member function and a derived class declares a member function with the same signature, then the base class member function is hidden (technically the same thing happens with virtual member functions, but in that case it hardly ever confuses people).

In the following example, `Base::f(float)` and `Base::g(float)` are virtual and therefore can be overridden by derived classes, but `Base::h(float)` is nonvirtual and therefore should not be redefined in derived classes.

```
#include <iostream>
using namespace std;

class Base {
public:
   virtual ~Base()          throw();
   virtual void f(float x) throw();
   virtual void g(float x) throw();
           void h(float x) throw();
};

Base::~Base() throw()
   { }
void Base::f(float x) throw()
   { cout << "Base::f(float)\n"; }
void Base::g(float x) throw()
   { cout << "Base::g(float)\n"; }
void Base::h(float x) throw()
   { cout << "Base::h(float)\n"; }
```

In the following code, member function `Derived::f(float)` is a normal override of virtual `Base::f(float)`. However, `Derived::g(int)` hides (rather than overrides or overloads) `Base::g(float)` and `Derived::h(float)` hides (rather than overrides or overloads) `Base::h(float)`.

```
class Derived : public Base {
public:
   virtual void f(float x) throw();  ←——— Good: Overrides Base::f(float)
   virtual void g(int x)   throw();  ←——— Bad: Hides Base::g(float)
           void h(float x) throw();  ←——— Bad: Redefines a nonvirtual function
};
```

```
void Derived::f(float x) throw()
  { cout << "Derived::f(float)\n"; }
void Derived::g(int x) throw()
  { cout << "Derived::g(int)\n"; }
void Derived::h(float x) throw()
  { cout << "Derived::h(float)\n"; }
```

Because `Derived::f(float)` is a normal override of `Base::f(float)`, calling `f(3.14f)` on a `Derived` object does the same thing independent of whether the reference to the `Derived` object is of type `Base&` or type `Derived&`. Said simply, the behavior depends on the type of the object, not on the type of the reference. This is the normal (and desirable) effect of dynamic binding, and it is shown in `sampleOne()`.

```
void sampleOne(Base& b, Derived& d)
{
  b.f(3.14f);  ◄──────── Good: If the object is a Derived, calls Derived::f(float)
  d.f(3.14f);
}

int main()
{
  Derived d;
  sampleOne(d, d);
}
```

Unfortunately, `Derived::g(int)` neither overrides nor overloads `Base::g(float)` but rather *hides* `Base::g(float)`. Therefore the compiler calls `g(float)` if someone tries to call `g(int)` on a `Derived&`. This behavior is surprising to many developers; it is shown in `sampleTwo()`.

```
void sampleTwo(Base& b, Derived& d)
{
  b.g(3.14f);
  d.g(3.14f);  ◄──────── Bad: Converts 3.14 to 3 and calls Derived::g(int)
}

int main()
{
  Derived d;
  sampleTwo(d, d);
}
```

Also unfortunately, `Derived::h(float)` is a redefinition of the nonvirtual function `Base::h(float)`. Since `Base::h(float)` is nonvirtual, `Derived::h(float)` is not an override, and dynamic binding does not occur. Therefore, the compiler calls `Base::h(float)` if someone tries to call `h(float)` on a `Derived` object using a `Base&`. This behavior is surprising to many developers; it is shown in `sampleThree()`.

```
void sampleThree(Base& b, Derived& d)
{
   b.h(3.14f);  ◄——— Bad: Calls Base::h(float)—does not use dynamic binding
   d.h(3.14f);
}

int main()
{
   Derived d;
   sampleThree(d, d);
}
```

The root problem with `sampleTwo()` and `sampleThree()` is that the behavior depends on the type of the reference rather than on the type of the object. For example, in `sampleThree()` the member function that gets invoked is the one associated with the reference's type, not the one associated with the object's type. These behaviors surprise users, since users normally expect behavior to depend on the type of the object rather than on the type of the reference or pointer used to access that object.

The hiding rule may not seem intuitive, but it prevents worse errors, especially in the case of assignment operators. If, for example, the hiding rule were removed, it would be legal to assign a `Circle` with a `Square` (the `Shape` part of the `Square` would be copied into the `Shape` part of the `Circle`).

FAQ 29.03

How should the hiding rule be handled?

Avoid triggering the hiding rule when possible, and use the following work-arounds   *new*
when the hiding rule can't be avoided.

Avoid hiding inherited `public:` member functions whenever possible. When it cannot be avoided, it is important not to surprise the class's users. The guiding principle is to avoid confusing users: when a `Base*` can be used to call a member function on a `Derived` object, calling it via a `Derived*` shouldn't alter the observable behavior.

In the case of redefining a nonvirtual member function, as in `Base::h(float)` from the previous FAQ, the simplest way to avoid surprising users is to use the `virtual` keyword when declaring the base class member function. In those rare cases where the base class function cannot be virtual, ensure that the observable behavior of the derived class function is identical to that of the base class.

For example, an experienced C++ programmer might use a nonvirtual member function to avoid the (small) overhead of a virtual function call, yet might also redefine that member function in a derived class to make better use of the derived class's resources. To avoid surprising users, there must not be any differences in the observable behavior of the two functions. Note: These relationships are somewhat subtle; if the code will be maintained by less experienced programmers, a normal, virtual function is probably a better choice.

In the case where a base class and a derived class declare member functions with the same name but different signatures, as in `Base::g(float)` and `Derived::g(int)` in the previous FAQ, a using declaration (FAQ 29.04) should be employed.

The following shows how these guidelines can be applied to the example from the previous FAQ.

```
#include <iostream>
using namespace std;

class Base {
public:
  virtual ~Base()         throw();
  virtual void f(float x) throw();
  virtual void g(float x) throw();
  virtual void h(float x) throw();
};

Base::~Base() throw()
  { }
void Base::f(float x) throw()
  { cout << "Base::f(float)\n"; }
void Base::g(float x) throw()
  { cout << "Base::g(float)\n"; }
void Base::h(float x) throw()
  { cout << "Base::h(float)\n"; }

class Derived : public Base {
public:
  virtual void f(float x) throw();
  virtual void g(int x)   throw();  ←—— Normally this would hide g(float) (bad!)
  using Base::g;  ←———————————————————— But this line unhides g(float) (good!)
};

void Derived::f(float x) throw()
  { cout << "Derived::f(float)\n"; }
```

```
void Derived::g(int x) throw()
  { cout << "Derived::g(int)\n"; }
```

After applying these fixes, users are not confused because the behavior depends on the type of the object rather than on the type of the pointer used to access that object.

```
void sample(Base& b, Derived& d)
{
  b.f(3.14f);
  d.f(3.14f);

  b.g(3.14f);
  d.g(3.14f);  ◄──────────── This is not hidden (good!)

  b.h(3.14f);
  d.h(3.14f);
}

int main()
{
  Derived d;
  sample(d, d);
}
```

The output of this program demonstrates that the behavior depends on the type of the object, not the type of the reference:

```
Derived::f(float)
Derived::f(float)
Derived::g(float)
Derived::g(float)
Derived::h(float)
Derived::h(float)
```

These guidelines apply only to public inheritance; hiding base class member functions is fine for private or protected inheritance (see FAQ 37.01).

FAQ 29.04

What should a derived class do when it redefines some but not all of a set of overloaded member functions inherited from the base class?

The derived class should use the using syntax.

If the base class has an overloaded set of member functions and the derived class over-rides some but not all of that set, the redefined member functions will hide the other overloads. The work-around is to use the using syntax. The following example shows class Base with two overloaded member functions called f.

```
#include <iostream>
using namespace std;

class Base {
public:
  virtual ~Base()          throw();
  virtual void f(int x)    throw();
  virtual void f(float x) throw();
};

Base::~Base() throw()
{ }

void Base::f(int x) throw()
{ cout << "Base::f(int)\n"; }

void Base::f(float x) throw()
{ cout << "Base::f(float)\n"; }
```

Now suppose the author of class Derived wants to override one of the two f() member functions. In this case the derived class should also say using Base::f; to avoid confusing users:

```
class Derived : public Base {
public:
  virtual void f(int x) throw();
  using Base::f; ◄─── This unhides f(float) (good!)
};

void Derived::f(int x) throw()
{ cout << "Derived::f(int)\n"; }
```

Because of the using Base::f; line in the derived class, f(float) is not hidden:

```
void sample(Base& b, Derived& d)
{
  b.f(42);
  d.f(42);
  b.f(3.14f);
  d.f(3.14f); ◄─────── This is not hidden (good!)
}
```

```
int main()
{
  Derived d;
  sample(d, d);
}
```

The output of this program demonstrates that the behavior depends on the type of the object, not the type of the reference:

```
Derived::f(int)
Derived::f(int)
Base::f(float)
Base::f(float)
```

This guideline applies only to `public` inheritance; hiding base class member functions is fine for `private` or `protected` inheritance (see FAQ 37.01).

— **FAQ 29.05**

Can virtual functions be overloaded?

Yes, but it's often easier to use nonvirtual overloads that call nonoverloaded virtuals.

As was discussed in FAQ 29.02, when virtual member functions are overloaded, the hiding rule forces derived classes to do a bit more work than necessary. In these situations, it is often easier if the overloads are nonvirtuals that call virtuals that aren't overloaded. These nonoverloaded virtuals are normally `protected:`.

The following code shows how to apply this guideline to the situation in the previous FAQ where `Base::f(int)` and `Base::f(float)` are overloaded virtuals. These functions are now nonvirtuals that call nonoverloaded virtuals `f_i(int)` and `f_f(float)`. (Don't redefine nonvirtual member functions; see FAQ 29.02.)

```
#include <iostream>
using namespace std;

class Base {
public:
  virtual ~Base() throw();
  void f(int x)   throw();
  void f(float x) throw();
protected:
  virtual void f_i(int x)   throw();
  virtual void f_f(float x) throw();
};
```

```
inline void Base::f(int x) throw()          Overloaded nonvirtuals
  { f_i(x); }
inline void Base::f(float x) throw()
  { f_f(x); }
void Base::f_i(int x) throw()               Nonoverloaded virtuals
  { cout << "Base::f(int)\n"; }
void Base::f_f(float x) throw()
  { cout << "Base::f(float)\n"; }

Base::~Base() throw()
  { }
```

In class `Derived`, the behavior of `f(int)` is changed by overriding `Base::f_i(int)`; redefining `f(int)` itself would be wrong, since a redefinition would hide `Base::f(float)`.

```
class Derived : public Base {
public:
                                            Derived classes never redefine f(int)
protected:
  virtual void f_i(int x) throw();          Derived classes may override f_i(int)
};

void Derived::f_i(int x) throw()
  { cout << "Derived::f(int)\n"; }
```

Now when member function `f(int)` is invoked on a `Derived` object, it expands inline as the code of `Base::f(int)`, which calls protected member function `f_i(int)`, and since `f_i(int)` is virtual, it resolves to the correct member function using dynamic binding (see FAQ 2.24). The message here is that both `f(int)` and `f(float)` work correctly on both a `Derived&` and on a `Base&`:

```
void sample(Base& b, Derived& d)
{
  b.f(42);
  d.f(42);

  b.f(3.14f);
  d.f(3.14f);                               This is not hidden (good!)
}

int main()
{
  Derived d;
  sample(d, d);
}
```

The output of this program demonstrates that the behavior depends on the type of the object, not the type of the reference:

```
Derived::f(int)
Derived::f(int)
Base::f(float)
Base::f(float)
```

This approach is more scalable than the approach presented in the earlier FAQ. It is scalable in two ways, with respect to the code and with respect to the people. With respect to the code, the root of the inheritance hierarchy has a few extra lines of code, but none of the (potentially many) derived classes need have any extra code to handle the hiding rule. This is a good trade-off since an inheritance hierarchy often has many derived classes. With respect to the people, the developer of the root class of the inheritance hierarchy needs to understand the hiding rule, but all the writers of all the derived classes can remain relatively ignorant of it—they need to know only that they are to override the virtual member functions rather than the nonvirtual member functions. This is a good trade-off because the developers who build the root classes in the inheritance hierarchies are normally more sophisticated than the developers who build the derived classes.

Note that this approach does not imply any performance overhead, since the overloaded `public:` member functions are normally `inline` nonvirtuals.

As before, this guideline applies only to `public` inheritance; hiding base class member functions is fine for `private` or `protected` inheritance (see FAQ 37.01).

Chapter 30

The Big Three

What is the purpose of this chapter?

new

The purpose of this chapter is to show you how to eliminate a nasty category of bugs from your software. The bugs discussed in this chapter are quite subtle—the compiler normally does not give any warning or error messages—and disastrous, often causing the application to crash or behave chaotically.

The specific details involve three infrastructure routines that the C++ compiler automatically defines when the developer leaves them undefined. A guideline is provided so readers can tell when those automatic definitions will cause problems and when they won't cause problems.

It is essential that every C++ programmer understand the material in this chapter.

What are the Big Three?

Destructor, copy constructor, and assignment operator.

These infrastructure routines provide the death and copy semantics for objects of the class. Here is some sample syntax:

```
class Fred {
public:
```

```
   ~Fred() throw();                          // Destructor
   Fred(const Fred& x) throw();              // Copy Constructor
   Fred& operator= (const Fred& x) throw();  // Assignment Operator
};

Fred::~Fred() throw()
{ /*...*/ }

Fred::Fred(const Fred& x) throw()
{ /*...*/ }

Fred& Fred::operator= (const Fred& x) throw()
{
  // ...
  return *this;
}
```

FAQ 30.03

What happens when an object is destroyed that doesn't have an explicit destructor?

The compiler synthesizes a destructor for the object's class.

For example, if an object of class Fred is destroyed and class Fred doesn't provide an explicit destructor, the compiler synthesizes a destructor that destroys all the Fred object's member objects and base class subobjects. This is called *memberwise destruction*. Thus, if class Fred doesn't have an explicit destructor and an object of class Fred contains an object of class Member that has an explicit destructor, then the compiler's synthesized Fred::~Fred() invokes Member's destructor.

The built-in types (int, float, void*, and so on) can be regarded as having destructors that do nothing.

```
#include <iostream>
using namespace std;

class Member {
public:
  ~Member() throw();
};

Member::~Member() throw()
{ cout << "destructing a Member object\n"; }
```

```
class Fred {
public:
            ———— Fred doesn't have an explicit destructor
protected:
  Member member_;
};

int main()
{
  {
    Fred x;
    cout << "before destructing a Fred\n";
  } ←——————— Compiler-synthesized destructor Fred::~Fred() called here
  cout << "after destructing a Fred\n";
}
```

The compiler's synthesized `Fred::~Fred()` calls `Member::~Member()` automatically, so the output is

```
before destructing a Fred
destructing a Member object
after destructing a Fred
```

FAQ 30.04

What happens if an object is copied but doesn't have an explicit copy constructor?

The compiler synthesizes a copy constructor for the object's class.

For example, if an object of class `Fred` is copied and class `Fred` doesn't provide an explicit copy constructor, the compiler synthesizes a copy constructor that copy constructs all the `Fred` object's member objects and base class subobjects. This is called *memberwise copy construction*. Thus, if class `Fred` doesn't have an explicit copy constructor, and an object of class `Fred` contains an object of class `Member` that has an explicit copy constructor, then the compiler's synthesized `Fred::Fred(const Fred&)` invokes `Member`'s copy constructor.

Built-in types (`int`, `float`, `void*`, and so on) can be viewed as having copy constructors that do a bitwise copy.

```
#include <iostream>
using namespace std;
```

```
class Member {
public:
  Member() throw();
  Member(const Member&) throw();
};

Member::Member() throw()
{ cout << "constructing a Member\n"; }

Member::Member(const Member&) throw()
{ cout << "copying a Member\n"; }

class Fred {
public:
  Fred() throw();
```
← ——————————— Fred doesn't have an explicit copy constructor
```
protected:
  Member member_;
};

Fred::Fred() throw()
: member_()
{ }

int main()
{
  Fred a;
  Fred b = a;  ←——— Compiler-synthesized copy constructor Fred::Fred(const Fred&) called here
}
```

The compiler's synthesized `Fred::Fred(const Fred&)` calls `Member::Member(const Member&)` automatically, so the output is

```
constructing a Member
copying a Member
```

FAQ 30.05

What happens when an object that doesn't have an explicit assignment operator is assigned?

The compiler synthesizes an assignment operator for the object's class.

For example, if an object of class `Fred` is assigned and class `Fred` doesn't provide an explicit assignment operator, the compiler synthesizes an assignment operator that assigns all the `Fred` object's member objects and base class subobjects. This is called *memberwise assignment.* Thus if class `Fred` doesn't have an explicit assignment operator and an object of class `Fred` contains an object of class `Member` that has an explicit assignment operator, then the compiler's synthesized `Fred::operator= (const Fred&)` invokes `Member`'s assignment operator.

Built-in types (`int`, `float`, `void*`, and so on) can be viewed as having assignment operators that do a bitwise copy.

```
#include <iostream>
using namespace std;

class Member {
public:
  Member() throw();
  Member& operator= (const Member&) throw();
};

Member::Member() throw()
  { cout << "constructing a Member\n"; }
Member& Member::operator= (const Member&) throw()
  { cout << "assigning a Member\n"; return *this; }

class Fred {
public:
  Fred() throw() : member_() { }
    ◄─────────────── Fred doesn't have an explicit assignment operator
protected:
  Member member_;
};

int main()
{
  Fred a;
  Fred b;
  a = b;  ◄─────── Compiler-synthesized assignment operator Fred::operator= (const Fred&) called here
}
```

The compiler's synthesized `Fred::operator= (const Fred&)` calls `Member::operator= (const Member&)`, so the output is

```
constructing a Member
constructing a Member
assigning a Member
```

FAQ 30.06

What is the Law of the Big Three?

If a class needs any of the Big Three, it needs them all.

This doesn't mean that every class should have all three of the Big Three. On the contrary, the Big Three are needed only in a relatively small percentage of classes. That is one of the reasons this is such an insidious error. Programmers see these infrastructure routines in only some of their classes, so they don't remember the critical Law of the Big Three.

This law first appeared in 1991 in the `comp.lang.c++` FAQ, and it seems to be rediscovered every six months or so. Violations almost always lead to incorrect behavior and often lead to disasters.

In particular, violations of the Law of the Big Three often corrupt the heap. This usually means that the program does not crash until much later in the program's execution (and simple test programs may not crash at all). By the time the programmer goes in with a debugger, the root cause is hard to identify and the heap has so many things wrong with it that it's difficult to trace what's going wrong.

FAQ 30.07

Which of the Big Three usually shows up first?

An explicit destructor.

Developers typically discover the need to do something special during a normal constructor, which frequently necessitates undoing the special action in the destructor. In almost all cases, the class needs a copy constructor so that the special thing will be done during copying, and the class also needs an assignment operator so that the special thing will be done during assignment.

The destructor is the signal for applying the Law. Pretend that the keyboard's ~ (tilde) key is painted bright red and is wired up to a siren.

In the following example, the constructor of class `MyString` allocates memory, so its destructor `delete`s the memory. Typing the ~ of `~MyString()` should sound a siren for the Law of the Big Three.

```
#include <new>
#include <cstring>
using namespace std;
```

```
class MyString {
public:
  MyString(const char* s) throw(bad_alloc);
 ~MyString() throw();
  MyString(const MyString& s) throw();
  MyString& operator= (const MyString& s) throw();
protected:
  unsigned len_;      // ORDER DEPENDENCY; see FAQ 22.10
  char*    data_;     // ORDER DEPENDENCY; see FAQ 22.10
};

MyString::MyString(const char* s) throw(bad_alloc)
: len_(strlen(s))
, data_(new char[len_ + 1])
{ memcpy(data_, s, len_ + 1); }

MyString::~MyString() throw()
{ delete[] data_; }

int main()
{ MyString s = "xyzzy"; }
```

Classes that own allocated memory (hash tables, linked lists, and so forth) generally need the Big Three (see FAQ 30.08).

FAQ 30.08

What is remote ownership?

Remote ownership is the responsibility that comes with being the owner of something allocated from the heap.

When an object is the logical owner of something allocated from the heap (known as the referent), the object is said to have remote ownership. That is, the object owns the referent. When an object has remote ownership, it usually means that the object is responsible for deleteing the referent.

Any time a pointer is added to an object's member data, the class's author should immediately determine whether the object owns the referent (that is, whether the object has remote ownership). If this determination is delayed, the class's implementation can become schizophrenic—some of the object's member functions assume that the object owns the referent, others assume that someone else owns the referent. This is usually a mess and sometimes a disaster.

FAQ 30.09

How is remote ownership special?

It requires a deep copy, not a shallow copy.

When an object has remote ownership, the object needs the Big Three (destructor, copy constructor, and assignment operator). These routines are responsible for destroying the referent, creating a copy of the referent, and assigning the referent, respectively.

The copy semantics for remote ownership require the referent to be copied (a.k.a. deep copy) rather than just the pointer (a.k.a. shallow copy). For example, if class `MyString` has a pointer to an array of characters, copying the `MyString` object should copy the array. It is not sufficient to simply copy the pointer to the array, since that would result in two objects that both think they are responsible for `deleteing` the same array.

When an object contains pointers for which it does not have remote ownership, the copy semantics are usually straightforward: the copy operation merely copies the pointer. For example, an iterator object might have a pointer to a node of a linked list, but the node is owned by the list rather than by the iterator, so copying an iterator merely needs to copy the pointer; the data in the node is not copied to the new iterator.

When an object doesn't contain pointers, the copy semantics are usually straightforward: the corresponding copy operation is called on each member object. This is what the compiler does automatically if the class doesn't have any copy operations (see FAQs 30.04, 30.05), which is why the Big Three are not usually needed in these cases.

FAQ 30.10

What if a class owns a referent and doesn't have all of the Big Three?

Trouble is brewing.

The following `EvilString` class doesn't have an explicit copy constructor or assignment operator, so the compiler synthesizes a copy constructor and/or assignment operator when it sees an `EvilString` being copy initialized and/or assigned, respectively. Unfortunately the compiler-synthesized copy constructor and assignment operators copy only the pointer (shallow copy) rather than the referent (deep copy).

```
#include <new>
#include <cstring>
```

```
#include <stdexcept>
using namespace std;

class EvilString {
public:
  EvilString(const char* s) throw(bad_alloc);
  ~EvilString() throw();
```
◄——————— Since this contains remote ownership, it needs an explicit copy constructor
◄——————— But pretend the developer failed to provide an explicit copy constructor
◄——————— Similar comments for the assignment operator
```
protected:
  unsigned len_;      // ORDER DEPENDENCY; see FAQ 22.10
  char* data_;        // ORDER DEPENDENCY; see FAQ 22.10
};

EvilString::EvilString(const char* s) throw(bad_alloc)
: len_(strlen(s))
, data_(new char[len_ + 1])
{ memcpy(data_, s, len_ + 1); }

EvilString::~EvilString() throw()
{ delete[] data_; }
```

If an EvilString is copied (passed by value, for example; see FAQ 20.07), then the copy points to the same string data as the original. When the copy dies, the data they are sharing is deleted, leaving the original EvilString object with a dangling reference. Any use of the original object, including the implicit destruction when the original dies, will probably corrupt the heap, which will eventually crash the program.

```
void sample(EvilString b) throw(bad_alloc)
{
  // Since EvilString lacks a proper copy constructor,
  // changes to b's string data will also change a's string
}

int main()
{
  EvilString a = "xyzzy";
  sample(a);
  // Any use of a might corrupt the heap
}
```

Note that the problem is not with pass-by-value. The problem is that the copy constructor for class EvilString is broken. Similar comments can be made regarding the assignment operator.

FAQ 30.11

Are there any C++ classes that help manage remote ownership?

 Yes, `auto_ptr`.

The standard template class `auto_ptr<T>` is a partial solution to managing remote ownership. `auto_ptr<Fred>` acts like a `Fred*`, except the referent (the `Fred` object) is automatically `deleted` when the `auto_ptr` dies. `auto_ptr<T>` is known as a *managed pointer*.

Managed pointers are useful whenever a referent is allocated by `new` and when the owner of the pointer owns the referent. In other words, `auto_ptr<T>` is useful for managing remote ownership.

The most important issue isn't that `auto_ptr<T>` saves the one line of `delete` code. The most important issue is that `auto_ptr<T>` handles exceptions properly: the referent is automagically `deleted` when an exception causes the `auto_ptr<T>` object to be destructed. In the following example, class `Noisy` throws exceptions randomly to simulate the fact that we can't always predict when an exception is going to be thrown (hopefully your classes don't have this property).

Here is a function that randomly returns `true` and `false` with 50–50 probability:

```
#include <memory>
#include <iostream>
#include <cstdlib>
#include <ctime>
using namespace std;

bool heads()    //Coin-toss: true with 50-50 probability
{ return (rand() >> 4) % 2 ? true : false; }
```

Here is a class that prints messages and possibly throws exceptions in its functions.

```
class Noisy {
public:
  Noisy() throw();
 ~Noisy() throw();
  void g() throw(int);
  friend void h(Noisy& n) throw(int);
  Noisy& operator= (const Noisy&) throw();
  Noisy           (const Noisy&) throw();
};
```

```
Noisy::Noisy() throw()
  { cout << "Noisy::Noisy(); "; }
Noisy::~Noisy() throw()
  { cout << "Noisy::~Noisy(); "; }
void Noisy::g() throw(int)
  { cout << "Noisy::g(); "; if (heads()) throw 5; }
void h(Noisy& n) throw(int)
  { cout << "h(Noisy&); "; if (heads()) throw 7; }
```

Here is a function that wisely chooses to use the managed pointer
auto_ptr<Noisy>.

```
void usingManagedPointers() throw(int)
{
  cout << "using an auto_ptr<Noisy>: ";
  auto_ptr<Noisy> p(new Noisy());
  p->g();
  h(*p);
  cout << "didn't throw\n";
} ◄──────── The delete is automagic (no need to worry)
```

Here is the same function, but this time using a raw Noisy* pointer. Note how much more complex this code is, even though it is doing the same thing. A significant portion of this code exists solely to ensure that the referent is deleted properly, whereas in the previous example the managed pointer enabled most of this scaffolding to disappear.

```
void usingRawPointers() throw(int)
{
  cout << "using a Noisy* pointer: ";
  Noisy* p = new Noisy();

  try {
    p->g();
    h(*p);
  }
  catch (...) {
    delete p;
    throw;
  }

  delete p; ◄──── Here the delete is explicit
  cout << "didn't throw\n";
}
```

Here is main() that repeatedly calls the foregoing routines.

```
int main()
{
  srand(time(NULL));    // Randomize the random number seed

  for (int i = 0; i < 10; ++i) {
    try {
      usingRawPointers();
      usingManagedPointers();
    } catch (int i) {
      cout << "caught " << i << '\n';
    }
    cout << '\n';
  }
}
```

FAQ 30.12

Does auto_ptr enforce the Law of the Big Three and solve the problems associated with remote ownership?

new   No. auto_ptr<T> plugs leaks, but it doesn't enforce the Law of the Big Three.

When a class uses a plain T* to implement remote ownership, forgetting any of the Big Three causes the compiler to silently generate wrong code. The result is often a disaster at runtime.

Unfortunately, replacing the T* with a managed pointer such as auto_ptr<T> does not correct the problem. The root of the problem is that when an auto_ptr<T> is copied, ownership of the referent is transferred to the copy and the original object's auto_ptr<T> becomes NULL. This is often undesirable. What is needed instead is for the referent to be copied or for a compile-time error to be generated that flags the problem.

The safest solution is to define and use a strict auto_ptr<T>. For example, the following could go into file strict_auto_ptr.h and could be reused whenever anyone wanted a strict auto_ptr<T>. Note that the copy constructor and assignment operator are private: and are undefined, thus making it impossible to copy a strict_auto_ptr<T> object.

```
#include <memory>
using namespace std;
```

```
template<class T>
class strict_auto_ptr : public auto_ptr<T> {
public:
  strict_auto_ptr(T* p=NULL) throw() : auto_ptr<T>(p) { }
private:
  strict_auto_ptr(const strict_auto_ptr&) throw();
  void operator= (const strict_auto_ptr&) throw();
};
```

When `strict_auto_ptr<T>` is used, the compiler either synthesizes the Big Three correctly or causes specific, compile-time errors; it does not allow run-time disasters.

The following example shows a class that implements remote ownership by the managed pointer `strict_auto_ptr<Noisy>` rather than the plain pointer `Noisy*`.

```
#include <iostream>
using namespace std;

class Noisy {
public:
  Noisy() throw();
 ~Noisy() throw();
  Noisy& operator= (const Noisy&) throw();
  Noisy            (const Noisy&) throw();
};

Noisy::Noisy() throw()
   { cout << "Noisy::Noisy()\n"; }
Noisy::~Noisy() throw()
   { cout << "Noisy::~Noisy()\n"; }

typedef strict_auto_ptr<Noisy> NoisyPtr;

class Fred {
public:
  Fred() throw(bad_alloc);
  //No destructor needed: The Noisy will automagically get
  //deleted. The compiler won't synthesize a copy ctor or
  //assignment operator, since the strict_auto_ptr version of these
  //are private.
protected:
  NoisyPtr ptr_;   // Like Noisy* ptr_ but better
};

Fred::Fred() throw(bad_alloc)
 : ptr_(new Noisy())
```

```
  { }

  void sample()
  {
    Fred x;   //OK: Allocates a new Noisy
  }           //OK: x is destructed, so its Noisy is deleted

  int main()
  { sample(); }
```

Because `strict_auto_ptr<Noisy>`'s destructor `deletes` the referent, `Fred` doesn't need an explicit destructor. The `Fred::~Fred()` synthesized by the compiler is correct.

Because `strict_auto_ptr<Noisy>`'s copy constructor and assignment operator are `private:`, the compiler is prevented from synthesizing either the copy constructor or the assignment operator for class `Fred`. Copying or assigning a `Fred` produces a specific, compile-time error message. Compare this to using a `Noisy*`, in which case the compiler silently synthesizes the wrong code, producing disastrous results.

For example, when the GENERATE_ERROR symbol is `#defined` in the following function, the compiler gives an error message rather than silently doing the wrong thing.

```
  void disasterAverted(const Fred& x) throw()
  {
    #ifdef GENERATE_ERROR
      Fred y = x;  //gives a compile-time error message
      y = x;       //gives a compile-time error message
    #endif
  }
```

`strict_auto_ptr<T>` effectively automates the proper `delete` and prevents the compiler from synthesizing improper copy operations. It plugs leaks and enforces the Law of the Big Three.

FAQ 30.13

Are there cases where one or two of the Big Three may be needed but not all three?

Yes, but define them all anyway.

There are cases where one or two of the Big Three may be needed but not all three. All three should usually be defined anyway so that people don't have to think so hard during code reviews and maintenance activities. Here are four common times when this happens: `virtual` destructors, `protected:` assignment operators, recording creation or destruction, and unnecessary or illogical copy operations.

Virtual destructors: A base class often has a `virtual` destructor to ensure that the right destructor is called during `delete basePointer` (see FAQ 21.05). If this explicit destructor exists solely to be made `virtual` (for example, if it does what the synthesized destructor would have done, namely `{ }`), the class may not need an explicit copy constructor or assignment operator.

Protected assignment operators: An ABC often has a `protected:` assignment operator to prevent users from performing assignment using a reference to an ABC (see FAQ 24.05). If this explicit assignment operator exists solely to be made `protected:` (for example, if it does what the synthesized assignment operator would have done, namely memberwise assignment), the class may not need an explicit copy constructor or destructor.

Recording creation or destruction: A class sometimes has an explicit destructor and copy constructor solely to record the birth and death of its objects. For example, the class might print a message to a log file or count the number of existing objects. If the explicit destructor or copy constructor exists solely to perform this information recording (for example, if these operations do what the synthesized versions would have done), the class may not need an explicit assignment operator, since assignment doesn't change the number of instances of a class.

Unnecessary or illogical copy operations: There are cases where a class simply doesn't need one or both copy operations. Sometimes the copy operations don't even make logical sense. For example, the semantics of class `File` may mean that it is nonsensical to copy `File` objects; similarly for objects of class `Semaphore`. In these cases, the unnecessary copy operations are normally declared in the `private:` section of the class and are never defined. This prevents the compiler from synthesizing these operations in the class's `public:` section and causes compile-time error messages whenever a user accidentally calls one of these member functions. In this case, it is not strictly necessary to define the other members of the Big Three just because one or both copy operations are declared in the `private:` section of the class.

FAQ 30.14

Are there any other circumstances that might explicitly warrant the Big Three?

Yes, when the Big Three need to be non-`inline`.

When the compiler synthesizes the Big Three, it makes them `inline`. If the application's classes are exposed to customers (for example, if customers `#include` the application's header files rather than merely using an executable), the application's `inline` code is copied into their executables. If you want to maintain binary compatibility between releases of your library, you must not change any visible `inline` functions, including the versions of the Big Three that are synthesized by the compiler. Therefore, explicit, non-`inline` versions of the Big Three should be used.

FAQ 30.15

Why does copying an object using `memcpy()` cause a program crash?

Because bitwise copying is evil.

A class's copy operations (copy constructor and assignment operator) are supposed to copy the logical state of an object. In some cases, the logical state of an object can be copied using a bitwise copy (e.g., using `memcpy()`). However a bitwise copy doesn't make sense for a lot of objects; it may even put the copy in an incoherent state.

If a class X has a nontrivial copy constructor or assignment operator, bitwise copying an X object often creates wild pointers. One common case where bitwise copying of an object creates wild pointers is when the object owns a referent (that is, it has remote ownership). The wild pointers are a result of the bitwise copy operation, not some failure on the part of the class designer.

For example, consider a class that has remote ownership, such as a `string` class that allocates an array of `char` from the heap. If `string` object a is bitwise copied into `string` b, then the two objects both point to the same allocated array. One of these `string`s will die first, which will `delete` the allocated array owned by both of them. BOOM!

```cpp
#include <string>
using namespace std;

int main()
{
  string a = "fred";
  string b;

  #if 1
    // Good: let the object copy itself:
    b = a;
  #else
```

```
    // Bad: manipulate the object's bits:
    memcpy(&b, &a, sizeof(string));
  #endif
}
```

Note that a bitwise copy is safe if the object's exact class is known and the object is (and will always remain!) bitwise copyable. For example, class `string` might use `memcpy()` to copy its string data because `char` is and will always remain bitwise copyable (assuming that the string data is a simple array of `char`).

FAQ 30.16

Why do programs with variable-length argument lists crash?

Because variable-length argument lists use bitwise copy, which is dangerous in many cases. There are times where variable-length argument lists don't cause a problem (`printf` comes to mind). But it is wise to avoid using them unless there is some compelling reason.

Objects passed into ellipses (. . .) are passed via bitwise copy. The parameter objects are bitwise copied onto the stack, but the `va_arg` macro uses the copy constructor to copy the pile of bits from the stack. The technical term for this asymmetry is *ouch*.

```
#include <cstdarg>

class Fred {
public:
  Fred() throw();
  Fred(const Fred& x) throw();
  Fred& operator= (const Fred& x) throw();
  ~Fred() throw();
};

void doSomethingWith(Fred x) throw();

void f(int count, Fred first...) throw()
{
  va_list ap;
  va_start(ap, first);
  doSomethingWith( first );
  for (int i = 1; i < count; ++i) {
    Fred x = va_arg(ap, Fred);
    doSomethingWith( x );
  }
```

```
   }

   int main()
   {
     Fred a, b, c;
     f(3, a, b, c);
   }
```

"Ladies and gentlemen, this is your pilot speaking; please fasten your seat belts in preparation for the air turbulence ahead."

main()'s three Fred objects are constructed via Fred::Fred(). The call to f(int,Fred...) passes these Freds using bitwise copy. The bitwise copies may not be properly initialized Fred objects and are not logical copies of a, b, and c. Inside f(int,Fred...), the va_arg macro uses a pointer cast (shudder) to create a Fred*, but this Fred* doesn't point to a valid Fred object because it points to a bitwise copy of a Fred object. The va_arg macro then dereferences this (invalid) pointer and copies the pile of incoherent bits (via Fred's copy constructor) into the local variable, x.

If Fred has nontrivial copy semantics, the chances that the bitwise copy is the same as a logical copy is remote at best.

Variable-length argument lists are evil.

FAQ 30.17

Why do programs that use realloc() to reallocate an array of objects crash?

When realloc() needs to move the storage that is being reallocated, it uses bitwise copy rather than invoking the appropriate constructor for the newly allocated objects.

Use realloc() only for objects guaranteed to be bitwise copyable.

Chapter 31

Using Objects to Prevent Memory Leaks

When are memory leaks important?

When the application is important and its lifetime has some duration.

A memory leak occurs when a program allocates memory off the heap and does not return the memory when it is no longer needed. As a result, the system eventually runs out of heap memory and crashes or hangs up. In general, memory leaks cannot be tolerated, particularly for long-running applications. "Reboot every few hours" is not a practical solution to the problem, so it is important to understand how leaks occur and what can be done to prevent them. It is very, very difficult to cure these problems after the fact, but a modicum of solid engineering applied in the early stages of development can eliminate almost all the grief.

Note that there are cases when memory leaks can be ignored. Applications that are extremely short-lived don't need to worry about memory leaks. For example, they might run for only a fraction of a second and allocate less memory than the target machine has. When the application terminates, all the memory that was allocated is automatically returned to the operating system, so the only thing to worry about is whether destructors have other side effects. In cases like this it might make sense to use new but simply never use delete. However, remember: if someday some requirements require the leaks to be plugged, it is very, very difficult to do after the application has been written.

FAQ 31.02

What is the easiest way to avoid memory leaks?

   Place pointers inside objects and have the objects manage the pointers.

The pointer returned from new should always be stored in a member variable of an object. That object's destructor should delete the allocation.

The beauty of this approach is that objects have comprehensive creation and destruction semantics (including constructors and destructors), whereas pointers have extremely rudimentary creation and destruction semantics. By putting pointers in objects it is possible to guarantee that the destructor will always be executed and the memory will be properly deallocated.

In the example that follows, whitespace-terminated words are read from the standard input stream cin (see FAQ 2.16), and the unique words are printed out in sorted order. For example, if the standard input stream contains the words "on and on and on he went," the output will contain the unique words "and he on went."

The preferred way to produce a sorted list of unique words is to use the string class (see FAQ 2.16) and a container class (in this case, the standard set<T> template; see FAQ 28.14):

```
#include <iostream>
#include <set>
#include <string>
using namespace std;

void theRightWay() throw()
{
  typedef set<string> StringSet;
  StringSet unique;
  string word;
  while (cin >> word)
    unique.insert(word);
  for (StringSet::iterator p = unique.begin();
       p != unique.end(); ++p)
    cout << *p << '\n';
}

int main()
{ theRightWay(); }
```

Note that there are no explicit pointers in this code, and there are no chances for memory leaks. For example the `string` object contains a `char*`, but there is no possibility of a leak since the `string` object is local and it has a proper destructor—it handles its own memory management. Similarly for the `set<string>`: this object may contain many pointers and may use many memory allocations, but since the object is local and since it has a proper destructor, it manages its own memory without any possibility of memory leaks.

In contrast, the undesirable approach would be to use explicit pointers to explicitly allocated memory. The following example is more or less equivalent to the example shown above, but it is rife with opportunities for both wild pointers and memory leaks. Making this code safe would be quite a bit more difficult than the relatively simple solution shown above (the problems cited are described after the code):

```
// a and b point to char*s
int compareCharPtr(const void* a, const void* b) throw()
{ return strcmp(*(char**)a, *(char**)b); }

void theWrongWay() throw()
{
  const unsigned maxNumWords = 1000;
  const unsigned maxWordLen = 100;
  char word[maxWordLen];
  unsigned uniqueSize = 0;
  unsigned uniqueCapacity = 100;
  char** unique = (char**) malloc(uniqueCapacity * sizeof(char*));
  if (unique == NULL)  ←──────────────────── Problem 1
    return;
  while (cin >> word) {  ←──────────────────── Problem 2
    unsigned i;
    for (i = 0; i < uniqueSize; ++i)
      if (strcmp(unique[i], word) == 0)  ←──── Problem 3
        break;
    if (i == uniqueSize) {
      if (uniqueSize == uniqueCapacity) {
        uniqueCapacity *= 2;
        unique = (char**)realloc(unique, uniqueCapacity * sizeof(char*));
        if (unique == NULL)  ←──────────── Problem 4
          return;
      }
      unique[uniqueSize++] = strdup(word);
    }
  }
  qsort(unique, uniqueSize, sizeof(unique[0]), compareCharPtr);
  for (unsigned i = 0; i < uniqueSize; ++i)
    cout << unique[i] << '\n';
  for (unsigned j = 0; j < uniqueSize; ++j)
```

```
        free(unique[j]);
    free(unique);
}
```

Most programmers will notice these major problems with this code.

1. If it runs out of memory in the `malloc()` step, it should probably throw an exception rather than silently returning; see FAQ 12.06.

2. If the length of a word exceeds `maxWordLen`, the program overwrites memory and probably crashes.

3. If the file contains null bytes (`'\0'`), `strcmp()` and `strdup()` give the wrong answers.

4. If it runs out of memory in the `realloc()` step, all the previously allocated memory is lost—a leak. Plus the routine should probably throw an exception rather than silently returning; see FAQ 12.06.

All these problems can be fixed, but fixing them makes the code even more complex. Note that `theRightWay()` doesn't have any of these problems and is much simpler. It properly handles running out of memory, and it can handle arbitrarily long words, arbitrarily many characters within long words (including null bytes), and arbitrarily many words.

The more subtle problem with `theWrongWay()` is its use of explicit pointers. If a maintenance programmer changes the code so that it exits before the last `for` loop, such as throwing an exception, perhaps from another routine, this code will leak memory. The code could protect against exceptions with a large `try` block around the whole routine except the last `for` loop, but it would be much harder to protect against an early `return`. Note that `theRightWay()` doesn't have this problem: it won't leak when an exception is thrown or an early `return` is executed.

But even if `theWrongWay()` is made safe, it will still be much slower than `theRightWay()`, especially with large numbers of unique words. This is because `theWrongWay()` uses a linear search (doubling the number of unique words typically quadruples the time); `theRightWay()` uses a much more efficient algorithm.

FAQ 31.03

What are the most important principles for resource management?

Ownership, responsibility, and focus.

Ownership: Every allocated resource is owned by exactly one resource manager object, which must be a local (`auto`) variable in some scope (or a member object of some local).

Responsibility: The resource manager object is charged with the responsibility of releasing the allocated resource. This is the only place the resource is released.

Focus: The resource manager object does nothing other than manage the individual resource.

A leak is simply a `new` that lacks a corresponding `delete`. Either the `delete` isn't physically in the source code or it is in the source code but is bypassed due to run-time control flow. Both situations are handled by the resource management discipline since the destructor for a local object always runs when control leaves the scope where the local object was created. In other words, the resource management discipline relies on the guarantees provided by the language rather than the good intentions of programmer self-discipline.

This resource management discipline can be applied to the management of all kinds of resources (e.g., files, semaphores, memory, database connections, and so on). "Memory" is used here only as a concrete example of a manageable resource.

_____ **FAQ 31.04**

Should the object that manages a resource also perform operations that may throw exceptions?

Not usually.

In the following example, class `Fred` both manages a resource (an `X` allocation) and performs some operations that may throw exceptions (it calls the function `mayThrow()`). In other words, `Fred` violates the guideline. When `Fred`'s constructor throws an exception (as a result of calling `mayThrow()`), there is a resource leak.

```
#include <new>
#include <iostream>
using namespace std;

class X { };

void mayThrow() throw(int)
  { throw 42; }

class Fred {
public:
  Fred() throw(bad_alloc, int);
  ~Fred() throw();
```

```
        Fred(const Fred& f) throw();
        Fred& operator= (const Fred& f) throw();
    private:
      X* p_;
    };

    Fred::Fred() throw(bad_alloc, int)
      : p_(new X()) { mayThrow(); }
    Fred::~Fred() throw()
      { cout << "Not reached #1\n"; delete p_; }

    int main()
    {
      try {
        Fred f;
        cout << "Not reached #2\n";
      }
      catch (int e) {
        cout << "Exception caught: " << e << "\n";
      }
    }
```

Because the guideline is violated, the X object leaks: the `delete p_` instruction in `Fred::~Fred()` is never executed. Either `Fred` should focus on being a resource manager—and nothing but a resource manager—or `Fred` should delegate the resource management responsibility to some other class. In other words, either get rid of the code that calls `mayThrow()` from `Fred`, or change the `X*` to an `auto_ptr<X>`.

In those cases where it is not possible to abide by the discipline, a `try` block can be put in the constructor initialization list. Use this only as a last resort.

FAQ 31.05

Should an object manage two or more resources?

 Not usually.

An object that manages a resource should manage exactly one resource. Use composition to combine multiple "pure" resource manager objects (for example, multiple `auto_ptr<T>` objects, `File` objects, and so forth). This guideline is a corollary of the guideline presented in the previous FAQ.

If an object manages two or more resources, the first resource may leak if the second allocation throws an exception. In particular, when an exception occurs during the execution of a constructor, the object's destructor is not executed so the destructor won't release the resource that was successfully allocated. In the following example, class `Fred` manages two resources; an `X` allocation and a `Y` allocation. When `Fred`'s constructor throws an exception as a result of allocating a `Y`, the `X` resource leaks.

```cpp
#include <new>
#include <iostream>
using namespace std;

class X { };

class Y {
public:
  Y() throw(int);
};

Y::Y() throw(int)
  { throw 42; }

class Fred {
public:
  Fred() throw(bad_alloc, int);
 ~Fred() throw();
protected:
  X* x_;
  Y* y_;
};

Fred::Fred() throw(bad_alloc, int)
  : x_(new X())
  , y_(new Y())
  { }
Fred::~Fred() throw()
  { cout << "Not reached #1\n"; delete y_; delete x_; }

int main()
{
  try {
    Fred f;
    cout << "Not reached #2\n";
  }
  catch (int e) {
    cout << "Exception caught: " << e << "\n";
  }
}
```

Because the guideline is violated, the `X` object leaks: the `delete x_` instruction is never executed. Either `Fred` should focus on being a manager of a resource—not two or more resources—or `Fred` should delegate the resource management responsibility to some other class. In other words, either get rid of the `Y` resource from `Fred` or change the `X*` to an `auto_ptr<X>`.

In those cases where it is not possible to abide by the discipline, a `try` block can be put in the constructor initialization list. Use this only as a last resort.

FAQ 31.06

What if an object has a pointer to an allocation and one of the object's member functions `deletes` the allocation?

That member function must immediately restore the integrity of the object holding the pointer.

If some member function (other than the destructor) `deletes` memory allocated from the heap, then the member function must either reassign the pointer with a *previously* allocated (`new`) object or set a flag that tells the destructor to skip the `delete`. Setting the pointer to NULL can be used as such a flag.

For example, some assignment operators need to `delete` an old allocation as well as allocate a new one. In such cases, the new allocation should be performed *before* the old is `deleted` in case the allocation throws an exception. The goal is for the assignment operator to be atomic: either it should succeed completely (no exceptions, and all states successfully copied from the source object), or it should fail (throw an exception) without changing the state of the `this` object. It is not always possible to meet the goal of atomicity, but the assignment operator must never leave the `this` object in an incoherent state.

A related guideline is to use a local `auto_ptr<T>` to point to the new allocation. This will ensure that the new allocation is `deleted` if an exception is thrown by some subsequent operation in the member function. The ownership of the allocated object can be transferred to the `this` object by assigning from the local `auto_ptr` into the `auto_ptr<T>` in the `this` object.

FAQ 31.07

How should a pointer variable be handled after being passed to `delete`?

The pointer variable should immediately be put into a safe state.

After calling `delete p`, immediately set `p = NULL` or `p = anotherAutoPtr` (unless the pointer p is just about to go out of scope). The goal is to prevent a subsequent operation from following the pointer p (which now points at garbage) or calling delete p a second time.

Note that setting p = new Fred() is not acceptable, since the Fred allocation may throw an exception before p is changed to a safe state.

We recommend setting p = NULL immediately, in case an exception subverts the normal flow of control.

FAQ 31.08

What should be done with a pointer to an object that is allocated and deallocated in the same scope?

It should be placed in a managed pointer object that is local to the scope.

The goal is to make the code *exception safe,* that is, safe in the presence of exceptions (see FAQ 9.03). As a pleasant side effect, it becomes unnecessary to remember (and therefore, in a sense, impossible to forget) to make sure that the temporary object is deleted. Using a managed pointer (for example, an auto_ptr<T>) meets these goals since the managed pointer's destructor automatically deletes the temporary object. Here's an example.

```
#include <new>
#include <iostream>
#include <memory>
using namespace std;

class Fred {
public:
  ~Fred() throw();
};

Fred::~Fred() throw()
  { cout << "Fred dtor\n"; }

void sample() throw(bad_alloc)
{
  auto_ptr<Fred> ptr( new Fred() );

  if (rand() % 2) {
    cout << "randomly doing an 'early return'\n";
    return;
  }
```

```
      cout << "randomly NOT doing an 'early return'\n";
  ◄──────── In either case, we do NOT say delete ptr, since ptr is a managed pointer
}

int main()
{ sample(); }
```

────────────────────────────────────

How easy is it to implement reference counting with pointer semantics?

new   It is relatively easy, and the result is worthwhile.

If the application tends to pass around pointers to dynamically allocated objects and possibly store some of the pointers in containers, it is quite possible that there will be either memory leaks or dangling references. Often a simple reference-counting scheme suffices in these circumstances.

Reference counting means that each object keeps track of how many pointers are pointing at it, and when the object no longer has any pointers pointing at it, the object deletes itself. With a little discipline, this means that the object dies when it becomes unreachable, which is precisely what is desired. A very simple implementation of this technique follows.

```
class FredPtr;

class Fred {
public:
  Fred() throw()
    : count_(0) /*...*/ { }  // All ctors set count_ to 0 !
  // ...
private:
  friend FredPtr;     // A friend class
  unsigned count_;
  // count_ must be initialized to 0 by all constructors
  // count_ is the number of FredPtr objects that point at
  // the this object
};

class FredPtr {
public:
  FredPtr(Fred* p) throw()
    : p_(p) { if (p_) ++p_->count_; }
 ~FredPtr() throw()
    { if (p_ && --p_->count_ == 0) delete p_; }
```

```
    FredPtr(const FredPtr& p) throw()
       : p_(p.p_) { if (p_) ++p_->count_; }
    FredPtr& operator= (const FredPtr& p) throw();
    Fred* operator-> () throw() { return p_;  }
    Fred& operator* () throw()  { return *p_; }
    Fred* getRaw() throw()      { return p_;  }
  private:
    Fred* p_;
  };

  FredPtr& FredPtr::operator= (const FredPtr& p) throw()
  {
    // DO NOT CHANGE THE ORDER OF THESE STATEMENTS!
    // (This order properly handles self-assignment; see FAQ 24.02)
    if (p.p_) ++p.p_->count_;
    if (p_ && --p_->count_ == 0) delete p_;
    p_ = p.p_;
    return *this;
  }
```

This simple reference-counting mechanism provides users with a pointer-oriented view of the Fred objects. In other words, users always allocate their Fred objects via new and point to the Fred objects via FredPtr "smart pointers." Users can make as many copies of their FredPtr pointers as they wish, including storing some FredPtrs in containers, and the pointed-to Fred objects are automatically deleted when the last such FredPtr object vanishes.

To hide the pointers from users so that users see objects rather than pointers to objects, use reference counting with copy-on-write semantics (see FAQ 31.10).

Note that the constraint that all Fred objects be allocated via new can be enforced using the named constructor idiom (see FAQ 16.08). In this case, it means making all Fred constructors private: and defining each named constructor as a public: static create() member function. The public: static create() member function would allocate a new Fred object and would return the resulting pointer as a FredPtr (not a Fred*). Users would then use FredPtr p = Fred::create() rather than FredPtr p = new Fred().

FAQ 31.10

Is reference counting with copy-on-write semantics hard to implement?

It's a bit involved, but it's manageable.

Copy-on-write semantics allows users to think they're copying `Fred` objects, but in reality the underlying implementation doesn't actually do any copying unless and until some user actually tries to modify the copied `Fred` object. This approach provides users with reference semantics; the previous FAQ used reference counting to provide users with pointer semantics.

Nested class `Fred::Data` houses all the data that would normally go into a `Fred` object. `Fred::Data` also has an extra data member, `count_`, to manage the reference counting. Class `Fred` ends up being a *smart reference:* internally it points to the `Fred::Data`, but externally it acts as if it has the `Fred::Data` data within itself.

```cpp
#include <new>
#include <cassert>
#include <stdexcept>
using namespace std;

class Fred {
public:
  Fred() throw();                            // Default constructor
  Fred(int i, int j) throw();                // Normal constructor
  Fred(const Fred& f) throw();
  Fred& operator= (const Fred& f) throw();
 ~Fred() throw();
  void sampleInspectorMethod() const throw();
  void sampleMutatorMethod() throw(bad_alloc);
  // ...

private:

  class Data {
  public:
    Data() throw();
    Data(int i, int j) throw();
    Data(const Data& d) throw();

    // Since only Fred can access Fred::Data,
    // the Fred::Data members can be public:.
    // If that feels uncomfortable, the members can be made
    // private: and class Fred can be made a friend class
    // (see FAQ 19-02)
    // ...

    unsigned count_;
    // count_ is the number of Fred objects that point at this
```

```
    // count_ must be initialized to 1 by all constructors
    // (starts at 1 because of the Fred object that created the this)
  };

  Data* data_;
};

Fred::Data::Data() throw()                     : count_(1) /*...*/ { }
Fred::Data::Data(int i, int j) throw()   : count_(1) /*...*/ { }
Fred::Data::Data(const Data& d) throw() : count_(1) /*...*/ { }

Fred::Fred() throw()                         : data_(new Data()) { }
Fred::Fred(int i, int j) throw()     : data_(new Data(i, j)) { }
Fred::Fred(const Fred& f) throw() : data_(f.data_) { ++data_->count_; }

Fred& Fred::operator= (const Fred& f) throw()
{
  // DO NOT CHANGE THE ORDER OF THESE STATEMENTS!
  // (This order properly handles self-assignment; see FAQ 24.02)
  ++f.data_->count_;
  if (--data_->count_ == 0) delete data_;
  data_ = f.data_;
  return *this;
}


Fred::~Fred() throw()
{ if (--data_->count_ == 0) delete data_; }

void Fred::sampleInspectorMethod() const throw()
{
  // This member function promises not to change anything in *data_
  // Other than that, any data access would simply use "data_->..."
}

void Fred::sampleMutatorMethod() throw(bad_alloc)
{
  // This member function might need to change things in *data_
  // Thus it first checks if this is the only pointer to *data_
  if (data_->count_ > 1) {
    Data* d = new Data(*data_);     // Invoke Fred::Data's copy ctor
    -- data_->count_;
    data_ = d;
  }
  assert(data_->count_ == 1);

  // Now the member function proceeds to access "data_->..." as normal
}
```

If it is fairly common to call Fred's default constructor, those new calls can be avoided by sharing a common Fred::Data object for all Freds that are constructed via Fred::Fred(). To avoid static initialization order problems (see FAQ 2.10), this shared Fred::Data object is created "on first use" inside a function. Here are the changes that need to be made (note that the shared Fred::Data object's destructor is never invoked; if that is a problem, either hope that there are no static initialization order problems, drop back to the approach described above, or use the nifty counter idiom (see FAQ 16.17)).

```
class Fred {
public:
  // ...
private:
  // ...
  static Data* defaultData() throw();
};

Fred::Fred() throw()
 : data_(defaultData())
{ ++ data_->count_; }

Fred::Data* Fred::defaultData() throw(bad_alloc)
{
  static Data* p = NULL;
  if (p == NULL) {
    p = new Data();
    ++ p->count_;    // Make sure it never goes to zero
  }
  return p;
}
```

The point of all this is that users can freely copy Fred objects, but the actual data isn't copied unless and until a copy is actually needed. This can help improve performance in some cases.

To provide reference counting for a hierarchy of classes, see FAQ 31.11.

FAQ 31.11

How can reference counting be implemented with copy-on-write semantics for a hierarchy of classes?

new   Through an extension of the technique for a single class.

The previous FAQ presented a reference-counting scheme that provided users with reference semantics but did so for a single class rather than for a hierarchy of classes. This FAQ extends the technique to allow for a hierarchy of classes. The basic difference is that Fred::Data is now the root of a hierarchy of classes, which probably means that it has some virtual functions. Note that class Fred itself still does not have any virtual functions.

The virtual constructor idiom (FAQ 21.07), is used to make copies of the Fred::Data objects. To select which derived class to create, the sample code uses the named constructor idiom (FAQ 16.08), but other techniques are possible (a switch statement in the constructor, for example). The sample code assumes two derived classes, Der1 and Der2. Member functions in the derived classes are unaware of the reference counting.

```cpp
#include <cassert>
#include <string>
using namespace std;

class Fred {
public:
  static Fred create1(string s, int i); // Named ctors (see FAQ 16.08)
  static Fred create2(float x, float y);
  Fred(const Fred& f);
  Fred& operator= (const Fred& f);
 ~Fred();
  void sampleInspectorMethod() const;    // Does not change this
  void sampleMutatorMethod();             // Changes this object

private:

  class Data {
  public:
    Data() : count_(1) { }
    Data(const Data& d) : count_(1) { }
    Data& operator= (const Data&) { return *this; }
    virtual ~Data() { assert(count_ == 0); }        // Virtual dtor
    virtual Data* clone() const = 0;                // Virtual ctor
    virtual void sampleInspectorMethod() const = 0;  // See FAQ 21.11
    virtual void sampleMutatorMethod() = 0;
  private:
    unsigned count_;    // count_ doesn't need to be protected:
    friend Fred;
  };

  class Der1 : public Data {
  public:
```

```
      Der1(string s, int i);
      virtual void sampleInspectorMethod() const;
      virtual void sampleMutatorMethod();
      virtual Data* clone() const;
      // ...
    };

    class Der2 : public Data {
    public:
      Der2(float x, float y);
      virtual void sampleInspectorMethod() const;
      virtual void sampleMutatorMethod();
      virtual Data* clone() const;
      // ...
    };

    Fred(Data* data);
    // Creates a Fred smart reference that owns *data
    // It is private: to force users to use createXXX()
    // Requirement: data must not be NULL

    Data* data_;    // Invariant: data_ is never NULL
    friend Der1;
    friend Der2;
  };

Fred::Fred(Data* data)
  : data_(data)     { assert(data != NULL); }
Fred::Fred(const Fred& f)
  : data_(f.data_) { ++ data_->count_; }
Fred Fred::create1(string s, int i)
  { return Fred(new Der1(s, i)); }
Fred Fred::create2(float x, float y)
  { return Fred(new Der2(x, y)); }

Fred::Data* Fred::Der1::clone() const { return new Der1(*this); }
Fred::Data* Fred::Der2::clone() const { return new Der2(*this); }

Fred& Fred::operator= (const Fred& f)
{
  // DO NOT CHANGE THE ORDER OF THESE STATEMENTS!
  // (This order properly handles self-assignment; see FAQ 24.02)
  ++ f.data_->count_;
  if (--data_->count_ == 0) delete data_;
  data_ = f.data_;
  return *this;
}
```

```
Fred::~Fred()
{ if (--data_->count_ == 0) delete data_; }

void Fred::sampleInspectorMethod() const
{
  // This member function promises not to change anything in *data_
  // Therefore we simply "pass the member function through" to *data_:
  data_->sampleInspectorMethod();
}

void Fred::sampleMutatorMethod()
{
  // This member function might need to change things in *data_
  // Thus it first checks if this is the only pointer to *data_
  if (data_->count_ > 1) {
    Data* d = data_->clone();   // Virtual ctor idiom (see FAQ 21.07)
    -- data_->count_;
    data_ = d;
  }
  assert(data_->count_ == 1);

  // Now we "pass the member function through" to *data_:
  data_->sampleMutatorMethod();
}
```

Naturally the constructors and sampleXXX member functions for Fred::Der1
and Fred::Der2 should be implemented in whatever way is appropriate. The point
is that users can copy Fred objects (pass them by value, assign them, and so on) even
though they really represent a hierarchy of objects, yet the underlying data isn't actually
copied unless and until a copy object is changed—that is, unless and until the copy is
necessary to maintain the desired observable semantics. This can improve performance
in some situations.

Chapter 32

Wild Pointers and Other Devilish Errors

What is a wild pointer?

A wild pointer is a pointer that refers to garbage.

There are three ways to get a wild pointer.

1. An uninitialized pointer that contains garbage bits

2. A pointer that gets inadvertently scribbled on (for example, by another wild pointer; this is the *domino effect*)

3. A pointer that refers to something that is no longer there (a dangling reference)

In C, the classic example of a dangling reference (3) occurs when a function returns a pointer to a local variable or when someone uses a pointer that has already been passed to free. Both situations can occur in C++, too.

Wild pointers are bad news no matter how they are created. Bad enough that we devote this entire chapter to the subject.

FAQ 32.02

What happens to a program that has even one wild pointer?

A wild pointer is to software what a car bomb is to a busy street: both cause indiscriminate pain and suffering.

After a program spawns its first wild pointer, an awesome chain reaction begins. The first wild pointer scribbles on a random memory location, which probably corrupts the object at that location, creating other wild pointers. Eventually—almost mercifully—one of these wild pointers attempts to scribble on something protected by the operating system or the hardware, and the program crashes.

By the time that happens, finding the root cause of the error with a debugger is nearly hopeless; what was once a cohesive system of objects is now a pile of rubble. The system has literally blown itself to bits.

Wild pointers create unstable systems. Arbitrarily small changes, such as inserting an extra semicolon, running the program on a different day of the week, or changing the way you smile as you press the Enter key can cause arbitrarily large changes in how the system behaves (or misbehaves). Sometimes the program deletes user files, sometimes it just gives the wrong answer, sometimes it actually works!

Wild pointers are a problem worth avoiding.

FAQ 32.03

What does the compiler mean by the warning "Returning a reference to a local object"?

It means "Pay attention to me or you'll regret it!"

A local (`auto`) object is an object local to a routine (and it is usually allocated on the stack). Never return a reference or a pointer to a local (`auto`) object. As soon as the function returns, the local object is destructed, and the reference or pointer refers to garbage. A program working with garbage eventually gets very, very sick.

Note that returning a copy of a local object (returning "by value") is fine.

How should pointers across block boundaries be controlled?

Avoid storing the address of a local object created in an inner scope in a pointer in an outer scope. Here's an example.

```
class Fred {
public:
  void method() throw();
};

void doSomething(Fred& x) throw();

void f()
{
  Fred* p;
  {
    Fred a;
    p = &a;          ◀──────────── Suspicious . . .
  }
  doSomething(*p);   ◀─────── Bang!
  p->method();       ◀─────── Bang!
}
```

When control flow leaves the inner block, a will be destroyed and p will be pointing at garbage. Because control can leave the inner scope a number of different ways (including an uncaught exception), setting the outer scope's pointer to point to an inner scope's object can lead to subtle errors and should be avoided on principle.

If the address of an inner scope's object has to be stored in an outer scope's pointer, then the outer scope's pointer should be changed to NULL (or some other safe value) before leaving the inner scope. Generally speaking, you should guarantee that the pointer is set to NULL by creating a pointer-like class whose destructor sets the pointer to NULL, then replace the Fred* local variable with a local object of that class.

Note that the problem addressed by this FAQ can occur only with pointers, not with references. This is because a reference is permanently bound to its referent at the moment it is initialized. This is yet another reason to prefer references to pointers (see FAQ 11.09).

FAQ 32.05

Is the reference-versus-pointer issue influenced by whether or not the object is allocated from the heap?

new No, there is very little relationship between these issues.

Occasionally, the claim is made that if an object is allocated via new then it should be passed via pointer; otherwise it should be passed by reference. This is not correct. There are two separate questions, when to delete the object and how to pass it.

First consider the issue of deleting the object. If an object is allocated from the heap (e.g., p = new Fred();), then some routine has to be responsible for deleting it (e.g., delete p;), and the routine must have a pointer (e.g., p) to it. There are three common situations.

1. The routine responsible for deleting the object is the same routine that created it, in which case a local auto_ptr is the easy solution: e.g.,
   auto_ptr<Fred> p(new Fred());

2. The routine responsible for deleting the object is the destructor of the same object that created the object. In this case put an auto_ptr in the this object and define a copy constructor and assignment operator that allocate a copy of the object from the heap (see FAQ 30.12).

3. There is no clear responsibility for the delete, but the newed object should be deleted when there are no pointers to it. In this case, use reference counting and avoid passing raw pointers to the object. (See FAQ 31.09.)

Now consider how the object should be passed. Assume that the routine f() takes a Fred object. Which is better, f(Fred* p) or f(Fred& r)? The key criterion is this: Does f() want to handle the case when it gets passed a nonobject (that is, the NULL pointer)? If it does, then the pointer form is indicated because it can use NULL to indicate the nonobject case. If f() always needs an actual Fred object, then the best way to signal this is to use a reference, which guarantees that it can't be passed a NULL since a reference can't legally be NULL.

Notice that the issues of deletion and passing are almost completely independent. Obviously, if reference counting is used to handle the deletion problem, then pointer-like objects are typical. But otherwise the questions aren't related. References can be used even if the object was allocated off the heap, and pointers can be used even if the object was not allocated from the heap, since it is always possible to have a pointer to a local or global object (so long as the object outlives the pointer to it).

FAQ 32.06

When should C-style pointer casts be used?

Rarely, probably only when interfacing with other languages. Any casting that *must* be done should use the C++ facilities for type-safe casting.

C-style pointer casts are the `goto` of OO programming. A `goto` complicates the control flow, making it difficult to statically reason about the flow of control. To determine the code's behavior, the dynamic flow of control has to be simulated. A pointer cast complicates the type flow, making it difficult to statically reason about the type of an object. To determine the code's behavior, the dynamic flow of types must be simulated. Use a C-style pointer cast as often as you would use a `goto`.

C-style pointer casts are also error prone. The basic problem is that the compiler meekly accepts C-style pointer casts without using runtime checks to see if they are correct. This can create wild pointers. Shudder.

Developers with a background in untyped (a.k.a. *dynamically typed*) languages tend to produce designs whose implementations employ an excessive number of pointer casts. These old habits must be terminated without prejudice. The lowest levels of memory management are among the few places where pointer casts are necessary.

Reference casts are just like pointer casts and are equally dangerous.

FAQ 32.07

Is it safe to bind a reference variable to a temporary object?

Yes, as long as that reference isn't copied into another reference or pointer.

In the following example, an unnamed temporary `string` object is created at line 1. A (`const`) reference (`main()`'s x) is bound to this temporary. The language guarantees that the unnamed temporary will live until the reference x dies, which in this case is at the end of `main()`. Therefore, line 2 is safe: the compiler isn't allowed to destruct the unnamed temporary `string` object until line 3.

```
#include <iostream>
#include <string>
using namespace std;

string createTemp()
{ return "fred"; }
```

```
int main()
{
   const string& x = createTemp();  ◄─── Line 1: Reference bound to temporary
   cout << "x = " << x << "\n";  ◄─────── Line 2: This is safe
}  ◄──────────────────────────────────── Line 3: Temporary destructed here
```

There is a caveat—don't copy reference x into a pointer variable that's out of the scope in which the temporary was created. For a subtle example of this, see the next FAQ.

FAQ 32.08

Should a parameter passed by `const` reference be returned by `const` reference?

No; it might create a dangling reference, which could destroy the world.

Returning an object by reference is not dangerous in and of itself, provided that the lifetime of the referent exceeds the lifetime of the returned reference. This cannot be guaranteed when a `const` reference parameter is returned by `const` reference, because the original argument might have been an unnamed temporary.

In the following example, an unnamed temporary `string` object is created at line 1. Parameter x from function `unsafe()` is bound to this temporary, but that is not an explicit, local reference in the scope of `main()`, so the temporary's lifetime is governed by the usual rules—the temporary dies at the `;` of line 1. Unfortunately, function `unsafe()` returns the reference x, which means `main()`'s y ends up referring to the temporary, even though the temporary is now dead. This means that line 2 is unsafe: it uses y, which refers to an object that has already been destructed—a dangling reference.

```
#include <string>
#include <iostream>
using namespace std;

string createTemp()
{ return "fred"; }

const string& unsafe(const string& x)
{ return x; }

int main()
{
   const string& y = unsafe( createTemp() );  ◄─── Line 1
```

```
    cout << "y = " << y << "\n";  ◄───────── Line 2: BOOM!
}
```

Note that if a function accepts a parameter by non-const reference (for example, f(string& s)), returning a copy of this reference parameter is safe because a temporary cannot be passed by non-const reference.

─── **FAQ 32.09**

Should template functions for things like min(x,y) or abs(x) return a const reference?

No!

When the following example is compiled and the symbol UNSAFE is defined, min(x,y) avoids an extra copy operation by returning a const reference parameter by const reference. As discussed in the previous FAQ, this can create a dangling reference, which can destroy the world.

```
#ifdef UNSAFE
  template<class T> inline const T& min(const T& x, const T& y)
  { return x < y ? x : y; }
#else
  template<class T> inline T min(const T& x, const T& y)
  { return x < y ? x : y; }
#endif
```

Returning a const reference to a const reference parameter is normally done as an optimization to avoid an extra copy operation. If you're willing to sacrifice correctness, you can make your software very fast!

─── **FAQ 32.10**

When is zero not necessarily zero?

When dealing with pointers.

When the token 0 appears in the source code at a place where a pointer should be, the compiler interprets the token 0 as the NULL pointer. However, the bit pattern for the

NULL pointer is not guaranteed to be all zeros. More specifically, setting a pointer to NULL may set some of the bits of that pointer to 1.

Depending on the hardware, the operating system, or the compiler, a pointer whose bits are all zeros may not be the same as the NULL pointer. For example, using memset() to set all the bits of a pointer to zero may not make that pointer equal to NULL.

In the following program, all conforming C++ compilers produce code that prints 0 is NULL, then NULL is NULL, but some may produce code that prints memsetPtr is not NULL.

```cpp
#include <iostream>
#include <string>
using namespace std;

void checkForNull(const string& nameOfPointer, char* p)
{
  cout << nameOfPointer;
  if (p == NULL)
    cout << " is NULL\n";
  else
    cout << " is not NULL\n";
}

int main()
{
  checkForNull("0", 0);             // OK: NULL pointer
  checkForNull("NULL", NULL);       // OK: NULL pointer

  char* memsetPtr;
  memset(&memsetPtr, '\0', sizeof(memsetPtr));   // BAD: Undefined pointer!
  checkForNull("memsetPtr", memsetPtr);
}
```

Another common way to generate a pointer whose bits are all zero that is equally dangerous is with unions. For example, the following is wrong on two levels. First, it accesses the char* member of the union even though it was the unsigned long member that was set most recently. Second, it assumes that a pointer whose bits are all zero is the same as a NULL pointer—the output may be unionPtr is not NULL on some machines.

```cpp
union Fred {
  unsigned long n;
  char* p;
};
```

```
void badForm()
{
  Fred x;
  x.n = 0;          ◄──────────────── OK: Set the unsigned long member to 0
  char* unionPtr = x.p;   ◄──────── BAD: The char* member isn't defined!
  checkForNull("unionPtr", unionPtr);
}
```

Chapter 33

High-Performance
Software

Is bad performance a result of bad design or bad coding?

All too often, bad performance is due to bad design.

When bad performance is due to bad coding practices, the correction is relatively inexpensive. However, when OO has been used improperly, the design is usually broken and performance problems are not easily repaired.

Improper inheritance is a common cause. When inheritance is used improperly, the design often becomes brittle and performance-related changes are prohibitively expensive. For example, some designs use inheritance as the means to put objects into a container. To put objects in a List, for example, they inherit from a particular base class, often called ListElement, ListItem, or Listable. The apparent motivation is to share the next pointer among all the derived classes, but the cost is enormous. In particular, the List class loses type safety (not all things that are listable should be linked into the same list), and most important, user code becomes tacitly aware of the technique used to implement the list. This implementation dependency can inhibit performance tuning. These costs are manageable on a small ("toy") project, but in a larger, more sophisticated application or system, the costs of improper inheritance become unbearable.

A better solution for the container problem is to use templates for type safety and design a proper abstraction that hides the "listness" from users. If abstractions are properly designed, the answer to "Would it disturb user code if I changed this particular data structure from a linked list to an array?" is "No." This means that the abstraction allows *late life-cycle performance tuning*, since it allows changing data structures or algorithms on an individual container-by-container basis. Code sharing among template classes can be accomplished by inheriting from a nontemplate base class.

FAQ 33.02

What are some techniques for improving performance?

new

The first step is knowing where the bottleneck is and then trying some of the following techniques. For example, if the bottleneck is CPU cycles, the application is said to be *CPU bound;* if the bottleneck is the network, the application is said to be *network bound.* Applications can also be *database bound, I/O bound, memory space bound* (a.k.a. *thrashing*), and so on. The important insight is that the techniques that work in one situation will either be a waste of time or perhaps even make performance worse in another situation. Measure, measure, measure. *Then* make your changes.

One technique that sometimes helps is reducing the number of expensive operations by using more CPU cycles. If the application is I/O bound, database bound, or network bound, making the application run fast means minimizing these expensive operations even if that might increase the number of CPU cycles consumed. For example, implementing a caching scheme increases the number of CPU cycles consumed, but it can reduce the number of expensive database operations required.

Another technique that can sometimes make an application run faster is making it more flexible. A flexible system can often be twisted to work around unnecessary requests that hit the database or network. This is counterintuitive: most developers equate increased flexibility with greater processing overhead. Nonetheless, flexibility can help make things faster in many (but not all) situations.

If the application is network bound or database bound, it may help to increase the granularity of objects that are transmitted through the wire and/or to a database and to decrease the granularity of in-memory-only objects.

If the application is thrashing (that is, using most of the computer's available memory), the goal is to reduce the size of the *working set* (that is, the number of pages that need to be in memory to execute the application's typical operation). There are two normal cases: either the pages that need to be in memory are mostly code or they are mostly data. In the case where most pages of memory are code pages, paradoxically making more functions `inline` can sometimes help. This is because the goal is to reduce the working set, not to reduce the size of the executable. If the application has improved locality, the working set can sometimes go down even though the application's executable size goes up. This is counterintuitive: most developers assume that applications that are thrashing need to be made smaller. Measure, measure, measure.

Another technique that can sometimes reduce thrashing is reorganizing the physical placement of member functions within source files. For example, a profiling tool can determine which member functions are called often and which are called rarely; then the commonly used member functions can be moved into a single source file. Even though this makes it harder to find all the member functions of a class, it has the effect of bringing all the commonly used code into the same group of memory pages, thus reducing the size of the working set.

In the case where most pages of memory are data, caches should be avoided, deeply nested function calls should be avoided, freestore should be limited, and care should be taken to avoid fragmenting memory. And of course memory leaks should be plugged (see FAQ 31.01).

If the bottleneck is the machine's CPU (that is, the application is CPU bound), start with limiting unnecessary use of freestore and using initialization lists in constructors (see FAQ 22.01). Most of the remaining FAQs in this chapter deal with CPU-bound applications, but some also help database-bound, I/O-bound, network-bound, and memory-bound applications as well.

In any event, the process cannot even begin until everyone agrees on the problem. The tuning effort should be focused on areas that deliver the most bang per hour invested.

FAQ 33.03

What is an advantage of using pointers and references?

Flexibility, with a likely cost in CPU cycles.

Almost all flexibility in software comes with an extra layer of indirection (arrays, dynamic data structures, recursion, and so on). Not surprisingly, dynamic binding also depends on an extra layer of indirection. So using pointers and references, as opposed to using local and member objects directly, offers additional flexibility in the form of polymorphism and dynamic binding (see FAQ 5.04).

Here is a small hierarchy with a base class and a derived class.

```
#include <new>
#include <iostream>
#include <memory>
using namespace std;
```

```
class Base {
public:
  virtual ~Base() throw();
  virtual void f() throw() = 0;
};

typedef auto_ptr<Base> BasePtr;

Base::~Base() throw()
{ }

class Derived : public Base {
public:
  virtual void f() throw();
};

void Derived::f() throw()
{ cout << "Derived::f()\n"; }
```

Here is a class whose objects have-a pair of `Derived` objects. One of these has-a relationships uses a pointer to an object allocated from the heap (remote ownership; see FAQ 30.08); the other uses a direct member object.

```
class Fred {
public:
  Fred() throw(bad_alloc);
  ~Fred() throw();
  Fred& operator= (const Fred& a) throw();
  Fred(const Fred& a) throw();
  void method() throw();
  void blahBlah() throw(bad_alloc);
private:
  BasePtr x_;  ◄——————— Has-a via remote ownership (see FAQ 30.08)
  Derived y_;  ◄——————— Has-a via direct object containment
};

Fred::Fred() throw(bad_alloc)
: x_(new Derived())
, y_()
{ }

void Fred::method() throw()
{
  x_->f();  ◄——————— May or may not invoke Derived::f() depending on the exact class of *x_
  y_.f();   ◄——————— Cannot be changed at runtime; always calls Derived::f()
}
```

Note that the behavior of `Fred::method()` depends on which type of object is pointed to by member `x_`. Even though the constructor initializes `x_` to point to a

`Derived` object, other member functions may change this pointer so that it points to an object of a different derived class, thus changing the behavior of `Fred::method()` as the following example shows. First, here is a second derived class.

```
class Derived2 : public Base {
public:
  virtual void f() throw();
};

void Derived2::f() throw()
{ cout << "Derived2::f()\n"; }
```

Here is a member function of class `Fred` that changes pointer `x_` so that it points to a `Derived2` object rather than a `Derived` object.

```
void Fred::blahBlah() throw(bad_alloc)
{
  BasePtr x2( new Derived2() );
  x_ = x2; ←——————— Safe: Automagically deletes the object formerly pointed to by x_
} ←——————————— Safe: x2 will be NULL, so this doesn't delete the new object

int main()
{
  Fred a;
  a.method(); ←——————— a.x_ will point to a Derived
  a.blahBlah(); ←——— Changes a.x_
  a.method(); ←——————— a.x_ will point to a Derived2
}
```

This shows the flexibility advantages of using pointers and freestore. If the application is database bound or network bound or I/O bound, this sort of flexibility can be used to improve performance in some cases (see FAQ 33.02). However if the application is CPU bound and the `Fred` object happens to be a bottleneck, read the next FAQ.

FAQ 33.04

What is a disadvantage of lots of references and pointers?

In some cases, they may degrade the application's performance if it is CPU bound.

In the previous FAQ, member `y_` is a `Derived` object rather than a pointer to an object. In addition to reducing flexibility, embedding an object inside another object like this makes it more expensive to copy a `Fred` object (the state of the `Derived` object must be copied, rather than just a pointer to the object). However objects are usually accessed more often than they are copied, so reducing the number of layers of indirection can make the application perform better.

One way that embedding an object inside another (as in y_ in the previous FAQ) can improve performance over using a pointer (as in x_ in the previous FAQ) is by inlining virtual function calls. Virtual function calls can be inlined only when the compiler can statically bind to the function, that is, when it knows the object's exact class. If a function doesn't do very much (a good candidate for inlining), then inline expansion of the function can improve performance significantly. As an extreme example, a simple fetch function (which might occur in a member function that gets a data member's value) might do only 3 CPU cycles worth of work, yet including the overhead of the virtual function call might cost a total of 30 cycles. In this case, it would take 27 + 3 cycles to do 3 cycles worth of work. If this were on a critical path and the operation could be inlined, reducing the overhead of this operation by a factor of 10 could be significant.

In the example that follows, the call x.sample() in main() can be statically bound to Fred::sample(), because the exact class of local object x is known to be Fred. Furthermore, since that member function is defined inline, the call can be inlined. Similarly the call d_.f() in Fred::sample() is known statically to invoke Derived::f(), this time because member d_ is known to be exactly a Derived; since Derived::f() is also inline, the call can be inlined. Thus the entire call graph starting at main()'s x.sample() collapses into nothing: the only code that will be executed is the code that happens to be within Derived::f(). However the call to b_->f() in sample2() cannot be inlined even though b_ apparently points to a Derived, since the compiler has to assume that some other member function might change b_ so that it points to some other derived class (see FAQ 33.03).   .

```
#include <memory>
using namespace std;

class Base {
public:
  virtual ~Base() throw();
  virtual void f() throw() = 0;
};
typedef auto_ptr<Base> BasePtr;

Base::~Base() throw()
{ }

class Derived : public Base {
public:
  virtual void f() throw();
};
```

```
inline void Derived::f() throw()          This is inline even though it's virtual
{
                                          If this is short, the inlining can make a significant
                                          difference
}
class Fred {
public:
  Fred() throw();
  virtual void sample() throw();
  virtual void sample2() throw();
protected:
  Derived d_;
  BasePtr b_;
};

Fred::Fred() throw()
: d_()
, b_(new Derived())
{ }

inline void Fred::sample() throw()
{ d_.f(); }                               The call to d_.f() can be inlined
inline void Fred::sample2() throw()
{ b_->f(); }                              The call to b_->f() cannot be inlined

int main()
{
  Fred x;
  x.sample();
  x.sample2();
}
```

Not all compilers are guaranteed to perform these optimizations, but many do in practice.

<hr>

FAQ 33.05

How else can member objects improve performance over pointers?

By reducing the number of freestore allocations and the fragmentation of memory.

In a CPU-bound application, freestore operations are generally very slow primitives: the more objects that are allocated from the freestore, the worse the performance. By moving the member object physically inside the outer object, as shown in d_ in FAQ 33.04, there are fewer freestore operations.

In addition, memory can become fragmented when the freestore is used excessively. For example, an entire page of memory may need to be brought into RAM just because a small piece is being used, even though 99% of the page is not being used. If this happens frequently, it can lead to thrashing, which can significantly degrade performance. By moving the member object physically inside the outer object, as shown in FAQ 33.04 the memory is less fragmented.

In some extreme performance-sensitive applications, cache misses can be a significant problem. In these cases, data structures must be carefully laid out to minimize the number of cache lines that need to be brought into the CPU, which again means minimizing fragmentation.

FAQ 33.06

Which is better, ++i or i++?

++i is better unless the old value of i is needed.

The expression i++ usually returns a copy of the old state of i. This requires that an unnecessary copy be created, as well as an unnecessary destruction of that copy. For built-in types (for example, int), the optimizer can eliminate the extra copies, but for user-defined (class) types, the compiler retains the extra constructor and destructor.

If the old value of i is needed, i++ may be appropriate; but if it's going to be discarded, ++i makes more sense. Here's an example.

```
#include <iostream>
using namespace std;

class Number {
public:
  Number() throw();
 ~Number() throw();
  Number(const Number& n) throw();
  Number& operator= (const Number& n) throw();
  Number& operator++ () throw();
  Number  operator++ (int) throw();
};

Number::Number() throw()
  { }
Number::~Number() throw()
  { cout << "dtor "; }
```

```
Number::Number(const Number& n) throw()
  { cout << "copy "; }
Number& Number::operator= (const Number& n) throw()
  { cout << "assign "; return *this; }
Number& Number::operator++ () throw()
  { cout << "increment "; return *this; }

Number Number::operator++ (int) throw()
{
  Number old = *this;
  ++(*this);
  return old;
}

int main()
{

  Number n;
  cout << "++n: ";  ++n;  cout << '\n';
  cout << "n++: ";  n++;  cout << '\n';
}
```

The output of this program follows.

```
++n: increment
n++: copy increment copy dtor dtor
dtor
```

The postfix increment creates two copies of the Number—the local object inside Number::operator++(int)—and the return value of the same (a smarter compiler would notice that the returned object is always the local variable old, thus avoiding one of the two temporary copies). The final output line is the destruction of main()'s n.

Note that the postfix increment operator, Number::operator++(int), can be made to return void rather than the Number's former state. This puts the performance of n++ on a par with ++n but forfeits the ability to use n++ in an expression.

FAQ 33.07

What is the performance difference between `Fred x(5);` and `Fred y = 5;` and `Fred z = Fred(5);`?

In practice, none. Therefore, use the one that looks most intuitive. This looks-most-intuitive notion depends on the situation—there is no one-size-fits-all guideline as to which is best.

Each of the three declarations initializes an object of type `Fred` using the single-parameter constructor that takes an `int` (that is, `Fred::Fred(int)`). Even though the last two definitions use the equal sign, none of them use `Fred`'s assignment operator. In practice, none of them creates extra temporaries either.

```
#include <iostream>
using namespace std;

class Fred {
public:
  Fred(int) throw();
  Fred(const Fred&) throw();
  void operator= (const Fred&) throw();
};

Fred::Fred(int) throw()
  { cout << "Fred ctor "; }
Fred::Fred(const Fred&) throw()
  { cout << "Fred copy "; }
void Fred::operator= (const Fred&) throw()
  { cout << "Fred assign "; }

int main()
{
  cout << "1: ";   Fred x(5);          cout << '\n';
  cout << "2: ";   Fred y = 5;         cout << '\n';
  cout << "3: ";   Fred z = Fred(5);   cout << '\n';
}
```

For most commercial-grade C++ compilers, the copy constructor is not called and the output of the program is as follows.

```
1: Fred ctor
2: Fred ctor
3: Fred ctor
```

Because they cause the same code to be generated, use the one that looks right. If class `Fred` is actually `Fraction` and 5 is the value of the numerator, the clearest is the second or third. If `Fred` is actually `Array` and 5 is the length of the `Array`, the clearest is the first or the third.

Note that if the user cannot access the copy constructor (for example, if the copy constructor is `private:`), only the first example is legal. Assuming that the compiler makes the appropriate optimization (a fairly safe assumption), the copy constructor isn't actually called; the user needs access to it *as if* it were called.

FAQ 33.08

What kinds of applications should consider using final classes and final member functions?

Performance-sensitive applications that are CPU bound.

Final classes and final member functions can squeeze a bit of extra CPU performance out of flexible applications. They are useful only in applications that are CPU bound (see FAQ 33.02) and even there, only on the critical path through those applications.

FAQ 33.09

What is a final class?

A *final class* (also known as a *leaf class*) is a class that permanently forbids derived classes.

A class should be declared final only if the designers have decided to permanently forbid any future classes from deriving from the final class. A class should not be declared final merely because it doesn't happen to have any derived classes in the current application. An example follows.

```
class Shape {
  //...
};

/*final*/ class Circle : public Shape {
  //...
};
```

C++ doesn't support a keyword for "final," so a comment is typically used. This means that the finality of a class is enforced by code reviews rather than by the compiler. However, it is not hard to get the compiler to enforce the class's finality: simply make the constructors `private:` and provide `public: static create()` member functions (the named constructor idiom; see FAQ 16.08). This will prevent derived classes from existing since the derived class wouldn't be able to call the (`private:`) constructor of the final class.

A final class should not have any `protected:` data members—all its data members should be `private:`. Similarly, a final class should not declare any new virtual functions (though it often overrides inherited virtual functions).

Caution should be used before declaring a class to be final. Nonetheless, doing so is sometimes useful, as demonstrated in FAQ 33.12.

FAQ 33.10

What is a final member function?

A *final member function* (also known as a *leaf member function*) is a member function that derived classes are permanently forbidden from overriding.

A member function should be declared final only if the designers have decided to permanently forbid any future class from overriding the member function. A member function should not be declared final merely because it doesn't happen to be overridden in the current application. An example follows.

```
class Shape {
public:
  virtual void draw() const throw() = 0;
  virtual ~Shape() throw();
};

Shape::~Shape()
{ }

class Circle : public Shape {
public:
  /*final*/ void draw() const throw();
};
```

Non-`virtual` member functions are implicitly final since a non-`virtual` member function should generally not be redefined in a derived class (see FAQ 29.02). Similarly, all member functions of a final class are implicitly final member functions because a final class isn't allowed to have derived classes (see FAQ 33.09).

As with classes, the finality of member functions is enforced by code reviews rather than by the compiler.

A final member function should not be marked with the `virtual` keyword even if it happens to be an override of a `virtual` function. If the final member function is not an override of a `virtual` from a base class, the easiest way to make it final is to not use the `virtual` keyword.

Caution should be used before declaring a member function to be final. Nonetheless doing so is sometimes useful, as demonstrated in FAQ 33.12.

FAQ 33.11

How can final classes and final member functions improve performance?

By eliminating the overhead associated with dynamic binding.

Final member functions can be called using full qualification ("`::`"). This allows the compiler to employ static binding, thereby reducing or even eliminating the cost of dynamic binding. If care is taken, this can allow virtual functions to be inlined, thus effectively eliminating the CPU overhead associated with the added flexibility brought by virtual functions. An example follows.

```
class Shape {
public:
  virtual void draw() const throw() = 0;
  virtual ~Shape() throw();
};

Shape::~Shape() throw()
{ }

class Circle : public Shape {
public:
  /*final*/ void draw() const throw();
};

inline void Circle::draw() const throw()    ◄——— Note the inline even though it is virtual
{
  // ...
}
```

```
void sample(Circle& c) throw()
{
  c.Circle::draw();
}
```

The full qualification (that is, the `Circle::` part of `c.Circle::draw()`) is safe because final member functions are never overridden in derived classes. Function `sample(Circle&)` would also be safe if class `Circle` were final, since all members of a final class, including `Circle::draw()`, are implicitly final.

Note that it is (hopefully) somewhat uncommon to have lots of functions that take derived class references, such as `sample(Circle&)` in the example (see FAQ 33.14).

FAQ 33.12

When should a nonfinal virtual function be invoked with a fully qualified name?

Almost never. The one situation where full qualification is appropriate and useful is where a derived class needs to invoke a member function from a base class. In this case the derived class uses full qualification ("`::`") to make sure the base class member is invoked, particularly in cases when the member function has been overridden in a derived class.

However, normal user code should avoid full qualification. That is, when x is a `Fred&` and `f()` is a virtual member function of class `Fred`, normal user code should use `x.f()` rather than `x.Fred::f()`. This is because full qualification subverts dynamic binding. If the actual class of the referent is something derived from `Fred`, the wrong member function may be invoked. An example follows.

```
class Shape {
public:
  virtual void draw() throw() = 0;
  virtual void hide() throw() = 0;
  virtual ~Shape() throw();
};

Shape::~Shape() throw()
{ }

class Circle : public Shape {
public:
  /*final*/ void draw() throw();
```

```
    virtual void hide() throw();
};

void sample(Circle& c) throw()
{
  c.Circle::draw();  ←——— GOOD: Circle::draw() is a final
  c.Circle::hide();  ←——— EVIL: Subverts dynamic binding
  c.hide();  ←——————— GOOD: Always calls the right hide() implementation
}
```

In `sample(Circle& c)`, if c actually refers to a derived class of `Circle` that overrides the `hide()` member function, the call to `c.Circle::hide()` invokes the wrong member function.

```
class FancyCircle : public Circle {
public:
  virtual void hide() throw();
};

int main()
{
  FancyCircle x;
  sample(x);
}
```

FAQ 33.13

Should full qualification be used when calling another member function of the same class?

Only if the called member function is a final member function.
If `D::f()` calls `this->g()`, full qualification (for example, `this->D::g()`) should be used only if `D::g()` is a final member function or D is a final class.

```
class B {
public:
  virtual void f() throw() = 0;
  virtual void g() throw() = 0;
  virtual void h() throw() = 0;
  virtual ~B();
};

class D : public B {
public:
```

```
   virtual void f() throw();
   virtual void g() throw();
   /*final*/ void h() throw();
};

void D::f() throw()
{
   g();        ←——————— GOOD: Nonfinal member function called without full qualification
   D::h();     ←——————— GOOD: Final member function called with full qualification
   D::g();     ←——————— EVIL: Do not call nonfinal member function with full qualification!
}
```

Although it seems as if `D::f()` should be able to use full qualification when calling `D::g()`, such a thing is dangerous and invokes the wrong function in some cases. For example, if the `this` object were actually of a further derived class that has an override of `g()`, the wrong function would be invoked:

```
class D2 : public D {
public:
   virtual void g() throw();
};

int main()
{
   D2 x;
   x.f();
}
```

Note that this is simply a specialization of the guideline presented in FAQ 33.12.

FAQ 33.14

Do final classes and final member functions cause a lot of code duplication?

 Some, but in practice the cost is insignificant if the application is designed according to the guidelines presented in this FAQ.

First, here is a description of the problem we're trying to solve. It seems inevitable that someone someday somewhere may come up with a reason to inherit from a final class and/or override a final member function. When this becomes desirable, the workaround will probably involve some code duplication. From the example in FAQ 33.12, if someone someday somewhere found it useful to override the `Circle::draw()` member function, they would instead have to copy the `Circle` class's code and create a modified `draw()` member function.

This code duplication has a nonzero cost. Indeed in small projects the volume of code within the derived classes is a significant portion of the whole system, which means that the cost can be noticeable on a small enough project. And for those unfortunate souls who believe that inheritance is for reuse (it's not; see FAQ 8.12), disallowing inheritance is equivalent to saying, "Don't reuse this."

However, on a large project that is designed according to the principles in this book, the cost of this sort of code duplication is normally insignificant, especially if final classes and member functions are used judiciously (see FAQs 33.09, 33.10). This is one of the many ways in which large projects differ from small projects. In particular, in a large project the most important goal is the stability of the design, not the reusability of the code; and within the code the most important asset is the code that uses base class references, not the code in the derived classes. On small projects, reuse is more important than stability, and the code within the derived classes is a large portion of the total, but that mentality is not scalable. Applying a small project mentality to a large project is a recipe for project failure. When working on a large project, do not extrapolate lessons learned on small projects (see FAQ 39.08).

A key design goal of most OO applications, especially large OO applications, is to allow new derived classes to be added without affecting existing code (remember: stability, not reuse per se). Part of this goal is achieved by building the bulk of the software so that it is ignorant of the derived classes. What this normally boils down to is making most parameters to be references/pointers to the abstract base classes rather than references/pointers to the concrete derived classes. Continuing the example from FAQ 33.09 the application as a whole should contain very few (ideally no) functions with parameters of type `Circle&` or `Circle*`; a much larger number of functions should take parameters of type `Shape&` or `Shape*`.

The next step in a good OO design is minimize the amount of complex decision logic within the functions (see FAQ 27.03). Part of this goal can be achieved by including important functionality of the derived classes in the base class's interface. This is a balancing act—adding too many member functions to the base class makes it difficult for some derived classes, but adding too few requires the users of the base class to use dynamic typing. Nonetheless, the flexibility and value of the system rest on the ability of the designer to find the best possible balance.

The result of applying these rules is both stability *and* reuse. But the reuse is what the derived classes can give, not what they can get. The reuse is the reuse of all the code that uses the abstract base class references and pointers, which (hopefully) is the bulk of the system. In other words, the derived classes don't inherit so that they can have what the base class has; they inherit so that they can be what the base class is. Inheritance is not about what the derived class can get; it is about providing a stable and consistent set of semantics to users of base class references and pointers. Inheritance is not for reuse (see FAQ 8.12).

FAQ 33.15

Why do some developers dislike final member functions and final classes?

Because they don't see the big picture and/or because they don't follow the design guidelines presented in FAQ 13.14.

Suppose class `Circle` inherits from abstract base class `Shape`, and suppose `Circle` is declared to be final (see FAQ 33.09 for the code). If the system was designed using the principles from FAQ 33.14, then there are very few `Circle&` used in the application as a whole. Therefore, there is no inherent pressure for new classes to inherit from `Circle`; they can just as easily inherit from `Shape`.

Even if a new derived class could have benefited from inheriting some code from `Circle`, the code bulk of class `Circle` would be very small compared to the rest of the system, particularly on large systems, so any cost savings would be insignificant. The larger the system, the less significance any individual class has.

The moral is to focus on the big picture.

FAQ 33.16

Can a programming language—rather than just the compiler— affect the performance of software?

Yes.

Sometimes it is assumed that software performance is limited only by the compiler, not by the programming language. However, this is generally not the case. The efficiency of the executable is, at least in part, due to the language as well as the compiler. For example, compilers for dynamically typed OO languages cannot statically resolve member function invocations, because every member function is `virtual` and every object is passed by pointer. Therefore, every member function dispatch needs to go through the dynamic-binding mechanism, which generally costs a function call. Thus, a member function with 10 statements in many OO languages almost necessarily costs at least 10 function calls. The efficiency of the dynamic-binding mechanism can be improved, but it rarely can be improved enough to inline-expand these calls (a technique called *customization* can alleviate some of these issues in dynamically typed OO programming languages).

Languages such as C++ require the compiler to work harder, since not all member functions are necessarily `virtual`, and even if they are all `virtual`, not all objects are allocated from the heap. In addition, statically bound member functions can be expanded inline (see FAQ 13.01).

Chapter 34

COM and ActiveX

Who should read this chapter?

Developers who are wondering about COM and ActiveX and how to take advantage of them.

The purpose of this chapter is to provide C++ developers with an introduction to COM and ActiveX. Long-time Unix developers will want to read it to get an overview of COM and ActiveX and the role they play in building C++ applications for Windows. Windows developers who have not taken the COM plunge will want to read this chapter to see how they can exploit COM and ActiveX to build reusable components that are easy to share in the Windows environment.

What is the Component Object Model?

The Component Object Model (COM) is the Windows standard that defines—at the most fundamental level—what components are, how they are identified, how they are located, how they are loaded, how they are accessed, and how they communicate. COM is the most widely used component model in the world.

In this context, components are reusable chunks of software with well-defined interfaces and encapsulated implementations, are defined in a language-independent manner, and are distributed in binary form.

To better understand COM, it is crucial to bear in mind that it is not an object-oriented language but rather a standard for defining components (however, the components are often referred to as objects). C++ is a programming language with a compiler. COM is a set of programming conventions. Therefore, many of the things that the C++ compiler does automatically COM requires the programmer to do manually. For example, the C++ compiler/linker can guarantee that all class names are unique. COM, on the other hand, relies on a mechanism that generates unique class names (called Class Identifiers; see FAQ 34.08) independent of any compile time or link time checks.

COM is language independent in that it does not prescribe any particular programming language for either developing or using COM classes. COM provides location transparency in that it allows callers to create and access COM objects without regard for where the objects are running (whether they are in the same process or in other processes or even on remote machines).

COM has survived and is thriving due to the growing interest in component technology. COM is important because it is the core technology on which all other ActiveX and OLE technologies are built. And understanding COM is the key to understanding and effectively exploiting all the other ActiveX and OLE technologies.

FAQ 34.03

What are ActiveX and OLE?

In the beginning, OLE stood for Object Linking and Embedding. OLE2 was an umbrella term that covered a family of Microsoft technologies for building software components and linking applications:

- Component Object Model (COM), Structured Storage

- Uniform Data Transfer, Drag and Drop

- Error Reporting and Exception Handling

- OLE Automation

- OLE Compound Documents

- OLE Custom Controls (OCXs)

At the time OLE was popular, the future of the desktop computer was GUIs and compound documents. You might even remember that OLE and OpenDoc (from IBM and Apple) were jousting to see who would rule the compound document kingdom.

Well, since that time, the Internet and the World Wide Web have replaced compound documents as the future of desktop computing, and ActiveX (which is web-centric) has replaced OLE (which is compound-document-centric) as the marketing buzzword du jour. OLE still exists, but these days its meaning is restricted to compound document technology.

ActiveX is a loosely defined umbrella term Microsoft uses to refer to a number of initiatives and technologies related to (but not limited to) the Web/Internet and Microsoft's component strategy. The important thing to remember is that ActiveX is a marketing term whose meaning can (and does) shift as it suits the suits in Redmond.

The aspects of ActiveX discussed in this book are those that are related to Microsoft's component strategy. This chapter does not try to explain and justify the numerous ambiguities surrounding ActiveX—call your local Microsoft representatives and ask them for an explanation.

FAQ 34.04

What does the name Component Object Model mean?

Microsoft's component architecture.

Component: Refers to the fact that COM defines reusable chunks of software in a language-independent manner according to a binary object model.

Object: Refers to the fact that the software components being defined resemble objects in the sense that they have a well-defined interface that encapsulates the implementation and allows multiple instances to be created and used.

Model: Refers to the fact that COM is primarily a specification (rather than an implementation) of how to build and use component objects.

COM provides a way of defining components in a way that is more or less language independent, location independent, operating system independent, and hardware independent.

By the way, there is an equally valid and less grandiose way of looking at COM. COM can be viewed simply as a packaging technology that consists of a set of conventions and supporting libraries that allow chunks of software to locate one another and interact in an object-oriented manner. It is sometimes worthwhile to remember this, since it helps to explain why COM is the way it is.

FAQ 34.05

What is a "binary object model"?

Component architecture defined at the machine level.

COM is called a binary object model because the COM specification defines how objects are laid out in memory (hence binary). This permits any programming language or any development tool to create a COM object as long as it is capable of laying out the memory in a manner that conforms with the COM specification and calling the appropriate COM routines.

Compare this to an object-oriented language, like C++, which defines classes and objects using a language object model. Specifically, C++ defines what constitutes a legal class definition in terms of the syntax and semantics of a programming language and then leaves it up to the compiler to translate the source code into an executable program.

In reality, COM is not Windows-specific; there are COM implementations for other operating systems (in particular, Software AG has ported COM/DCOM to Sun Solaris, 64-bit Digital Unix, and IBM's OS 390), but COM was designed with Windows as its first and foremost priority.

FAQ 34.06

What are the key features of COM?

Language transparency, location transparency, program to the interface rather than to the implementation, unique naming of classes and interfaces, meta data, and a system registry.

Language transparency: COM defines object interfaces in a manner that is independent of any particular programming language. This means that a caller can use a COM object without knowing or caring what programming language it is implemented in. Conversely, the COM class can be implemented in a variety of programming languages without concern for what programming language will be used by callers.

Location transparency: COM provides the infrastructure so that callers can create and access COM objects no matter whether the COM object is running in the caller's process as an in-process object or running in another process on the same computer or running remotely on another computer.

Interface definition: A COM interface is a set of related methods that have a well-defined contract but no implementation (see FAQ 34.09). The signatures for the methods of a COM interface can be defined using a programming language (such as C++ and C) or the Microsoft Interface Definition Language (MIDL), which is based on the Distributed Computing Environment Interface Definition Language (DCE IDL) specification of the Open Software Foundation.

Unique Naming of Classes and Interfaces: COM classes and interfaces have unique "names" called globally unique identifiers (GUIDs; see FAQ 34.07). Unique names are required so that the names of components being developed by different groups in different organizations and in different parts of the world do not accidentally clash.

Meta data: COM provides support for meta data (that is, information about interfaces and classes) in the form of type libraries (see FAQ 34.29). Type libraries contain machine-readable definitions of COM interfaces and/or COM classes and can be accessed programmatically at runtime.

System Registry: COM stores static information about classes, interfaces, and type libraries in a registry so that it can be looked up at runtime. The information in the registry can be accessed prior to any objects being created. In fact, the registry contains the information necessary for loading COM servers (see FAQ 34.12), locating class objects, and creating COM objects. The registry is a hierarchy of key/value pairs and contains information such as the name of the file containing a COM class and the name of the file that contains a type library that defines a particular COM interface.

FAQ 34.07

What are GUIDs?

Unique names that are about as user friendly as a bar code.

Globally Unique Identifiers (GUIDs) are 128-bit, globally unique identifiers (in this context, "globally" literally means globally).

GUIDs are based on the universally unique identifiers developed and used by OSF for DCE. COM uses GUIDs for several purposes but the two most important are Class Identifiers and Interface Identifiers. Class Identifiers (CLSIDs) are used to give COM classes unique class names. Similarly, Interface Identifiers (IIDs) are used to give unique names to COM interfaces.

Since GUIDs identify COM classes and COM interfaces, they are part of the definition of the class or interface and must be available to the calling program. This is usually done by distributing the GUIDs in header files and/or Type Libraries.

Although GUIDs are 128-bit numbers, they are usually referred to using mnemonics (i.e., symbolic names). Hey, look, there are a couple of GUIDs going by right now.

```
#include "wtypes.h"

// {FC3B3F61-BCEC-11D1-91FE-E1CBED988F66}
DEFINE_GUID(IID_IStack,
```

```
    0xFC3B3F61, 0xBCEC, 0x11D1, 0x91, 0xFE,
    0xE1, 0xCB, 0xED, 0x98, 0x8F, 0x66);

// {FC3B3F62-BCEC-11D1-91FE-E1CBED988F66}
DEFINE_GUID(CLSID_CoStack,
    0xFC3B3F62, 0xBCEC, 0x11D1, 0x91, 0xFE,
    0xE1, 0xCB, 0xED, 0x98, 0x8F, 0x66);
```

This defines two GUIDs using the COM macro DEFINE_GUID. The macro has several parameters—the first parameter defines the mnemonic for the GUID and the remaining parameters define the 128-bit number (the numbers can be generated using the COM utility program guidgen.exe).

The first GUID defines an interface identifier called IID_IStack for the COM interface IStack. The second GUID defines a class identifier called CLSID_CoStack for the COM class CoStack. After these definitions, the GUIDs can be referred to using IID_IStack and CLSID_CoStack without having to write out the 128-bit number.

COM uses class identifiers in the same way C++ uses class names. For example, when a caller wishes to create a COM object, it specifies the CLSID for the COM class and COM uses this CLSID to locate and create the correct type of COM object.

Besides class identifiers and interface identifiers, COM defines several other types of GUIDs including Type Library Identifiers (LIBIDs) and Category Identifiers (CATIDs).

FAQ 34.08

Why does COM need GUIDs (and CLSIDs and IIDs)?

To uniquely identify software components.

In C++, classes have names and the name of a class must be unique in the context of a linked program (otherwise the compiler or the linker will detect the duplicate names and report an error). Namespaces have been added to C++ to reduce the chances of name conflicts, but they don't eliminate the possibility of name conflicts. If there are name conflicts, you have to come up with some way to make all the class names unique before you can get your program to compile and link.

The situation is slightly more complex with COM. With COM, you have thousands of developers working around the world and defining thousands of components that are delivered to users as binary components. Imagine if COM used nice short text names (like C++ does) for class names and interface names. How many COM classes and COM interfaces, worldwide, do you think would be called String? List? Date? So, the chances of name clashes are high.

Furthermore, COM classes are delivered to you as binary components, so you can't modify them to resolve name conflicts. After all, what are you going to do? Edit the binary? That seems a little extreme. Or maybe you could call the vendor and have them change the name of the class and ship you a new version? That's impractical.

So the solution is to have names that are 128 bits long (giving a namespace of 2^{128} unique names) and to employ a method that makes sure that everyone generates different names. One of these methods is to have programmers use the utility program `guidgen.exe` to generate GUIDs. This program generates GUIDs based on unique information built into the network card of the computer. Another method is to call the COM routine `CoCreateGuid` to generate new GUIDs (there are some other methods we won't discuss here, but you get the general idea).

Of course these methods can be compromised, but in practice, the likelihood of two developers creating duplicate GUIDs is so small that no one worries about it.

FAQ 34.09

What is an interface?

Pure specification without any implementation.

A COM interface is a set of related methods that have a well-defined contract but have no implementation. A COM class implements one or more interfaces, and all the services a COM class exports are defined by the interfaces it implements. Callers access the services of a COM object by calling the methods defined by its interfaces. COM interfaces serve to decouple the caller's view of the services provided by a COM class from how the COM class implements those interfaces.

In C++ terms, an interface is an abstract class that defines a set of `public`, pure virtual functions and contains no data members. By convention, the names of COM interfaces begin with a capital I (for interface). The following interface is called `IUnknown` and it defines three methods—`QueryInterface`, `AddRef`, and `Release` (for more information on `IUnknown`, see FAQ 34.10).

```
class IUnknown {
public:
    virtual HRESULT QueryInterface(REFIID riid, void** ppv) = 0;
    virtual unsigned long AddRef() = 0;
    virtual unsigned long Release()= 0;
};
```

COM interfaces and COM classes are distinct concepts, and COM interfaces are specified independently of any particular COM class and independently of any particular implementation of the interface. In this way, COM interfaces resemble Java interfaces. Unfortunately, C++ provides only one construct, the class, for representing classes and interfaces, and therefore a certain amount of programmer discipline is required when using C++ to achieve the same effect.

Once defined, a COM interface and its contract can never change. Thus, every implementation of the interface must satisfy the same contract no matter what programming language is used, no matter what operating system is used, no matter what data structures are used, and no matter what performance optimizations are performed. In this way, objects and their callers can work together even when they are implemented by different people using different tools and working in different organizations and who don't know or communicate with each other. In other words, COM interfaces are substitutable.

Notice that an interface cannot define concrete data members (whereas C++ permits data members to be declared in the class body). However, an interface can define get/set member functions, thus indicating that there is some abstract state that can be manipulated through the interface. The COM class that implements the interface is responsible for defining the concrete data members.

A key element of the COM standard is the binary specification of COM interfaces. A COM interface is an array of function pointers similar to the virtual function table generated by most C++ compilers. With COM interfaces, unlike C++ virtual function tables, the location of the interface pointer is not linked to the location of the object's data. COM makes the location of the COM object's data invisible to the caller in the interests of decoupling and guaranteeing language and location transparency. This separation of the interface from the concrete data promotes location transparency because it means that a COM interface can be accessed by a caller (through a proxy) even when the actual COM object (and the object's data) is located in another process.

Microsoft has defined a set of COM interfaces (usually referred to as the *standard interfaces*) that cover a wide range of services including object creation, memory allocation, structured storage, and compound documents, and more are being added all the time. You can define your own interfaces, too; these are referred to as *custom interfaces*.

FAQ 34.10

What is the `IUnknown` interface?

The `IUnknown` interface is the interface from which all other interfaces are derived. Here is the C++ definition of the `IUnknown` interface.

```
class IUnknown {
public:
  virtual HRESULT QueryInterface(REFIID riid, void** ppv) = 0;
  virtual unsigned long AddRef() = 0;
  virtual unsigned long Release()= 0;
};
```

The IUnknown interface defines the following three methods.

1. QueryInterface: Allows the caller to dynamically discover whether a particular object supports a particular interface. The caller passes the IID of the interface it is looking for to QueryInterface (via riid, which is a reference to an IID), and if the COM object implements the specified interface, QueryInterface returns a pointer to it (via ppv, which is a pointer to a pointer to a void); otherwise it returns NULL.

2. AddRef: Increments the reference count of a COM object, and the object uses this reference count to know when it can remove itself from memory.

3. Release: Decrements the reference count of a COM object and causes the object to destroy itself when the reference count is reduced to zero.

The pervasive nature of this interface has a profound impact on COM.

First, a COM object that has multiple interfaces may have multiple implementations of the IUnknown interface. This is because each interface is derived from IUnknown and therefore might have its own implementation of IUnknown.

Second, all calls to QueryInterface for a single COM object must behave in the same manner at all times. For example, if at one point QueryInterface returns non-NULL when asked whether this COM object supports the IStack interface, then it must always return a valid interface pointer and cannot return NULL. As another example, suppose a caller has a pointer to one interface of a COM object and uses that interface pointer to call QueryInterface to ask if that object supports IStack. Then, all the other implementations of QueryInterface provided by all the other interfaces of the COM object must respond in the same manner (it would be illegal for some implementations of QueryInterface to return an interface pointer and for other implementations to return NULL).

Third, in a very loose sense, QueryInterface is similar to the RTTI mechanism of C++. It is the mechanism by which a caller gains access to the other services defined by an object.

Fourth, AddRef and Release point to the fact that the lifetimes of COM objects are controlled through reference counting. Thus, AddRef must be called whenever an interface pointer for a COM object is created or copied, and Release must be called whenever an interface pointer is destroyed (by the way, AddRef is called implicitly by CoCreateInstance() and QueryInterface()).

Fifth, the IID for `IUnknown`, is called `IID_IUnknown`, and it is defined in the COM header files since it is a standard interface defined by Microsoft.

FAQ 34.11

How many ways are there to specify COM interfaces?

For better or worse there are several ways to define a COM interface.

Suppose we want to define the interface `IStack`, which provides facilities for pushing and popping integers. One technique is to define the COM interface as a C++ abstract base class.

```
#include "wtypes.h"

/* {FC3B3F61-BCEC-11D1-91FE-E1CBED988F66} */
DEFINE_GUID(IID_IStack,
    0xFC3B3F61, 0xBCEC, 0x11D1, 0x91, 0xFE,
    0xE1, 0xCB, 0xED, 0x98, 0x8F, 0x66);

class IStack : public IUnknown {
public:
    virtual HRESULT Push(long value) = 0;
    virtual HRESULT Pop(long* value) = 0;
    virtual HRESULT Empty(long* flag) = 0;
};
```

This technique would be the most familiar to C++ programmers. Notice how `IStack` is derived from `IUnknown` (all COM interfaces must be derived either directly or indirectly from `IUnknown`). The problem with this definition is that it is language specific and can't be used by callers written in other languages. Also you'd have to provide code for marshaling the parameters if the caller using `IStack` and the COM object implementing `IStack` were running in different processes.

Another technique is to define the interface using a set of COM-defined macros. This technique defines the interface in a manner that hides the differences between programming languages (e.g., C and C++) and operating systems (e.g., Windows and Macintosh).

```
#include "wtypes.h"

/* {FC3B3F61-BCEC-11D1-91FE-E1CBED988F66} */
DEFINE_GUID(IID_IStack,
```

```
    0xFC3B3F61, 0xBCEC, 0x11D1, 0x91, 0xFE,
    0xE1, 0xCB, 0xED, 0x98, 0x8F, 0x66);

DECLARE_INTERFACE_(IStack, IUnknown)
{
    // *** IStack methods *** //
    STDMETHOD(Push)  (THIS_ long  value) PURE;
    STDMETHOD(Pop)   (THIS_ long* value) PURE;
    STDMETHOD(Empty) (THIS_ long* flag)  PURE;
};
```

The tags such as `DECLARE_INTERFACE_`, `STDMETHOD`, `THIS_`, and `PURE` are COM macros that expand differently based on the operating system and programming language. This is a better approach than the pure C++ approach because it allows the same interface definition to be used in multiple environments without changes. But you'd still have to provide code for marshaling the parameters if the caller using `IStack` and the COM object implementing `IStack` were running in different processes.

A third technique is to define the interface using the Microsoft Interface Definition Language (MIDL). MIDL allows interfaces to be defined in a language-independent manner. MIDL is based on DCE's IDL syntax and includes extensions to support COM programming. MIDL is used for defining COM interfaces, defining what interfaces a COM class implements (see FAQ 34.12), defining dispatch interfaces (see FAQ 34.25), and generating type libraries (see FAQ 34.29). Here is the MIDL definition of the `IStack` interface.

```
[   object,
    uuid(FC3B3F61-BCEC-11D1-91FE-E1CBED988F66)
]
interface IStack : IUnknown
{
    import "unknwn.idl";
    HRESULT Push([in] long value);
    HRESULT Pop([out, retval] long* pVal);
    HRESULT Empty([out, retval] boolean* pVal);
};
```

MDL has some major advantages.

- MIDL is language independent.

- MIDL clearly separates interface from implementation.

- MIDL provides Microsoft-specific features that are not found in other IDLs.

- The MIDL compiler can automatically generate proxies and stubs (see FAQ 34.15 for more information regarding proxies and stubs) capable of marshaling parameters across process boundaries. More specifically, for a caller running in one process to talk to a COM object in another process, the COM communication layer needs to understand the exact size and nature of the data involved in the interprocess communication. COM provides built-in support for marshaling standard interfaces (such as IUnknown). However, no such built-in support exists for custom interfaces (such as IStack). By defining a COM interface using MIDL and compiling it with the MIDL compiler, you get source code for a proxy/stub DLL as a by-product. The communication layer uses this proxy/stub pair to marshal parameters between objects and their callers.

MIDL also has some limitations, including the fact that it is relatively complex, all out parameters must be pointers (which is an issue only for programmers and programming languages who are pointer challenged), function name overloading is not supported, and the return type for methods in object interfaces must be an HRESULT (although methods can return any number of results by defining one or more parameters as out parameters or in/out parameters).

Define interfaces using MIDL when possible: it is the most general and the easiest to work with.

FAQ 34.12

What are COM classes and COM objects?

 The concrete implementation of one or more COM interfaces.

A COM class is a body of code that implements all the functions of at least one COM interface. Every COM class has a unique CLSID and callers use the unique CLSID when they want to create objects that are instances of the COM class.

In the following example, the COM class CoStack implements the IUnknown interface and the IStack interface. The following code fragment declares the external interface including the CLSID for CoStack, the IStack interface, and the IID for the IStack interface.

```
#include "wtypes.h"

extern HRESULT STACK_E_UNDERFLOW;

/* {FC3B3F61-BCEC-11D1-91FE-E1CBED988F66} */
DEFINE_GUID(IID_IStack,
```

```
    0xFC3B3F61, 0xBCEC, 0x11D1, 0x91, 0xFE,
    0xE1, 0xCB, 0xED, 0x98, 0x8F, 0x66);

DECLARE_INTERFACE_(IStack, IUnknown)
{
    // *** IStack methods *** //
    STDMETHOD(Push)  (THIS_ long  value) PURE;
    STDMETHOD(Pop)   (THIS_ long* value) PURE;
    STDMETHOD(Empty) (THIS_ long* flag) PURE;
};
// {FC3B3F62-BCEC-11D1-91FE-E1CBED988F66}
DEFINE_GUID(CLSID_CoStack,
    0xFC3B3F62, 0xBCEC, 0x11D1, 0x91, 0xFE,
    0xE1, 0xCB, 0xED, 0x98, 0x8F, 0x66);
```

Class CoStack declares all the methods of the IUnknown interface (by the way, ULONG is a typedef for unsigned long) and the IStack interface. It also declares two private data members—refCnt_ is used to implement reference counting for the object and data_ is the data structure used to hold the elements of the stack.

```
#include <stack>
using namespace std;

class CoStack : public IStack {
public:
    // *** IUnknown methods *** //
    STDMETHOD(QueryInterface) (REFIID riid, void** ppv);
    STDMETHOD_(ULONG,AddRef) ();
    STDMETHOD_(ULONG,Release) ();
    // *** IStack methods *** //
    STDMETHOD(Push) (long  value);
    STDMETHOD(Pop)  (long* value);
    STDMETHOD(Empty)(long* flag);

    CoStack();
private:
    ULONG refCnt_;
    stack<long> data_;
};

CoStack::CoStack()
: refCnt_(0)
, data_()
{ }
```

Note that class CoStack has a constructor even though the COM specification does not define constructors for COM classes. In this case, the implementation is taking advantage of a C++ feature. In particular, the C++ constructor initializes the data structures of the C++ object, which happens to initialize the data structures of the COM object at the same time. The lesson here is that class CoStack is a mix of COM features and C++ features, and sometimes it is hard to tell them apart.

The COM class implements the three methods of the IUnknown interface. QueryInterface tests to see if the caller is requesting one of the two interfaces that this class implements. If the caller is requesting a legitimate interface for this class, QueryInterface returns a pointer to that interface; otherwise, it returns NULL. Notice that QueryInterface copies an interface pointer so that it calls AddRef. AddRef increments the reference count for this object. Release decrements the reference count and destroys the object if the reference count is zero.

```
STDMETHODIMP CoStack::QueryInterface(REFIID riid, void** ppv)
{
    if (riid == IID_IUnknown)
        *ppv = this;
    else if (riid == IID_IStack)
        *ppv = this;
    else {
        *ppv = NULL;
        return E_NOINTERFACE;
    }
    AddRef();
    return S_OK;
}


STDMETHODIMP_(ULONG) CoStack::AddRef()
{ return ++refCnt_; }

STDMETHODIMP_(ULONG) CoStack::Release()
{
    ULONG result = --refCnt_;
    if (result == 0)
        delete this;
    return result;
}
```

The COM class also implements the methods of the IStack interface. These all look pretty normal except for the fact that the return values for the methods are status codes (S_OK if the call succeeds, STACK_E_UNDERFLOW if an underflow condition is detected).

```
STDMETHODIMP CoStack::Push(long value)
{
    data_.push(value);
```

```
        return S_OK;
}

STDMETHODIMP CoStack::Pop(long* value)
{
    if (data_.empty())
        return STACK_E_UNDERFLOW;
    *value = data_.top();
    data_.pop();
    return S_OK;
}

STDMETHODIMP CoStack::Empty(long* flag)
{
    *flag = data_.empty() ? 1 : 0;
    return S_OK;
}
```

Every COM class has a *class object* that acts as the meta class for the COM class. The most important function that the class object plays is that it provides the class factory for its COM class by implementing the `IClassFactory` interface (or the `IClassFactory2` interface). Here is the class object for class `CoStack` (some details have been left out of this example code).

```
class CoStackClassObject : public IClassFactory {
public:
    STDMETHOD(QueryInterface) (REFIID riid, void** ppv);
    STDMETHOD_(ULONG,AddRef) ();
    STDMETHOD_(ULONG,Release) ();
    STDMETHOD(CreateInstance) (IUnknown* outer, REFIID riid, void** ppv);
    STDMETHOD(LockServer) (BOOL b);
};

STDMETHODIMP CoStackClassObject::QueryInterface(REFIID riid, void** ppv)
{
    if (riid == IID_IUnknown || riid == IID_IClassFactory)
        *ppv = this;
    else {
        *ppv = NULL;
        return E_NOINTERFACE;
    }
    AddRef();
    return S_OK;
}

STDMETHODIMP_(ULONG) CoStackClassObject::AddRef() { /*...*/ }

STDMETHODIMP_(ULONG) CoStackClassObject::Release() { /*...*/ }
```

```
STDMETHODIMP CoStackClassObject::CreateInstance
                    (IUnknown* outer, REFIID riid, void** ppv)
{
    *ppv = NULL;
    if (outer != NULL)
        return CLASS_E_NOAGGREGATION;
    CoStack* p = new CoStack;
    if (p == NULL)
        return E_OUTOFMEMORY;
    p->AddRef();
    HRESULT hr = p->QueryInterface(riid, ppv);
    p->Release();
    return hr;
}

STDMETHODIMP CoStackClassObject::LockServer(BOOL b) { /*...*/ }
```

The class object is registered in the system registry (see FAQ 34.06) and is used during object creation. Callers create COM objects by calling the API function `CoGetClassObject`, obtaining a pointer to the class object's `IClassFactory` interface, and calling `CreateInstance` (callers may also call `CoCreateInstance`, which is a helper function that performs this series of actions).

Every COM class and its class object live within a *COM server* (on Windows this means either a DLL or an EXE), which contains the executable code that implements the class and the class object. When the COM server is a DLL, COM locates and loads the DLL when the caller creates the first object of any class that lives within the server. When the COM server is an EXE, COM locates and runs the EXE when the caller creates the first object of any class that lives within the server.

Most COM classes implement more than one interface. Typically this is done in C++ using nested classes or multiple inheritance. For details, refer to a book dedicated to COM.

FAQ 34.13

How hard is it for callers to create and use a COM object?

Not that hard. To create and use a COM object, a caller needs to

- Include the external interface of the COM class. In this case the caller declares the IID for the `IStack` interface, the CLSID for `CoStack`, and the `IStack` interface. Usually all these declarations are provided by the writer of the COM class in an include file.

- Create the object (line 1). The program calls CoCreateInstance passing it the class identifier for the COM class that is being created (CLSID_CoStack in this case), the interface identifier for IUnknown (IID_IUnknown), and a pointer to an interface pointer (&unknownPtr in this case), which CoCreateInstance uses to return a pointer to the IUnknown interface for the newly created object.

- Query the object for one or more of its interfaces (line 2). The program calls QueryInterface passing it the interface identifier for the interface it wants access to (IID_IStack in this case) and a pointer to an interface pointer (&stackPtr in this case), which QueryInterface uses to return a pointer to the requested interface for the object (the interface pointer is NULL if the object does not support the requested interface).

- Use the services provided by the interface (lines 3 and 4). The program calls the Push and Pop methods of the IStack interface using the interface pointer returned by QueryInterface.

- Release the object (lines 5 and 6). The program holds two interface pointers for the Stack object (stackPtr and unknownPtr in this case), and therefore it calls Release once for each interface pointer it holds.

```
#include "wtypes.h"
#include <initguid.h>

// {FC3B3F61-BCEC-11D1-91FE-E1CBED988F66}
DEFINE_GUID(IID_IStack,
    0xFC3B3F61, 0xBCEC, 0x11D1, 0x91, 0xFE,
    0xE1, 0xCB, 0xED, 0x98, 0x8F, 0x66);
// {FC3B3F62-BCEC-11D1-91FE-E1CBED988F66}
DEFINE_GUID(CLSID_CoStack,
    0xFC3B3F62, 0xBCEC, 0x11D1, 0x91, 0xFE,
    0xE1, 0xCB, 0xED, 0x98, 0x8F, 0x66);

class IStack : public IUnknown {
public:
    STDMETHOD(Push) (long  value);
    STDMETHOD(Pop)  (long* value);
    STDMETHOD(Empty)(long* flag);
};

void useStack()
{
    IUnknown* unknownPtr = NULL;
    HRESULT hr = CoCreateInstance(CLSID_CoStack,       //Line 1
        NULL, CLSCTX_ALL, IID_IUnknown, (void**)&unknownPtr);
```

```
        if (SUCCEEDED(hr)) {
            IStack* stackPtr = NULL;
            hr = unknownPtr->QueryInterface(IID_IStack,  //Line 2
                                    (void**)&stackPtr);

            if (SUCCEEDED(hr)) {
                hr = stackPtr->Push(10);        //Line 3
                long val;
                hr = stackPtr->Pop(&val);       //Line 4
                stackPtr->Release();            //Line 5
            }
            unknownPtr->Release();              //Line 6
        }
    }
```

The caller must take a couple of steps to initialize COM and signal when it is finished using COM:

1. Initialize COM (line 7). The program loads the COM libraries by calling CoInitialize.

2. Uninitialize COM (line 8). The program unloads the COM libraries by calling CoUninitialize.

```
int main()
{
    HRESULT hr = CoInitialize(NULL);    //Line 7
    if (SUCCEEDED(hr)) {
        useStack();
    }
    CoUninitialize();                   //Line 8
    return 0;
}
```

Of course, there are a zillion details that we don't have space to go into here.

FAQ 34.14

How does COM provide language transparency?

 The COM binary object model.

COM is language independent due to its binary specification of how COM classes and interfaces are laid out in memory. For example, the binary definition of an interface is a pointer to a table of function pointers.

Thus, even though the examples use C++ to define the `IUnknown` and `IStack` interfaces, the key step is for the C++ compiler to turn the C++ class definitions into a pointer to a table of function pointers (or a virtual function table).

This binary definition of classes and interfaces makes it possible for any language that can create the correct memory structures to define COM classes and interfaces. For example, the C language can define a COM interface using `structs` and pointers to functions; many other languages use similar features. Languages that cannot build these constructs cannot be used for defining COM classes.

This binary specification also means that a COM class can be used by any programming language that can call functions using a function pointer. Clearly, C++ and C are capable of this trick.

All this makes C++ a natural programming language for defining and using COM classes since C++ compilers are capable of automatically constructing the virtual function tables (so that the programmer does not have to lay them out by hand) and calling functions through virtual function tables.

Of course, other programming languages and development environments can automate the definition of COM classes in the same way. For instance, Visual Basic can be used for creating COM classes since the Visual Basic development environment can interpret the Visual Basic code and emit the correct interface declarations, class declarations, MIDL code, and so on.

FAQ 34.15

How does COM provide location transparency?

Proxies and stubs.

COM provides location transparency because a caller can use a COM object without knowing or caring where the object is running. The object could be running in the same process or in another process running on the same machine or in another process running on another machine (this is where Distributed COM comes into play; see FAQ 34.39).

COM facilitates location transparency by defining an architecture that uses proxies and stubs for linking callers to COM objects in a location-transparent manner and marshaling parameters between callers and objects. A proxy is an object that runs in the caller's address space and serves as a surrogate for the actual object. The proxy has an interface that is identical to the interface of the actual object. Stubs are objects that run in the server process where a COM object is running and handle all member function calls coming from other processes.

During execution, when a caller creates a COM object in another process, the COM runtime system also creates a proxy for the just created object in the caller's address space and a stub object in the server process. The caller is then given an interface pointer to the corresponding interface on the proxy object. When the caller calls a member function using this interface pointer, the proxy object transmits the parameters to the stub object, which makes the actual call on the corresponding interface of the actual COM object. Similarly, any results are returned from the COM object to the stub object, which transmits them to the proxy object, which returns them to the calling program.

Marshaling refers to the transmission of parameters from the caller to the object and the transmission of return values back again along with conversion of the parameters and return values, as necessary. There are two types of marshaling. *Standard marshaling* is provided by COM, and it is provided, by default, for all standard interfaces. *Custom marshaling* is defined by programmers for situations that standard marshaling does not cover (e.g., marshal a data type that the standard marshaler doesn't understand) and for performing optimizations that standard marshaling does not support.

This architecture defines the roles and responsibilities of the proxies and stubs and defines how they are created and destroyed and how parameters are marshaled between the caller and the COM object. Proxies and stubs can also come into play when the caller and the object are running on separate threads in the same process. Except for highly specialized situations, proxies and stubs are invisible to programmers and can be ignored.

FAQ 34.16

What types of errors occur due to reference counting?

Reference counting is a powerful mechanism, but it can lead to errors that are extremely hard to detect.

First, a caller might call `AddRef` too often or forget to call `Release`. In this case, there is a memory leak since the COM object never knows when to destroy itself.

Second, a caller might call `Release` too often. In this case, the reference count of the COM object is reduced to zero prematurely, and the COM object destroys itself leaving a dangling pointer since other callers have interface pointers to the COM object.

Reference counting is made more complicated by performance optimizations. For example, sometimes it is not necessary to call `AddRef` and `Release` for a temporary interface pointer if it is going to be created and destroyed within the lifetime of another interface pointer. This sort of optimization creates a dependency between the two interface pointers, and in the future it can become the source of a reference counting error if some invariant associated with the dependency changes.

None of this should be a surprise to C++ programmers. After all, C++ programmers have to deal with the same conditions in C++ programs if the calls to new and delete are not properly coordinated. Forgetting to call delete results in memory leaks and calling delete prematurely results in dangling pointers.

However, the situation in COM is more insidious since COM components can be running in different processes than the ones their callers are running in. For example, a memory leak caused by a caller running in one process may result in a server process continuing to run when it should have shut down, thus consuming operating system resources as well as memory resources. Or worse, a bug in one caller can release a server process prematurely, causing it to shut down while it is still being used by other callers.

Note that Distributed COM (see FAQs 34.39, 34.40) has a security option that performs callbacks to the client to authenticate distributed reference count calls, ensuring that objects are not released maliciously.

FAQ 34.17

What mechanism does COM define for error handling?

COM sends us right back to the Dark Ages, since COM functions return error codes for doing error handling. Or, stated in a positive way, COM defines a mechanism for handling errors that is language and location transparent and is consistent with its binary standard.

The return value of most COM methods (AddRef and Release are two exceptions) is an HRESULT (a "handle to a result object"). An HRESULT is a 32-bit value that is divided into three fields. The first field (1 bit) can be tested to determine whether or not a function succeeded. The second field (15 bits) indicates what subsystem returned the error code. The third field (16 bits) is the return code. The biggest drawback of using this mechanism is that it requires the caller to explicitly test the value of the HRESULT after each COM method call.

Just because COM uses HRESULT does not prevent programmers from using C++ exception handling in the C++ code *within* the implementation of a method of a COM class, provided the exceptions are caught and handled by the COM method. In any event, C++ exceptions cannot be used for transmitting the error to the caller or to another COM object.

FAQ 34.18

How are interfaces versioned?

 This is one of the more straightforward elements of COM—*YOU CAN'T.*

Interface versioning refers to the COM conventions for changing and modifying interfaces. COM's rule for versioning interfaces is simple: interfaces cannot be versioned; a modified interface is a new interface with a new and unique IID.

In this context, modifying an interface includes any change to the interface's specification, including adding or removing methods, adding or removing parameters, or changing the contract for a method (even if none of its parameters change). At the same time, the rule does not prevent multiple implementations for the same interface, as long as all the implementations satisfy the interface's contract.

The reasoning behind the rule regarding versioning interfaces is to maintain backward compatibility and guarantee that there are no conflicts between existing interfaces and new interfaces. The rule makes a lot of sense since it allows callers to program to a well-defined interface knowing that the interface will never change.

The fact that COM interfaces can't be versioned is really no different from the current situation with C++ class libraries, except that it is presented in a slightly different way. Suppose a system defines a COM interface called `IDate` for handling date-related information. Later the interface is modified, producing `IDate2`. Also suppose that there is a C++ class library that has a `Date` class and people write programs using the `Date` class. Now the vendor of the class library releases a new and improved C++ class library (version 2) with a `Date` class with a modified interface. Under these circumstances, what are the trade-offs between the C++ approach and the COM approach?

First, suppose the new version of `Date` simply adds methods so that it is completely substitutable with the earlier version. In the case of COM, existing callers continue to use `IDate` and new callers can choose between `IDate` and `IDate2`. In the case of the C++ class library, existing callers and new callers simply use version 2 of class `Date`. Easy.

Second, suppose the new version of `Date` is not completely backward compatible with the older version. In the case of COM, existing callers continue to use `IDate` and new callers can choose between `IDate` and `IDate2`. We might also decide to review some of the existing caller code and revise it to use `IDate2`. The choices are almost the same for the caller code using the C++ class library. Existing callers continue to use class `Date Version One` and new callers can choose between class `Date Version One` and class `Date Version Two`. We might also decide to review some of the existing caller code and revise it to use class `Date Version Two` (instead of class `Date Version One`).

In some ways, the COM approach is better. If one subsystem of a program uses the COM interface `IDate` and another subsystem of a program uses the COM interface `IDate2`, no incompatibilities occur when the subsystems are linked together. In contrast, if the two subsystems use different and incompatible versions of the C++ class `Date`, linking the two subsystems probably will create some conflicts. Typically this sort of problem forces the users of the C++ class library to choose between the two incompatible versions of the `Date` class, which may require one of the subsystems to be updated.

In the case of COM the two interfaces are distinguished using 128-bit IIDs, and in the case of C++ the two interfaces need to be distinguished by their names. In the end, both approaches amount to pretty much the same thing, and each has its champions.

FAQ 34.19

Is COM object oriented?

Yes, COM delivers all the major benefits of object technology (although some purists disagree).

Each *COM class* has a unique *class identifier* and implements one or more *interfaces*. An interface is a group of functions that provide a set of related services. A *COM object* is an instance of a COM class. A COM class can be used to create many separate COM objects. These definitions are similar to C++ where classes have unique identifiers and objects are instances of classes.

Most developers using COM could not care less about whether or not COM is "truly" object oriented. As far as they are concerned, it gives them the benefits of object orientation and that is all that counts:

- You can define classes.

- You can use the classes to create objects.

- The classes have well-defined interfaces and the implementations of the classes are fully encapsulated.

- Interfaces can be defined using inheritance and interface pointers are polymorphic.

FAQ 34.20

What is the biggest problem with COM?

 Complete confusion for beginners.

Programmers can expect to experience a *COM haze* when they first work with COM. This comes from having to mentally juggle all the different issues:

- COM is relatively large and has its own way of doing things, and often its approach is unlike other systems (including C++ and CORBA).

- COM terminology is Humpty-Dumpty terminology (if you remember, Humpty-Dumpty said, "When *I* use a word it means just what I choose it to mean—neither more nor less"). Thus, COM uses many of the same terms as C++ and other object technologies but uses them in its own way. This can lead to misunderstandings.

- Most COM examples are written in C++, and this makes it hard to figure out where COM stops and where C++ begins. Programmers often find themselves wondering which of the five C++ classes in a COM example represent COM interfaces, which ones represent COM classes, and which ones are internal classes that are used only within the implementation of the COM classes.

- Different C++ class libraries use different approaches for declaring and implementing COM classes and offer different trade-offs. Some class libraries (like MFC, the Microsoft Foundation Class library) use numerous macros for defining COM classes, whereas other libraries (like ATL, the ActiveX Template Library) use C++ templates.

- There are numerous ways of declaring and implementing COM classes, and it is sometimes hard to figure out how they fit together. Examples in books don't always make it clear whether they are describing a new and distinct feature of COM or are simply describing another way of implementing a feature described earlier.

FAQ 34.21

What are the major differences between COM and C++?

 COM is a component standard while C++ is an object-oriented language, and even though they have much in common, they really do have different roles in life.

As a programming language, C++ defines classes and objects, defines a complete syntax and semantics, and has a compiler that translates source text into executable code. In addition, C++ has a relatively small runtime system and restricts its view of the world to the objects in a single process.

As a component standard, COM defines classes and objects, has a minimal syntax and a minimal compiler (the MIDL compiler) for defining interfaces, defines an architecture for creating, locating, and accessing objects running in different processes, defines interfaces for marshaling parameters when calls are made to a different process (see FAQ 34.15 for more information regarding marshaling), and defines several threading models.

Therefore COM and C++ are completely different in their scope, but fortunately, they are compatible technologies: COM is well suited to defining components and interfaces, and C++ provides a rich language for implementing components and classes.

C++ FEATURE	COM FEATURE
A C++ class name is an identifier.	A COM class name is a CLSID or a 128-bit number.
C++ classes are not required to support a common interface.	COM classes are required to support the `IUnknown` interface.
C++ classes have constructors that are automatically called when objects are created.	COM classes do not have constructors (although the language used for implementing a COM class may provide a mechanism for executing an initialization routine when instances of the class are created).
C++ classes have destructors that are automatically called when objects are destroyed.	COM classes do not have destructors (although the language used for implementing a COM class may provide a mechanism for executing a finalization routine when instances of the class are destroyed).
A C++ class can declare pure virtual functions, virtual functions, nonvirtual functions, overloaded functions, static functions, data members, and friends.	A COM interface declares pure virtual functions only.

continued

C++ FEATURE	COM FEATURE
A C++ class represents an interface, although the interface does not have a distinct and explicit name or identifier.	A COM interface has an explicit identifier (IID).
A C++ class normally has one virtual function table that contains pointers to all the virtual functions defined by the object.	A COM class can be implemented using a separate virtual function table for each interface.
C++ callers can safely navigate to other interfaces using `dynamic_cast`.	COM callers can safely navigate to other interfaces using `QueryInterface`.
C++ callers can use `new` to create objects; this mechanism ends up calling the class's constructor. C++ callers can also create objects in a local scope.	COM callers typically use `CoCreateInstance` to create objects; this mechanism ends up calling the `IClassFactory` interface, which must be implemented for every COM class. COM callers can also directly call the `CreateInstance` method of the `IClassFactory` interface.
C++ callers use `delete` to destroy objects created using `new`; objects in a local scope are destroyed automatically.	COM callers do not destroy COM objects directly; instead they call `Release()` when they no longer need an interface pointer, and the COM object destroys itself.
When a caller creates a C++ object using `new`, the caller gets a pointer to the object.	When a caller creates a COM object, the caller gets a pointer to one of the object's interfaces; however, it never gets a pointer to the object—no such pointer exists.
Error handling is normally accomplished using `throw` and `catch`; Return codes are supported but are undesirable.	Error handling is required to use return codes.
C++ supports both reference semantics and value semantics.	COM supports reference semantics only.
C++ does not define a meta data facility	Type libraries contain meta data.

C++ FEATURE	COM FEATURE
C++ defines features such as templates, overloaded functions, operator overloading, default parameters, namespaces, try/catch exception handling, const declarations, references, private inheritance, protected inheritance, etc.	These features are not part of COM but they can be used by C++ programs that implement COM interfaces and COM classes.
C++ supports interface inheritance.	COM supports interface inheritance.
C++ supports multiple inheritance.	COM supports only single inheritance (although there are several techniques for building COM classes that implement multiple interfaces).
C++ supports implementation inheritance.	COM does not support implementation inheritance; however, COM does not prevent an implementation of a COM class (using C++, for example) from using implementation inheritance.
C++ does not use a system registry.	COM uses a system registry for storing static information about classes, interfaces, and type libraries.
C++ classes and namespaces reduce name clashes.	COM GUIDs eliminate name clashes.
C++ does not define any mechanisms for creating objects in other processes.	COM defines an architecture for creating out-of-process objects (both on the local machine and on remote machines).
C++ does not define any mechanisms to support communication between objects running in different processes.	COM defines an architecture for invoking methods on out-of-process objects, marshaling parameters from the caller to the object, and marshaling return values from the object to the caller.
C++ does not define a threading model.	COM defines several threading models for governing how COM objects execute.

FAQ 34.22

When should a class be defined as a COM class?

 Here are some guidelines.

1. The development organization needs to buy into the idea of adopting a component-oriented architecture based on COM; otherwise, it can be pretty lonely if you're the only wolf in the pack trying to use COM. The development organization must also buy into the idea of using one of the 32-bit Windows operating systems (probably Windows NT) as a development and deployment platform.

2. Start by developing a system or application architecture and make your decisions regarding where and when to use COM based on the architecture. Don't worry about deciding where to use COM on a class-by-class basis. Instead, look for the larger components of your system and think about the interfaces to these components. Try out subsystems as a first approximation.

   For example, it might not make sense to define an Account class, whereas it might make sense to define an Account server. The Account server might run as an out-of-process COM server that can be shared by multiple callers and exposes a rich set of domain objects including account objects, customer objects, sales objects, invoice objects, and so on (where all of these objects are COM objects).

3. Sticking with the software architecture theme, use COM when the goal is to improve reliability by running the classes/objects in a separate process or on a separate machine. For example, running the caller and the COM objects in the same process allows a bug in one to bring down the other. Using COM to run the objects/services in separate processes helps to protect the objects from the callers and the callers from the objects—if one of them crashes it does not necessarily bring down the other.

4. Use COM when language transparency is important. Use COM when the callers and the objects might be written in different programming languages.

5. Use COM when location transparency is important or when the objects need to be shared by callers running in separate processes. Use COM when it is important to be able to rehost the classes/objects in an in-process server, in a local server, or in a remote server without affecting the callers.

6. Define the interfaces for your components from the caller's perspective rather than from the perspective of the developer. Limit the number of COM classes to classes that are visible from outside the component. For example, if the component includes account objects, customer objects, sales objects, and invoice objects, the component might internally utilize many other C++ classes for accessing a database and caching data, but there may be no reason to expose these internal C++ classes as COM classes.

7. Be aware of performance issues and the fact the COM is sensitive to whether or not the caller and the object are running in the same process and whether or not the caller and the object are using the same threading model. For example, calling a method of a COM object that is running in process and is using a compatible threading model takes about the same amount of time as calling a virtual function of a C++ object (tens of millions of calls per second). For callers and servers using different threading models, the time cost is greater (tens of thousands of calls per second).

8. Be aware of packaging issues. Multiple COM classes are packaged into a COM server, and the server is loaded/activated when the first COM object is created using the server. Since loading/activating a COM server can be time-consuming, make sure that all related COM classes are packaged together in the same server. That means that after the first COM object is created using the server, the time needed to create other objects will be less because the server is already loaded/activated. Putting related COM classes into separate servers can hurt performance.

9. If the COM objects are expected to be running in an out-of-process server, then define the interfaces to accommodate it. For example, provide methods that get/set multiple properties in one call to minimize the number of round-trip method calls that must cross process boundaries.

FAQ 34.23

What is Automation?

Automation is a set of facilities that sits on top of COM and that can be used by programming tools that cannot use the lower-level COM interfaces and facilities (such as high-level scripting tools).

The goals for Automation and COM are almost identical: define components with well-defined interfaces in a location-transparent and language-independent manner.

The main difference between Automation and COM is that Automation is targeted at enabling callers that are high-level scripting tools to manipulate objects, whereas COM is targeted at lower-level languages such as C++ and C.

Automation was originally developed to allow Visual Basic to bind to COM components through a special interface. The name "Automation" is something of an anachronism since Automation has grown beyond its original goals of simply allowing scripting languages to automate common tasks. Automation is becoming more important with the growing use of scripting languages in Web browsers, server side scripting, and office suites.

FAQ 34.24

What are dispatch interfaces?

The interfaces exposed by Automation objects. In particular, Automation objects expose dispatch interfaces rather than vtable interfaces.

There are two different kinds of COM interfaces. First, there are *vtable interfaces,* which work well for callers written in C++ (and, ironically, Visual Basic). Vtable interfaces are normal (nondispatch) COM interfaces, and they get their name from the fact that their binary layout is the same as the binary layout of the virtual function table (vtable) produced by most C++ compilers.

Second, there are *dispatch interfaces.* Dispatch interfaces get their name from the fact that they are implemented using the COM interface IDispatch.

Dispatch interfaces make it *much* easier for tools such as Visual Basic and Power-Builder to be adapted to use and support dispatch interfaces compared to using and supporting vtable interfaces for COM objects. Today, higher-level scripting languages such as Visual Basic for Applications and VBScript rely on dispatch interfaces, while Visual Basic supports both vtable interfaces and dispatch interfaces.

A dispatch interface allows callers to query an object at runtime for a list of its Automation methods and parameters and then invoke these methods. This facility is vital for allowing callers to invoke methods on objects when the methods were not known when the caller was compiled.

COM objects that expose dispatch interfaces are referred to as Automation objects or Automation servers. Callers that use Automation objects are referred to as Automation controllers. Automation objects are COM objects in every sense. They have a CLSID and a class factory, they implement IUnknown, their lifetime is controlled by reference counting, they can be implemented as in-process servers (in DLLs) or as out-of-process servers (in EXEs). It is important to realize that Automation is a protocol built on top of COM; in many ways, Automation is reminiscent of CORBA's Dynamic Invocation Interface (DII).

FAQ 34.25

When should a class expose a Dispatch interface?

When its callers say so.

The most obvious reason for implementing dispatch interfaces is that certain tools (such as VBScript, JScript, and older versions of Visual Basic) can interact with COM objects only through dispatch interfaces. Furthermore, ActiveX Controls (see FAQ 34.33) are required to expose their properties and methods through dispatch interfaces.

Dispatch interfaces define both dispatch methods and dispatch properties. Because COM interfaces can define only COM methods and dispatch interfaces are implemented using the `IDispatch` interface, dispatch properties are "virtual properties": they are manipulated indirectly by calling the methods of the `IDispatch` interface (see FAQ 34.27). Note that the programming language used by the caller may make it appear as if the property is being manipulated directly, but underneath it is still using COM methods. This illustrates, once again, that dispatch interfaces are at a higher level of abstraction than vtable interfaces and that Automation is a protocol that is implemented in terms of COM.

Dispatch interfaces can be declared using IDL. Here is the Microsoft IDL definition of the `IStack` dispatch interface.

```
[ uuid(FC3B3F51-BCED-11D1-91FE-E1CBED988F66) ]
library StackLib
{
    importlib("stdole32.tlb");

    [ uuid(FC3B3F31-BCEC-11D1-91FE-E1CBED988F66) ]
    dispinterface IStack
    {
        properties:
            [id(1), propget] boolean Empty;
        methods:
            [id(2)] void Push(long value);
            [id(3)] long Pop();
    };
};
```

The dispinterface statement is used to create type information for a dispatch interface. For this reason, dispatch interfaces must be declared inside library declarations. Dispatch interfaces, like all other COM interfaces, must have an IID, and it is declared using the [uuid] attribute.

Dispatch interfaces are derived from IDispatch (the dispinterface statement implicitly derives the interface from IDispatch). The declarations for the IDispatch interface are loaded from the Automation type library using the statement importlib("stdole32.tlb");.

The dispinterface statement has two sections; one for declaring properties and one for declaring methods. Each property must have an Automation-compatible type (see FAQ 34.32). The types of the parameters and return value for each method must also be Automation-compatible. Every method and property has a DISPID, which is assigned using the [id] attribute.

You may have noticed that the syntax for the dispinterface statement is unlike other IDL statements. This is because the dispinterface statement was originally part of an earlier tool called the Object Definition Language (ODL), which has been merged into Microsoft IDL.

Dispatch interfaces use Type Library Marshaling (see FAQ 34.29) using the built-in Automation Marshaler; therefore the MIDL compiler does not need to generate proxy/stub code.

The best way for COM classes to expose dispatch interfaces is as dual interfaces. As discussed in FAQ 34.31, this allows a COM class to have its cake and eat it, too.

FAQ 34.26

How does Automation work?

The IDispatch interface is what makes Automation work.

The IDispatch interface is a regular COM interface and is declared as follows.

```
interface IDispatch : public IUnknown {
public:
    virtual HRESULT GetTypeInfo(....) = 0;

    virtual HRESULT GetTypeInfoCount(....) = 0;

    virtual HRESULT GetIDsOfNames(....) = 0;

    virtual HRESULT Invoke(
        /* [in] */ DISPID dispIdMember,
        /* [in] */ REFIID riid,
```

```
              /* [in] */ LCID lcid,
              /* [in] */ WORD wFlags,
              /* [out][in] */ DISPPARAMS *pDispParams,
              /* [out] */ VARIANT *pVarResult,
              /* [out] */ EXCEPINFO *pExcepInfo,
              /* [out] */ UINT *puArgErr) = 0;
       };
```

When a caller wants to call a dispatch method defined by an Automation server, it first calls the server's implementation of IDispatch::GetIDsOfNames, supplying it with the string name of the dispatch method it wants to call. The result returned by GetIDsOfNames is the Dispatch Identifier (DISPID) for that dispatch method. The caller then calls the dispatch method by calling IDispatch::Invoke, supplying it with the DISPID for the dispatch method, the type of each parameter, and the values of each parameter. The implementation of IDispatch::Invoke performs a table lookup using the DISPID and executes the dispatch method.

When a caller wants to access a dispatch property, it first calls the server's implementation of IDispatch::GetIDsOfNames, supplying it with the string name of the dispatch property it wants to access. The result returned by GetIDsOfNames is the DISPID for that dispatch property. The caller then calls IDispatch::Invoke and supplies it with a flag indicating whether it wants to get the value of the dispatch property or set a new value for the dispatch property. The implementation of IDispatch::Invoke performs a table lookup using the DISPID and accesses the corresponding dispatch property.

Once a caller obtains a DISPID for a particular dispatch method (or property), it can cache it and use it repeatedly for calling the same method (or accessing the same property) without having to bother calling GetIDsOfNames again for that dispatch method (or dispatch property).

The good news is that most callers never call Invoke directly (the calls to Invoke are usually hidden behind a layer of abstraction). In the case of environments like Visual Basic, the Visual Basic syntax hides all the interactions with IDispatch. In the case of programming languages like C++, the development environment should automatically generate "automation proxy classes" that hide all the interactions with IDispatch. If your development environment cannot automatically generate automation proxy classes, you can always build them yourself.

FAQ 34.27

How does `Invoke` accomplish all of this?

`IDispatch::Invoke` declares a very general interface that has a large number of formal arguments that allow the caller to specify a wide range of parameters—including the `DISPID` for the operation, the type of operation (method call versus property get versus property put), the return value, exception information, and so on. The Automation object's implementation of `IDispatch::Invoke` must unpackage these parameters, call the method or access the property, and handle any errors that occur. When the property or method returns, the Automation object passes its return value back to the caller through another parameter of `IDispatch::Invoke`.

`Invoke` is similar in spirit to `printf`: callers pass a bunch of information, and the implementation of `IDispatch::Invoke` (like `printf`) ends up interpreting the incoming parameters to decide what to do. This makes `IDispatch::Invoke` capable of doing almost anything.

After `IDispatch::Invoke` interprets the parameters passed to it, it calls a method defined by the server—in this way `IDispatch::Invoke` does nothing. All `IDispatch::Invoke` does is look up the right routine, and that routine performs the useful work.

Notice that dispatch interfaces reverse the usual notions associated with COM interfaces. COM interfaces tend to have a small set of well-defined methods that are semantically related to one another. Dispatch interfaces tend to group together a large number of methods that are not necessarily related and funnel them through the `IDispatch` interface.

FAQ 34.28

What is a type library?

A type library is a compiled version of an IDL file that can be accessed programmatically.

COM provides a facility called type libraries that allows programs to dynamically access interface definitions and query for information on interfaces, components, methods, and parameters. Most Automation components create type libraries. A type library has a unique identifier (that is, a GUID) called a `LIBID`.

Type libraries can be generated by the Microsoft IDL compiler. After creating the type library, it can be included in the application as a resource or it can be a stand-alone file (in which case, the file name of the type library needs to be registered in the system registry so that the type library can be located when necessary).

COM defines interfaces for creating type information (`ICreateTypeInfo`, `ICreateTypeInfo2`), accessing type information (`ITypeInfo`, `ITypeInfo2`), creating type libraries (`ICreateTypeLib`, `ICreateTypeLib2`), and accessing type libraries (`ITypeLib`, `ITypeLib2`).

A caller can ask a COM object at runtime if it supports the `ITypeInfo` interface. Through this interface, the caller can interrogate the object to find out what methods and properties it provides. This facility is useful for scripting languages.

FAQ 34.29

What are the benefits of using type libraries?

Discover type information for a COM class without having to load the class.

new

A type library is the Automation standard for describing the objects, properties, and methods exposed by an Automation object. Type libraries provide important benefits.

- Type checking can be performed at compile time. This helps developers of Automation callers to write fast, correct code to access objects.

- Type browsers can scan the type library, allowing others to see the characteristics of the classes.

- Browsers and compilers can use the type information to display and access the classes.

- Automation callers that cannot use vtable interfaces can read and cache `DISPID`s at compile time, improving runtime performance.

- Visual Basic applications can take advantage of early binding by creating objects with specific interface types, rather than the generic `Object` type.

- Implementation of `IDispatch::Invoke` for the interface is faster and easier.

- Access to out-of-process servers is improved because Automation uses information from the type library to package the parameters that are passed to an object in another process.

Another benefit of type libraries is type library marshaling. Type library marshaling allows a custom interface to use the built-in Automation marshaler for the `IDispatch` interface, thus avoiding the need to build a proxy/stub DLL for the custom interface and then having to register it on each machine—the Automation marshaler is automatically available on Windows machines. To use this option, you need only register a type library for the interface on the client machines and restrict the interface to using the Automation–compatible data types (see FAQ 34.32).

FAQ 34.30

How do type libraries improve performance?

The Automation controller can avoid calling `GetIDsOfNames` at runtime.

An Automation controller can bind to a dispatch interface in one of two ways. One way is for the Automation controller to get the `DISPIDs` by calling the `IDispatch::GetIDsOfNames` function. This is called *late binding* because the controller binds to the property or method at runtime. Late binding works when nothing is known about the dispatch interface at compile time.

The other way is for the Automation controller to use *ID binding*. When using ID binding, the Automation controller extracts type information about the Automation object from its type library and maps the names of dispatch methods and properties to `DISPIDs`. More specifically, the `DISPID` of each property or method is fixed and is part of the object's type description. If the object is described in a type library, an Automation controller can read the `DISPIDs` from the type library and does not have to call `GetIDsOfNames` at runtime.

FAQ 34.31

What are dual interfaces?

A great way to have your cake and eat it, too.

A dual interface is an interface that combines a dispatch interface and a direct vtable interface.

One advantage of dual interfaces is that they let the caller choose the binding mechanism it wants to use. Scripting languages can use the dispatch interface while C++ callers can use the direct vtable interface. This means that objects that export dual interfaces are more useful since they can be used by a wider range of callers.

`IDispatch` offers support for late binding, whereas vtable binding offers much higher performance because the method is called directly instead of going through `IDispatch::Invoke`.

IDL supports the definition of dual interfaces. This is done by deriving the interface from `IDispatch` and attaching the [dual] attribute to the `interface` statement (notice that the `dispinterface` statement is not used). Here is the IDL declaration of `IStack` suitable for a dual interface.

```
[ uuid(FC3B3F51-BCED-11D1-91FE-E1CBED988F66) ]
library StackLib
{
    importlib("stdole32.tlb");
    [   object, dual,
        uuid(FC3B3F51-BCEC-11D1-91FE-E1CBED988F66)
    ]
    interface IStack : IDispatch
    {
        [id(1)] HRESULT push([in] long value);
        [id(2)] HRESULT pop([out, retval] long* value);
        [id(3)] HRESULT empty([out, retval] long* pVal);
    };
};
```

Since dual interfaces are COM interfaces, they must abide by the rules for COM interfaces.

- A dual interface must have an IID, and it is declared using the [uuid] attribute.

- The return type for a method is `HRESULT`, and all other results need to be returned through the parameter list (see `pop` and `empty`).

Since dual interfaces are dispatch interfaces, they must abide by the rules for dispatch interfaces.

- The declarations for the `IDispatch` interface are loaded from the Automation type library using the statement `importlib("stdole32.tlb");`.

- Each method has a `DISPID`, which is assigned using the [id] attribute.

- The types of the parameters for each method must be Automation-compatible data types.

- Dual interfaces are able to use type library marshaling (see FAQ 34.29) so that the interface can be accessed across process boundaries or across machine boundaries automatically (this is not automatically true for all custom-defined vtable interfaces). This is done using the type library for the interface in conjunction with a generic universal proxy/stub implementation.

A dual interface inherits from `IDispatch` and also implicitly inherits from `IUnknown` (since `IDispatch` inherits from `IUnknown`). At a binary level, the first three entries in the vtable are the members of `IUnknown`, the next four entries are the members of `IDispatch`, and the subsequent entries are pointers to the custom methods of the dual interface. Thus Automation controllers can access the `IDispatch` interface (including `GetIDsOfNames` and `Invoke`) since the entries for the dispatch interface are at the same locations in the vtable whether or not this is a dual interface. Other callers who are aware of dual interfaces can bind directly to the custom methods in the COM interface. Information about the physical layout of the vtable is obtained from a type library or a header file.

Direct vtable binding can be two to five times faster than Automation binding for in-process calls.

FAQ 34.32

What limitations are there on dual interfaces?

The primary limitation of dual interfaces is that arguments and return types are restricted to the Automation-compatible data types:

- boolean
- unsigned char
- short, int, long
- float, double
- currency, Date
- text strings
- status codes
- pointers to COM interfaces
- pointers to dispatch interfaces
- arrays of these types
- references to these types

These data types are defined by COM; they are not C++ data types, although there is a mapping from these data types to C++ data types. The reason that dual interfaces are restricted to these data types is that these are the data types that can be passed to `IDispatch::Invoke`, and every custom method of a dual interface has a corresponding automation method that is invoked using `IDispatch::Invoke`.

FAQ 34.33

What are OLE custom controls and ActiveX controls?

The word "control" has evolved in the same way the term OLE has evolved. About the only thing that can be said for sure is that a control is a software component. Early controls tended to be used as GUI widgets in Visual Basic programs, but now there are many non-GUI controls and they are used in non-Visual Basic programs. Controls are in-process objects and must execute in some kind of control container (see FAQ 34.35), a program specially designed for hosting controls and working with controls.

In the beginning there were Visual Basic Controls (VBXs). VBXs are a mechanism for packaging non-Visual Basic code (usually C routines) and calling them from 16-bit versions of Visual Basic. As such, VBXs are DLLs written in a prescribed manner so that they can be easily incorporated into and called from Visual Basic programs.

And VBXs begat OLE Custom Controls (or OCXs). OCXs have a number of advantages over VBXs.

- OCXs are based on COM, which means that they take advantage of all of the COM facilities for defining interfaces, developing components, creating components, and accessing components.

- OCXs are 32-bit custom controls (VBXs were 16-bit). Therefore OCXs are better suited to 32-bit applications and 32-bit Windows operating systems.

- OCXs can be written in any language that can be used for writing COM components (VBXs were almost always written in C).

- OCXs can be used from any program that is a custom control container (VBXs were pretty much limited to being used from Visual Basic).

- The OCX architecture defines a large number of mandatory interfaces that an OCX must support, and these interfaces provide a great deal of integration between the OCX and the control container.

And OCXs begat ActiveX Controls. ActiveX controls are a slimmed-down version of OCXs that are better suited to Web-based applications. The ActiveX architecture defines a minimal set of interfaces for an ActiveX control and, in fact, ActiveX controls are required to implement only one interface: IUnknown. All other interfaces are optional. More specifically,

- An ActiveX Control must have a CLSID (required for all COM objects).

- An ActiveX Control must support the IUnknown interface (required for all COM objects).

- An ActiveX Control must have a class object that implements IClassFactory (required for all COM objects).

- An ActiveX Control must expose its properties, methods, and events via dispatch interfaces or dual interfaces. In other words, ActiveX Controls are Automation objects.

- If a control has any persistent state, it must, as a minimum, implement either IPersistStream or IPersistStreamInit. The latter is used when a control wants to know when it is created new as opposed to being reloaded from an existing persistent state

- An ActiveX Control must be a self-registering, in-process component that implements the routines DllRegisterServer and DllUnregisterServer.

- An ActiveX Control must use the component categories API to register itself as a control, and it must register the component categories it requires a control container to support and any categories the control implements.

FAQ 34.34

Why do ActiveX controls differ from OLE custom controls?

Mostly to support the World Wide Web.

First, some background. OCXs are COM components that must implement many well-defined COM interfaces. This has both good and bad consequences. It is good because it means that OLE control containers (see FAQ 34.35) can rely on every OCX implementing a core set of interfaces, allowing the Control Container and the OCX to interact seamlessly and provide richer interactions with the user. It is bad because it makes OCXs into fairly heavyweight objects and it makes writing OCXs fairly complicated (but tools are evolving to ease this problem).

The OCX architecture makes several assumptions. First, it assumes that when an OCX is loaded, its state information is available on a local file system. Second, the OCX architecture provides for only synchronous loading of OCX state information. For desktop components this is irrelevant since it is assumed that the control container and the OCX are loaded onto the same machine.

Then the Web exploded and everything changed. It is no longer safe to assume that the control container and the control reside on the same machine. Instead, the control may reside on another machine and the control container may have to dynamically download the control across the Web/Internet.

For these reasons (and many more), the ActiveX control architecture replaced the OCX architecture. As mentioned already, ActiveX controls dispense with most of the baggage associated with OCXs. This permits smaller executables so that ActiveX control can be downloaded over the Web/Internet faster.

While the ActiveX architecture makes ActiveX controls more Web/Internet friendly, it has side effects. For example, now control containers have to be "smarter" since they have to "negotiate" with every ActiveX control to determine its capabilities. This, in turn, sometimes results in less integration between the control and its container than was previously possible using the OCX architecture.

The ActiveX architecture also supports situations where the control's state information is stored on a distant machine across the Web/Internet. In particular, the ActiveX architecture defines interfaces for asynchronously loading a control's state information and asynchronous notification of the container regarding the progress of loading this information

FAQ 34.35

What is a control container?

An ActiveX control container is an application or component capable of hosting (or containing) an ActiveX control. Control containers must implement a mandatory set of COM interfaces for hosting and interacting with ActiveX controls. Control containers may also implement a number of optional COM interfaces, depending on the functionality they provide and the level of integration they wish to provide.

Control containers cannot rely on an ActiveX control supporting any specific interfaces other than IUnknown. Determining what interfaces an ActiveX control supports is part of the negotiation process that occurs between a control container and a control.

Control containers must degrade gracefully when an ActiveX control does not support a particular interface, even if this means it cannot perform its designated job. At a minimum, "degrade gracefully" means that the control container continues to operate and does not fail. As you can see, the ActiveX architecture assigns many responsibilities to the control container.

Some containers provide container-specific private interfaces for additional functionality or improved performance. Controls that rely on container-specific interfaces should also work without the container-specific interfaces so that the control can function in different containers.

FAQ 34.36

What are component categories?

Component categories are a COM mechanism that allows a control to register the types of services it provides. Although the following discussion is phrased in terms of controls and control containers, it applies to any COM component and any COM caller.

Component categories are particularly valuable for control containers since it allows them to determine the capabilities of a control without having to create the control and enter into a lengthy discovery process involving querying the components for the interfaces it supports.

Every component category has a unique category identifier or CATID (which is a GUID) and a list of interfaces a control must implement before it can belong to that component category. Any control that implements all the interfaces defined for a particular component category is then able to register itself as belonging to and supporting the component category.

This permits control containers to look up the component categories for a particular control in the system registry and immediately determine whether or not it provides the services the control container requires so that the control container can adapt its behavior as necessary.

FAQ 34.37

What are events?

Asynchronous actions that are fired by ActiveX controls and handled by control containers.

ActiveX Controls (and OCXs) define "events" in addition to properties and methods. Events are asynchronous actions that are fired by the ActiveX control and are handled by the control container. An event is like a method in that it has a name, parameters, and a return value, and is implemented using Automation. Events are different from methods in that methods are defined by the control and implemented by the control, whereas events are defined by the control and implemented by the control container.

Some events are GUI events: if the user clicks on a button that is an ActiveX control, the button could fire an event notifying its control container. Other events are database events: if an ActiveX control is bound to a record in a database and the record is updated by another program, the control could fire an event notifying its control container and the container might query the database and update its display. Many other asynchronous actions can be implemented as events including timer events and network events.

Events are asynchronous. In this context, asynchronous means that the control can fire the event at any time and the firing of the event is not initiated by (or stimulated by) the control container. Asynchronous does not mean nonblocking, as it might in the context of asynchronous message queueing.

FAQ 34.38

What is DCOM?

Distributed COM—the distributed version of COM.

new

Distributed COM extends COM to support communication between callers and components that are located on different computers. DCOM does not really change much about how callers create and interact with COM objects, and therefore, DCOM lets callers remain unaware of where a COM object is running. The one noticeable difference is, of course, that network latency means that accessing a remote object is slower than accessing a local object. DCOM does introduce some differences, especially in the areas of security and the registry.

DCOM uses reference counting and pinging (pinging is a technique whereby one computer or one program sends ping messages to another computer or another program to determine whether or not it is running and to verify that there is a valid connection between the two) to handle garbage collection of objects and the servers in which the objects are running. As always, callers call `AddRef` when they obtain pointers to interfaces and call `Release` when they no longer need the pointer to the interface. When the reference count on an object hits zero, it can be garbage collected and its resources can be freed. Since reference-counting schemes are vulnerable to machine crashes and network problems, DCOM also uses a mechanism that sends pings on a computer-by-computer basis to detect nonexistent callers and dangling references so that unneeded objects can be garbage collected.

Although DCOM extends COM across machine boundaries it does not try to solve every possible distributed programming problem. Some of these other problems are handled by Microsoft Transaction Server and Microsoft Message Queueing.

Software AG has ported DCOM to Sun Solaris, 64-bit Digital Unix, and IBM's OS 390.

FAQ 34.39

How stable is DCOM's infrastructure?

new

DCOM is based on the Distributed Computing Environment (DCE) Remote Procedure Call (RPC) mechanism, thus inheriting a stable and proven cross-platform communication protocol. DCE RPC has been in use for a number of years and has proven its worth.

Although DCE RPC is complex, it brings a wealth of capabilities to DCOM. DCOM uses DCE-compatible RPCs for marshaling data and operates over a variety of protocols including TCP/IP, IPX, UDP, and NetBIOS (see FAQ 34.15 for more information regarding marshaling). Although DCOM uses DCE as its RPC mechanism by default, much of DCOM can be overridden and customized. For instance, a DCOM system might handle data marshaling on its own or it might decide not to use DCE at all and provide its own RPC mechanism.

DCOM includes a distributed security mechanism providing authentication and data encryption. DCOM includes provision for using naming services for locating class and objects on other machines, including both Domain Name System (DNS) and Active Directory with NT 5.0.

FAQ 34.40

What is COM+?

new

It is the second generation of COM.

The purpose of COM+ is to make it easier to write COM-based components and applications using any COM+-compliant programming language. COM+ attempts to make the development of COM components more like developing language-specific components. The tools you use and the COM+ runtime take care of turning those classes into COM+ components and applications. For example, a C++ development environment that is COM+ compliant can produce a COM+ class from a C++ class, and a Visual

Basic development environment that is COM+ compliant can produce a COM+ class from a Visual Basic class. COM+ is language neutral and doesn't care what syntax is used to implement a component—that's up to the tools you use.

When using a COM+-compliant tool there is no need to explicitly write a class factory—the COM+ runtime provides one. Nor is it necessary to create a type library—COM+-aware languages and tools use the COM+ runtime to generate meta data that fully describe the COM+ class. In COM+, there is no need to specify the CLSID and other GUIDs explicitly—COM+ tools generate them and may use GUIDs internally, but programmers generally use class names in the source code.

A COM+ class, unlike a COM class, defines data members, properties, methods, and events. Data members and properties collectively describe an object's state. Methods are the actions that may be performed on an object. Events are notifications that something interesting has happened. COM+, unlike COM, defines a common set of data types no matter what language is used. Your tool may need to provide some sort of mapping between its native type definitions and those used by COM+. In addition, COM+ classes are completely described by meta data, and COM+ can use this information to coerce values you supply into the types it expects.

COM+ methods allow overloading of method names within a COM+ class. Methods in COM+ can be decorated with modifiers such as static and virtual. Static methods are class methods rather than instance methods. Virtual methods are object methods that can be overridden in derived classes. COM+ also recognizes two special types of methods: constructors and destructors.

COM+ lets programmers use two types of inheritance, interface inheritance and implementation inheritance. COM+ retains the notion of interfaces, and interfaces are still the recommended way to define the public behavior of COM+ classes. In implementation inheritance, a COM+ class inherits both interface and implementation from another COM+ class. COM+ supports single implementation inheritance and does not permit multiple inheritance of COM+ classes.

COM+ understands exceptions. COM+ allows the types of exceptions that may be thrown by a method to be specified. Whenever boundaries between COM+ and non-COM+ execution environments are encountered, exceptions are translated to and from COM IErrorInfo, Win32 Structured Exception Handling, or C++ exceptions as needed.

Another key concept for COM+ is interception. Whenever the compiler sees a method being called or a property being accessed, it generates a call to the COM+ object services rather than generating a direct call to the class code. This lets COM+ intercept and manage all method invocations and property accesses between callers and components. This can be used by external services. For example, a performance-monitoring service could log the number of calls to each method and the time required to process the calls. A security service could determine whether the caller was authorized to call a particular function.

From the caller's perspective, COM+ objects are created using the same mechanism used to allocate native objects. For example, a C++ program uses syntax such as `new Fred()`. Furthermore, the object reference is managed by COM+. When the program is finished with the reference, it just sets the pointer to NULL and COM+ takes care of cleaning up the object. This means that COM-style reference counting is not needed—COM+ takes care of it.

It is important to note that all COM+ objects are COM objects. Furthermore, Microsoft will add some new features and keywords to its C++ specifically for writing COM+ classes and supporting the services described here.

Chapter 35

Transitioning to
CORBA

What is CORBA?

CORBA stands for *Common Object Request Broker Architecture*. It is a standardized way for objects to communicate with one another even if the objects exist on different computers and/or if they are written in different programming languages.

CORBA is a specification rather than an implementation—the various CORBA vendors have created software that complies with (or tries to comply with) the CORBA specification. There are numerous CORBA implementations on the market and CORBA is readily available on most platforms.

What is an ORB?

ORB stands for *Object Request Broker*. The ORB is the plumbing that enables member functions to be called on objects that may be remote and/or may be written in different programming languages.

A key feature of the ORB is transparency. The caller of a member function does not need to know whether the object is local or remote (location transparency), the programming language used to implement the object (implementation transparency), or the type of computer that the object is running on (hardware transparency). The overall effect is to provide seamless communication among objects that may be distributed on a heterogeneous network of computers.

FAQ 35.03

What is IDL?

new

IDL stands for *Interface Definition Language*. It allows developers to define the interfaces for distributed services along with a common set of data types for interacting with the distributed services. Syntactically, IDL looks a lot like C++, but unlike C++, IDL is a specification language rather than an implementation language (see FAQ 35.10).

FAQ 35.04

What is COS?

new

COS stands for *Common Object Services*. COS is also known as CORBA Services. These services are common components that handle things like creating objects, controlling access to objects, keeping track of relocated objects, managing objects and their relationships, and so on.

Typical CORBA Services include Naming, Event Management, Lifecycle Management, Transaction Management, Persistence, and Security. CORBA Services provide infrastructure utilities that improve application consistency and programmer productivity.

FAQ 35.05

What is OMA?

new

OMA stands for *Object Management Architecture*. It's the big picture architecture that includes the CORBA (the ORB itself), CORBA Services (COS), and CORBA Facilities. It ties all the pieces together.

FAQ 35.06

What is OMG?

OMG stands for *Object Management Group*. OMG is an international consortium with nearly 1000 members, including software vendors, software developers, and users. OMG is the organization that develops and standardizes the OMA.

This chapter will be deliberately loose in distinguishing between CORBA, OMA, and IDL. Technically, IDL is a proper subset of CORBA, which is a proper subset of OMA, but it is easier to speak of some IDL issues as CORBA questions than it is to use precise wording that could confuse a newcomer to the subject.

FAQ 35.07

What is the purpose of this chapter?

The purpose of this chapter is to help developers and development organizations avoid some of the common pitfalls that can occur when they first encounter distributed objects and CORBA. It is not intended to be a tutorial that provides all the details of using CORBA. Rather, this chapter skims a few of the important issues without getting into technical detail.

Entire books are devoted to using CORBA, and readers interested in the details of, for example, static versus dynamic member function invocation or the proper use of the _var and _ptr suffixes should consult them. Another good way to get general information on CORBA is to visit the Web site of the Object Management Group (OMG) by pointing the browser at http://www.omg.org.

FAQ 35.08

What is the most important message of this chapter?

CORBA is nontrivial and requires serious effort, even for experienced C++ programmers.

Because CORBA's Interface Definition Language (IDL) looks so similar to C++, many programmers assume that CORBA doesn't have a steep learning curve. This is far from the truth, and most of this chapter is dedicated to showing why there are and have to be major differences between C++ and CORBA. Most of these differences are inherent in any approach to distributed objects.

Also, it's important to understand where CORBA fits into the grand scheme of things. It offers critical middleware and useful components for developing major systems, but the technical differences between the various CORBA implementations or between CORBA and COM are usually less important than business considerations.

FAQ 35.09

What are the important concepts behind CORBA?

 The key concepts are

1. Platform and language independence

2. Location transparency

3. An OO approach that includes interface inheritance within IDL

4. Interoperability between ORBs

5. A consensus-based industry standards process

CORBA uses the proxy design pattern to achieve platform and language independence. A proxy is a stand-in, or surrogate, for a "real" object and provides a client-side reference for accessing a server object that could be located anywhere. By decoupling the software architecture from the runtime environment, the software becomes more flexible and decisions such as which objects reside where can be controlled by a network administrator armed with time sensitive information that was not available to the software architects when they were designing the system.

IDL is a language for defining the interfaces for distributed objects, where the interfaces are similar to C++ abstract base classes with only pure virtual member functions. The IDL compiler converts the interface specification into the target language, which can be C, C++, Java, and so on. CORBA IDL supports interface inheritance, but since it is not an implementation programming language, it does not support inheritance of implementation (however implementation inheritance is normally used when implementing an IDL interface in an OO programming language such as C++).

ORBs from different vendors can communicate seamlessly because of the Internet Inter-ORB Protocol (IIOP), which runs over TCP/IP. The specification also supports DCE as the communications layer, but most CORBA users choose TCP/IP.

FAQ 35.10

Isn't OMG IDL pretty much the same as C++?

No.

IDL does have a C++-like syntax, and it includes these familiar features:

1. Basic data types such as short, long, float, char and others

2. Modules, which are roughly equivalent to namespaces

3. Exceptions (but see FAQ 35.13)

4. Strings, arrays, enumerations, typedefs, and so on

Despite these surface similarities, OMG IDL is not a programming language and it should not be compared as such with C++. OMG IDL is a platform-neutral specification language. OMG IDL can handle only interface issues—parameter types, return types, member function names. It cannot handle implementation issues such as member data, local variables, implementation code, and so on.

Furthermore, it is important to note that CORBA data types do not necessarily correspond to the similarly named C++ data types. For example, a long in IDL may or may not be equivalent to the C++ type long. A long in IDL corresponds to the C++ type CORBA::Long. For these reasons, C++ programmers who are implementing CORBA classes should be careful to use the CORBA data types rather than the C++ data types when necessary.

As another paradigm shift, C++ programmers who are new to CORBA tend to think of the CORBA data types (such as CORBA::Long) as aberrations that should be avoided. In reality the opposite is true: in a sense the CORBA data types are more portable than the C++ data types. For example, sizeof(CORBA::Long) is guaranteed to be 4 bytes on all hardware platforms, whereas sizeof(long) might not be exactly 4 bytes.

In addition, CORBA is responsible for transmitting data values between various machines as necessary and dealing with any data transformation issues. For example, different machines use different byte orderings for different data types (little-endian vs. big-endian), and different programming languages may represent data types differently than C/C++ does. CORBA manages all this transparently—if the communicating objects are on different machines it uses a process called marshaling to convert the source machine's binary data to the IIOP (the standard usually allows others) representation, and a reverse process called demarshaling to convert the IIOP representation at the destination machine back into the appropriate binary data format. One performance trick used by some ORBs is recognizing situations where these processes can be safely eliminated (such as when everything is on the same hardware and the networking can be avoided). Other performance tricks, such as receiver-makes-right semantics, avoid unnecessary message translations between machines using the same byte order and are part of the specification.

Finally, C++ programmers need to be aware that IDL does not support overloading, overriding, or pointers. So even though IDL looks a lot like C++, there are significant differences.

FAQ 35.11

Is the lifecycle of a CORBA object the same as the life cycle of a C++ object?

No, and this requires some mental adjustments.

C++ programmers are accustomed to objects that are known to exist because they were instantiated or known to be gone because they went out of scope or were programmatically destroyed. Reference counting (see FAQ 31.09) confuses the argument a little, but the point remains that the programmer feels that the object life cycle is under control.

But in the CORBA world, objects, particularly server objects, have much more of a life of their own. They may be brought to life once and never die because there is no scope to exit, or they may have a brief existence and commit suicide. It is also important to distinguish between a CORBA object and a servant for a CORBA object. A servant is a C++ object that provides the body of and implementation for one or more CORBA objects, and many C++ programmers stumble over this distinction. A CORBA object may have one or more servants, and a servant may represent (the proper technical term is *incarnate*) several CORBA objects during its lifetime. These are separate but related entities.

Emotionally, the experience for most developers is similar to the one they went through when they made the shift from procedural programming to OO. For example, programmers coming to OO (say, programming in C++) from procedural programming (say, programming in C) usually feel that they have "lost control." The top-down command-and-control approach was part of their old programming paradigm, and an adjustment is needed. Eventually this uncomfortable feeling disappears. The shift from a traditional monolithic program to a distributed program is similar.

FAQ 35.12

Is the C++ code that interacts with the CORBA implementation portable to a different CORBA vendor?

No, but the situation has improved because of the Portable Object Adapter.

Unfortunately, the C++ code that interacts with a particular CORBA vendor's ORB is not 100% portable to other CORBA vendors. In the early days, it could be said that there was no such thing as a CORBA programmer, there was only an Orbix programmer or a VisiBroker programmer. Many of the differences between CORBA implementations could be traced to the imprecise specification of the *Basic Object Adapter* (BOA). In mid-1997, the OMG adopted a replacement for the BOA called the *Portable Object Adapter* (POA). The POA specification is voluminous as well as precise, and it introduces some unifying concepts for the CORBA paradigm. The reader is cautioned that many excellent CORBA books were written prior to POA and that BOA has been deprecated.

The net result of the POA is that conforming vendors do not have the same latitude as before and programs are much more portable than in earlier days.

FAQ 35.13

How do CORBA exceptions compare to C++ exceptions?

The same but different.

At first glance, it appears that C++ exceptions and CORBA/IDL exceptions are pretty much the same. For example the semantics of instantiating, throwing, and catching exceptions are the same as with C++. But there are also differences, some minor and some major.

As a minor difference, C++ implementations of CORBA member functions need to include `CORBA::SystemException` in the exception specification (either that or not have an exception specification; see FAQ 9.04). Another minor difference is that each CORBA exception must be mapped to a C++ class that inherits from the abstract base class `CORBA::UserException`.

A major difference is that normal C++ exceptions have both state and behavior but CORBA/IDL exceptions cannot have behavior. This is because exceptions may get transmitted to different computers (e.g., when the thrower and the catcher are on different computers), and it's easier for the implementation to copy pure data objects than to copy objects that have behavior.

IDL does not support inheritance in exception declarations, which can get quite nasty when C++ exceptions are mapped to CORBA exceptions and then thrown around the ORB. Finally, memory management is tough enough with C++ exceptions, but the issues become substantially more complex in a distributed object environment.

So don't be lulled into a false sense of security because the words sound the same. Exceptions in CORBA require a great deal of knowledge and experience that the beginner does not have and does not gain easily, no matter how familiar they are with C++ exceptions.

FAQ 35.14

Which CORBA implementation is best? Is CORBA better than COM?

The fact that these questions are being asked implies that they do not have a clear answer.

If there were one approach to distributed objects that was clearly superior in all respects, then the market would have gravitated to that solution and people wouldn't be asking, "Which is better?" But that hasn't happened, and there is probably a time and place for each alternative to shine. Many articles have been written about the technical differences between CORBA and COM, and each CORBA implementation has its voluble critics and fans. And there are intelligent technical people on both sides of these arguments.

So the only proper answer to the question is to take an open-minded approach to ORB selection, as opposed to the one-size-fits-all mentality favored by bigots. Also, it is important to recognize that, in many cases, the technical differences can be relatively small and that nontechnical issues such as pricing, vendor support, or training may dominate the decision process.

Chapter 36

C Language Considerations

What are the main issues when mixing C and C++ code in the same application?

The main issues are

- The C++ compiler must be used to compile main(). This allows the C++ compiler to deal with static initialization and other magical things that main() has to do.

- The C++ compiler must be used to direct the linking process. This allows the C++ compilers to deal with templates and also to link in the C++ libraries.

- The C++ and C compilers probably need to come from the same vendor and have compatible versions. This allows them to use compatible calling conventions in the binary code they generate, as well as compatible naming strategies.

- The interface between the two languages should be kept reasonably small. For example, it is unwise to enable all C++ routines in the entire application to be callable from C, although the reverse is possible: it is not that hard to make C routines callable by C++.

- Read the rest of this chapter for more details.

FAQ 36.02

How can C++ code call C code?

The C++ compiler must know that the function has C linkage.

If the C code that is being called is part of the standard C library, such as `printf()`, simply `#include` the correct C header file and call the function.

If the C code that is being called is not part of the standard C library, the C++ compiler needs to know that the function is a C function. To do this, include an `extern "C"` block in the C++ code, and declare the C function inside the block:

```
extern "C" {
  void myCfunction(int x, int y);
  void yourCfunction(float z);
}
```

An entire C header file can be included within an `extern "C"` block:

```
extern "C" {
  #include "my-C-header.h"
  #include "your-C-header.h"
}
```

If a C header file needs to be included in a lot of C++ locations, the `extern "C"` part can be moved into the header file, provided only the C++ compiler sees it. The simplest way to do this is to create a new C++ header file that includes the C header file. For example, if "`Fred.h`" is a C header file, "`Fred.hpp`" can be created as a C++ header file:

```
// Fred.hpp
extern "C" {
  #include "Fred.h"   ◄──────── Include the C header file
}
```

The other approach is to modify the C header file directly, which obviously can only be done if the team has control over the C header file. The `extern "C"` part is wrapped in an `#ifdef` to make sure these lines are seen only by C++ compilers, not by C compilers. The idea is simple: insert the following lines near the top of the C header file.

```
#ifdef __cplusplus
  extern "C" {
#endif
```

Then insert the following near the bottom of the C header file.

```
#ifdef __cplusplus
 }
#endif
```

This works because the C++ compiler automatically #defines the preprocessor symbol __cplusplus.

─── **FAQ 36.03**

How can C code call C++ code?

The C++ compiler must be told to compile the C++ function using C-compatible calling conventions (also known as *C linkage*). This is done using the same extern "C" construct as detailed in the previous FAQ, only this time the extern "C" goes around the declaration of the C++ function rather than the declaration of the C function. The C++ function is then defined just like any other C++ function:

```
// This is C++ code
extern "C" {
  void sample(int i, char c, float x) throw();
}

void sample(int i, char c, float x) throw()
{
  ◄──────── The C++ code that defines the function goes here
}
```

The extern "C" declaration causes the C++ compiler to use C calling conventions and name mangling. For example, the C++ compiler might precede the name with a single underscore rather than the usual C++ name-mangling scheme.

The C code then declares the function using the usual C prototype:

```
/* This is C code */
void sample(int i, char c, float x);

void myCfunction()
{
  // ...
  sample(42, 'a', 3.14);
  // ...
}
```

There can be overloaded C++ functions with the same name as the function that was exported to the C code, but only one of these overloads can be declared as extern "C". Also, the C code cannot access more than one of these since C doesn't support name overloading. Member functions cannot be exported to C code using the extern "C" syntax.

FAQ 36.04

Why is the linker giving errors for C functions called from C++ functions and vice versa?

main() should be compiled with the C++ compiler, and the C++ compiler should direct the linking process.

The C++ compiler should be used to compile main() because it normally embeds C++-specific operations inside the compiled code (for example, to deal with static initialization; see FAQ 2.10). The C++ compiler should direct the linking process since it needs to deal with things such as C++ libraries, static initialization, and templates.

FAQ 36.05

How can an object of a C++ class be passed to or from a C function?

With a layer of glue code.

The example that follows is a bilingual header file, readable by both a straight C compiler and a C++ compiler. Bilingual header files often use the preprocessor symbol __cplusplus, which is automatically #defined by C++ compilers but left undefined by C compilers.

```
/****** Bilingual C/C++ header file: Fred.h ******/
#ifdef __cplusplus
  class Fred {
  public:
    Fred() throw();
    void wilma(int i) throw();
  protected:
    int i_;
  };
```

```
  inline Fred::Fred() throw() : i_(0) { }
  inline void Fred::wilma(int i) throw() { i_ = i; }
#else
  struct Fred {
    int i_;
  };
  typedef  struct Fred  Fred;
#endif

#ifdef __cplusplus
  extern "C" {
#endif

extern void cppCallingC(Fred* p);
extern void cCallingCpp(Fred* p, int param);

#ifdef __cplusplus
  }
#endif
```

The function cCallingCpp() might be defined in a C++ file, such as
c++-code.cpp.

```
// This is C++ code
#include "Fred.h"

void cCallingCpp(Fred* p, int param) throw()
{ p->wilma(param); }
```

The function cppCallingC() might be defined in a C file, such as c-code.c.

```
/* This is C code */
#include "Fred.h"

void cppCallingC(Fred* p)
{ cCallingCpp(p, 3); }
```

A Fred might be passed to the C code by main() (recall that main() must be compiled by the C++ compiler).

```
// This is C++ code
#include "Fred.h"

int main()
{
  Fred x;
```

```
        cppCallingC(&x);
    }
```

Note that C code should not cast pointers that refer to C++ objects because doing so can introduce errors, especially in cases where the pointer is returned to C++. For example, most compilers adjust the pointer during certain pointer casts involving multiple and/or virtual inheritance; the C compiler doesn't know how to do these adjustments.

The example assumes that the C compiler supports ANSI-C function prototypes. Use `#ifdef __STDC__` for those rare legacy situations that require selecting code that supports only the outdated K&R C style.

FAQ 36.06

Can a C function directly access data in an object of a C++ class?

Sometimes.

First read the previous FAQ on passing C++ objects to and from C functions. A C++ object's data can be safely accessed from a C function if all of the following are true.

- The C++ class has no virtual base classes anywhere in the inheritance graph.

- The C++ class has no virtual functions (including inherited virtual functions).

- The C++ class has all its data in the same access level section (`private:`, `protected:`, or `public:`).

- The C++ class has no fully contained member objects that have either virtual functions or virtual base classes.

If the C++ class or its member object have any base classes, accessing the data will be technically nonportable, because the language does not mandate a specific class layout in the presence of inheritance. However, at least with nonvirtual inheritance, all C++ compilers do it the same way—the base class subobject appears first (in left-to-right order in the event of multiple inheritance), and member objects follow.

If the class has any virtual base classes, it is more complicated and even less portable.

By far the safer and easier way is to use an access function from C. This costs a function call to access the datum (that is, these calls from C cannot be inlined), but unless the application is CPU bound (see FAQ 33.02), it is probably best to make the application code safe and portable.

FAQ 36.07

Can C++ I/O (`<iostream>`) be mixed with C I/O (`<stdio.h>`)?

Yes, but be careful.

`<iostream>` and `<stdio.h>` can be used in the same program. The easiest way to mix them is to make sure that no single file is manipulated using both `<iostream>` routines and `<stdio.h>` routines.

If any given file needs to be manipulated by both `<iostream>` routines and `<stdio.h>` routines, special considerations must be taken into account. Make sure that `ios::sync_stdio(false)` has not been called. If it has then call `ios::sync_with_stdio()` as shown.

```
#include <iostream>
#include <cstdio>
using namespace std;

int main()
{
  ios::sync_with_stdio();  ←———— No I/O should occur before this line
  // ...
}
```

Note that this synchronization can degrade I/O performance, so it should be used only if `<iostream>` routines and `<stdio.h>` routines are manipulating the same file. For example, synchronization is needed if the program reads from both `cin` and `stdin`, or if it writes to both `cout` and `stdout`. But if `<iostream>` routines and `<stdio.h>` routines are not manipulating the same file, synchronization is unnecessary and should not be used.

FAQ 36.08

Which is safer: `<iostream>` or `<stdio.h>`?

`<iostream>` is safer than `<stdio.h>` due to improved type safety and less redundancy.

The `<stdio.h>` functions `scanf()` and `printf()` are interpreters of a tiny language, made up mainly of "`%`" fields (format specifiers). These functions select the correct I/O primitive at runtime by assuming that the format specifier and the actual argument are compatible; if they aren't compatible, garbage is printed or the program crashes. Thus, the programmer is required to provide duplicate information in the format specifier and the actual argument.

The `<iostream>` routines are different. Users provide only the object to be read or written; the compiler selects the correct I/O primitive at compile time via the rules of function overloading. Therefore, `<iostream>` is type safe since the selected primitive is always compatible with the actual argument.

FAQ 36.09

Which is more extensible: `<iostream>` or `<stdio.h>`?

`<iostream>` is more extensible than `<stdio.h>` since `<iostream>` allows I/O with user-defined types as well as built-in types.

The `<stdio.h>` functions `scanf()` and `printf()` work with a predefined set of types. In contrast, `<iostream>` allows new, user-defined data types to be written and read using the same syntax used for built-in types (that is, using `<<` and `>>`). This extensibility is analogous to adding new "`%`" fields to the `switch` statement that is used within the implementation of `scanf()` and `printf()`.

C++ allows user-defined types (`class` types) to look and act like built-in types.

FAQ 36.10

Which is more flexible: `<iostream>` or `<stdio.h>`?

`<iostream>` is more flexible than `<stdio.h>` since `<iostream>` separates the code that formats an object from the code that performs I/O of the character stream produced or consumed by formatting. This separation allows replacement of the underlying I/O mechanisms without the need to rewrite the formatting code.

For example, `<iostream>` uses real classes, hence users can create derived classes. User-defined types can thus look and act like streams but don't necessarily have to use the same underlying I/O mechanisms. The formatting code written for both user-defined and built-in types works correctly with these new classes.

FAQ 36.11

Why does it seem that C++ programming feels farther away from the machine than C?

Because it is.

Because C++ is an object-oriented programming language, it is designed to allow the creation and manipulation of objects from the problem domain. Thus, C++ allows programmers to operate at a higher level of abstraction: there is effectively a greater distance between the software and the machine. This higher level of abstraction allows programmers to develop software in the language of the problem domain rather than in the language of the computer. It is considered a feature, not a bug.

FAQ 36.12

Why does C++ do more things behind your back than C does?

Because the goal of programming in C++ is different than the goal of programming in C.

One of C's great strengths is that it has no hidden mechanism. What you see is what you get. You can read a C program and see every clock cycle.

This is not the case in C++. As an OO programming language, C++ has different goals than C. For instance, C++ calls constructors and destructors to initialize objects. Overloaded operators are another case in point—they provide a level of abstraction and economy of expression that lowers maintenance costs without destroying runtime performance. Longtime C programmers are often ambivalent about these features, but they soon realize their benefits.

Naturally, bad code can be written in any language. C++ doesn't guarantee any particular level of quality, reusability, abstraction, or any other measure of goodness.

C++ enables reasonable developers to write superior software. It doesn't make it impossible for bad programmers to write bad programs.

Chapter 37

Private and Protected
Inheritance

What are private inheritance and protected inheritance?

Has-a, not is-a. From the user's perspective, private and protected inheritance are semantically similar to composition, but they are very different from normal public inheritance. Thus private and protected inheritance are a lot more like "has-a" than "is-a" (more precisely, than "is-substitutable-for"). Here are the ways they are like "has-a".

Like normal composition, private and protected inheritance cause an inner object to be contained inside the outer object. With normal composition, this inner object is called a *member object*. The syntax for doing this with private inheritance is different than the syntax for normal composition, but the idea is the same. With private and protected inheritance, the inner object is called the *base class subobject*. The important thing to note is that the outer object contains the inner object in both cases.

Like normal composition, private and protected inheritance prevent normal users from directly accessing the inner object. With normal composition, this is normally done by declaring the member object in the `private:` or `protected:` part of the outer object. The syntax for doing this with private inheritance is different than the syntax for normal composition, but the idea is the same. With private and protected inheritance, this encapsulation is done automagically: normal users are not allowed to convert a derived pointer to its private or protected base class pointer (this is different than the normal is-a conversion of public inheritance; see FAQ 2.24).

Like normal composition, private and protected inheritance allow the outer object to select specific features of the inner object that users can access, and users are prevented from accessing any other features than the ones explicitly allowed by the outer object. With normal composition, the outer object grants normal users access to specific features of the inner object by *call-through member functions.* A call-through member function is often a one-line function that simply calls the corresponding member function on the inner object. The syntax for doing this with private inheritance is different than that for normal composition, but the idea is the same. With private and protected inheritance, there are two options: either the derived class defines a call-through member function that calls the corresponding member function of the private or protected base class subobject, or the `using` syntax can be used to make a base class member function `public:` (see FAQ 37.06).

FAQ 37.02

What is the difference between private inheritance and protected inheritance?

In private inheritance, the relationship with the base class is a `private` decision; only members and friends of the privately derived class can exploit the relationship with the private base class. In protected inheritance, the relationship with the base class is a `protected` decision, so members and friends of the protected derived class and members and friends of classes derived from the protected derived class can exploit the protected inheritance relationship, but normal users cannot.

Protected inheritance is less restrictive than private inheritance and therefore introduces more coupling between the derived class and the base class. With protected inheritance, if the relationship between the protected base class and the derived class is changed (or if the protected operations of the protected base class change), the effects may reach beyond the protected derived class and its friends to classes derived from the protected derived class, classes derived from those derived classes, and so on.

This is a for-better-for-worse situation; derived classes have more coupling, but they also have the ability to exploit the relationship between the derived class and the base class.

FAQ 37.03

What is the syntax and semantics for private and protected inheritance?

The following example shows a simple has-a relationship between a car object and its engine object; it uses normal composition, where the `Engine` member object appears in the `private:` section of the `Car` class.

```
class Engine {
public:
  void publ() throw();
protected:
  void prot() throw();
};

class CarA {
public:
  // ...
private:
  Engine e_;
};
```

Obviously composition does not create an is-a relationship: a `CarA` is *not* a kind-of an `Engine`. In particular, users cannot legally convert a `CarA*` to an `Engine*`. Also note that a `CarA` object contains exactly one `Engine` object (though it could be made to contain more than one).

Private inheritance accomplishes essentially the same thing. In the following example, `CarB` is said to *privately inherit* from `Engine` (if the symbols : `private Engine` are changed to : `protected Engine`, `CarB` is said to *protectedly inherit* from `Engine`).

```
class CarB : private Engine {
public:
  // ...
};
```

Just as with normal composition, there is no is-a relationship: a `CarB` is *not* a kind-of `Engine`. In particular, normal (nonfriend) users cannot legally convert a `CarB*` to an `Engine*`. Also like normal composition, a `CarB` object contains exactly one `Engine` object (however, unlike normal composition, private and protected inheritance does not allow a second `Engine` subobject to appear as a second private and/or protected base class).

The main difference between composition and private/protected inheritance is access to the protected members of `Engine`. With private/protected inheritance, members and friends of `CarB` can access the `protected:` members of `Engine` (in this case, they can access both `Engine::publ()` *and* `Engine::prot()`). However, with normal composition, members and friends of `CarA` can only access `Engine::publ()`; they are forbidden to access `Engine::prot()`. The usual reason people use private/protected inheritance is for this additional access authority; but note that the extra authority carries with it extra responsibility.

Another difference between composition and private/protected inheritance is the ability to convert a `CarB*` to an `Engine*`. With private/protected inheritance, members and friends of `CarB` can convert a `CarB*` to an `Engine*`. With normal composition this is not possible: no one can legally convert a `CarA*` to an `Engine*`.

There are several caveats when using private/protected inheritance. Simple composition (has-a) is needed if it is necessary to contain several member objects of the same class; private or protected inheritance can introduce unnecessary multiple inheritance.

FAQ 37.04

When should normal has-a be used, rather than private or protected inheritance?

Use normal has-a when you can; use private or protected inheritance when you have to.

Normal composition (has-a) is preferred because it leads to fewer dependencies between classes. Private and protected inheritance are more expensive to maintain because they increase the number of classes that have access to the protected parts of other classes—they increase coupling.

Private or protected inheritance is often used when the goal is has-a but the interface of the contained class is insufficient. In this case, an alternative to private or protected inheritance is improving the public interface of the base class so that simple composition can be used. If you cannot change the interface of the base class (for example, because the source code is not available), you can create one derived class (often using public inheritance) that has an improved interface. This derived class with its improved interface is then used via simple composition (has-a).

FAQ 37.05

What are the access rules for public, protected, and private inheritance?

In the following example, class B has a `public:` member, a `protected:` member, and a `private:` member.

```
class B {
public:
  void publ() throw();
protected:
  void prot() throw();
private:
  void priv() throw();
};
```

Class `PrivD` privately inherits from B, class `ProtD` protectedly inherits from B, and `PublD` publicly inherits from B.

```
class PrivD : private   B { };
class ProtD : protected B { };
class PublD : public    B { };
```

With private inheritance, the public and protected parts of B become private in `PrivD`. This means that `PrivD` can access these member functions, but user code and classes derived from `PrivD` cannot access them.

With protected inheritance, the public and protected parts of B become protected in `ProtD`. This means that members and friends of `ProtD` can access these member functions, as can classes derived from `ProtD`, but user code cannot access them.

With public inheritance, the public parts of B become public on `PublD`, and the protected parts of B remain protected in `PublD`.

In all three cases, the private parts of B are inaccessible to the derived classes (`PrivD`, `ProtD`, and `PublD`) as well as to user code.

FAQ 37.06

In a private or protected derived class, how can a member function that was public in the base class be made public in the derived class?

The name (not the entire signature) of the member function should be declared in the public interface of the derived class preceded by the keyword using. For example, to make the member function B::f(int,char,float) public in PrivD, say this:

```
class B {
public:
   int f(int, char, float) throw();
protected:
   int g(double, char) throw();
};

class PrivD : private B {
public:
   using B::f; ◄——— Note: Omit the parameter declarations
};
```

The syntax for doing this with protected inheritance is identical.

There are two limitations to this technique: overloaded names can't be distinguished, and a base member cannot be made public if it was protected in the base class (that is, this technique cannot be used to make Base::g(double,char) public in the derived class). When necessary, both these limitations can be avoided by defining a call-through member function in the privately/protectedly derived class, as shown in the following example.

```
class PrivD2 : private B {
public:
   int g(double d, char c) throw();
};

inline int PrivD2::g(double d, char c) throw()
{ return B::g(d, c); }
```

FAQ 37.07

Should a pointer be cast from a private or protected derived class to its base class?

No.

Within a member function or friend function of a private or protected derived class, the relationship to the base class is known and the upward pointer or reference conversion takes place automatically without a cast.

In normal user code, the relationship to a private or protected base class is inaccessible and the conversion is illegal. Users should not perform a cast because private or protected inheritance is a nonpublic decision of the derived class. The cast will subtly break at some future date if/when the private or protected derived class chooses to change or remove the private/protected inheritance relationship.

The conclusion is that only a class and its friends have the right to convert a pointer to the class's nonpublic base class. The member functions and friend functions of the privately/protectedly derived class don't need a cast because the relationship with the base class is directly accessible to them.

Here's an even simpler conclusion—don't use pointer casts unless there is an overriding reason to do so!

Chapter 38

Pointers to Member Functions

What is the type of a pointer to a nonstatic member function?

The most important thing to understand is that the type is different from that of a pointer to a C-style (non-member) function. Simply understanding that they are completely different and have incompatible types will prevent the most common and dangerous errors with pointers to member functions.

A pointer to the nonstatic member function with signature `void Fred::f(int)` has type `void(Fred::*)(int)`. In particular, the type of the pointer to a nonstatic member function includes the class of the member function because nonstatic member functions have an implicit parameter that points to the object (the `this` pointer).
  Here's an example.

```
#include <iostream>
using namespace std;

class Fred {
public:
  void f(int i) throw();
  void g(int i) throw();
```

```
    void h(int i) throw();
};

void Fred::f(int i) throw()
    { cout << "Fred::f(int); i=" << i << '\n'; }
void Fred::g(int i) throw()
    { cout << "Fred::g(int); i=" << i << '\n'; }
void Fred::h(int i) throw()
    { cout << "Fred::h(int); i=" << i << '\n'; }

typedef void(Fred::*FredMemberPtr)(int);
```

Note the use of the `typedef`. Because of the rather obscure syntax of pointers to non-static member functions, it is highly recommended that a `typedef` be used to represent the pointer type.

In the following example, a pointer `p` is created to point to `Fred::g`. This pointer is then used to call the member function.

```
void sample(Fred& x, FredMemberPtr p) throw()
{ (x.*p)(42); }  ←——— If p is &Fred::g, this is the same as x.g(42)

int main()
{
   FredMemberPtr p = &Fred::g;
   Fred x;
   sample(x, p);
}
```

The output of this program is as follows.

```
Fred::g(int); i=42
```

A pointer to a nonstatic member function of class `Fred` has a totally different type from a pointer to a function. For example, the pointer type `void(Fred::*)(int)` is totally different from the pointer type `void(*)(int)`. Do *not* use a cast to try to convert between the two types. You have been warned.

A pointer to a static member function of class `Fred` has the same type as a pointer to a C-like function. In other words, a C-like function or static member function can be converted to the same pointer to function type, such as `void(*)(int)`. But a pointer to a nonstatic member function cannot be converted to a normal pointer to a function type.

FAQ 38.02

Can pointers to nonstatic member functions be passed to signal handlers, X event call-back handlers, and so on, that expect C-like function pointers?

A pointer to a nonstatic member function cannot be passed into a routine that is expecting a pointer to a C-like function, since a nonstatic member function is meaningless without there being an object to which the nonstatic member function can be applied.

To simulate this behavior, pass a pointer to a C-like function, and have that function obtain the object pointer through some other technique (such as storing it in a global). The C-like function would then call the desired nonstatic member function. For example, suppose x.f(int) were to be called on interrupt, where f(int) is a nonstatic member function of the class of object x. The following would accomplish the call (note that a static member function has the same type as a C-like function).

```cpp
#include <iostream>
#include <signal.h>
using namespace std;

class Fred {
public:
  void f(int n) throw();
  static void staticMethod(int n) throw();
  static void registerHandlerObject(Fred* p) throw();
private:
  static Fred* signalHandlerObject_;      //the handler object
};

void Fred::f(int n)
  { cout << "Fred::f()\n"; }
void Fred::registerHandlerObject(Fred* p)
  { signalHandlerObject_ = p; }
void Fred::staticMethod(int n)
  {
    Fred* p = Fred::signalHandlerObject_;
    p->f(n);
  }
Fred* Fred::signalHandlerObject_ = NULL;

int main()
{
```

```
    //signal(SIGINT, Fred::f);  ◄──────────── ERROR: Cannot do this
    Fred x;
    Fred::registerHandlerObject(&x);
    signal(SIGINT, Fred::staticMethod); ◄──── Good
}
```

FAQ 38.03

What is one of the most common errors when using pointers to member functions?

Trying to pass the address of a nonstatic member function into a function that is expecting a pointer to function, and sometimes the inverse of this scenario.

Nonstatic member functions have an implicit parameter that points to the object—the pointer called this inside the member function. Nonstatic member functions can be thought of as having a different calling convention from that of normal C functions, so the types of their pointers are different and incompatible—pointer to nonstatic member function versus pointer to function.

C++ introduces a new type of pointer, called a pointer to nonstatic member, which can be invoked only by providing an object. Do not attempt to cast a pointer that points to a nonstatic member function into a pointer to function or vice versa; the result is undefined and probably disastrous. For example, a pointer to nonstatic member function probably doesn't contain the machine address of the appropriate function. As noted in the last example, if a regular C function pointer is needed, use either a static member function or a nonmember function.

FAQ 38.04

How is an array of pointers to nonstatic member functions declared?

Use a typedef.

Consider the following class example.

```
#include <iostream>
using namespace std;
```

```
class Fred {
public:
  void f(int i);
  void g(int i);
  void h(int i);
};

void Fred::f(int i)
  { cout << "Fred::f(int); i=" << i << '\n'; }
void Fred::g(int i)
  { cout << "Fred::g(int); i=" << i << '\n'; }
void Fred::h(int i)
  { cout << "Fred::h(int); i=" << i << '\n'; }

typedef void (Fred::*FredMemberPtr)(int);
```

Since `FredMemberPtr` is a `typedef`, it can be used like most other data types. In particular, an array of `FredMemberPtr` can be created using the following syntax.

```
FredMemberPtr array[3] = { &Fred::f, &Fred::g, &Fred::h };
```

To call one of the nonstatic member functions, supply a `Fred` object, and use the .* operator.

```
int main()
{
  Fred x;
  for (int i = 0; i < 3; ++i) {
    FredMemberPtr p = array[i];
    (x.*p)(42 + i);
  }
}
```

The output of this program is as follows.

```
Fred::f(int); i=42
Fred::g(int); i=43
Fred::h(int); i=44
```

Chapter 39

The Transition to
OO and C++

FAQ 39.01

Who should read this chapter?

People who are learning OO and C++, but also experienced developers who have to get others through the paradigm shift.

This chapter is partially written for people who are learning OO and C++, but it is also aimed at those who already have the technical knowledge, but are trying to guide others through the cycle. It is based on our experience training and mentoring thousands of developers in different environments. Our insights are as much psychological as they are technical, because the goal is to set realistic expectations and then help as many people as possible succeed.

FAQ 39.02

What are the key messages of this chapter?

The key messages are

1. Know the stages of development, and set appropriate goals.

2. Books are necessary but not sufficient.

3. Courses might help but are not sufficient.

4. Experience on significant projects led by competent mentors is very important.

5. Small projects build the wrong skills and attitudes for success on large projects.

6. C expertise can hurt more than it helps.

FAQ 39.03

How many stages of technical expertise are there in the transition?

 There are at least four different stages of technical expertise.

1. The first objective is to be able to play a useful role on a project, with technical assistance from others. Sometimes referred to as "grunt programming" or "blue-collar programming," there is a need for solid citizens who can take work direction and do most simple tasks on their own.

2. The next step corresponds to the "senior developer" role, and the main difference from level 1 is the ability to work without detailed technical direction on all but the most difficult problems. People at this level have usually worked on at least three significant C++ projects and have made a fair number of mistakes. Most developers attain this level of competence eventually.

3. At the next level, the developer is thought of as the "resident guru" or technical expert in one or more aspects of C++ development. These are the people who come up with the bright ideas and technical leadership for their organization, and are usually spread across several projects. Their salaries can be quite high, and they usually have no interest in management career paths. The good ones have a large amount of scar tissue and arrow wounds in their back. Very few programmers have the intelligence and dedication necessary to reach this level of expertise.

4. At the final level, the person is the "industry thought leader," and very few organizations can afford one of these exotic specialists. These are the true experts who are well known in their peer group. It is unrealistic for most developers to aim for this level of expertise, and those who achieve it spend almost every waking hour maintaining their craft. People of this caliber are usually brought in as consultants rather than hired as full-time employees.

Why bother defining levels of expertise?

Because it is important to set realistic targets for the transition plan.

In the early years of OO and C++, many organizations decided that they needed to develop expertise quickly, and many poor souls were "chosen" to become resident experts. They were given a book to read, subjected to an intensive two- or three-week training course and a few months of experience with a trivial project. These battlefield promotions did not work very well, and the organizations have suffered from having created anointed "experts" out of people who are actually at level 1 in their development. These organizations have a hard time developing legitimate skills at any level because their "top" people are clueless.

So the first task is to get the trainee to level 1 and to recognize that not everyone will make even this transition. The hard part is recognizing that everyone, no matter how experienced or talented, has to start off at the bottom rung. OO is radically different from functional decomposition and requires a "paradigm shift" that can be quite difficult for strong-willed people. C++, if used properly, is quite different than traditional C, even though it can be used as "a better C" (this latter approach does not deliver the promises of OO, however). Finally, object modeling is quite different than data modeling. People who were strong in the older technologies have significant emotional and intellectual hurdles to leap, and they should not be expected to immediately reach their previous level of expertise in the new technologies.

In our opinion, organizations should focus on getting people to level 1 through training, reading, and mentoring. With experience and additional mentoring, many of the level 1 people can eventually attain level 2. Anything beyond that is beyond the scope of this book and probably depends more on talent and attitude than on organizational process.

Can OO/C++ be learned from a book?

A good book can teach syntax and semantics, and a great book can open your eyes, but that isn't good enough.

We think the book you are reading is a good book, maybe even better than that. But a book can't reinforce its messages like practice does, and a book can't answer questions like a good mentor can. It has been our experience that incremental technology, such as going from FORTRAN to C, can be picked up by good people from reading a book and experimenting a bit. But a paradigm shift, such as transitioning to OO and C++, doesn't lend itself to this traditional approach.

So, learn by reading, but become proficient by doing, particularly under the tutelage of a pro. A book alone cannot get you even to level 1.

FAQ 39.06

Can OO/C++ be learned from a course?

No. Courses are like books, helpful only if the objective is very limited.

We have found that courses are a great way to learn specific skills, such as how to use a tool. But they can't convey the depth of knowledge that is needed for learning something as deep as OO and C++ in a reasonable time frame. Most of the instructors aren't up to the task technically (they are educators, not developers, and lack the experience and scar tissue that is needed). Even if the instructors are great (we think we've been pretty good instructors ourselves) and the material is wonderful (but when was the last time a great developer knew how to develop great pedagogical material?), the key is still to do something real.

One of our classroom experiences was predictable: we preached the gospel about OO design and the students nodded their heads approvingly. But when we gave them their first miniproject, they did things the way they always had. It takes time and repeated effort to break old habit patterns.

In our opinion, it is possible to get a talented person to level 1 with a combination of good courses and good books, but it takes both ingredients.

FAQ 39.07

What is the key to learning OO/C++?

Serve an apprenticeship on a real project with a top professional.

A good mentor has level 3 to level 4 technical skills, good one-on-one communications skills, and a practical orientation backed by sound judgment. Mentoring is difficult because it requires patiently responding to off-beat questions while still getting work accomplished. The apprentice has the opportunity to ask questions in a real-world environment, and learning when "rules" should be broken in the name of practicality.

Another part of the learning process is listening to "war stories" and tales of failure that cannot be discussed formally.

Real projects are important because classroom exercises and books fit the subject matter into neat theoretical compartments. A live project is essential to see how theory and practice coincide and overlap and to develop the background for making practical trade-offs.

Good mentors are worth whatever they charge, but watch out for the bad ones. Avoid technology bigots who know the answers before they've heard the question: a good example would be people who automatically hate anything from Microsoft (or, equally bad, automatically love anything from Microsoft). Also, there are many people who talk a good game but have never finished anything of significance. In particular, there are people who will put their version of OO theory and "purity" ahead of project success. Look for practical mentors who have built something and lived with the consequences of their actions. Avoid people who have been on lots of projects but never saw anything through to completion.

FAQ 39.08

Are small projects a good way to get your feet wet?

No. Small projects can set you up to drown later on.

Small projects, whose intellectual content can be understood by one intelligent person, build exactly the wrong skills and attitudes for success on large projects. In terms of thousands of lines of code (KLOC), anything under 20KLOC is clearly small, and anything over 100KLOC is not small. The experience of the industry has been that small projects succeed most often when there are a few highly intelligent people involved who use a minimum of process and are willing to rip things apart and start over when a design flaw is discovered. A small program can be desk-checked by senior people to discover many of the errors, and static type checking and const correctness on a small project can be more grief than they are worth. Bad inheritance can be fixed in many ways, including changing all the code that relied on the base class to reflect the new derived class. Breaking interfaces is not the end of the world because there aren't that many interconnections to start with. Finally, source code control systems and formalized build procedures can slow down progress.

On the other hand, big projects require more people, which implies that the average skill level will be lower because there are only so many geniuses to start with, and they usually don't get along with each other that well, anyway. Since the volume of code is too large for any one person to comprehend, it is imperative that processes be used to formalize and communicate the work effort and that the project be decomposed into manageable chunks. Big programs need automated help to catch programming errors, and this is where the payback for static type checking and const correctness can be significant. There is usually so much code based on the promises of base classes that there is no alternative to following proper inheritance for all the derived classes; the cost of changing everything that relied on the base class promises could be prohibitive. Breaking an interface is a major undertaking, because there are so many possible ripple effects. Source code control systems and formalized build processes are necessary to avoid the confusion that arises otherwise.

So the issue is not just that big projects are different. The approaches and attitudes to small and large projects are so diametrically opposed that success with small projects breeds habits that do not scale and can lead to failure of large projects.

FAQ 39.09

Does being a good C programmer help when learning OO/C++?

 No. A good C programmer is almost always a horrible OO/C++ programmer.

One of the early ideas behind C++ is that it could be used as a "better C" without using its OO or modern software engineering features. We don't think this is a desirable approach in most instances, and this book is written for organizations which want "good" OO software using C++, not just C++ programs that compile and execute correctly. With that perspective, this is the new reality for C programmers:

- The use of arrays is evil. C++ now uses container classes.

- The use of pointers is evil. References are "in." When pointers are used, reference counting is "in."

- The beloved type casts of all sorts are bad.

- Using code to find code is evil (that is, using type information and `if` and `switch` statements and downcasts to locate the right routine to call). In C++ we use virtual functions and dynamic binding.

- Good old-fashioned `char*` delimited by `'\0'` is evil. In C++ we have strings from the class library.

- Familiar functions such as `memcpy()` and `strlen()` either have nasty behavior or are obsolete.

So, what's left from C that's "good" C++? Curly braces and semicolons, and that's about it. Not only do C programmers have to throw away quite a bit of old technique, they also have to pick up a few new ideas:

- Templates

- Exceptions

- Mutable

- Inheritance and hiding rules

- Operator overloading

- Virtual functions, abstract base classes

- Special characteristics of STL or the class library of your choice

- Constructors and destructors, `new[]` and `delete[]`

- Declare at first use, where no one can find it

- And on and on and on.

Okay, we'll admit that we've had our tongue planted firmly in our cheek while writing this FAQ. It isn't quite that gloomy, and hundreds of thousands of C programmers have learned to program successfully in C++. But, our message is that the transition isn't automatic or easy, and C programmers better be prepared for a major intellectual challenge if they want to become good C++ programmers.

FAQ 39.10

What skills help when learning OO/C++?

Being able to see the big picture and solid software engineering skills.

Invariably the most successful OO/C++ developers (those that reach levels 3 and 4) share a set of core beliefs.

- They love designing interfaces, they use programming by contract techniques, and they see the value of decoupling as an architectural goal.

- They understand why interface reuse is more valuable than code reuse.

- They are committed to building high-quality software systems in a team-oriented environment rather than just making sure their small piece compiles and runs.

- They are willing to try new techniques, rather than rejecting new ideas because they've never used them before.

- They understand the costs of using code to find code and they avoid it religiously.

- They realize that requirements are always changing and they work hard at designing interfaces that are flexible and extensible.

- They know what they know and they know what they don't know, and they are willing to seek out good advice in an effort to find better solutions.

- They would rather understand how and why something works than be satisfied with simply getting something to compile and run.

- They put the good of the many (the client code) ahead of the good of the few (the system code), and they understand that "breaking client code" is very expensive.

- They understand the cost and benefits and risks of alternative approaches and factor them into their decision-making process.

- They design changeability into the fabric of the system architecture and design, rather than thinking of "change" as an afterthought or maintenance activity.

- They do not believe that one size fits all.

- They listen before they speak—they do not have an answer before they hear the question.

- They want to understand *why* the software is being built—the underlying business case—in addition to simply knowing what the requirements are.

- They consistently put business considerations ahead of technology considerations.

Developers with these skills will thrive when using C++ no matter what their background was—C programmer, Smalltalk programmer, Cobol programmer, former CEO, or itinerant sheepherder.

Index

Addison-Wesley Computer and Engineering Publishing Group

How to Interact with Us

1. Visit our Web site

http://www.awl.com/cseng

When you think you've read enough, there's always more content for you at Addison-Wesley's web site. Our web site contains a directory of complete product information including:

- Chapters
- Exclusive author interviews
- Links to authors' pages
- Tables of contents
- Source code

You can also discover what tradeshows and conferences Addison-Wesley will be attending, read what others are saying about our titles, and find out where and when you can meet our authors and have them sign your book.

2. Subscribe to Our Email Mailing Lists

Subscribe to our electronic mailing lists and be the first to know when new books are publishing. Here's how it works: Sign up for our electronic mailing at **http://www.awl.com/cseng/mailinglists.html**. Just select the subject areas that interest you and you will receive notification via email when we publish a book in that area.

We encourage you to patronize the many fine retailers who stock Addison-Wesley titles. Visit our online directory to find stores near you or visit our online store: **http://store.awl.com/** or call **800-824-7799**.

3. Contact Us via Email

cepubprof@awl.com

Ask general questions about our books.
Sign up for our electronic mailing lists.
Submit corrections for our web site.

bexpress@awl.com

Request an Addison-Wesley catalog.
Get answers to questions regarding your order or our products.

innovations@awl.com

Request a current Innovations Newsletter.

webmaster@awl.com

Send comments about our web site.

mikeh@awl.com

Submit a book proposal.
Send errata for an Addison-Wesley book.

cepubpublicity@awl.com

Request a review copy for a member of the media interested in reviewing new Addison-Wesley titles.

Addison Wesley Longman
Computer and Engineering Publishing Group
One Jacob Way, Reading, Massachusetts 01867 USA
TEL 781-944-3700 • FAX 781-942-3076